D1404914

20-2004

RD

Microsoft®
Outlook® 2000
Programming Bible

Microsoft® Outlook® 2000 Programming Bible

Jeffrey A. Kent
David G. Jung

IDG Books Worldwide, Inc.
An International Data Group Company

Foster City, CA ✦ Chicago, IL ✦ Indianapolis, IN ✦ New York, NY

Microsoft® Outlook® 2000 Programming Bible

Published by
IDG Books Worldwide, Inc.
An International Data Group Company
919 E. Hillsdale Blvd., Suite 400
Foster City, CA 94404
www.idgbooks.com (IDG Books Worldwide Web site)

ISBN: 0-7645-4650-3

Printed in the United States of America

10 9 8 7 6 5 4 3 2 1

1B/RU/QZ/QQ/FC

Distributed in the United States by IDG Books Worldwide, Inc.

Distributed by CDG Books Canada Inc. for Canada; by Transworld Publishers Limited in the United Kingdom; by IDG Norge Books for Norway; by IDG Sweden Books for Sweden; by IDG Books Australia Publishing Corporation Pty. Ltd. for Australia and New Zealand; by TransQuest Publishers Pte Ltd. for Singapore, Malaysia, Thailand, Indonesia, and Hong Kong; by Gotop Information Inc. for Taiwan; by ICG Muse, Inc. for Japan; by Intersoft for South Africa; by Eyrolles for France; by International Thomson Publishing for Germany, Austria, and Switzerland; by Distribuidora Cuspide for Argentina; by LR International for Brazil; by Galileo Libros for Chile; by Ediciones ZETA S.C.R. Ltda. for Peru; by WS Computer Publishing Corporation, Inc., for the Philippines; by Contemporanea de Ediciones for Venezuela; by Express Computer Distributors for the Caribbean and West Indies; by Micronesia Media Distributor, Inc. for Micronesia; by Chips Computadoras S.A. de C.V. for Mexico; by Editorial Norma de Panama S.A. for Panama; by American Bookshops for Finland.

For general information on IDG Books Worldwide's books in the U.S., please call our Consumer Customer Service department at 800-762-2974. For reseller information, including discounts and premium sales, please call our Reseller Customer Service department at 800-434-3422.

For information on where to purchase IDG Books Worldwide's books outside the U.S., please contact our International Sales department at 317-596-5530 or fax 317-572-4002.

For consumer information on foreign language translations, please contact our Customer Service department at 800-434-3422, fax 317-572-4002, or e-mail rights@idgbooks.com.

For information on licensing foreign or domestic rights, please phone +1-650-653-7098.

For sales inquiries and special prices for bulk quantities, please contact our Order Services department at 800-434-3422 or write to the address above.

For information on using IDG Books Worldwide's books in the classroom or for ordering examination copies, please contact our Educational Sales department at 800-434-2086 or fax 317-572-4005.

For press review copies, author interviews, or other publicity information, please contact our Public Relations department at 650-653-7000 or fax 650-653-7500.

For authorization to photocopy items for corporate, personal, or educational use, please contact Copyright Clearance Center, 222 Rosewood Drive, Danvers, MA 01923, or fax 978-750-4470.

Library of Congress Cataloging-in-Publication Data

Kent, Jeffrey A. (Jeffrey Alan), 1952-
    Microsoft Outlook 2000 programming bible /
Jeffrey A. Kent, David G. Jung.
        p.   cm.
    ISBN 0-7645-4650-3 (alk. paper)
    1. Microsoft Outlook--Handbooks, manuals, etc.
2. Business--Computer programs--Handbooks,
manuals, etc.   I. Jung, David G., 1966-   II. Title.
HF5548.4.M5255 K46   2000
005.369--dc21

00-058128

Trademarks: All brand names and product names used in this book are trade names, service marks, trademarks, or registered trademarks of their respective owners. IDG Books Worldwide is not associated with any product or vendor mentioned in this book.

is a registered trademark or trademark under exclusive license to IDG Books Worldwide, Inc. from International Data Group, Inc. in the United States and/or other countries.

R0174735979

ABOUT IDG BOOKS WORLDWIDE

Welcome to the world of IDG Books Worldwide.

IDG Books Worldwide, Inc., is a subsidiary of International Data Group, the world's largest publisher of computer-related information and the leading global provider of information services on information technology. IDG was founded more than 30 years ago by Patrick J. McGovern and now employs more than 9,000 people worldwide. IDG publishes more than 290 computer publications in over 75 countries. More than 90 million people read one or more IDG publications each month.

Launched in 1990, IDG Books Worldwide is today the #1 publisher of best-selling computer books in the United States. We are proud to have received eight awards from the Computer Press Association in recognition of editorial excellence and three from Computer Currents' First Annual Readers' Choice Awards. Our best-selling ...For Dummies® series has more than 50 million copies in print with translations in 31 languages. IDG Books Worldwide, through a joint venture with IDG's Hi-Tech Beijing, became the first U.S. publisher to publish a computer book in the People's Republic of China. In record time, IDG Books Worldwide has become the first choice for millions of readers around the world who want to learn how to better manage their businesses.

Our mission is simple: Every one of our books is designed to bring extra value and skill-building instructions to the reader. Our books are written by experts who understand and care about our readers. The knowledge base of our editorial staff comes from years of experience in publishing, education, and journalism — experience we use to produce books to carry us into the new millennium. In short, we care about books, so we attract the best people. We devote special attention to details such as audience, interior design, use of icons, and illustrations. And because we use an efficient process of authoring, editing, and desktop publishing our books electronically, we can spend more time ensuring superior content and less time on the technicalities of making books.

You can count on our commitment to deliver high-quality books at competitive prices on topics you want to read about. At IDG Books Worldwide, we continue in the IDG tradition of delivering quality for more than 30 years. You'll find no better book on a subject than one from IDG Books Worldwide.

John J. Kilcullen
John Kilcullen
Chairman and CEO
IDG Books Worldwide, Inc.

Eighth Annual Computer Press Awards ≥1992

Ninth Annual Computer Press Awards ≥1993

Tenth Annual Computer Press Awards ≥1994

Eleventh Annual Computer Press Awards ≥1995

IDG is the world's leading IT media, research and exposition company. Founded in 1964, IDG had 1997 revenues of $2.05 billion and has more than 9,000 employees worldwide. IDG offers the widest range of media options that reach IT buyers in 75 countries representing 95% of worldwide IT spending. IDG's diverse product and services portfolio spans six key areas including print publishing, online publishing, expositions and conferences, market research, education and training, and global marketing services. More than 90 million people read one or more of IDG's 290 magazines and newspapers, including IDG's leading global brands — Computerworld, PC World, Network World, Macworld and the Channel World family of publications. IDG Books Worldwide is one of the fastest-growing computer book publishers in the world, with more than 700 titles in 36 languages. The "...For Dummies®" series alone has more than 50 million copies in print. IDG offers online users the largest network of technology-specific Web sites around the world through IDG.net (http://www.idg.net), which comprises more than 225 targeted Web sites in 55 countries worldwide. International Data Corporation (IDC) is the world's largest provider of information technology data, analysis and consulting, with research centers in over 41 countries and more than 400 research analysts worldwide. IDG World Expo is a leading producer of more than 168 globally branded conferences and expositions in 35 countries including E3 (Electronic Entertainment Expo), Macworld Expo, ComNet, Windows World Expo, ICE (Internet Commerce Expo), Agenda, DEMO, and Spotlight. IDG's training subsidiary, ExecuTrain, is the world's largest computer training company, with more than 230 locations worldwide and 785 training courses. IDG Marketing Services helps industry-leading IT companies build international brand recognition by developing global integrated marketing programs via IDG's print, online and exposition products worldwide. Further information about the company can be found at www.idg.com.   1/26/00

Credits

Acquisitions Editor
Greg Croy

Project Editors
Matt Lusher
Andy Marinkovich
Neil Romanosky

Technical Editor
Allen Wyatt

Copy Editor
S. B. Kleinman

Project Coordinators
Joe Shines
Danette Nurse

Media Development Coordinator
Marisa Pearman

Media Development Specialist
Megan Decraene

Permissions Editor
Carmen Krikorian

Media Development Manager
Laura Carpenter

Graphics and Production Specialists
Bob Bihlmayer
Darren Cutlip
Jude Levinson
Michael Lewis
Victor Pérez-Varela
Ramses Ramirez

Quality Control Technician
Dina F Quan

Illustrators
Shelley Norris
Gabriele McCann

Proofreading and Indexing
York Production Services

Cover Illustration
Peter Kowaleszyn

About the Authors

Jeff Kent is an Assistant Professor of Computer Science at Los Angeles Valley College in Valley Glen, CA. He teaches a number of programming languages, including Visual Basic, C++, Java, and, when he's feeling masochistic, Assembler. He also manages a network for a Los Angeles law firm whose employees are guinea pigs for his Outlook/Exchange Server applications. Jeff has co-authored programming books, is a lawyer, and is a former professional chess master.

David Jung has been programming on computers since the early 1980s. A graduate of California State Polytechnic University, Pomona, David has a Bachelor of Science degree in Business Administration, with an emphasis in computer information systems. His development expertise is in architecting and constructing cross-platform client/server and distributed database solutions using Visual Basic, XML, Access, SQL Server, Oracle, DB2, and Internet technology. He is a member of the Pasadena IBM Users Group's technical staff and leads its Visual Basic Special Interest Group. David has co-authored a number of books on Visual Basic ranging from introductory and reference titles to client/server development.

I would like to dedicate this book to my wife, Devvie, who tolerated my lousy outlook (pun intended) and crashes of the home network while I was experimenting with Outlook/Exchange Server applications.

—Jeff Kent

I would like to dedicate this book to my son, Nicholas Hitoshi, who managed to make it safely into this world during the creation of this book.

—David Jung

Preface

We did not write the *Microsoft Outlook 2000 Programming Bible* as a road to riches or fame. We are misguided, but not that misguided. We wrote this book because we believe it fills a need. There already are many good books about how to *use* Outlook 2000, but comparatively few books on *programming* Outlook 2000.

While Outlook serves well "out of the box" as a personal information manager (PIM), Outlook exposes a rich object model that enables you, the programmer, to harness and expand on the power of Outlook in your custom applications in desktop, client-server, and Web environments. Given the many tasks that Outlook does well, the primary limitation to using Outlook in your applications is your imagination!

Who This Book Is For

This book is for you, the programmer who wants to use and extend Outlook in your applications. While this book has much for experienced programmers, you do not need to be an experienced programmer to benefit from this book. You can use this book to start writing Outlook programs even if you are programming at an introductory level or if it's been a while since you've written programs. This book includes sidebars on programming topics to introduce you to or refresh your memory on the object-oriented programming concepts you will need to know.

How This Book Is Organized

This book is divided into three parts:

✦ Outlook 2000 Object Model (Chapters 1-5)

✦ Outlook Applications (Chapters 6-8)

✦ Web Enabling Outlook (Chapters 9-11)

Part I: Outlook 2000 Object Model

This part provides you with an in-depth understanding of Outlook 2000's rich and complex object model. First on our list are the top-level objects, Application and NameSpace, which are the gateways to the remainder of the object model. Next are Folders, used by Outlook to organize information, and Items, which represent the information stored in Outlook. Finally, we'll show you how to create Outlook forms, which are the interface for users to add or change that information.

Part II: Outlook Applications

This part shows you how to develop desktop and COM-enabled applications using Outlook, as well as how to integrate Outlook with other Office 2000 applications. In this part you also will learn how to develop COM Add-Ins for Outlook and to create a Command Bar COM Add-In.

Part III: Web Enabling Outlook

This part first examines the Outlook Web Components: Outlook Today, Outlook Folder Home Pages, and the Outlook View Control. Next, you will learn to configure Outlook Web Access so users can access an "Outlook-like" application over the Internet without even having Outlook on their computer. You then will learn how to use the HTML Form Converter so you can reuse your Outlook forms on Outlook Web Access. Finally, you will learn Active Server Pages (ASP) and Collaboration Data Objects (CDO), two technologies critical to the development of web applications using Outlook.

How You Can Use This Book

If you are not familiar with the Outlook 2000 Object Model, Part I is a good place to begin (that's why it's Part I). The Outlook 2000 Object Model is the basis of developing Outlook applications in all environments, so you will need to understand the object model before you begin developing applications.

If you already reasonably familiar with the Outlook 2000 Object Model, then you can always return to Part I as a reference and instead go straight ahead to developing applications. Which part of the book you go to next depends on the environment for which you are developing:

+ You are developing for desktop or client/server environments: Part II

+ You are developing for the Web, either in Internet or Intranet environments: Part III

Conventions Used in This Book

Throughout the book, keywords are highlighted in **bold**. Variables, function parameters, control names, and so on are formatted in different ways, such as by being italicized or appearing in `code font` (like that!).

Several icons are used throughout this book to alert you to special information:

 A Tip icon points out a helpful hint or technique you will find useful in your programming.

 A Note icon identifies an interesting point that you will find worth remembering.

 A Caution icon will alert you to a possible problem.

 A Cross-Reference icon refers to further information on a topic that you can find outside of the current chapter.

Contacting the Authors

We enthusiastically welcome gushing praise. We also are receptive to comments, suggestions, grunts, groans, and yes, even criticism. The best way to contact us is via e-mail; you can use `books@vb2java.com`. Alternately, visit our Web site, `http://www.vb2java.com`, which contains resources and updated information about the code and contents of this book.

We hope you enjoy this book as much as we enjoyed writing it.

Acknowledgments

Our heartfelt thanks to Greg Croy, without whose help, guidance, and patience this book in the Bible series would not exist. A special thanks goes to Andy Marinkovich, Neil Romanosky, and Matt Lusher for shepherding this book through to completion.

Thanks to S. B. Kleinman for wading through mounds of pages of our manuscript and keeping our writing as honest as it could possibly be.

There are a lot of other talented people behind the scenes who also helped to get this book out to press, and like in an Academy Awards speech, we're bound to forget to mention them. That doesn't mean we don't appreciate all their hard work, because we do.

Jeff would like to personally give thanks to his co-author, David Jung, for yet another interesting book collaboration. He also would like to give thanks to his family for tolerating him while he was grumbling about deadlines or cracking corny jokes about having a "lousy Outlook," and for not having him committed when he talks about writing his "next" book.

David would like to personally give thanks to his co-author, Jeff Kent, for his constant encouragement and words of guidance during this endeavor. He would also like to give thanks to this friends and family for putting up with him during the writing of this book and understanding that he "couldn't come out and play." As strange as it may sound, he'd like to thank his dogs for always showing up with toys in the middle of the night to provide a good distraction for all the late night coding sessions. But most importantly, he would like to thank his wife, Joanne, for her enduring love, encouragement, and support. And through the midst of this project, she gave birth to their first child, Nicholas Hitoshi.

Contents at a Glance

Contents

Part II: Outlook Applications   237

Chapter 6: Building Outlook Applications 239

Outlook 2000 Object Model

◆   ◆   ◆   ◆

◆   ◆   ◆   ◆

Introduction to Outlook 2000

Welcome to the *Microsoft Outlook 2000 Programming
Bible*. Outlook 2000 is the third incarnation of
Microsoft's e-mail and scheduling client. Outlook is generally
regarded as a personal information manager (PIM), but unlike
most other PIMs, Outlook is also a development tool. If you're
new to Outlook as a PIM or as a development tool, this chapter will provide you with an overview of many of its features
and lay the path for the rest of the book.

Introduction

Outlook is a program with an identity crisis. Most applications
perform one primary task. Microsoft Word is a word processing program. Microsoft Excel is a spreadsheet program. By
contrast, Outlook is not limited to a single purpose, or even
two or three purposes. Its mail messaging capabilities make
it a superior e-mail application. Its ability to store detailed
contact and appointment information makes it an excellent
contact manager. Its ability to record and track tasks makes
it a project management application. It also enables its users
to record notes and, through journals, track e-mail and other
activities.

Some people call Outlook a PIM. That might be accurate if
you're thinking of using it as a standalone application. However,
as powerful as Outlook is as a standalone application, its power
and uses increase almost exponentially when it is used with
Microsoft Exchange Server in an intranet, or even Internet,
environment.

Additionally, Outlook is also programmable. It offers a rich object model and enables you to create objects that inherit the capabilities of its built-in objects. Furthermore, Outlook provides a development environment that enables you to create custom forms and write code. Thus, you can create custom applications using Outlook that leverage its wide-ranging capabilities as an application. Indeed, the programmer's imagination is the main limitation to the applications that can be created with Outlook.

Quick Tour of Outlook 2000

Outlook can be installed and configured into three different versions: PIM only, PIM with Internet e-mail, and Corporate or Workgroup e-mail client. Each version has different features:

✦ PIM only — This version enables only the Contacts, Calendar, and Tasks features of the product.

✦ PIM with Internet e-mail — This version enables the Contacts, Calendar, and Tasks features. It can also be used as an Internet e-mail client and a Newsgroup reader, and it enables you to send and receive faxes and access your Web browser.

✦ Corporate or Workgroup e-mail client — This version provides you with all the features included in PIM with Internet e-mail, with additional e-mail support for Lotus cc:Mail, Lotus Notes, Microsoft Exchange, Microsoft Mail, and more.

Many features have been carried over from previous versions of Outlook. Although this book specifically refers to Outlook 2000, in this quick tour we will discuss features that were available in previous versions but have been changed or enhanced in Outlook 2000.

 Note   The three versions described are included as part of Outlook 2000. You don't need to purchase any additional licenses or upgrades to change from one installation type to the next. You can change the configuration at any time.

Contacts

This feature allows you to store names, snail mail and e-mail addresses, phone numbers and other business and personal information about customers, family, friends, and enemies. You can link any Outlook item or Office document to a contact to help you track your activities associated with that contact. If you are migrating from another e-mail client, like Lotus cc:Mail or Qualcomm Eudora, you can import its contact lists into Outlook.

In previous versions of Outlook, contact information could be stored in either of two different areas, the Contacts folder or the Personal Address Book. This was a problem because Outlook (or perhaps you) never quite knew where your contact information should reside. Since the two repositories for contact information were separated, it was all too easy for contact information to be duplicated or out of sync. Having two different repositories for contact information was clumsy. Also, to create a distribution list for a group, you would create them in the Personal Address Book, and only the contact people in the Personal Address Book could be added to the group. By eliminating the two repositories, you can now create a distribution list for a group for one source.

You can define how you view your contact information. You can view your contact information in several predefined ways, such as sorted by the name of companies, by name and phone number, or by category title you defined a contact person to. A category is a keyword or phrase that helps group items. For example, you might assign a number of contacts under the category of "Cal Alumni" group them as everyone you know who graduated with you from the University of California, Berkeley. Figure 1-1 shows contact information that displays only the contact name and address. Just as in Windows Explorer, you can change the layout of the information as well, so that each person's contact information looks like a Rolodex card or is displayed in a spreadsheet.

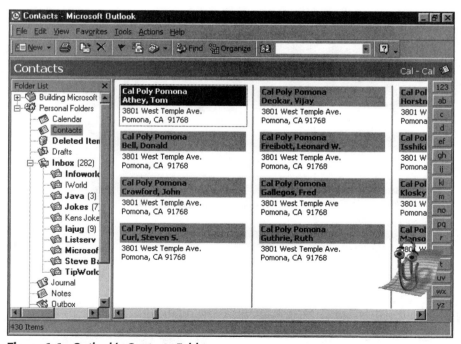

Figure 1-1: Outlook's Contacts Folder

Calendar

The Calendar allows you to schedule appointments, meetings, and all-day events, and to track holidays, special occasions, and other important dates. You can also receive notifications to alert you when a calendar event is about to occur.

You face a very daunting task when trying to arrange a meeting that accommodates everyone's schedule. Scheduling meetings and appointments with correspondents in your Outlook Contacts folder is not limited to your Microsoft Exchange environment. Outlook has the important feature of being able to share Calendar free/busy information over the Internet, and to send and receive meeting requests and responses over the Internet using the iCalendar Internet standard. You can use this feature to schedule meetings and appointments with colleagues who are all on different environments.

If your work environment provides you with the ability to teleconference through Microsoft NetMeeting, Outlook's Calendar can schedule real-time, online meetings over the Internet with video, audio, and chat capabilities. Outlook also can schedule times to show broadcasts on Microsoft NetShow Services, and automatically start them at the designated times.

Figure 1-2 illustrates the Calendar folder and Figure 1-3 shows the appointment detail of a NetMeeting appointment.

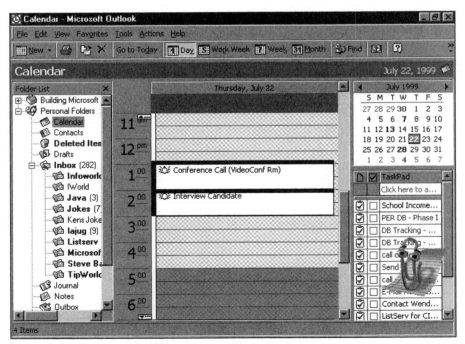

Figure 1-2: Outlook's Calendar folder

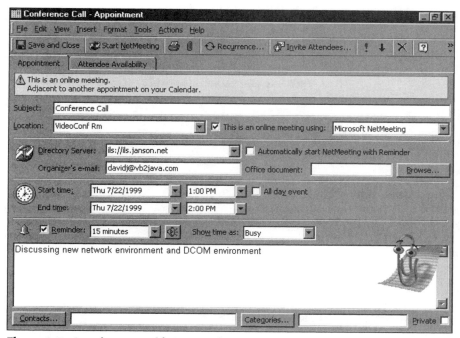

Figure 1-3: Appointment with NetMeeting

Tasks

The Tasks feature allows you to create and maintain a to-do list, categorize and prioritize your tasks, set reminders for deadlines, and track your progress. You can also assign tasks to other people, monitor their progress as they update the tasks properties, and receive status reports summarizing the tasks.

You can set tasks to be recurring, such as a reminder indicating "shuttle maintenance report is due" that repeats at either regular intervals, a specified number of times, or a specified amount of time after the task is complete. Outlook can also generate an e-mail message that summarizes the status of a task and then address the message to everyone on the update list for the task. Figure 1-4 illustrates a number of tasks and when they are due.

Journal

The Journal is a unique feature in Outlook capable of automatically recording activities performed by Outlook, like sending e-mail messages, meeting requests and responses, and task requests and responses. It can also record activity related to other Microsoft Office documents you work on.

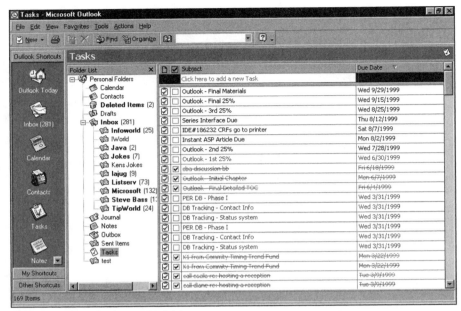

Figure 1-4: Outlook's Tasks folder

The Journal can automatically record the activities you've performed. It records the date the activity took place and what was done. For example, Journal can track e-mail you send, Office documents you create or modify, and activities you want to remember that might not be stored in a file on your computer, such as phone conversations or handwritten letters you mailed or received. The Journal is especially convenient when you want to track all the activities related to a particular contact—such as for billing purposes. Figure 1-5 is an example of the activities the Journal recorded.

Notes

Notes is probably one of the simplest features within Outlook. The Notes feature's sole purpose is to allow you to keep quick notes about anything without having to write them down on a piece of paper. You most likely have seen sticky yellow notes stuck to computers and furniture in other people's work areas (of course not your own). These notes can easily be misplaced or lost. The Notes feature enables you to reduce the amount of clutter in your work area and, if you're a mobile computer user, to have the notes with you wherever you go. Figure 1-6 shows a note being viewed within the Notes folder.

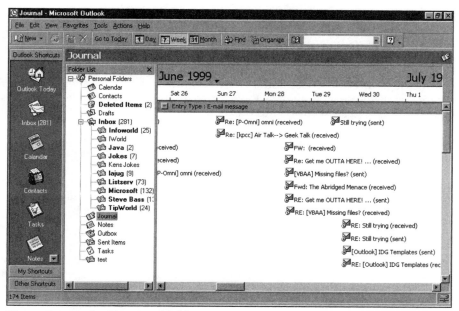

Figure 1-5: Outlook's Journal folder

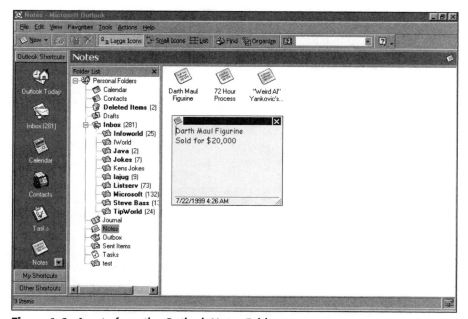

Figure 1-6: A note from the Outlook Notes Folder

E-Mail

Most Outlook users regard the e-mail feature as the heart and soul of Outlook. Indeed, many users use Outlook only for e-mail. Managing e-mail can be very time-consuming. Therefore, Outlook includes many features that help you keep your messages organized and under control. Outlook also offers a variety of tools for enhancing your e-mail, such as tools for decorating and enhancing messages or for building special security into them.

When Outlook is first installed, there are four basic folders that are used for managing your e-mail. They are the Inbox, Draft, Outbox, and Sent Items.

✦ Inbox — The Inbox is the heart of the e-mail system. All messages that you receive first arrive in this folder. From there, you can set up rules to filter messages into other folders, denote messages from senders by color, and so on.

✦ Drafts — This folder is used as a repository for all unfinished messages. This is useful when you have not have finished a message but have to turn to another task or even leave. The Drafts folder also is useful when you have typed a scathing message to your boss but then wisely decide to wait and cool off before you decide whether to send it. The Drafts folder makes it easy for you to identify and view your unfinished messages.

✦ Outbox — This folder is the staging area where your e-mail waits before it is sent out into your mail server. You can configure Outlook to send messages as soon as they enter the Outbox, or to send items in the Outbox at regular intervals. Keep in mind that if you have Outlook configured for the Corporate and Workgroup client, your e-mail messages are sent as soon as they enter the Outbox folder.

✦ Sent Items — This folder is the repository of all e-mail messages you have sent. This folder can fill up the fastest and it is a good idea to archive and/or purge its contents regularly.

There are a number of features that enable users to be more productive with their e-mail. Here some of the e-mail features you can use:

✦ AutoPreview — This feature shows messages in the folder with their first few lines displayed. AutoPreview is especially useful if you receive a lot of e-mail (50 or more messages a day), because it allows you to gauge the importance of a message before you decide to read or respond to it.

✦ Preview Pane — This feature splits the folder into two panes so that you can read the entire contents of a message in a separate pane in the Inbox without opening the message. If there is an attached file, you can quickly get to the information you need by opening and viewing the attachment without having to open the e-mail message first. Both AutoPreview and the Preview Pane are shown in Figure 1-7.

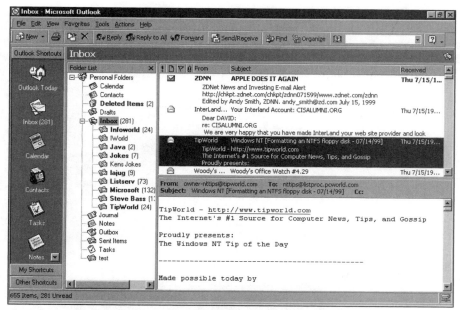

Figure 1-7: The Outlook Inbox with the AutoPreview and Preview Pane features enabled

✦ Rules Wizard — As mentioned earlier, you can create rules to automatically move, delete, highlight, forward, or flag incoming and outgoing messages. You can run rules at any time to process messages that you've already received, including those you've moved to other folders.

✦ HTML mail — This feature was added in Outlook 98 and enhanced in Outlook 2000. This allows you to send messages that contain items that a Web browser can display, such as animated graphics, pictures, and multimedia objects.

Message expiration and deferred delivery — If you're using Microsoft Exchange Server, you can mark a message that you're sending to be deleted at a certain time, or send a message now that Outlook will deliver at a later time.

Newsreader

Just as in previous versions, Outlook itself does not support newsgroup reading; therefore, you will still need to use Outlook Express. Outlook Express is a scaled-down e-mail client with newsgroup capabilities. When used in conjunction with Outlook, the Internet e-mail portion of Outlook Express is disabled so it's not confusing to the user.

To view newsgroups, select News from View ⇨ Go To menu item. If you don't see the News selection in the menu, select the double arrows pointing down to extend the menu. Figure 1-8 shows Outlook Express as the Newsgroup client. Notice that the user interface looks a lot like Outlook itself. Microsoft did that on purpose so you don't have to learn a new user interface.

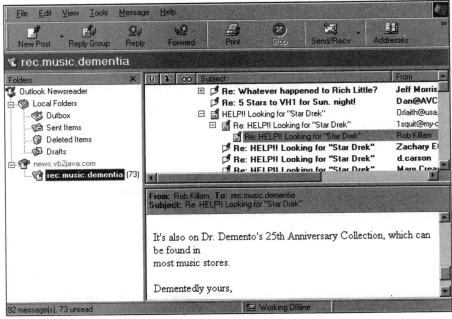

Figure 1-8: Outlook Express as Newsgroup client

Public Folders (Corporate or Workgroup Version)

Outlook stores different types of information in separate folders. For example, contact information is stored in the Contacts folder and task information is stored in the Tasks folder.

The Corporate or Workgroup version of Outlook provides you with access to folders beyond the folders within your local environment. Maintaining public folders on the server is an easy and effective way to collect, organize, and share information with others on your team or across your organization. You can use public folders to store any type of file or Outlook item. Figure 1-9 shows a public folder displaying a message in the same format it would use if the message were just a plain Outlook item.

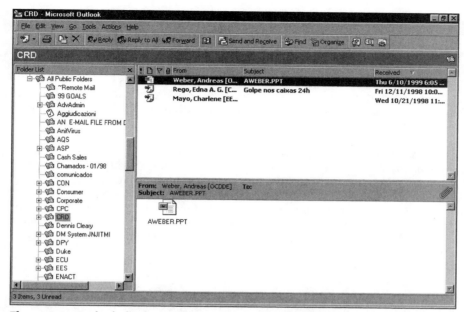

Figure 1-9: Outlook displaying the contents of a public folder

Public folders are created and designed by administrators and others in your workgroup or organization who have the appropriate permission. If you have the appropriate server permission, you can set up your own public folders and give other people permission to use them. You can customize them by applying your own custom views, forms, fields, and rules to your public folders.

Public folders are stored on the Microsoft Exchange Server in an area called the *Exchange Store*. The Exchange Server provides up to 16 gigabytes of space for public folders. Your Exchange administrator can limit the size of individual public folders.

Cross-Reference

The details of creating public folders are not within the scope of this book. For more information about this, there are a number of good books that specifically cover Exchange Server, such as *Exchange Server 5.5 Secrets* by Robert Guaraldi, also published by IDG Books Worldwide (1998).

Overview of Tools

Ask a community of application and Office developers about developing applications for Outlook. You'll either get a lot of blank stares or people will talk to you about the great mail merge macros they built to send letters to everyone in the Contact folder based on category. As you will find throughout this book, we will cover more topics than just sending e-mail, coordinating meetings, and chatting with newsgroups.

While Outlook is powerful as a standalone tool in its own right, it also can be a powerful component within a Component Object Model (COM) development environment. COM is a general architecture that lays the foundation upon which OLE and ActiveX components are built. It establishes a common model for interaction among software and reusable components. Its fundamental principle is to promote binary components that can be built in any programming language, not just Visual Basic. COM objects can be built using C++, Delphi, and even Assembler. They can be executed from any location as either in-process, cross-process, or cross-machine, and have no centralized authority.

Since Outlook can be used as a COM component, there are a number of tools at your disposal. This section will cover the tools you can use with Outlook and how they fit into the grand scheme.

Microsoft BackOffice

Microsoft BackOffice is a suite of Microsoft Windows NT/2000 server products. It provides a fully integrated foundation for building document, collaboration, and data analysis–driven business solutions for branch offices, departments, and mid-sized organizations with the use of Microsoft Office 2000. The products that make up the BackOffice suite are Exchange Server, Proxy Server, Site Server, SNA Server, SQL Server, and Systems Management Server. This section is only going to focus on a few components.

Exchange Server

Exchange Server provides a reliable, enterprise-wide infrastructure for collaboration and information sharing. When used with Office 2000, Exchange Server enables secure replication and sharing of Office 2000 documents, integrated group scheduling, real-time collaboration, team-based contact management, and easily created collaborative discussions. Exchange Server used with Outlook 2000 provides a unified experience for the Office and Exchange Server user, with integrated e-mail, scheduling, contact management, task management, and collaboration. Exchange Server also extends Office's Web integration by providing a set of messaging and collaboration services that are tightly integrated with Microsoft Internet Information Server.

See Chapter 10, "Outlook Web Access and Forms," for information on integrated Web technology with Exchange Server.

Internet Information Server

The Microsoft Internet Information Server (IIS) is actually part of the Microsoft Windows NT Option Pack. This is Microsoft's premier Internet Web server program. It has become an integral part of Microsoft's Internet strategy. Its latest version allows you access COM components through its server-side technology. This technology, called Active Server Pages (better known as ASP) plays an integral part in Outlook Web access. It allows you to do calculations or information manipulation using ActiveScript technology that is executed on the Web server rather than through the user's browser. ActiveScript technology encompasses JavaScript, Perl, and VBScript. By accessing COM objects, HTML writers can now access business rules or functions that were normally available to traditional client/server applications.

See Chapter 10 for more information on Outlook Web access and Chapter 11 for a more detailed discussion of ASP.

SQL Server

SQL Server 7.0 is Microsoft's database management system that brings scalable business solutions, powerful data warehousing, and integration with Microsoft Office 2000 to your enterprise. Version 7.0 provides seamless integration with Microsoft Access, Microsoft Excel, and other Microsoft Office 2000 components, and provides key competitive advantages by bringing decision-making data to all organizational levels. One of the advanced features is SQL Server's ability to autotune. This frees database administrators from the burden of constantly monitoring database queries and transactions for efficiency as users increase their access to crucial data. Decisions can be made quicker because of the built-in OLAP (On-Line Analytic Processing) components and integration with Excel 2000. It's scalable from general database users to enterprise-wide data access to mobile applications computer users.

Microsoft Transaction Server

The Microsoft Transaction Server (MTS), like IIS, comes with the Microsoft Windows NT Option Pack. MTS is a middleware object broker that offers process isolation, transaction control, security, and resource pooling for COM components across your network. Middleware is a program that allows different applications to communicate. It is also one of the key components of the Microsoft development architecture known as Distributed interNet Architecture, better known as Microsoft DNA.

You're probably wondering why you would need to be concerned with a transaction server. If you only plan to create Outlook applications with Microsoft Office 2000, then you don't need to use MTS. But as an application developer who creates Outlook applications using COM components for Corporate or Workgroup e-mail client solutions, you will want to consider using MTS. When you build Outlook applications for e-mail client solutions, you need to consider breaking your application into components, commonly known as client/server or *n*-tier development. The *n* refers to the number of server or business process layers your application is built upon.

The most common model is the three-tier model, where you have user services, business services, and data services. Components that fall into the user services tier provide the visual interface that a user will use to view and interact with information. These components are responsible for contacting and requesting services from components in either the user services tier or the business services tier. Since user services should not directly contact the data services tier, the business services tier serves as a bridge between the other tiers. Business components with this tier provide business services that complete business tasks, such as validating that customers have not exceeded their credit limits. They also serve to buffer the user from direct interaction with the database. From a development standpoint, this is useful for building reusable components that can be used by more than just one application. Data services involve all the typical data chores, including the retrieval and modification of data as well as the full range of other database-related tasks. The key to data services is that the rules of business are not implemented here. While data services are responsible for managing and satisfying the requests submitted by a business component, implementing the rules of business is not one of their responsibilities.

When you develop reusable business components that reside on the business tier, they are usually encapsulated within COM components. Many times, you want to group these business components into a transaction, also referred to as a *unit of work*. A transaction can have many components, and all the components must successfully execute in order for the transaction to be valid or the information must be rolled back to its original state before the transaction began. *Rollback* is a term that describes the transaction process that allows any particular transaction to be returned to its original state. Figure 1-10 illustrates the steps that make up a transaction.

So where does MTS fit into this model? MTS allows you to encapsulate COM components into a single transaction. MTS monitors the progress of the transaction. If any one of the components fails or the transaction itself does not complete, MTS will roll back all the changed information. For example, assume you're entering information into a Help Desk application. Figure 1-11 illustrates the steps and the components used to close out a help desk call.

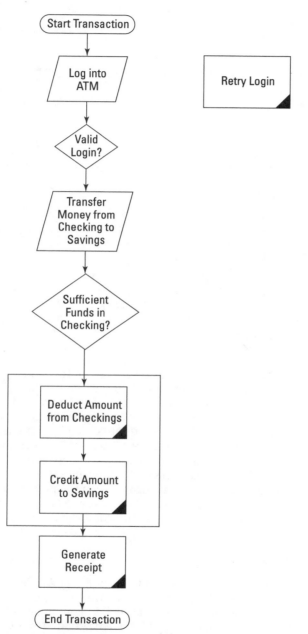

Figure 1-10: Simple transaction workflow

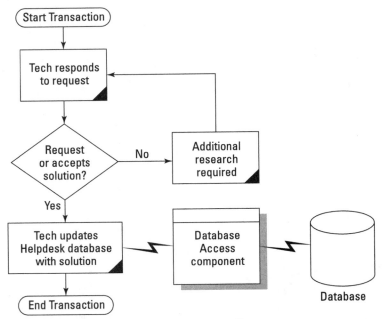

Figure 1-11: Steps to close a Help Desk call

You just finished troubleshooting one of the vice president's computers and you're entering the solution and trying to close out the Help Desk call. In the middle of entering the information about the VP's computer and what you did to it, one of your colleagues in the wiring closet accidentally overloads the power grid you're on and shuts it down. Because you could not send the "commit" statement to the server, the transaction is not complete. After a preset time, MTS determines that a transaction has been started but has not been completed. Since records in the database have been modified, MTS rolls back the entire transaction so that the database looks the way it did before the transaction began. When the power comes back on, you will have to reenter all the information. But at least you know that the transaction was not committed and that the integrity of the database is sound.

Microsoft Visual Studio

Visual Studio is Microsoft's integrated development suite for building Windows and Web-based applications. You can quickly build collaborative solutions that can take advantage of the products available in BackOffice as well as components that interact with Office 2000. Visual Basic (VB) and Visual InterDev (VI) are two development products within the suite that you will use the most to make high-powered Windows applications and dynamic, interactive Web solutions. VB can also be used to create components that other COM-enabled tools can use, as well as Office 2000 applications.

VB is probably the most commonly used and popular Windows rapid application development tool on the market. Since its first incarnation in 1989, it has become much more than just a way to make Windows applications through the use of the BASIC programming language. It has been developed to a common macro language across all their end-user applications (Word, Access, Excel, and so on), known as Visual Basic for Applications (VBA). It's based on VB, but the procedures and macros you develop can only run within the application's environment — unlike VB, which can compile the code into a standalone application. VBA allows users to create macros and work with other programs faster and more easily than they could in the past. Before there was a common macro language, there was WordBasic to create Word macros, AccessBasic for Access coding, and a separate language for Excel. Now that all the products use VBA, you only have to learn one macro language and the different object models the various applications use. VBA has also been made available to other products available from Independent Software Vendors (ISVs), making application extendibility more efficient.

The final incarnation of VB is the form of a scripting language for the Internet, called VBScript, sometimes referred to as Visual Basic Scripting Edition. This is Microsoft's answer to Netscape's JavaScript, which is loosely based on Sun MicroSystems' Java development language. VBScript is based on VB's language in many ways, but ultimately adheres to the Internet model in that a scripting language does not hold *state*. A *state* can be thought of as a snapshot of a system at a given point in time. Internet browsers work in a *stateless* environment, which means that the browser does not know the value of a variable from one HTML page to the next, even though you have cleared the variable and are reusing it from page to page. The browser thinks the variable is a different variable each time. When you define a variable in Visual Basic, however, you have complete control over when a variable is defined and how long the value will persist within your application. Outlook 2000 now allows you use VBA for most of your programming automation, but you still need to use VBScript if you plan to create any Outlook forms or work with ASP files.

 Note For more information about the different versions and features of VBScript and how it compares to VB and VBA, visit the Microsoft Web site at http://msdn. microsoft.com/scripting.

Overview of Technology

With all the tools available to you to extend Outlook, there are a number of different types of technology at your disposal as well. You can access information through a Web using Active Server Page (ASP) technology that is part of IIS. To assist ASP in deploying messages, there is the Collaborative Data Object (CDO). To add functionality to the Outlook user interface, you can develop COM Add-Ins.

Active Server Pages and Collaboration Data Objects

Active Server Pages is an integral part of the IIS and provides powerful server-side scripting capabilities. ASPs are standard text files that contain HTML and script. You can write the script with any ActiveScript language—VBScript, JScript, or Perl. ASP Web-based applications are powerful, not because the code is executed on the Web server and can access information on database servers, but because the code on an ASP page can call and interact with COM objects. One of the object libraries it can interact with is the Collaboration Data Objects, or CDO. CDO enables you to develop messaging and collaboration applications for the Web, as well as client-based and server-based applications.

Like all COM objects, CDO is an object library. Its purpose is to expose the interfaces of the Messaging Application Programming Interface, better known as MAPI. If you've done any programming with MAPI in the past using Microsoft Visual C++ or Visual Basic, you'll realize that the CDO object model isn't anything new. That's right! Microsoft has yet again come up with a new name for a product that's been around for a while. First it was called OLE Messaging. Then during the phase when Microsoft starting changing every name that had "OLE" in front of it to "Active," it changed the name of OLE Messaging to Active Messaging. Now that Microsoft is giving products and object models meaningful names, it has changed Active Messaging to Collaboration Data Objects. This actually makes sense because this technology is designed for collaborative messaging and workflow development, not just messaging functionality. Though the names have changed, Microsoft had done its best to make CDO as compatible as possible with previous versions of the object model.

Installing Outlook 2000, Outlook Web Access, or IIS with SMTP and NNTP components on your Web server installs CDO on your system. There are three distinct CDO components. Two consist of DLLs (dynamic link libraries) and the third is an NT Server service: CDO.DLL, CDOHTML.DLL, and CDO for NTS respectively. CDO.DLL contains the core collaborative functions of CDO, such as the ability to send messages and access folders. CDOHTML.DLL is the CDO Rendering library that allows you to automatically convert information stored inside Exchange Server to HTML by using custom views, colors and formats. CDO for NTS is a library that allows you to quickly build applications that don't require the complete functionality of CDO. CDO.DLL is installed with Outlook 2000. CDOHTML. DLL is installed with Outlook Web Access. CDO for NTS is installed with IIS with the optional components SMTP and NNTP installed.

CDO.DLL and CDOHTML.DLL both provide the same thing, but for two different platforms. Both provide the ability to render data into HTML, create multiple-user server-based collaborative applications, access information stored on Exchange Server. CDO for NTS, on the other hand, allows you to quickly build applications that don't require the complete functionality of CDO. For example, if you wanted to create a Web page that allows a visitor to send an e-mail to the Web master without using an e-mail client or the "MailTo:" HTML hypertext reference, you would use CDO for NTS. If you didn't want to use CDO for NTS, you would have to write a CGI (Common Gateway Interface) script to accomplish the same thing.

See Chapter 11, "Active Server Pages (ASP) and Collaborative Data Objects (CDO)," for a much more in-depth look at how to use CDO's object model and how it works within an application.

COM Add-Ins

In the past, when it came to developing applications that link into the application's environment, you would need to a lot of hardcore programming as well as a complete understanding of the target application's software development kit (SDK) — assuming one was available. With Windows applications, you would have to poke around the parent form's environment and write routines that would "hook" themselves to the application's main form and write callback routines to make your add-in appear to be a seamless component. This is very time-consuming and very risky: time-consuming because of all the time invested to learn the SDK, write the add-in, and test it; risky because if you didn't hook into the interface just right, you could crash your system or your target audience's system.

Then came COM. Outlook and Office 2000 are COM-enabled applications that support COM add-ins. A COM add-in is an ActiveX DLL containing a COM interface that can be integrated into Outlook and Office. They are used to provide additional functionality in an Office application that wasn't originally there. And because COM add-ins are based on COM, they can be used in other Office products.

COM add-ins are built using any COM-enabled development environment, such as Microsoft Visual C++, Visual Basic, or Inprise Delphi. COM add-ins are registered specifically to be used by Office 2000 applications, which means that they can't be used by any other end-user application. That might change, because ISVs may work with Microsoft to make the COM add-in feature available to them as well, but by the time this book goes to press, only Office 2000 applications support COM add-ins.

See Chapter 8, "COM Add-Ins," for more information about building COM add-ins.

Integration with Applications

We've talked a lot about what Outlook is. We briefly discussed how it can be used in a collaborative environment by using CDO and COM add-ins for adding features to Outlook. Yet for all of our discussion about this technology, the question still remains: How do I put all the pieces together? The rest of the book will cover that in much greater detail. This section will give you an idea of what is in store for you when you start building integration solutions with Outlook.

As you will find in Chapters 2 through 4, the object model Outlook 2000 is built upon is a vast improvement on previous versions. It currently has over 100 new methods and properties and a number of new events that your applications can interact with. Figure 1-12 shows Outlook 2000's hierarchical object model.

Through the use of the object model, you have access to almost any component within Outlook.

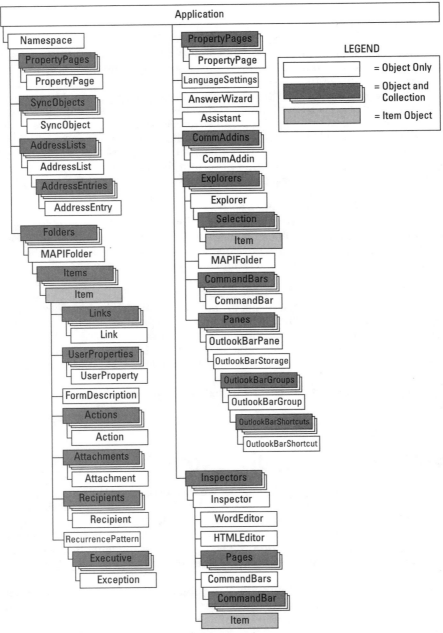

Figure 1-12: Outlook 2000 object model hierarchy

Understanding the object model is the first step toward making applications that interact or integrate with Outlook. If you are building application interfaces that will be used within Outlook, you will need to become familiar with designing Outlook Forms and its Form Components. Outlook provides you with four basic types of forms as templates that you can build upon. Chapter 5, "Outlook Forms," covers this subject in greater detail.

Though the use of the object model and VBA, you can integrate Outlook into your Office applications. Listing 1-1 is an example of the VBA code you would use to instantiate, or create an instance of, Outlook. This code can be used within a VB application, Office product, or any product that is "powered by VBA technology."

Listing 1-1: **Outlook_Open function using VBA**

```
Function Outlook_Open()

    Dim objOutlook As Outlook.Application
    Set objOutlook = New Outlook.Application

    If objOutlook Is Nothing Then
        ' Create a new instance of the object
        Set objOutlook = New Outlook.Application

        ' Check to make sure that object
        ' was created
        If objOutlook Is Nothing Then
            MsgBox "Error in starting Outlook"
            GoTo Err_Outlook_Open
        End If
    End If

    Outlook_Open = True

Exit_Outlook_Open:
    Exit Function

Err_Outlook_Open:
    Outlook_Open = False
    GoTo Exit_Outlook_Open

End Function
```

In Part II, "Outlook Applications," we will be covering in great depth how to integrate Outlook with Office 2000 products, Visual Basic, and non-Office products such as Visio.

Summary

Outlook has come a long way from its earlier predecessors. The object model has been expanded and enhanced with many new methods, properties, and events, making it easier than ever before to extend its features into your own custom solutions. COM add-ins really make it easy to build features into Outlook for a seamless integration. As a collaborative work product, Outlook enables you to tie into Exchange Server through CDO, which allows you extend your reach with other users either through your organization's intranet or through the Internet itself.

✦   ✦   ✦

The Gateway Objects – Application and NameSpace

You can access Outlook's functionality, from both inside and outside Outlook, through its *object model*. This chapter will examine the Application and NameSpace objects, which are the gateways to the remainder of Outlook's large object model, as well as the development environment that Outlook provides to enable you to create custom forms and write code.

Access to Application Code

An Outlook user can access the program's functionality by choosing menu commands, clicking toolbar buttons, and completing dialog boxes. For example, you can create a new blank contact item with the menu command File ⇨ New ⇨ Contact or by pressing the New toolbar button while the Contacts folder is selected. Choosing the File ⇨ New ⇨ Contact menu command or pressing the New toolbar button while the Contacts folder is selected opens a new blank contact item only because the user's action triggers the running of code. Indeed, complex programs may have thousands of lines of code.

You may want to access an application's code programmatically rather than through the application's graphical user interface (GUI). For example, you may write a custom application to be used by your employer's Human Resources department. The application's specifications call for the user of your application to be able to create, from your application, a new Outlook contact item when a new employee is hired. The user cannot create the new contact item using the Outlook GUI

File ➩ New ➩ Contact menu command or the New toolbar button because the user is running your application, not Outlook. Thus, your application must programmatically access the same code as these menu and toolbar items.

With many applications you would be out of luck. The application obviously has the code you need because you can perform the task in question through the application's GUI. The problem may be that the code is so intertwined with other code that it is not possible to access it as a discrete unit. However, the more likely reason is that the application does not permit access to the code, or, in other words, the code is private.

With Outlook you are in luck. The code is organized in a hierarchal model, so that the functionality you need is a discrete unit and not entangled with other code that you can't use in your application. Additionally, the functionality you need is public; it can be accessed by other applications. This is not to say that *all* of Outlook's code is public. However, enough of its functionality is public that you can harness Outlook's power in your own applications.

The benefit of being able to access Outlook's functionality programmatically is not limited to third-party applications. You can also customize Outlook itself. For example, you could create the Human Resources application discussed above as a custom Outlook application. The contact item created when a new employee is hired could be a customized contact form. Additionally, the creation of the form could trigger code that e-mails it to the company's security personnel to notify them of the new hire. Thus, you can leverage Outlook's wide-ranging capabilities as an application with forms and functionality tailored to your customer's requirements. Indeed, your imagination is the main limitation to the applications that you can create with Outlook.

As stated earlier, Outlook's functionality is accessed, whether from inside or outside, through its object model. Before we explore what's inside the object model (i.e., the objects themselves), it's worthwhile to consider what exactly an object model is.

What Are Object Models?

Automation, formerly known as OLE Automation and ActiveX Automation, is often defined as a data communication protocol for applications meeting the Component Object Model (COM) specification. In plain English, Automation allows different applications to talk to each other. For example, your application, using Automation, can command Microsoft Access to provide the last year's sales figures stored in a database, order Microsoft Excel to incorporate these sales figures into a formula, instruct Microsoft Word to put the formula results in a report, and finally tell Microsoft Outlook to e-mail the report to corporate headquarters.

Automation permits you to combine the best features of several applications. In the above example, your application, through Automation, used Microsoft Access for database services, Microsoft Excel for calculations, Microsoft Word as a report writer, and, of course, Microsoft Outlook for e-mail services.

All Microsoft Office 2000 applications support Automation. Many non-Microsoft applications also support Automation, including Visio and AutoCAD. Additionally, you do not need to rely on the existence of programs that support Automation. You can write your own applications that support Automation. The Human Resources application discussed earlier would use Automation to create contact items in Outlook. To do so, it first would have to access Outlook. It would do so through *objects*.

Applications that support Automation contain objects. Objects represent different parts of the application. For example, Outlook has an Application object that represents the Outlook application itself, the oddly named NameSpace object that represents the root of the Outlook folders, the Folder object that represents Outlook folders such as the Inbox, and Item objects that represent, depending on the type of item, mail messages, task requests, appointments, or contact information.

The Human Resources application would access Outlook through Outlook's Application object. However, accessing Outlook is not enough. The Human Resources application also needs to create an Outlook contact item. It does so through a *property*, *method*, or *event* of an object, in this case the Application object.

Properties

A property is a characteristic of an object. For example, a MailItem object has a Subject property whose value is the text in the subject line of a mail message. This property can be used to *return* the value of the text in the subject line so you can programmatically read this value. The ability to return the value of the Subject property could be used to find, among all mail messages in the Inbox, those having a particular subject. The Subject property also can be *set*, which means that you can programmatically set the value of the text in the subject line. The ability to set the value of the Subject property would be useful in, for example, a customized helpdesk form in which you would want the Subject property to state the name of the sender followed by "Help!!!" However, some properties can return, but not set, a value. An example would be the MailItem object's ReceivedTime property that represents when the mail message was received. Properties that can return but not set a value are referred to as *read-only*. It is logical that the ReceivedTime property is read-only since the time an item was received is an objective fact that should not be altered through code.

Methods

A method is an action that an object may take. For example, a MailItem object has a Send method that sends the mail message. This particular method is used to send a message programmatically.

Methods may have one or more parameters. A parameter is information that the method needs to take its action. For example, the CreateItem method of the Application object creates an item. However, Outlook has many types of items, such as a mail message item, appointment item, contact item, and task item. In order to create a contact item, the `CreateItem` method is passed a contact item parameter.

Events

An event is an incident that has occurred. For example, a MailItem object has a `Send` event that occurs when the item is being sent, either by the user clicking the `Send` button or by code in which the item's `Send` method is called. This relationship between the `Send` method and the `Send` event is not an unusual one between methods and events. Often a method will cause a corresponding event to occur, or "fire." However, while an object uses a method to do something, an event tells the object that something is happening.

The MailItem object just discussed may be one of many mail messages in an Inbox or other folder. Each folder contains an Items collection. A collection is a container for objects, usually the same kind of object. Outlook also has a Folders collection that contains subfolders, an Attachment collection that contains Attachment objects that are attached to an item, a Recipients collection that contains the Recipient objects that are the recipients of an item, and so on. A collection may have its own properties, methods, and events. For example, the Items collection has a Count property whose value is the number of objects in the collection, an `Add` method to add items to the collection, a `Remove` method to remove objects from a collection, and an ItemRemove event that fires when an item is removed from the collection. When the Human Resources application adds a contact item to the Contacts folder, the Count property of the Items collection of that folder increases by one.

The Outlook object model consists of the public collections, objects, properties, methods and events. Outlook has private collections, objects, properties, methods and events, but since these cannot be accessed programmatically, either within or outside Outlook, they are not considered part of the Outlook object model.

While the examples discussed above used Automation in an external, standalone application, Automation can just as easily be used by a custom Outlook application which, for example, incorporates into contact information an Excel spreadsheet or chart displaying data from Access and generates an e-mail using Word as an e-mail editor. Additionally, you can write an Outlook application, or code behind an Outlook form, which accesses Outlook's own collections, objects, properties, methods and events.

Automation has its limits. It won't make you thinner or better looking, though the authors haven't given up hope. However, Automation may make you richer. Programmers who understand Automation are in high demand. Given Outlook's ability to do many things, programmers who understand how to incorporate Outlook into business solutions are rarely found on freeway off ramps with cardboard signs proclaiming their willingness to program for food.

Now that you are properly motivated, let's start programming! After all, this is the Outlook 2000 *Programming* Bible!

Programming Languages and Development Environments

What programming language do you use? Do you use a Visual Basic or its relatives Visual Basic for Applications (VBA) or Visual Basic Script (VBScript)? Instead, should you use C++, Java, or Java Script? Additionally, where do you start writing your program? Do you fire up Visual Studio, Outlook, or both? Are the authors asking too many rhetorical questions? Leaving that last question alone, the good news is you do have many choices. The bad news is you have to choose. This section will help you make those choices wisely.

Choosing a Programming Language

The programming language you use depends on what you are trying to accomplish:

✦ *I want to write a standalone application that uses Outlook services.* Visual Basic is a good choice, though not the only choice. Other COM-compliant programming languages, like Visual C++, Java or Delphi, will do the job. This book will focus on Visual Basic. Visual Basic is the language generally used by Microsoft Office developers, partly because its ease of use facilitates Rapid Application Development (RAD), but also because, as you'll soon see, variants of Visual Basic are used for coding *within* Outlook.

✦ *I want to write a code component, which usually will be an ActiveX DLL.* Visual Basic again is a good choice, though also again, other COM-compliant programming languages will suffice. Outlook utilizes a specialized ActiveX DLL called a COM Add-In. As you'll see in Chapter 8, a COM Add-In is a specialized dynamic-link library (DLL) registered specifically to be loaded by Office 2000 applications.

✦ *I want to write an application within Outlook.* VBA is the answer. In Office 97 Outlook was the only Office application that did not support VBA and instead required its more limited relation, Visual Basic Script (VBScript). With Office 2000, Outlook joins its siblings in supporting VBA.

✦ *I want to write code for an Outlook form.* Visual Basic Script is the only choice. While Outlook applications support VBA, Outlook forms do not.

✦ *I want to automate Outlook actions.* VBScript again is a good choice. You might want to automate the e-mailing of a file when a user right-clicks the file in Windows Explorer and chooses a custom "Send by E-mail" option from the SendTo context menu. You can accomplish this with Windows Scripting Host (WSH), which supports, among script languages, VBScript.

✦ *I want a life.* That's a different book.

Finally, these alternatives are not mutually exclusive. Some concepts may be implemented either as a COM Add-In or as an Outlook VBA application, or VBScript code behind a form can call VBA application-level code.

Configuring Your Development Environment

The code examples in this chapter will use Visual Basic and VBA. VBScript will be used in the code examples for Outlook forms in Chapter 3.

 Note Our "sister" Bible series books, *Visual Basic 6 Bible* and *Visual Basic for Applications Bible*, both published by IDG Books Worldwide, are excellent resources on Visual Basic, VBA, and their respective development environments.

Visual Basic

These examples will use a Visual Basic program run outside of Outlook. Follow these steps to get started:

1. Start Visual Basic.

2. Select New Project from the File menu.

3. Select Standard EXE from the New Project dialog box.

4. Insert a Standard module. The module will have one procedure, Sub Main.

5. Select Project Properties under the Project Menu. On the General Tab, select Sub Main from the dropdown list labeled Startup Object. See Figure 2-1.

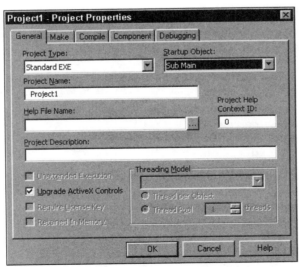

Figure 2-1: Selecting Sub Main as the Startup Object

6. Click the References under the Project menu. Check Microsoft Outlook 9.0 Object Library. See Figure 2-2.

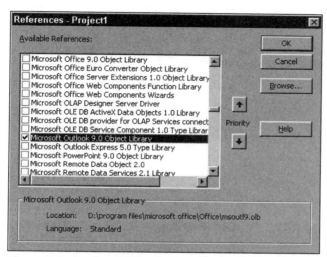

Figure 2-2: Setting a Reference to the Outlook 9.0 Object Library

The project will not use the default form, which you can keep or delete. Rather, the code will output information in the Immediate Window using the Print method of the Debug object. You activate the Immediate Window by selecting that menu item under the View menu or by the keyboard shortcut Ctrl-G.

You also should save the module, form (if you keep it), and project files before you run the project. Unlike in VBA, these Visual Basic files have no particular naming restrictions and do not have to be saved in any particular location.

VBA development environment

The VBA development environment is the Visual Basic Editor. Open this editor by selecting Macro from the Tools menu and then choosing Visual Basic Editor. The shortcut key Alt-F11 also opens the Visual Basic Editor.

Figure 2-3 shows the Visual Basic Editor with the Project Explorer in the top left-hand corner. If the Project Explorer does not appear, you can display it by selecting Project Explorer from the View menu or by using the keyboard shortcut Ctrl-R.

The Project Explorer has an object named ThisOutlookSession. ThisOutlookSession is a class module as opposed to a standard module. Most of your code will be written in this class module.

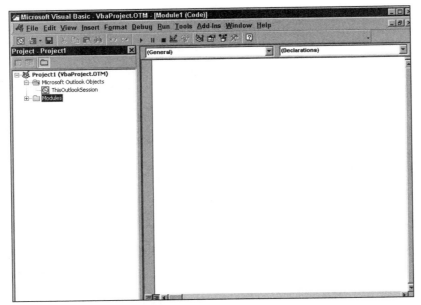

Figure 2-3: The Visual Basic Editor

While the nodes in the VBA Project Explorer are different from those in the typical Project Explorer for a Standard EXE Visual Basic project, the VBA development environment is quite similar to the Visual Basic development environment. However, there are significant differences between the two environments when you are saving a project. A VBA project is saved under the name VBAProject.otm. You cannot change the name of this file. Additionally, this file is binary, rather than a text file like a .vbp project file in Visual Basic. Further, the project file is saved in a specific location that you cannot change. Table 2-1 lists these locations:

Table 2-1		
Location for Saved VBA Project File VBA Project.otm		
Operating System	***Location for VBAProject.otm***	
Windows 95 and 98 without UserProfiles	`C:\Windows\Application Data\Microsoft\Outlook`	
Windows 95 and 98 with UserProfiles	`C:\Windows\Profiles\`*UserName*`\Application Data\ Microsoft\Outlook`	
Windows NT 4.0 or Windows 2000	`C:\Winnt\Profiles\`*UserName*`\Application Data\ Microsoft\Outlook`	

You would be correct if you came to the conclusion that since a VBA project can have only one name and must be saved in only one place, Outlook supports only one VBA project per user. This is different from Word and Excel, in which you can have a different VBA project for each .doc and .xls file. The reason is that in Word and Excel (among other Office applications) each .doc and .xls file is a separate entity within an instance of the application. For example, in Word you usually are working with one particular .doc file at a time. By contrast, in Outlook you generally are working on an application-wide basis rather than being limited to a particular item to the exclusion of the others. Therefore Outlook permits only one application-wide VBA project per user profile, or, if there are no user profiles, one VBA project.

The Outlook Object Model

Outlook 2000 is not the first version of Outlook to have an object model. Indeed, all prior versions of Outlook had an object model. However, the Outlook 2000 object model is clearly "new and improved." The improvements include numerous new collections, objects, properties, methods, and events. However, the most significant improvement is support for application-level events.

The previous versions of Microsoft Outlook provided event notifications only at the level of an individual Outlook item, such as a mail item or contact item. However, there were no event notifications for actions at the application level, such as the user switching folders or views or new mail arriving. Outlook 2000 added many new application-level events, including not only notifications of changes to views of folders and items, but also changes to the contents of the folder or the collection of items in it.

The addition in Outlook 2000 of application-level events goes hand in hand with the support in Outlook 2000 of VBA application-level programs. Outlook 98, consistent with its limited support of only item-level events, supported only VBScript code behind a form. Outlook 2000 still supports VBScript code behind a form, but also supports an application-level VBA project. An application-level program should be able to react to events at that level.

Figure 2-4 shows the objects and collections of the Outlook object model. It would take a wall-size chart to show, in one place, the properties, methods and events of all of these objects and collections.

The Outlook object model has a hierarchical structure typical of applications that support Automation. This hierarchy of objects is comparable to Windows Explorer, in which following the level of "My Computer" are, in succeeding order, the drives, the top-level directories (folders), the subdirectories (subfolders), and so on until the files of a directory or subdirectory are reached.

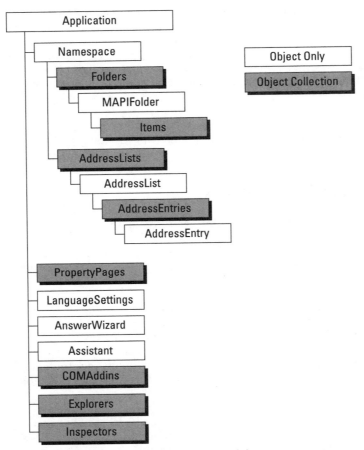

Figure 2-4: The Outlook 2000 Object Model

The top-level object in the Outlook object model is the Application object. This object is comparable to "My Computer" in Windows Explorer. A next-level object is the "NameSpace." This object is the root of the Outlook folders, and is comparable to a drive in Windows Explorer. The NameSpace object contains folders such as "Personal Folders" or "Public Folders," which themselves usually contain other folders. These top-level folders are comparable to the top-level directories in Windows Explorer. The top-level folders can be used to access the folders they contain, which are comparable to subdirectories (or subfolders) in Windows Explorer. Finally, folders contain Item objects, whether mail messages, task requests, appointments, or contact information. These Item objects are comparable to individual files in Windows Explorer.

In Windows Explorer, one method of accessing a file is "drilling down" through drives, directories, and subdirectories until you reach the file. Similarly, in Outlook, the top-level Application object is used to access the second-level NameSpace object. The

NameSpace object in turn is used to access the Folders collection. The Folders collection is used to access MAPIFolder objects. Each MAPIFolder object has an Items collection, which contains the folder's items, whether they are mail messages, contacts, appointments or other item types. The NameSpace object also is used to access the Outlook address books, which are contained in the Address Lists collection, which contains the address books, each an AddressList object that contains an AddressEntries collection that contains the address entries, which are AddressEntry objects.

Windows Explorer also provides an interface with which you can examine the contents of folders and files. Similarly, Outlook provides an Explorer object with which you can view the contents of folders and an Inspector object to view the contents of an item. Collections are present here also. The available Explorer objects are contained in an Explorers collection and available Inspector objects are contained in an Inspectors collection.

This chapter will focus on the properties, methods and events of these objects and collections of objects, which are the entry points to the many other objects and collections in the Outlook object model that will be discussed in the following chapters.

Application Object

The *Application* object (see Figure 2-5) represents the Outlook application. Outlook is a multi-use application. This means that only one instance of Outlook may be running at one time. This is in contrast to, for example, Visual Basic, in which multiple instances can run at one time, and sometimes should to test, for example, ActiveX EXE projects. Therefore, the Application object always represents the running instance of Outlook.

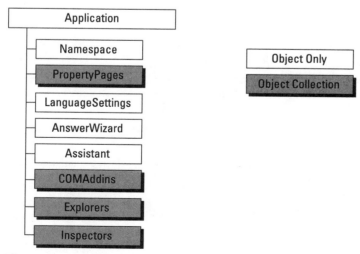

Figure 2-5: Application object

As Figure 2-5 depicts, the Application object is at the top of the Outlook object hierarchy. It is the only Outlook object that can be created from outside Outlook. All other Outlook objects must be created through the Application object or a descendant of the Application object. In other words, the Application object is the gateway through which all other objects in Outlook are accessed.

Properties

Table 2-2 lists the properties of the Application object:

Table 2-2 **Properties of Application Object**	
Name	**Description**
AnswerWizard	Returns the AnswerWizard object, which you can access through the Answer Wizard tab in Outlook Help.
Application	Returns an Application object that represents the parent application (Microsoft Outlook) for an object. This is also a property of other Outlook objects and more usefully accessed by them since the Application object already represents the parent application.
Assistant	Returns a Microsoft Office Assistant Wizard object that represents the (boo, hiss) Microsoft Office Assistant.
Class	Returns the `olObjectClass` constant corresponding to the object, in this case `olApplication` having a value of 0. This is also a property of other Outlook objects and more usefully accessed by certain collections. For example, this property is used with the Items collection to distinguish among the different types of items in the collection.
COMAddIns	Returns a collection of all Component Object Model (COM) Add-Ins currently loaded in Microsoft Outlook. COM Add-Ins are discussed in Chapter 8.
Explorers	Returns collection of all open Explorers. The Explorers collection and the Explorer object are discussed in Chapter 3.
Inspectors	Returns collection of all open Inspectors. The Inspectors collection and the Inspector object are discussed in Chapter 4.
LanguageSettings	Returns a LanguageSettings object from which the language-specific characteristics of the installed Outlook application can be determined.
Name	Returns application's name, "Outlook."

Name	Description
Parent	Returns the parent object. The Application object has no parent since it is at the top of the object hierarchy. This is also a property of other Outlook objects and more usefully accessed by them since they, unlike the Application object, do have parent objects.
ProductCode	Returns the Globally Unique Identifier (GUID) for Outlook.
Session	Returns the NameSpace object for current session of Outlook. The NameSpace object is discussed next in this section.
Version	Returns string representing the version number of the installed Outlook application.

The code in Listing 2-1 uses the Name and Version properties of the Application object to output to the Immediate Window the name and version number of the installed Outlook application, in this case "Outlook version 9.0.0.3011."

Listing 2-1: **Output Outlook Name and Version to Immediate Window**

```
Sub Main()

Dim myOutlook As Outlook.Application
Set myOutlook = New Outlook.Application
Debug.Print myOutlook.Name + " version " + myOutlook.Version
myOutlook.Quit
Set myOutlook = Nothing

End Sub
```

Binding

Visual Basic (or another COM-compliant programming language) must bind an object variable to a particular object. In essence, the application must determine if the type of object the variable is supports the particular property or method it is calling, since not all objects support identical properties and methods. This determination can be made either when the project is compiled or when the project is running. Making this determination at compile time is referred to as "early binding." Making this determination at run time is referred to as "late binding."

Continued

Continued

In order for the compiler to determine if the type of object the variable is supports a particular property or method (early binding), the variable must be declared as a particular object rather than as a generic object. The statement `Dim myOutlook As Outlook.Application` declares `myOutlook` as a particular object, Outlook.Application. However, the Visual Basic compiler will not know what an Outlook.Application even is, much less be able to determine if it supports a particular property or method, unless you set a reference to the Microsoft Outlook 9.0 Object Library using the References menu item under the Project menu.

The application can determine while it is running if the type of object the variable is supports a particular property or method (late binding). However, this is extra work for your application over and above whatever else it needs to do to run. With early binding this work has already been done by the compiler before the running of the application and therefore does not need to be done again while the application is running.

However, there are circumstances when you use late binding. One example is when the object you are attempting to reference does not have a type library. Another example is when you will not know until run time, based on a user choice, the precise type of object you will be trying to reference. Late-bound generic object variables are declared as generic objects, such as `Dim myOutlook As Object`. The object variable is then instantiated using either the `CreateObject` method or the `GetObject` method. Basically, the `GetObject` function is used when there is a current instance of the object or if you want to create the object with a file already loaded, and the `CreateObject` function is used if there is no current instance and you don't want the object started with a file loaded.

The code first declares a variable, `myOutlook`, whose type is an Application object of Outlook. Just as it is necessary to use an integer variable to store an integer value in memory, it is necessary to use an object variable to access the properties and methods of the object.

With primitive (built-in) Visual Basic variables such as integers, declaring a variable would be sufficient to allocate memory for the variable. However, Outlook.Application is not a primitive variable but instead an object. Therefore it is necessary to use the `Set` statement and `New` operator to allocate memory for the object variable. This also is referred to as "instantiating" the object variable.

After using `Debug.Print` to output the Application object's name and version to the Immediate Window, the `Quit` method of the Application object is used to close the Outlook session that was instantiated. This prevents the Outlook session from lingering in memory and draining system resources. The `Set myOutlook = Nothing` has the same purpose.

Methods

Table 2-3 lists the methods of the Application object:

Table 2-3
Methods of Application Object

Name	Action	Parameters
ActiveExplorer	Returns topmost Explorer object, or Nothing if no active Explorer.	None.
ActiveInspector	Returns topmost Inspector object, or Nothing if no active Inspector.	None.
ActiveWindow	Returns topmost Explorer or Inspector object, or Nothing if none.	None.
CreateItem	Creates and returns a new Outlook item	The type of standard Outlook item represented by one of the olItem Type constants, which are listed in Table 2-4.
CreateItemFromTemplate	Creates and returns a new Outlook item from a template.	Required: String representing the path and file name of the template file (*.oft). Optional: Folder in which item will be created. If omitted the folder will be the default folder for the item type.
CreateObject	Creates an object of the specified class. Used to create objects of other applications, such as Excel, and not Outlook.	String representing Class name of object to create. Example: "Excel. Application."
GetNameSpace	Returns a NameSpace Object.	The string "MAPI."
Quit	Closes the existing Outlook session.	None.

Table 2-4
olItemType Constants Representing Standard Item Types

Item Type	Constant	Value
Mail Message	OlMailItem	0
Appointment	OlAppointmentItem	1
Contact	OlContactItem	2
Task	OlTaskItem	3
Journal	OlJournalItem	4
Note	OlNoteItem	5
Post	OlPostItem	6

The ActiveExplorer method is used to return a reference to the currently active Explorer object. The Explorer object is discussed in Chapter 3. This object is a window that displays the contents of a folder, much as the list pane in Windows Explorer displays the files in the folder selected in the contents pane. Figure 2-6 shows the topmost Explorer object, which shows the contents of the Inbox folder.

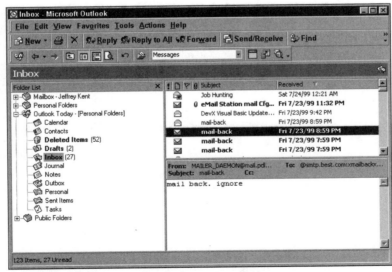

Figure 2-6: Explorer showing contents of Inbox

The code in Listing 2-2 maximizes the active Explorer if there is one:

Listing 2-2: **Maximize active Explorer**

```
Dim myOutlook As Outlook.Application
Dim myExplorer As Outlook.Explorer
Set myOutlook = New Outlook.Application
Set myExplorer = myOutlook.ActiveExplorer
If Not myExplorer Is Nothing Then _
    MyExplorer.WindowState = olMaximized
```

The check for `Is Nothing` is necessary since the `ActiveExplorer` method returns the `Nothing` keyword if there is no currently active Explorer object.

Like the `ActiveExplorer` method, the `ActiveInspector` method returns a reference to the currently active Inspector object. The Inspector object is discussed in Chapter 4. This object is a window that displays the contents of an item, much as opening a file in Windows Explorer displays the contents of a file. Figure 2-7 shows the topmost Inspector object, which shows the contents of a mail message typical of the fan mail the authors receive.

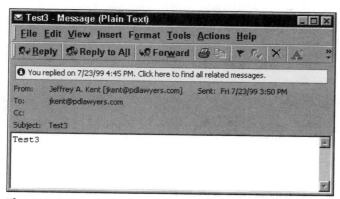

Figure 2-7: Inspector showing contents of fan mail message

The code in Listing 2-3 maximizes the active Inspector if there is one:

Listing 2-3: **Maximize active Inspector**

```
Dim myOutlook As Outlook.Application
Dim my Inspector As Outlook.Inspector
Set myOutlook = New Outlook.Application
Set my Inspector = myOutlook.ActiveInspector
If Not my Inspector Is Nothing Then _
    MyExplorer.WindowState = olMaximized
```

As with the code example of the `ActiveExplorer` method, the check for `Is Nothing` is necessary since the `ActiveInspector` method returns the `Nothing` keyword if there is no currently active Inspector object.

The `ActiveWindow` method returns the object that represents the currently active window, or `Nothing` if there is no currently active window. The active window may be an Explorer object or an Inspector object. In addition to checking for `Is Nothing`, because you do not know whether the type of object being returned is an Explorer object or an Inspector object, you need to test for which type of object is being returned before you assign the return value to an object variable. Otherwise, you risk assigning to an Explorer object variable a return value that represents an Inspector object, or vice versa. Either will result in an error. This checking is done by the `Class` property, as shown by the code in Listing 2-4:

Listing 2-4: **Using the ActiveWindow method and Class property**

```
Dim myOutlook As Outlook.Application
Dim my Explorer As Outlook. Explorer
Dim my Inspector As Outlook.Inspector
Set myOutlook = New Outlook.Application
If myOutlook.ActiveWindow.Class = olExplorer Then
    Set myExplorer = myOutlook.ActiveWindow
    If Not myExplorer Is Nothing Then _
        myExplorer.WindowState = olMaximized
End If
If myOutlook.ActiveWindow.Class = olInspector Then
    Set myInspector = myOutlook.ActiveWindow
    If Not myInspector Is Nothing Then _
        myInspector.WindowState = olMaximized
End If
```

The CreateItem method can be used to create an item directly from the Application object without having to drill down into the object hierarchy. The code in Listing 2-5 creates and displays a mail message:

Listing 2-5: **Using the CreateItem method**

```
Dim myOutlook As Outlook.Application
Dim myMsg As Outlook.MailItem
Set myOutlook = New Outlook.Application
Set myMsg = myOutlook.CreateItem(myMailItem)
myMsg.Display
```

Declaring an Object Variable

Listing 2-3, which showed how to maximize the active Inspector, declared and instantiated the Outlook Application object variable as follows:

```
Dim myApp As Outlook.Application
Set myApp = New Outlook.Application
```

Other code examples you may see, including some in the Microsoft Outlook Visual Basic Reference help file, declare and instantiate the Outlook Application object variable in one line and do not use the Set statement:

```
Dim myApp As New Outlook.Application
```

The above line declared and allocated memory for the object variable. The object variable is then created when it first calls a property or method, in this case the Name and Version properties:

```
Debug.Print myOutlook.Name + " version " + myOutlook.Version
```

We recommend the first way, declaring the object variable without the New keyword and then using the Set statement. The reason for this is that you know exactly where in the code (i.e., the Set statement) the object variable is created. By contrast, if you declare the object variable with the New keyword, and make changes to your code, exactly where the object variable is created could change, depending on where it first calls a property or method. This could present a problem if you are relying on the instantiation event of the object variable (such as the Startup event of the Application object) to perform other tasks in your program since when these tasks are performed could change, possibly to the detriment of your program.

Why then show another, debatably inferior method of dimensioning an object variable? The reason is that this method is often used in code examples, including the Microsoft Outlook Visual Basic Reference help file!

Listing 2-3, which maximized the active Inspector, did not invoke the Quit method of the Application object (myOutlook.Quit), as did code Listing 2-1 that output to the Immediate Window the name and version number of the installed Outlook application. The reason is that using the Quit method in code Listing 2-3 would cause the session to end before you could see the mail message the code creates. This was not a problem in Listing 2-1 because the output was to the Immediate Window rather than to Outlook itself. The CreateItemFromTemplate method is quite similar to the CreateItem method. The difference is that the required argument is the template path and file name rather than the constant representing the type of item. The code in Listing 2-6, which uses the CreateItemFromTemplate method, is similar to code Listing 2-5, in that both use the CreateItem method to create and display a mail message. The difference is that the code in Listing 2-6 uses the template file specified in the parameter to the method:

Listing 2-6: **Displaying a mail message using template**

```
Dim myOutlook As Outlook.Application
Dim myMsg As Outlook.MailItem
Set myOutlook = New Outlook.Application
Set myMsg = myOutlook.CreateItemFromTemplate _
    ("c:\MyDocuments\idg.oft")
myMsg.Display
```

Another difference between the CreateItemFromTemplate and CreateItem methods is that the CreateItem method can only create default Outlook items. It cannot be used to create new items based on a custom form. By contrast, the CreateItem FromTemplate method can be used to create a new item based on a custom form if a template file for that item was created.

As discussed in Chapter 4, a new item based on a custom form can be created by the Add method of the Items collection. The usual purpose of the CreateObject method is to use another application's objects. The following code snippet displays an existing file in Word:

```
Dim objWord As Object
Set objWord = CreateObject("Word.Application")
ObjWord.Visible = True
objWord.Documents.Open("C:\pleaformercy.doc")
```

Note   As discussed earlier in the "Binding" sidebar, another CreateObject method can be used to create an instance of Outlook when the object variable is late bound:

```
Dim objOutlook As Object
Se objOutlook = CreateObject("Outlook.Application")
```

However, this is not using the CreateObject method of the Outlook Application object. Rather, it is using the Visual Basic CreateObject method.

The GetNameSpace method is quite important. This method creates and returns a NameSpace object. The GetNameSpace method is used in a code example when we discuss the NameSpace object later in this chapter.

Events

Table 2-5 lists the events of the Application objects:

	Table 2-5 Events of Application Object	
Name	**Fires When ...**	**Cancelable?**
StartUp	Outlook is starting.	No.
Quit	Outlook is closing.	No.
ItemSend	An item is being sent.	Yes.
NewMail	An item arrives in the Inbox.	No.
Reminder	A reminder is about to be displayed.	No.
OptionPagesAdd	A page is about to be added to the property page in the dialog box displayed by selecting Options under the Tools menu.	No.

Some events can be "canceled." The word "canceled" is somewhat of a misnomer. The event still fires. It is the consequence of the event that is cancelled. For example, in the case of the Item_Send event, canceling this event results in the item not being sent.

The first VBA code example, like the preceding one using Visual Basic, will create and display a mail message, but this time in VBA. First, an Outlook.MailItem object variable should be declared. For reasons that will be explained shortly, declare it under General Declarations of ThisOutlookSession. Figure 2-8 shows the declaration of the Outlook.MailItem variable objMsg in the VBA code window, under General Declarations of ThisOutlookSession:

The Startup event is a logical place to instantiate variables. The Visual Basic editor can be used to create the stub of the code, that is:

```
Private Sub Application_Startup()

End Sub
```

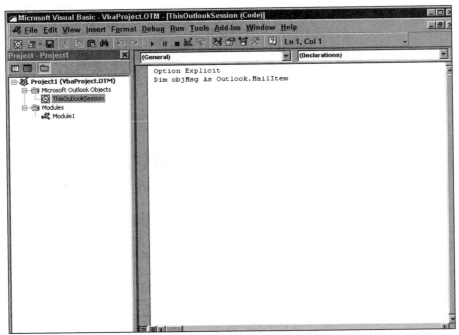

Figure 2-8: Declaration of Variable in VBA under General Declarations of ThisOutlookSession

Figure 2-9 shows how to create the code stub by choosing Application from the object dropdown box on the upper left of the code window and then choosing Startup from the event procedures dropdown box on the upper right of the code.

The Startup event is used to instantiate the MailItem variable objMsg and then display the mail message form:

```
Private Sub Application_Startup()

Set objMsg = Application.CreateItem(olMailItem)
objMsg.Display

End Sub
```

The Quit event is used to deallocate the memory previously allocated to the object variable objMsg when the Outlook session finishes:

```
Private Sub Application_Quit()

Set objMsg = Nothing

End Sub
```

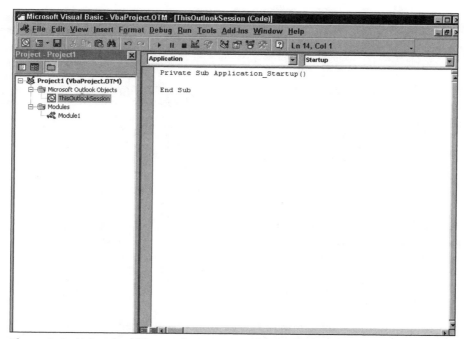

Figure 2-9: Using the object and event procedures dropdown lists to create a code stub

The variable objMsg was declared in General Declarations in order to give it scope in the entire class. This code would not compile if objMsg had been declared in the Startup event instead of in General Declarations because then the scope of objMsg would be limited to the Startup event procedure and would not extend to the Quit event procedure in which objMsg is used in the statement Set objMsg = Nothing.

As an observant reader you will note that this VBA example did not declare and instantiate an Application object. In the prior Visual Basic code examples it was necessary to declare and instantiate an Application object. By contrast, VBA provides without your even asking an Application object, and even conveniently calls it "Application." The reason is that ThisOutlookSession *is* a built-in and already instantiated Application object, which is referred to in VBA code as the "Application."

Additionally, were this example converted to Visual Basic, it would not be enough to declare and instantiate an Application object in the manner of the previous examples:

```
Dim myOutlook As Outlook.Application
Set myOutlook = New Outlook.Application
```

The Application object variable myOutlook would not respond to the Startup or Quit events. Indeed, these events would not appear in the Event Procedures drop-down list in the code window when myOutlook was chosen from the Objects dropdown list.

The reason is that a variable of an object that has events may (but need not) respond to those events. The object variable must be declared with the WithEvents keyword to respond to the events. Otherwise, while the events will continue to fire, the object variable will simply ignore them. Therefore, in the Visual Basic code, the Application object variable would have to be declared with the WithEvents keyword before it was instantiated:

```
Dim WithEvents myOutlook As Outlook.Application
Set myOutlook = New Outlook.Application
```

Once again, as an observant reader, you will note that in the VBA code the WithEvents keyword was not used. The reason is that the built-in, instantiated Application object was declared, behind the scenes, WithEvents. However, as further code examples will demonstrate, other object variables in VBA, which are not built in and therefore have to be declared explicitly as in Visual Basic, must be declared WithEvents in order to respond to events.

The ItemSend event, in addition to being subject to cancellation as discussed above, can be used to examine items before they are sent. The following code snippet cancels the sending of the message if the message has any attachments. More practical implementations of this event will be discussed later in the book after further objects and collections have been covered:

```
Private Sub Application_ItemSend _
    (ByVal Item As Object, Cancel As Boolean)

    If Item.Attachements.Count Then Cancel = True

End Sub
```

The NewMail event can be used to provide more conspicuous notification of the arrival of new mail than the rather mild dialog box Outlook provides (if enabled). One of the authors (we won't mention names) solved the problem of a user who ignored incoming messages on the company's internal e-mail by using the NewMail event to play a sound file that emitted a blood-curdling scream.

The Reminder event can be used to provide more conspicuous notification of a reminder than the mild bell and dialog box Outlook provides. One of the authors (again, we won't mention names) solved the problem of a user (yes, the same one) who ignored reminders by also using the Reminder event to play a sound file that emitted a blood-curdling scream. With the proper attitude, and a disregard for your personal well being, programming can be great fun!

NameSpace Object

The *NameSpace* object (see Figure 2-10) represents the Outlook data source. This object is at the second level of the Outlook object model. Therefore, it is accessed from the Application object. As the Application object is the gateway to the Outlook application, the NameSpace object is the gateway to the Outlook collections that contain data: Folders, AddressLists, PropertyPages, and SynchObjects.

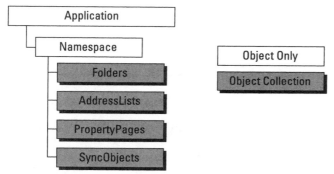

Figure 2-10: NameSpace object

Properties

Table 2-6 lists the properties of the NameSpace object:

Table 2-6 Properties of NameSpace Object	
Name	*Description*
AddressLists	Collection of AddressLists, such as the Global Address List and Contacts.
Application	Returns the Application object.
Class	The olObjectClass constant, in this case olNameSpace having a value of 1.
CurrentUser	Display name of current user.
Folders	Collection of top-level folders, such as Personal Folders and Public Folders.

Continued

Table 2-6 *(continued)*	
Name	**Description**
Parent	The parent object, in this case the Application object.
Session	Returns the NameSpace object for the current session. Therefore, this property would return the very NameSpace object that is calling it, which is not very useful. Other Outlook objects also have a Session property. This property is more useful when called by them.
SynchObjects	Collection of all synchronization profiles.
Type	"MAPI" is the only supported type.

The AddressLists property returns a reference to the AddressLists collection. This collection contains AddressList objects such as the Personal Address Book and the Global Address List. It provides access to the root of the address book hierarchy much as the NameSpace object provides access to the root of the Outlook folder hierarchy.

Cross-Reference The address book collections and objects are discussed in Chapter 4, "Outlook Items."

The CurrentUser property contains the name of the user who is currently logged on. The Visual Basic code in Listing 2-7 uses the CurrentUser property to output to the Immediate Window the name of the current user:

Listing 2-7: Output Current User's name to Immediate Window

```
Sub Main()

Dim myOutlook As Outlook.Application
Dim ns As Outlook.NameSpace
Set myOutlook = New Outlook.Application
Set ns = myOutlook.GetNameSpace("MAPI")
Debug.Print ns.CurrentUser
myOutlook.Quit
Set ns = Nothing
Set myOutlook = Nothing

End Sub
```

The object variable ns is declared as a variable whose type is a NameSpace object of Outlook. This is comparable to the declaration of the object variable myOutlook that represents the Application object.

In this code example the object variable ns is not declared WithEvents because it will not need to respond to events to output the value of the CurrentUser property to the Immediate Window. However, if the object variable ns needed to respond to events, it would have to be declared with the WithEvents keyword as follows:

```
Dim WithEvents ns As Outlook.NameSpace
```

As was the case with the Application object in prior Visual Basic code examples, an instance of the NameSpace object must be instantiated. However, the NameSpace object is not instantiated with the New keyword as was the Application object variable. The New keyword only can be used to instantiate a top-level object, i.e., the Application object. It cannot be used to instantiate a child object, and a NameSpace object is a "child" of the Application object. Instead, a child object is instantiated, using the Set statement, by a method of the parent object. Here, the NameSpace object variable ns is instantiated in a Set statement by the GetNameSpace method of the Application object:

```
Set ns = myOutlook.GetNameSpace("MAPI")
```

The GetNameSpace method returns a reference to a NameSpace object with a data source of the type specified in its one argument. The argument "MAPI" is an acronym for Mail Application Programming Interface, the only data source currently supported by Outlook. For the same reason, "MAPI" is the only value returned by the Type property.

Instantiating a NameSpace variable from an Application object is consistent with the hierarchal nature of the object model. Second-level objects are created from first-level objects, third-level objects are created from second-level objects, and so on.

GetNameSpace is not called by Outlook.Application, but rather from the object variable, myOutlook, which represents the Application object. The reason for this is that the methods of the Application object must be called from a living instance of that object. Outlook.Application is just an abstract representation of the object, much like a data type.

Finally, the GetNameSpace method is called with the dot syntax, in which the object variable and the method are separated by a dot.

The Folders property returns the Folders collection. This collection contains MAPIFolder objects such as the Personal Folders and Public Folders. This collection provides access to the root folders much as the NameSpace object provides access to the root of the Outlook folder hierarchy.

Cross-Reference The MAPIFolder objects that are accessed through the Folders collection will be discussed in Chapter 3, "Accessing and Viewing Folders."

The SynchObjects property returns the SynchObjects collection, which, you guessed it, contains SynchObject objects! These objects are new in Outlook 2000. Each SynchObject represents a synchronization profile for a user. A synchronization profile lets users configure different synchronization scenarios, selecting which folders and filters apply.

Methods

Table 2-7 lists the methods of the NameSpace object:

Table 2-7 Methods of NameSpace Object		
Name	*Action*	*Parameters*
AddStore	Adds a personal folder (.pst) file to the current profile.	The path to and name of the .pst file to be added to the profile.
CreateRecipient	Creates a new recipient object, which is a person or a distribution list.	The name of the recipient to be added.
GetDefaultFolder	Returns the default folder of the requested type.	One of the olDefaultFolder constants listed in Table 2-8.
GetFolderFromID	Returns a Folder object identified by the specified entry ID. Not discussed further since it exists for backward compatibility with earlier MAPI applications.	The EntryID and optionally the StoreID of the folder.
GetItemFromID	Returns an Item object identified by the specified entry ID. Not discussed further since it exists for backward compatibility with earlier MAPI applications.	The EntryID and optionally the StoreID of the item.

Name	Action	Parameters
GetRecipientFromID	Returns a Recipient object identified by the specified entry ID.	The EntryID of the recipient.
GetSharedDefaultFolder	Similar to GetDefaultFolder but applies to shared folder to which owner has delegated access to another user.	The Recipient object that owns the folder and one of the olDefaultFolder constants listed in Table 2-8.
Logoff	Logs the user off the current session.	None.
Logon	Logs the user on to a session	Four optional parameters listed in Table 2-9 and discussed in code example below.
PickFolder	Displays the Select Folder dialog box from which the user may pick a folder, and returns a reference to the folder chosen or to Nothing if no folder was chosen (the user pressed the Cancel button).	None.

The AddStore method adds a new personal folder (.pst file) to the current user's profile. This method accomplishes programmatically what the user can do by the menu commands File ➪ Open ➪ Personal Folders File (.pst). Personal folder files are often used to distribute items to other Outlook users.

The CreateRecipient method creates a Recipient object, a person or a distribution list, to which an item will be sent. However, the item will not be sent to the Recipient until the Recipient's name is *resolved*. A user resolves a Recipient's name by choosing Check Names from the Tools menu. A programmer resolves a Recipient's name programmatically by first creating the Recipient object with the CreateRecipient method, and then calling the Resolve method of the Recipient object, and finally checking the Resolved property of the Recipient object, which is True if the name is resolved, False if not. A Recipient's name is resolved if the name is in the user's default AddressList object (such as the Global Address List or Contacts), or, if not, at least is in an appropriate e-mail format such as our editor's, Godzilla@idgbooks.com. The code snippet in Listing 2-8 demonstrates the CreateRecipient and Resolve methods and Resolved property and outputs to the Immediate Window whether the Recipient object is valid:

Listing 2-8: Output to Immediate Window whether Recipient object is valid

```
Dim myOutlook As Outlook.Application
Dim myNS As Outlook.NameSpace
Dim myRecip As Outlook.Recipient
Set myOutlook = New Outlook.Application
Set myNS = myOutlook.GetNameSpace("MAPI")
Set myRecip = myNS.CreateRecipient("Godzilla")
myRecip.Resolve
If myRecip.Resolved Then
    Debug.Print "Valid Recipient"
Else
    Debug.Print "Invalid Recipient"
End If
```

The GetDefaultFolder method returns the default folder of a specified type, such as the Inbox or the Calendar. This method has one parameter, the specified type. The type can be referenced either by an olDefaultFolder constant or the constant's numerical value. Table 2-8 lists these constants and their associated values:

Table 2-8
olDefaultFolder Constants Representing Default Folders

Folder	Constant	Value
Deleted Items	olFolderDeletedItems	3
Outbox	olFolderOutbox	4
Sent Items	olFolderSentMail	5
Inbox	olFolderInbox	6
Calendar	olFolderCalendar	9
Contacts	olFolderContacts	10
Journal	olFolderJournal	11
Notes	olFolderNotes	12
Tasks	olFolderTasks	13
Drafts	olFolderDrafts	16

This code snippet calls the GetDefaultFolder method from an already instanti-ated NameSpace object variable olNS and assigns the return value of that method (a folder) to the already dimensioned variable fldCalendar:

```
Set fldCalendar = olNS.GetDefaultFolder(olFolderCalendar)
```

The GetDefaultFolder method enables you to obtain a reference to a folder without having to iterate through the Folders collection. However, the GetDefaultFolder method applies only to Outlook default folders. It cannot be used to access a private folder you have created or a public folder. If you need to access a custom folder, you will need to drill down further into the object hierarchy to the Folders collection. How to do so is discussed in Chapter 3.

The GetSharedDefaultFolder method (see Listing 2-9) is similar to GetDefault Folder method but applies to the shared folder to which the owner has delegated access to another user. Therefore, it requires, in addition to the olDefaultFolder parameter, a Recipient object representing the owner of the folder. This Recipient object has to be a valid recipient, or, in other words, has to be resolved. If you are thinking that the CreateRecipient code example above might be useful here, you are correct:

Listing 2-9: **Use of GetSharedDefaultFolder method**

```
Dim myOutlook As Outlook.Application
Dim myNS As Outlook.NameSpace
Dim myRecip As Outlook.Recipient
Dim myFolder As Outlook.MAPIFolder
Set myOutlook = New Outlook.Application
Set myNS = myOutlook.GetNameSpace("MAPI")
Set myRecip = myNS.CreateRecipient("Godzilla")
myRecip.Resolve
If myRecip.Resolved Then _
    Set myFolder = myNS.GetSharedDefaultFolder _
        (myRecip, olFolderInbox)
```

The Logon method is often used. This is not surprising since, after all, a user has to log on to Outlook to start using it. If Outlook is already running when the NameSpace object variable is created, the user has already logged on. However, if Outlook is not already running, then the user has to be logged on when the NameSpace object vari-able is created. The user can log on manually, or programmatically with the Logon method.

Table 2-9 describe the four optional parameters of the `Logon` method:

Table 2-9 Parameters of Logon Method		
Name	**Data Type**	**Description**
Profile	String	Name of profile to use for session.
Password	String	Password (if any) associated with profile.
ShowDialog	Boolean	If True, displays the MAPI logon dialog.
NewSession	Boolean	Default is False, and in any event, Outlook does not support multiple sessions.

Profiles

The Profile is analogous to UserProfiles in Windows 95 and 98, which were mentioned above in connection with where a VBA project file is stored. An Outlook profile lists the Information Services previously selected by the user, such as Microsoft Exchange Server, Internet Mail, Outlook Address Book and Personal Folders and the properties of these services. The profile also specifies the order in which the Information Services are used to send e-mail, where received e-mail is delivered, and where other Outlook items are saved. Additionally, the profile specifies which address book is used first to resolve recipient names and the address book in which new contact information is saved.

Profiles are used with Outlook's Corporate or Workgroup (C/W) service option. Outlook has two other service options: No e-mail when Outlook is used solely as a PIM (Personal Information Manager) and Internet Mail Only (IMO) when Outlook is used as an e-mail client but does not use a mail server such as Microsoft Exchange Server. The C/W service option is used if Outlook is a client of Microsoft Exchange Server or another MAPI mail server. Given Outlook's tight integration with Microsoft Exchange Server, it is likely that a business solution will utilize the C/W service option.

The C/W service option requires at least one Outlook profile, but often a user will have more than one profile. A typical example involves a laptop that you will be using in three different situations:

✦ In your office, where, working happy and contented, you are connected to Microsoft Exchange Server and don't need a dial-up connection as you can get to the outside world through the office LAN's T1 or DSL line.

✦ While flying the unfriendly skies, sitting between two sumo wrestlers with the person in front of you having his seat tilted all the way back. Here you are not connected to anything, perhaps not even your sanity.

✦ Staying at the Bates Motel, where your only connection to the outside world is a dial-up connection through POTS (Plain Old Telephone Service), and you hope and pray that the hotel room phone jack is to an analog line and not a modem-frying digital line, and that those sounds from the next room are not what you think they are.

Another circumstance in which different profiles are desirable is when other users share your computer, possibly because your employer is too cheap to buy everyone his or her own.

When there is more than one profile, a default profile can be selected. This profile will be used automatically when the user logs on. However, often a user will want to be able to select the profile when logging on. The user will be prompted for a profile if the "Prompt for a profile to be used" radio button is selected on the Mail Services tab of the Options dialog box (Tools ➪ Options).

This code snippet calls the `Logon` method from an already instantiated NameSpace object variable `olNS`. The profile name and password would be dependent on the particular user:

```
olNS.Logon "myProfile", "myPassword", True, True
```

A more generic call of the `Logon` method would omit the profile name and password as follows:

```
olNS.Logon , , True, True
```

The two commas after `Logon` are necessary as placeholders for the omitted parameters.

The `PickFolder` method displays the Select Folder dialog box shown in Figure 2-11. This folder also can be displayed by the user through the Outlook GUI by, for example, pressing the Browse button in the Advanced Find dialog box displayed by the Tools ➪ Advanced Find menu command.

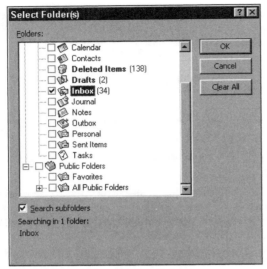

Figure 2-11: Select Folder dialog box

If the user picks a folder and presses the OK button, this method returns a reference to the folder chosen. If the user instead decides not to pick a folder and dismisses the Select Folder dialog box by pressing the Cancel button, the method returns Nothing. The code snippet in Listing 2-10 outputs, using Debug.Print, the name of the selected folder or a message stating that no folder was selected:

Listing 2-10: **Output name of selected folder**

```
Dim myOutlook As Outlook.Application
Dim myNS As Outlook.NameSpace
Dim myFolder As Outlook.MAPIFolder
Set myOutlook = New Outlook.Application
Set myNS = myOutlook.GetNameSpace("MAPI")
Set myFolder = myNS.PickFolder
If myFolder Is Nothing Then
    Debug.Print "No Folder selected"
Else
    Debug.Print MyFolder.Name
End If
```

Event

The NameSpace object supports only one event, OptionsPagesAdd, which is similar to the event of the Application object with the same name, the difference being that it pertains to the Properties dialog box of a folder.

Summary

In this chapter you learned how an object model can be used to program an application. Object models provide objects and collections whose properties, methods and events can be used to programmatically access an application's functionality from either outside or inside the application.

Outlook programming assignments may range from programming Outlook from an external application to creating a COM add-in to writing an application-level VBA program. This chapter showed you the programming language options and how they depend on your particular programming task.

Programs are written in development environments. Outlook 2000, like the other Microsoft Office 2000 applications, provides a Visual Basic editor for VBA application-level programs. This chapter showed you how to configure and use this development environment.

Finally, you learned how to create and use the Application and NameSpace objects, which are used to access the other objects and collections in the Outlook 2000 Object Model, including the Outlook folders, the subject of the next chapter.

✦   ✦   ✦

Accessing and Viewing Folders

Outlook, like the file system in Windows 9*x*/NT/2000, uses a folder metaphor to contain subfolders and, ultimately, data, which in Outlook, instead of being files, are Outlook items, such as mail messages, contact items, task items, and so on.

Each folder is an object with properties and methods that can be accessed through the Outlook 2000 object model. These folders are the gateway through which you access the Outlook items in the folder.

All folders at a particular level also are part of a Folders collection, another object with its own properties, methods, and events. You use the Folders collection to navigate to and access, or even add or delete, a particular folder.

The Outlook 2000 object model also provides the Explorer object, which represents the window through which the user views the contents of a folder. This object, which is contained in, you guessed it, an Explorers collection, has properties, methods, and events that permit you programmatic control over the user's view of the folders contents and the user's ability to navigate among folders and views of the folders.

The Outlook GUI includes an Outlook Bar, which may contain shortcuts to Outlook folders. New with Outlook 2000, the Outlook Bar also may contain shortcuts to non-Outlook folders or files on a local or network drive or even to URLs on the World Wide Web. Here too, the object model permits you programmatic control over the shortcut groups and individual shortcuts displayed in the Outlook Bar and the user's ability to navigate among these groups and shortcuts.

Outlook Folders

Each Outlook folder, in addition to being a MAPIFolder object, is part of a Folders collection of all folders at that particular level. A Folders collection does not contain data. Rather, it is used to locate the MAPIFolder objects that do contain data. Thus, in drilling down to data, you usually first will use the Folders collection, and then the MAPIFolder object. Therefore, the two are discussed in that order.

Folders Collection

A collection is a container, usually for objects of a particular type. The Folders collection contains MAPIFolder objects. Figure 3-1 shows the portion of the object model in which this collection and object are located.

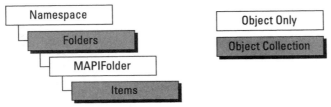

Figure 3-1: Folders collection

Outlook has many Folders collections. The top-level folders, such as the Public Folders and Personal Folders, which are present by default, are part of a Folders collection that you can access through the NameSpace object discussed in Chapter 2, "The Gateway Objects — Application and NameSpace." The folders under Personal Folders, such as Inbox, Contacts and Calendar, are part of another Folders collection. Additionally, you can create more Folders collections by, for example, creating a subfolder under your Inbox. However, these different Folders collections all have in common the properties, methods and events of the Folders collection.

Properties

Table 3-1 lists the properties of the Folders collection:

Table 3-1 Properties of the Folders Collection	
Name	**Description**
Application	Returns the Outlook Application object.
Class	Returns the olObjectClass **constant, in this case** olFolders **having a value of 15.**

Name	Description
Count	Returns the number of objects, in this case MAPIFolder objects, in the collection.
Parent	Returns the parent object, which is a NameSpace object for a top-level folder like Personal Folders and a MAPIFolder object for subfolders.
Session	Returns the NameSpace object for the collection, which you probably already have in order to access the Folders collection.

Listing 3-1 shows how to use the Count property with a For loop to iterate through the Folders in a folder collection, in this case to output to the Immediate Window the names of all of the folders in a Folders collection:

Listing 3-1: **Using Count Property and For Loop to Iterate through Folders in Collection**

```
Sub Main()

Dim myOutlook As Outlook.Application
Dim ns As Outlook.NameSpace
Dim counter As Integer
Set myOutlook = New Outlook.Application
Set ns = myOutlook.GetNameSpace("MAPI")
For counter = 1 to ns.Folders.Count
    Debug.Print ns.Folders(counter).Name
Next
myOutlook.Quit
Set myOutlook = Nothing

End Sub
```

The NameSpace object has a Folders property that returns a reference to the Folders collection. The counter variable starts at 1 because the Folders collection, like other Outlook collections, is one-based, not zero-based. Additionally, as discussed below, this code implicitly uses the Item method of the Folders collection.

Listing 3-2 shows another and perhaps simpler alternative to Listing 3-1, using the For Each ... Next syntax and the Count property to iterate through the collection:

Listing 3-2: Using Count Property and For Each ... Next syntax to Iterate through Folders in Collection

```
Sub Main()

Dim myOutlook As Outlook.Application
Dim ns As Outlook.NameSpace
Dim fld As Outlook.MAPIFolder
Set myOutlook = New Outlook.Application
Set ns = myOutlook.GetNameSpace("MAPI")
For Each fld In ns.Folders
    Debug.Print fld.Name
Next
myOutlook.Quit
Set myOutlook = Nothing

End Sub
```

The output of these code examples may be a bit surprising. While the output will vary depending on what folders you have on your Outlook application, on one of the co-authors' computers the output (with the folder names comma-delimited rather than being on separate lines) is: Public Folders, Mailbox - Jeffrey Kent, Internet Folders, Personal Folders.

The surprise is that not all of the folder names were output. For example, none of the names of the personal folders, such as the Inbox and Contacts, were output. The reason is that the Folders collection contains only the *top-level* folders. These folders may contain other folders, as is the case with Personal Folders and Public Folders.

The code in Listing 3-3 outputs the names of the folders in Personal Folders:

Listing 3-3: Output Names of Folders in Collection

```
Sub Main()

Dim myOutlook As Outlook.Application
Dim ns As Outlook.NameSpace
Dim fld As Outlook.MAPIFolder
Set myOutlook = New Outlook.Application
Set ns = myOutlook.GetNameSpace("MAPI")
For Each fld In ns.Folders("Personal Folders").Folders
    Debug.Print fld.Name
```

```
Next
myOutlook.Quit
Set myOutlook = Nothing

End Sub
```

The output is (with the folder names comma-delimited rather than being on separate lines) Deleted Items, Inbox, Outbox, Sent Items, Calendar, Contacts, Journal, Notes, Tasks, Drafts, Personal.

Objects in a collection are accessed either by index number or by name. Usually the index is not used unless you are looping through the collection (as in the code example above using the `For` loop) because there is no guarantee that a particular item will have a given index number. The statement `ns.Folders("Personal Folders")` refers, by name, to the MAPIFolder named Personal Folders. A MAPIFolder object, like a NameSpace object, has a Folders property that returns the collection of subfolders. Therefore, the statement `ns.Folders("Personal Folders").Folders` refers to the collection of folders under Personal Folders. These statements also implicitly use the `Item` method discussed below.

Methods

Table 3-2 lists the methods of the Folder collection:

	Table 3-2	
	Methods of Folders Collection	
Name	*Description*	*Parameter*
Add	Creates a new folder in the Folders collection, and returns the new folder as a MAPIFolder object.	Display name for new folder and optionally the `olDefaultFolder` constant on which the folder is based.
GetFirst	Returns the first folder in the collection, or `Nothing` if no folder exists.	None.
GetLast	Returns the last folder in the collection, or `Nothing` if no folder exists.	None.

Continued

Table 3-2 *(continued)*

Name	Description	Parameter
GetNext	Returns the next folder in the collection, or Nothing if no folder exists or at last folder.	None.
GetPrevious	Returns the previous object in the collection, or Nothing if no folder exists or at first folder.	None.
Item	Returns a folder from the collection.	Index or other identifier of folder to be accessed.
Remove	Removes folder from collection.	Index of folder to be removed.

The Add method programmatically adds a folder to a collection of folders. In the code in Listing 3-4, two folders are added under the default Tasks folder. The first new folder (firstNewFolder) contains Task items because, if the optional second parameter is missing, the new folder will default to the same type as the folder in which it is created. However, the second new folder (firstNewFolder secondNewFolder), while under the Tasks folder, will contain message items because optional second parameter specifies olFolderInbox:

Listing 3-4: **Adding Folders to Collection**

```
Dim existingFolder as Outlook.MAPIFolder
Dim firstNewFolder as Outlook.MAPIFolder
Dim secondNewFolder as Outlook.MAPIFolder
Set existingFolder = olNS.GetDefaultFolder(olFolderTasks)
Set firstNewFolder = existingFolder.Folders.Add("MoreWork")
Set secondNewFolder = existingFolder.Folders.Add _
    ("Gripes", olFolderInbox)
```

Not all of the olDefaultFolder constants can be used as the optional second parameter of the Add method. The constants for Deleted Items, Sent Items, and Outbox cannot be used.

The Item method is similar to the Add method except that it returns an existing folder from the Folders collection rather than adding a new folder to the Folders collection. The argument is the one-based index or name of the folder. Since Item is the default method of the Folders collection, the following two statements produce the same result:

```
Debug.Print ns.Folders(counter).Name
Debug.Print ns.Folders.Item(counter).Name
```

The Remove method's method, similarly, is the one-based index of the folder to be removed from the collection.

The four Get methods are used to navigate the Folders collection. You can use the Get methods without explicitly instantiating a Folders collection variable:

```
Set aFolder = myNameSpace.Folders.GetFirst
```

However, it is good programming practice to obtain a reference to the Folders collection before using these methods:

```
Set myFolders = myNameSpace.Folders
Set aFolder = myFolders.GetFirst
```

You can then use the GetNext method to return a reference to the remaining folders in the collection. The following code example outputs the names of the remaining folders:

```
Set myFolders = myNameSpace.Folders
Set aFolder = myFolders.GetFirst
Do Until aFolder Is Nothing
    Debug.Print aFolder.Name
    Set aFolder = myFolders.GetNext
Loop
```

The loop continues unless the reference returned by GetNext is Nothing, the keyword returned if no folder exists.

Similarly, you can iterate "backwards" through the Folders collection using the GetLast and GetPrevious methods:

```
Set myFolders = myNameSpace.Folders
Set aFolder = myFolders.GetLast
Do Until aFolder Is Nothing
    Debug.Print aFolder.Name
    Set aFolder = myFolders.GetPrevious
Loop
```

Events

Table 3-3 lists the three events of the Folders collection. None of these events can be cancelled.

Table 3-3
Events of Folders Collection

Name	Fires When ...
FolderAdd	Folder is added to collection.
FolderChange	Folder in collection is changed.
FolderRemove	Folder is removed from collection.

The FolderAdd event can be used to notify your application when a folder has been added as an item to the Deleted Items folder as a result of being deleted from its previous location. The code in Listing 3-5 moves the deleted folder back to the Inbox folder if it contains any unread items:

Listing 3-5: **Using the FolderAdd event**

```
Public ns As NameSpace
Public WithEvents ocolDeletedFolders As Folders

Private Sub Application_StartUp()

    Set ns = Application.GetNameSpace("MAPI")
    Set ocolDeletedFolders = ns.GetDefaultFolder _
        (olDeletedItems).Folders

End Sub

Private Sub ocolDeletedFolders_FolderAdd _
    (ByVal Folder As MAPIFolder)

    If Folder.UnReadItemCount Then
        MsgBox "Deletion prohibited. Unread items in folder."
        Folder.MoveTo ns.GetDefaultFolder(olFolderInbox)
    End If

End Sub
```

The object variable ocolDeletedFolders represents the Folders collection of the Deleted Items folder. It is declared WithEvents so it will receive the FolderAdd event. It then is instantiated in the StartUp event of the Application object. The FolderAdd event passes as a parameter the MAPIFolder object being added. The UnReadItemCount property of the MAPIFolder object (discussed in the next section) returns the number of unread items in the folder. If there are any, the MoveTo method of the MAPIFolder object moves the folder to the Inbox.

The FolderRemove event also could have been used to notify your application when the folder had been deleted. The code in Listing 3-6 assumes the folder had been deleted from the Inbox:

Listing 3-6: Using the FolderRemove event

```
Public ns As NameSpace
Public WithEvents ocolDeletedFolders As Folders

Private Sub Application_StartUp()

    Set ns = Application.GetNameSpace("MAPI")
    Set ocolDeletedFolders = ns.GetDefaultFolder _
        (olInbox).Folders

End Sub

Private Sub ocolDeletedFolders_FolderRemove()

    MsgBox "Folder removed from Inbox."

End Sub
```

The code in Listing 3-6 only displays a warning. It cannot be used to move the folder back. This is because unlike the FolderAdd event, the FolderRemove event does not pass the folder involved as a parameter. Therefore, the functionality of the FolderRemove event is more limited than that of the FolderAdd event. Nevertheless, the FolderRemove event could be used to do more than display a warning.

For example, the code in Listing 3-7 modifies the code in Listing 3-5 that illustrates the FolderAdd event by moving a folder back from the Deleted Items folder only if the folder came from the Inbox. If the folder came from another location, the folder remains in Deleted Items:

Listing 3-7: Using the FolderAdd and FolderRemove events together

```
Public ns As NameSpace
Public WithEvents ocolInboxFolders As Folders
Public WithEvents ocolDeletedFolders As Folders
Public blnFromInbox As Boolean
```

Continued

Listing 3-7 *(continued)*

```
Private Sub Application_StartUp()

    Set ns = Application.GetNameSpace("MAPI")
    Set ocolInboxFolders = ns.GetDefaultFolder _
        (olInbox).Folders
    Set ocolDeletedFolders = ns.GetDefaultFolder _
        (olDeletedItems).Folders
    blnFromInbox = False

End Sub

Private Sub ocolInboxFolders_FolderRemove()

    blnFromInbox = True

End Sub

Private Sub ocolDeletedFolders_FolderAdd _
    (ByVal Folder As MAPIFolder)

    If blnFromInbox Then
        Folder.MoveTo ns.GetDefaultFolder(olFolderInbox)
        blnFromInbox = False
    End If

End Sub
```

The FolderAdd and FolderRemove events work together in Listing 3-7 to complement each other. The FolderAdd event does not know where the added folder came
from. However, the FolderRemove event does know because it is an event of the
object variable that represents the specific Folders collection from which the folder
was removed. The FolderRemove event uses its "knowledge" of the origin of the
folder to set a Boolean variable that notifies the FolderAdd event of the Deleted
Items folders object variable that the added folder came from the Inbox. The Folder
Remove event does not have the folder involved as a parameter and therefore cannot
retrieve the folder. However, the folder is a parameter of the FolderAdd event.
Therefore, the FolderAdd event can use that parameter to return the folder to
the Inbox.

The FolderChange event fires when one of the following occurs:

✦ A folder in the Folders collection is renamed.

✦ An item is added to a folder in the Folders collection.

✦ An existing item is deleted from a folder in the Folders collection.

✦ An existing item in a folder in the Folders collection is modified.

The FolderChange event, like the FolderAdd event, has the MAPIFolder involved as a parameter. Therefore, the code stub for the FolderChange event, assuming ocolChangedFolders is an object variable of the Folders collection instantiated with the WithEvents keyword, is:

```
Private Sub ocolChangedFolders_FolderChange _
    (ByVal Folder As MAPIFolder)

End Sub
```

The parameter represents the folder *after* the change. Therefore, the FolderChange event cannot be used, at least by itself, to access the name or other property of the folder *before* the change. However, just as the FolderAdd and FolderRemove events worked together in the code example above, the FolderChange event can work together with other events.

MAPIFolder Objects

The Folders collection contains MAPIFolder objects, which are Outlook folders. The folder object is named a "MAPIFolder" because "MAPI" is the acronym for the only Outlook data source. A MAPIFolder may contain items, other MAPIFolder objects, or both.

A MAPIFolder object is accessed through the NameSpace object or, if not a top-level folder, through a Folders collection. Code examples in the preceding section on the Folders collection showed how to access a MAPIFolder object through the Item, GetFirst, and GetLast methods. Additionally, folders may be accessed by at least one of three methods of the NameSpace object. The following code assumes ns is a declared and instantiated NameSpace object variable and ofFolder was already declared as a MAPIFolder object variable:

✦ GetDefaultFolder — A default folder represented by an olDefaultFolder constants listed in Table 2-8 in Chapter 2:

```
Set ofFolder = ns.GetDefaultFolder(olFolderInbox)
```

✦ GetFolderFromID — Any folder.

```
Set ofFolder = ns.GetFolderFromID(strEntryID, _
    strStoreID)
```

✦ GetSharedDefaultFolder — A shared folder that is a default folder represented by one of the olDefaultFolder constants listed in Table 2-8 of Chapter 2.

```
Set ofFolder = ns.GetSharedDefaultFolder(aRecip, _
    olFolderInbox)
```

Properties

Table 3-4 lists the properties of the MAPIFolder object:

Table 3-4 Properties of MAPIFolder Object	
Name	**Description**
Application	Returns the Outlook Application object.
Class	Returns the olObjectClass constant, in this case olFolder having a value of 2.
DefaultItemType	Returns one of the olItemType constants listed in Table 2-8 in Chapter 2, representing the default Outlook item type contained in the folder.
DefaultMessageClass	Returns the default message class for items in the folder.
Description	Returns or sets the description of the folder.
EntryID	Returns the unique entry ID of the object.
Folders	Returns the collection of folders for the MAPIFolder object.
Items	Returns the collection of Outlook items in the folder.
Name	Returns or sets the display name for the item. The Name property is also the caption for a form.
Parent	Returns the parent object, which will be either a NameSpace object for a top-level folder or another MAPIFolder object for a subfolder.
Session	Returns the NameSpace object for the current session.
StoreID	Returns or sets the store ID for the folder, which is a unique ID set when the folder is created or moved.
UnReadItemCount	Returns the number of unread items in the folder.
WebViewAllowNavigation	Returns or sets the navigation mode of the Web view for a folder. True to allow navigation using Back and Forward buttons.
WebViewOn	Returns or sets the Web view state for a folder. True to display the Web page specified by the WebViewURL property.
WebViewURL	Returns or sets the URL of the Web page that is assigned to a folder.

The DefaultItemType identifies the default Outlook item type in a folder. For example, a Contacts folder by default contains Contact items. A newly created item will have the default type of the folder to which it is added unless explicitly speci-fied otherwise. The olItemType constants are listed in Table 2-8 in Chapter 2.

The DefaultMessageClass property returns the message class for the folder. Message classes will be discussed in Chapter 5, "Outlook Forms." This property is related to the DefaultItemType property in that it identifies the default item type in a folder. Table 3-5 lists the message classes for the default folders:

Table 3-5	
Message Classes for Default Folders	
Folder	*Default Message Class*
Calendar	IPM.Appointment
Contacts	IPM.Contact
Deleted Items	IPM.Note
Drafts	IPM.Note
Inbox	IPM.Note
Journal	IPM.Activity
Notes	IPM.StickyNote
Outbox	IPM.Note
Sent Items	IPM.Note
Tasks	IPM.Task

The Description property returns the text in the Description box of the General tab in the Properties box of a folder.

The Folders property was demonstrated in Listings 3-5 through 3-7 in connection with the Folders collection. It is used to obtain a collection of the subfolders of a folder.

The Name property returns or sets the name of the folder. The default Outlook folders, such as the Inbox, Outbox, Calendar, Contacts, Tasks, and Notes, are accessed by the GetDefaultFolder method of the NameSpace object. The code in Listing 3-8 acces-ses the Inbox and outputs to the Immediate Window the name of that folder, Inbox:

Listing 3-8: **Using the Name property**

```
Sub Main()

Dim olOutlook As Outlook.Application
```

Continued

Listing 3-8 *(continued)*

```
Dim ns As Outlook.NameSpace
Dim fld As Outlook.MAPIFolder
Set olOutlook = New Outlook.Application
Set ns = olOutlook.GetNameSpace("MAPI")
Set fld = ns.GetDefaultFolder(olFolderInbox)
Debug.Print fld.Name
olOutlook.Quit
Set olOutlook = Nothing

End Sub
```

While the `Name` property can set the name of a folder, the name cannot duplicate the name of another folder in the same collection. This is analogous to the rule that two files in the same folder cannot have the same name.

Both the `EntryID` and `StoreID` properties return a unique ID that is set when the folder is created or moved. Why there are two such properties when one would do is not clear.

The `UnReadItemCount` property returns the number of unread items in a folder. It can be used to determine and then notify the user of the existence and number of unread items.

The `WebViewAllowNavigation`, `WebViewOn`, and `WebViewURL` properties are used in Outlook WebFolders.

Methods

Table 3-6 lists the methods of the MAPIFolder object:

Table 3-6
Methods of MAPIFolder Object

Name	Action	Parameter
CopyTo	Copies the current folder in its entirety to the destination folder. Returns a MAPIFolder object that represents the new copy.	MAPIFolder representing destination folder.

Name	Action	Parameter
Delete	Deletes from the collection the MAPIFolder object that calls this method.	None.
Display	Displays a new Explorer object for the MAPIFolder object that calls this method.	Optional True to display as modal; that is, the object must be closed before the user can work with any other window of the application.
GetExplorer	Returns a new Explorer object to display the folder that calls it.	Optionally one of the olFolderDisplayMode constants listed in Table 3-7 to represent the display mode of the folder.
MoveTo	Moves a folder to the specified destination folder.	MAPIFolder representing destination folder.

The CopyTo, MoveTo, and Delete methods are useful for folder maintenance. The MoveTo method was demonstrated in the code example of the FolderAdd and FolderRemove events of the Folders collection. The CopyTo method can be used to create a backup of a folder. This VBA code example copies the "Special Messages" subfolder in the Inbox to a custom first-level "Backups" folder:

```
Dim ns As NameSpace
Dim ofSpecialFolder As MAPIFolder
Dim ofBackupFolders As MAPIFolder

Set ns = Application.GetNameSpace("MAPI")
Set ofSpecialFolder = ns.GetDefaultFolder _
    (olInbox).Folders("Special Messages")
Set ofBackupFolders = ns.Folders("Backup") _
OfSpecialFolder.CopyTo ofBackupFolders
```

The object variables ofSpecialFolder and ofBackupFolders are not declared WithEvents because the MAPIFolder object has no events.

The other methods concern the Explorers collection and Explorer object discussed in the next section. The Display method creates and displays a new Explorer window for the folder that calls the method. The GetExplorer method returns, but does not display, a new Explorer window for the folder that calls the method. The Explorer window is then displayed by the `Activate` method discussed later in this section in connection with Explorer objects. The `GetExplorer` method provides greater precision than the `Display` method on how the Explorer window is displayed because, unlike the `Display` method, the `GetExplorer` method has an additional (and optional) parameter, one of the `olFolderDisplayMode` constants listed in Table 3-7:

Table 3-7		
Folder Display Mode Constants		
Name	*Value*	*Description*
`olFolderDisplayNormal`	0	Default. Display includes Outlook Bar and Folder List.
`olFolderDisplayFolderOnly`	1	Display includes Folder List but not Outlook Bar.
`olFolderDisplayNoNavigation`	2	Display does not include Outlook Bar or Folder List.

There are no MAPIFolder events.

Outlook Explorers

Outlook folders have many built-in views. These views are listed under the CurrentView menu item of the View menu. Additionally, Outlook permits the user to customize a view by using the Customize Current View and Define Views submenu items under View ⇨ Current View.

The user may choose the folder view from the Current View menu item of the View menu. You as a developer may wish to know the folder view chosen by the user, or when the user changes to another view. Alternatively, you may want to choose the view for the user.

An Explorer object is an Outlook window that displays the contents of a folder. Figure 3-2 shows an Explorer object that displays the contents of one of the co-author's Deleted Items folder (someone obviously receives a lot of spam mail).

The Explorer object can be used to determine or control the user's view of a folder's contents. There may be, and often are, multiple Explorer objects, and they are contained in the Explorers collection. Figure 3-3 shows the location in the object model of the Explorers collection and the Explorer object.

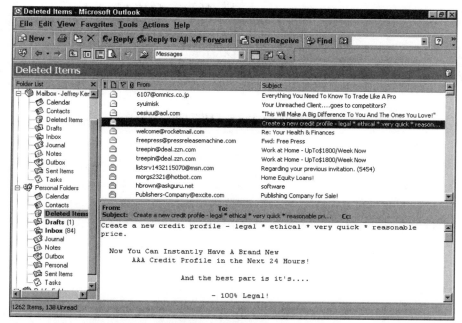

Figure 3-2: Explorer object displaying Deleted Items folder

Figure 3-3: Explorers collection

Explorers Collection

The Explorers collection has the properties and methods typical of collections, as well as one problematic event.

Properties

Table 3-8 lists the properties of the Explorers collection:

Table 3-8 Properties of Explorers Collection	
Name	**Description**
Application	Returns the Outlook Application object.
Class	Returns the olObjectClass constant, in this case olExplorers having a value of 60.
Count	Returns the number of Explorer objects in the collection.
Parent	Returns the Parent object, in this case the Application object.
Session	Returns the NameSpace object through which the Explorers collection was accessed.

These properties are quite similar to those of the Folders collection discussed above. The Count property in particular is useful to iterate through the Explorer objects in the collection.

Methods

Table 3-9 lists the methods of the Explorers collection:

Table 3-9 Methods of Explorers Collection		
Name	**Description**	**Parameter**
Add	Creates a new explorer window and returns the resulting Explorer object.	Required: MAPIFolder to display in explorer window. Optional: One of the olFolder DisplayMode constants listed in Table 3-7 for the display mode.
Item	Returns a folder from the collection.	One-based position within the collection of the Explorer object.

The code in Listing 3-9 displays the Tasks folder in an Explorer window. The use of the olFolderDisplay mode constant olFolderDisplayFolderOnly in the optional second argument of the Add method displays the Tasks folder with a Folder List but not an Outlook Bar:

Listing 3-9: **Using the Add Method of the Explorers Collection**

```
Dim olApp As Outlook.Application
Dim olExplorers As Outlook.Explorers
Dim olExpl As Outlook.Explorer
Set olApp = New Outlook.Application
Set olExplorers = olApp.Explorers
Set olFolder = olApp.GetNamespace("MAPI").GetDefaultFolder _
    (olFolderTasks)
Set olExpl = olExplorers.Add _
    (olFolder, olFolderDisplayFolderOnly)
olExpl.Display
```

The Explorers collection variable olExplorers is instantiated by the Explorers property of the Application object. This property returns an Explorers collection object that contains all open explorers. The Explorers collection object can be instantiated even if there are no open explorers. A collection may be empty of objects. This code example does not rely on there being any currently open Explorer. Instead, it uses the Add method to instantiate a new Explorer. The Display method, which is discussed later in connection with the Explorer object, is then called to make the new Explorer window visible.

Explicit vs. Implicit Instantiation

A number of preceding code examples explicitly declared and instantiated a NameSpace object with code such as:

```
Dim olNS as Outlook.NameSpace
Set olNS = olApp.GetNamespace("MAPI")
```

The last code example did not explicitly declare and instantiate a NameSpace object. However, it did implicitly create a NameSpace object in the line

```
Set olFolder = olApp.GetNamespace("MAPI").GetDefaultFolder _
    (olFolderTasks)
```

The GetNameSpace method of the Application object returns a NameSpace object. That NameSpace object variable then calls its GetDefaultFolder method.

An object variable is created implicitly when it will not be referred to again in the code. If there will be further use of the object variable, then as a general rule it should be declared and instantiated explicitly.

The Explorers collection's only event is NewExplorer. Like many events, it is not available in VBScript. The NewExplorer event fires after a new Explorer window is created, either as a result of user action or through program code, but before the explorer window appears.

The cmdShowInbox macro code in the preceding example instantiates a new Explorer object oeExplorer and then invokes the Add method of the Explorers collection to add oeExplorer to the collection. The parameters of the Add method indicate that the Explorer object represented by oeExplorer will display the Inbox and that the display will be with a Folder List but not an Outlook Bar. The addition of oeExplorer to the Explorers collection fires the NewExplorer event. This event is recognized by the Explorers collection object variable colExplorers because it was declared with the WithEvents keyword. This event passes the newly created Explorer object as a parameter. This parameter is used to maximize the Explorer object represented by the oeExplorer object variable.

Events

The Explorers collection has one event. The NewExplorer event fires when a new Explorer object is added to the Explorers collection, and before the new Explorer object is displayed.

The first step in using the NewExplorer event is to declare an Explorers collection variable with the WithEvents keyword:

```
Public WithEvents ocExplorers As Explorers
```

The next step is to instantiate the Explorers collection variable in the Initialize event of the class module:

```
Public Sub Class_Initialize()
    Set ocExplorers = Application.Explorers
End Sub
```

You then can use the NewExplorer event through the Explorers collection variable:

```
Public Sub ocExplorers_NewExplorer(ByVal oExplore As Explorer)
    'do something
End Sub
```

The parameter is the new Explorer object being added to the Explorers collection.

Unfortunately, we were not able to do anything constructive with this event, and from our research, we are not alone. The example in the Microsoft help file does nothing with the parameter either.

Macros

The following VBA code example involves a macro, cmdShowInbox. A macro is a Sub procedure with no parameters. Macros are often used to automate common tasks.

You can create a macro in a VBA project simply by inserting the Sub procedure in an existing or new module. The name of the Sub procedure is the name of the macro.

The macro may be run by either user action or being called through code. The macro may be run from the Macros dialog box. This dialog box is displayed by the Tools ➪ Macro ➪ Macros menu command or the Alt-F8 shortcut key in an Explorer (or Inspector) window, and lists the available macros. You can then select a macro from the list and run it by clicking the Run command button.

The macro can also be added to a toolbar so you can run it simply by clicking the toolbar icon. You can add a macro to the toolbar by following these steps:

1. In an Explorer window, choose the Customize menu item under the Tools menu.

2. Choose the Commands tab, and select Macros from the Categories list box.

3. The available macros appear in the Commands list box. Drag the macro to the desired position on the toolbar.

4. Right-click the toolbar button, choose Properties from the context menu, and set its properties as desired.

```
'General Declarations

Dim ofFolder As MAPIFolder
Dim WithEvents colExplorers AsExplorers
Dim oeExplorer as Explorer

Private Sub cmdShowInbox()

    Set ofFolder = Application.GetNameSpace("MAPI") _
        .GetDefaultFolder(olInbox)
    Set colExplorers = Application.Explorers
    Set oeExplorer = colExplorers.Add(ofFolder, _
        olFolderDisplayFolderOnly)

End Sub

Private Sub olExplorers_NewExplorer _
    (ByVal Explorer As Outlook.Explorer)

    Set oeExplorer = Explorer
    oeExplorer.WindowState = olMaximized

End Sub
```

Explorer Object

Figure 3-2 showed the Explorer object. This object is the window through which you view Outlook. Like Windows Explorer, the Outlook Explorer object often has the folder list in the left list pane and the items in the selected folder in the right content pane.

Properties

Table 3-10 lists the properties of the Explorer object:

	Table 3-10
	Properties of Explorer Object

Name	Description
Application	Returns the Outlook Application object. The Parent property below does the same.
Caption	Returns the window caption (title-bar text) of an explorer window.
Class	Returns the olObjectClass constant for this object, olExplorer having a value of 34.
CommandBars	Returns a CommandBars collection object that represents all the menus and toolbars in the Explorer.
CurrentFolder	Returns or sets a MAPIFolder object that represents the current folder displayed in the explorer. This property is used to change the folder the user is viewing.
CurrentView	Returns or sets the view for an explorer. When this property is set, two events occur: BeforeViewSwitch occurs before the actual view change takes place and can be used to cancel the change; ViewSwitch takes place after the change is effective.
Height	Returns or sets the height in pixels of the Explorer object.
Left	Returns or sets the position (in pixels) of the left vertical edge of an explorer from the edge of the screen.
Panes	Returns a Panes collection object representing the panes (Outlook Bar, Folder List or Preview Pane) displayed by the specified explorer.
Parent	Returns the parent object, in this case the Application object. The Application property above does the same.
Selection	Returns a collection consisting of the items selected in the current view.

Name	Description
Session	Returns the current session.
Top	Returns or sets the position (in pixels) of the top horizontal edge of an explorer from the edge of the screen.
Width	Returns or sets the width in pixels of the Explorer object.
WindowState	Returns or sets the window state of an explorer or inspector window using one of the olWindowState constants in Table 3-11.

Table 3-11
Window State Constants

Constant	Description	Value
OlMaximized	Maximized	1
OlMinimized	Minimized	2
OlNormal	Normal (default)	3

The CurrentFolder property may be used to change the folder the user is viewing. The code in Listing 3-10 changes the displayed folder to the Inbox:

Listing 3-10: **Using the CurrentFolder property of the Explorer object**

```
Dim olApp As Outlook.Application
Dim olExplorer As Outlook.Explorer
Dim olFolder As Outlook.MAPIFolder
Set olApp = New Outlook.Application
Set olFolder = olApp.GetNamespace("MAPI"). _
    GetDefaultFolder(olFolderInbox)
Set olExplorer = olApp.ActiveExplorer
If TypeName(olExplorer) <> "Nothing" Then
    Set olExplorer.CurrentFolder = olFolder
End If
```

This code *changes* the displayed folder to the Inbox. The word "changes" is emphasized because the CurrentFolder property, being a property of the Explorer object, requires that there be at least one existing Explorer object. This code, before calling the `CurrentFolder` property, checks to see if the `ActiveExplorer` method of the Application object returns `Nothing`, which it will do if there are no Explorer objects. The `TypeName` function returns information about the variable that is its one argument. That information may be the data type of the variable, or `Nothing` if the variable is an object variable that doesn't refer to an object.

Tip

The `GetExplorer` method of the Folder object should be used if there is no Explorer object. If you know there is at least one Explorer object, then an instantiated Application object variable can invoke the `CurrentFolder` method with only one line of code (using line continuation characters):

```
Set olApp.ActiveExplorer.CurrentFolder = _
OlApp.GetNameSpace("MAPI"). _
GetDefaultFolder(olFolderInbox)
```

The `CurrentView` property returns or sets the view of an Explorer by the string whose name identifies the view. The following example assumes an already instantiated Explorer object variable `olExplorer` and an existing view name of "Messages":

```
olExplorer.CurrentView = "Messages"
```

When this property is set, two events occur: `BeforeViewSwitch` occurs before the actual view change takes place and can be used to cancel the change; `ViewSwitch` takes place after the change is effective. We will discuss these events shortly.

Note

The names of the existing views are set forth in the "View Name" column of the Define Views dialog box displayed by the menu command sequence View ➪ CurrentView ➪ Define Views. The name of a custom view is set when the view is created in the Create a New View dialog box displayed when you click the New command button in the Define Views dialog box. Once the custom view is created and saved, you can change its name by clicking the Rename command button in the Define Views dialog box. However, the built-in views cannot be renamed; only custom views can be.

The Explorer object has a number of properties that control its appearance. The `WindowState` property, which was used in an Explorers collection code example, determines whether the window is minimized, maximized or normal. More granular control is obtained through the `Height`, `Width`, `Left`, and `Top` properties to specify the precise size and orientation on the screen. For example, setting the Left and Top properties to 0 will position the Explorer in the upper left-hand corner of the display window.

Caution

The `Height`, `Width`, `Left`, and `Top` properties measure in pixels. By contrast, most Visual Basic functions express these types of properties in twips. A twip is a device-independent unit of measurement used by Visual Basic, and is 1/20 of a printer's point (1,440 twips equal one inch, and 567 twips equal one centimeter). The `TwipsPerPixelX`, `TwipsPerPixelY` and `ScaleMode` properties in Visual Basic may be useful in this regard.

The Selection property returns a collection consisting of the items selected in the current view. You can iterate through these items, using the Count property of the Selection collection. Listing 3-11 outputs to the immediate window the subject of all items that were sent by one of the co-authors:

Listing 3-11: Using the Selection Property of the Explorer Object

```
Dim olApp As Outlook.Application
Dim olExplorer As Outlook.Explorer
Dim olSel As Outlook.Selection
Dim x As Integer
Set olApp = New Outlook.Application
Set olExplorer = olApp.ActiveExplorer
Set olSel = olExplorer.Selection
For x = 1 To olSel.Count
    If olSel.Item(x).SenderName "David Jung" Then _
        Debug.Print Item(x).Subject
Next x
```

Methods

Table 3-12 lists the Methods of the Explorer object:

Table 3-12
Methods of Explorer Object

Method Name	Action	Parameter
Activate	Makes an Explorer object the active window	None.
Display	Displays an Explorer object. Only retained for backward compatibility; use the Activate method instead.	None.
Close	Closes the Explorer object.	None.
IsPaneVisible	Determines if one of three panes is visible: (1) the Outlook Bar; (2) the Folder List; or (3) the Preview Pane.	One of the olPanes constants listed in Table 3-13.
ShowPane	Shows or hides one of the three panes.	One of the olPanes constants listed in Table 3-13, and True to make the pane visible, False to hide the pane.

The `Activate` method displays an Explorer by bringing it to the foreground and setting keyboard focus. It has superseded the `Display` method. The `Activate` method assumes the Explorer object that is calling the method represents an existing Explorer object. For example, the following VBA code will cause an error if there are no Explorer objects:

```
Dim oeExplorer as Explorer
Set oeExplorer = Application.ActiveExplorer
oeExplorer.Activate
```

Therefore, you should check to make surethat the `ActiveExplorer` method did not return `Nothing`, which it would return if there are no Explorer objects:

```
Dim oeExplorer as Explorer
Set oeExplorer = Application.ActiveExplorer
If Not oeExplorer Is Nothing Then oeExplorer.Activate
```

Table 3-13 lists the `olPanes` constants used by the `IsPaneVisible` and `ShowPane` methods:

Table 3-13
Outlook Panes Constants

Pane	Constant	Value
Outlook Bar	olOutlookBar	1
Folder List	olFolderList	2
Preview Pane	olPreviewPane	3

The code in Listing 3-12 uses the `IsPaneVisible` and `ShowPane` methods to toggle the visibility of the Outlook Bar:

Listing 3-12: Using the IsPaneVisible and ShowPane methods of the Explorer Object

```
Dim olApp As Outlook.Application
Dim olExplorer As Outlook.Explorer
Set olApp = New Outlook.Application
Set olExplorer = olApp.ActiveExplorer
If olExplorer.IsPaneVisible(olOutlookBar) = False Then
    olExplorer.ShowPane olOutlookBar,True
Else
    olExplorer.ShowPane olOutlookBar,False
End If
```

Events

Table 3-14 lists the events of the Explorer object:

Table 3-14 **Events of Explorer Object**		
Event Name	*Fires When ...*	*Cancelable*
Activate	Explorer becomes the active window.	No
Deactivate	Explorer ceases to be the active window.	No
Close	Explorer object is closed.	No
BeforeFolderSwitch	Before Explorer navigates to a new folder.	Yes
FolderSwitch	After Explorer navigates to a new folder.	No
BeforeViewSwitch	Before Explorer navigates to a new folder changes to a new view.	Yes
ViewSwitch	After Explorer navigates to a new folder changes to a new view.	No
SelectionChange	Occurs when the user selects an item in the current view.	No

The Activate event fires not only when the Explorer object first appears, but also every time the Explorer object becomes the active window. Since this event occurs early and often, the Activate event is not a good place for code that takes time to execute, or to show message boxes or the like. This event is useful for setting the initial size and screen location of the Explorer view. The code in Listing 3-13 maximizes the Explorer window using the WindowState property. The Height, Width, Left, and Top properties also could be set in this event:

Listing 3-13: **Using the WindowState property of the Explorer Object**

```
Private Sub myOlExp_Activate()

    If myOlExp.WindowState <> olMaximized Then _
        myOlExp.WindowState = olMaximized

End Sub
```

Similarly, the Deactivate event fires each time the Explorer window stops being the active window. Therefore, the caveats regarding the Activate event apply here also. This event could be used to minimize the Explorer window.

The events that occur immediately before movement to a new folder or view, BeforeFolderSwitch and BeforeViewSwitch, enable you to cancel the movement. The following code snippet cancels the movement to a folder named "Off Limits." You could also prohibit access to this folder by setting its permissions. However, folder permissions are essentially an "either/or" proposition: either you have permission or you don't. By contrast, the BeforeFolderSwitch event provides you with more granular control. The code in Listing 3-14 has a custom message box, which would not be possible with folder permissions, but even finer control is possible. The only limit is the developer's imagination.

Listing 3-14: Using the BeforeSwitch event of the Explorer Object

```
Private Sub myOlExp_BeforeFolderSwitch _
    (ByVal NewFolder As Object, Cancel As Boolean)

    If NewFolder.Name = "Off Limits" Then
        MsgBox "Access denied."
        Cancel = True
    End If

End Sub
```

Folder permissions are not even an alternative to the BeforeViewSwitch event. This event, like BeforeFolderSwitch, is not limited to the two alternatives of granting or denying access to a view. Access to a view may depend on, for example, the nature or number of items in a folder.

The FolderSwitch event occurs upon a change in the current folder displayed by the Explorer object. Thus, the BeforeFolderSwitch event occurs *before* the change, whereas the FolderSwitch event occurs *after* the change. Therefore, the FolderSwitch event, unlike the BeforeFolderSwitch event, cannot be canceled.

The FolderSwitch event is useful in determining which folder has become the current folder. The code in Listing 3-15 shows a custom toolbar only if the Sales Contacts folder is the current folder:

Listing 3-15: Using the FolderSwitch event of the Explorer Object

```
Private Sub myOlExp_FolderSwitch()


If MyOlExp.CurrentFolder.Name = "Sales Contacts" Then _
        MyToolsMenu.Visible = True
Else
        MyToolsMenu.Visible = False
End If

End Sub
```

The ViewSwitch event has a similar relationship with the BeforeViewSwitch Event. The BeforeViewSwitch event occurs before the view changes; the ViewSwitch event occurs after the view changes. Therefore, the ViewSwitch event, like the FolderSwitch event, cannot be cancelled.

The ViewSwitch event is useful in determining which view has become the current view. The code in Listing 3-16 hides the Preview Pane if it is visible when the user switches to the "Messages with AutoPreview" view:

Listing 3-16: Using the ViewSwitch event of the Explorer Object

```
Private Sub myOlExpl_ViewSwitch()

    If myOlExpl.CurrentView = "Messages with AutoPreview" _
        AndmyOlExpl.IsPaneVisible(olPreview) = True Then _
        myOlExpl.ShowPane olPreview, False
    End Sub
```

The SelectionChange event fires when the user changes the current selection in the active Explorer window, usually with the mouse or arrow key. This event can be used to determine the items selected by the user. The Selection property of the

Explorer object can then be used to iterate through the selected items, as shown by the code in Listing 3-17:

Listing 3-17: Using the SelectionChange event of the Explorer Object

```
Private Sub myOlExpl_ViewSwitch()

Dim counter As Integer
If myOlExpl.Selection.Count = 0 Then Exit Sub
For counter = 1 to myOlExpl.Selection.Count
    'Take desired action
Next counter

End Sub
```

Last but not least, the `Close` event is useful for "cleanup." For example, if an object variable `opPane` was created when the Explorer object was created, a `Set opPane = Nothing` statement cleans up the object variable. Often VB and VBA will clean up object variables for you when the object variable goes out of scope or the program terminates, but there are exceptions, so it is a good idea to do it yourself.

Selection Collection

The preceding discussions of the `SelectionChange` event and the `Selection` property of the Explorer object are a good introduction to the Selection collection. This collection represents the items selected in an Explorer object. Each Explorer object has its own Selection collection.

The Selection collection performs essentially the same function as the `Selection` property of an Explorer object. Indeed, the Selection collection is accessed from the `Selection` property:

```
Dim oeExpl As Explorer
Dim osSelect As Selection
Set osSelect = oeExpl.Selection
```

The difference between the Selection collection and the `Selection` property is that the Selection collection has several properties and one method of its own. Table 3-15 lists the properties of the Selection collection:

Table 3-15
Properties of the Selection Collection

Name	Description
Application	Returns the Outlook Application object.
Class	The olObjectClass constant, in this case olSelection, having a value of 74.
Count	The number of objects: in this case, the selected items.
Parent	The parent object, which is the Explorer object that contains the selected items.
Session	Returns the NameSpace object for the current session.

The one method is Item. This method returns a particular selected item. The Item method takes one parameter, which is either the position of the item in the Selection collection or the Subject property of the Outlook item if the Outlook item has a Subject property.

Outlook Bar

The Outlook Bar holds shortcuts to often-used Outlook folders such as the Inbox. However, any file can be represented by a shortcut on the Outlook Bar. Indeed, the Outlook Bar may contain URL shortcuts to Web pages.

Figure 3-4 depicts the three collections and four objects in the Outlook object model that directly relate to the Outlook Bar.

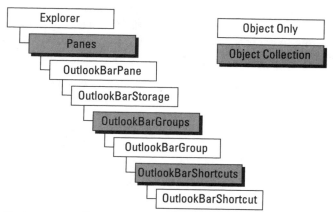

Figure 3-4: Collections and objects relating to the Outlook Bar

Panes Collection

The Outlook Bar is a pane (no, this is not a misspelling). There are two other Outlook panes, the FolderList and the Preview Pane. Figure 3-5 shows an Outlook window with all three panes.

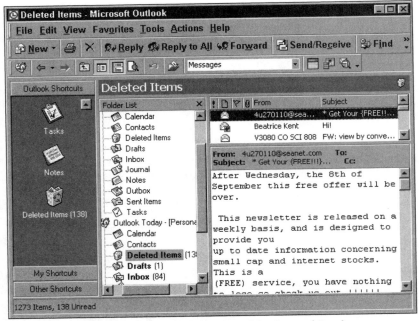

Figure 3-5: The three panes: Outlook Bar, FolderList, and Preview

Outlook has a Panes collection. However, while there are three Outlook panes, only one, the Outlook Bar, is accessible through the Panes collection. The FolderList and the Preview Pane only can be accessed through the Outlook GUI through the View menu command. Attempting to access either the FolderList or the Preview Pane through the Panes collection will cause an error.

Since a pane is part of an Explorer window, the Panes collection is accessed through the Panes property of the Explorer object:

```
Dim oeExpl As Explorer
Dim ocpPanes As Panes
'intervening code to instantiate oeExpl
Set ocpPanes = oeExpl.Panes
```

Table 3-16 lists the properties of the Panes collection:

Table 3-16	
Properties of the Panes Collection	
Name	*Description*
Application	Returns the Outlook Application object.
Class	Returns the olObjectClass constant, in this case olPanes having a value of 62.
Count	Returns the number of objects, in this case the number of panes. This property is only of limited utility, as in Outlook 2000 only the Outlook Bar can be accessed as an object in the Panes collection.
Parent	Returns the parent object, which is the Explorer object that displays the panes.
Session	Returns the NameSpace object for the current session.

The Panes collection has only one method, Item. This method, which is used by the code in Listing 3-18, returns a Pane object from the collection. It has one parameter, either the position or the name of the pane. Since in Outlook 2000 only the Outlook Bar can be accessed as an object in the Panes collection, the parameter will be either 1 or "OutlookBar":

Listing 3-18: Using the Item method of the Panes Collection

```
Dim oeExpl As Explorer
Dim ocpPanes As Panes
Dim obpPane As OutlookBarPane
'intervening code to instantiate oeExpl
Set ocpPanes = oeExpl.Panes
Set obpPane = ocpPanes.Item(1)
'or Set obpPane = ocpPanes.Item("OutlookBar")
```

This code returns a reference to an OutlookBarPane object, which we will discuss in the next section.

OutlookBarPane Object

The OutlookBarPane object represents the Outlook Bar and its groups and shortcuts. Table 3-17 lists the properties of the OutlookBarPane object:

Table 3-17
Properties of the OutlookBarPane Object

Name	Description
Application	Returns the Outlook Application object.
Class	Returns the olObjectClass constant, in this case olOutlookBarPane having a value of 63.
Contents	Returns the OutlookBarStorage object for the OutlookBarPane object. The OutlookBarStorage object, discussed in detail in this chapter, holds the shortcuts and groups for the Outlook Bar.
CurrentGroup	Sets and returns the OutlookBarGroup object for the OutlookBarPane object. Figure 3-5 shows three groups, "Outlook Shortcuts," "My Shortcuts," and "Other Shortcuts."
Name	Returns the name of the OutlookBarPane object.
Parent	Returns the parent object, which is the Explorer object that displays the pane.
Session	Returns the NameSpace object for the current session.
Visible	Sets and returns whether the Outlook Bar is visible using the Boolean values True and False.

The OutlookBarPane object has no methods, but it does have events, which are listed in Table 3-18:

Table 3-18
Events of OutlookBarPane Object

Name	Fires When ...	Cancelable?
BeforeGroupSwitch	User selects a new group.	Yes
BeforeNavigate	User selects a shortcut within the current group.	Yes

The BeforeGroupSwitch event may be used to prevent the user from switching to an Outlook group, as shown by the code in Listing 3-19:

Listing 3-19: **Using the BeforeGroupSwitch event of the OutlookBarPane Object**

```
Dim oeExpl As Explorer
Dim ocpPanes As Panes
Dim WithEvents obpPane As OutlookBarPane
'intervening code to instantiate oeExpl
Set ocpPanes = oeExpl.Panes
Set obpPane = ocpPanes.Item("OutlookBar")

Private Sub obpPane_BeforeGroupSwitch( _
    ByVal ToGroup As OutlookBarGroup, _
    Cancel As Boolean)

If ToGroup.Name = "My (Not Your) Shortcuts" Then
    MsgBox "They're my shortcuts, not yours"
    Cancel = True
End If

End Sub
```

The OutlookBarPane object variable obpPane was declared with the WithEvents keyword so that it could use the BeforeGroupSwitch event.

Similarly, the BeforeNavigate event may be used to prevent the user from accessing a particular Outlook folder via a shortcut on the Outlook Bar, as shown by the code in Listing 3-20:

Listing 3-20: **Using the BeforeNavigate event of the OutlookBarPane Object**

```
Dim oeExpl As Explorer
Dim ocpPanes As Panes
Dim ofFldr As MAPIFolder
Dim WithEvents obpPane As OutlookBarPane
'intervening code to instantiate oeExpl
Set ocpPanes = oeExpl.Panes
Set obpPane = ocpPanes.Item("OutlookBar")
```

Continued

Listing 3-20 *(continued)*

```
Private Sub obpPane_BeforeNavigate( _
    ByVal Shortcut As OutlookBar.Shortcut, _
    Cancel As Boolean)

On Error Resume Next
Set ofFlder = Shortcut.Target
If ofFlder.Name = "Top Secret Folder" Then
    MsgBox "Access Denied"
    Cancel = True
End If

End Sub
```

The code is assigning the `Target` property of the `Shortcut` parameter to a MAPI Folder object variable. However, the shortcut is not necessarily pointing to an Outlook folder. Shortcuts also may point to a file or Web URLs. Therefore, the `On Error Resume Next` statement is necessary to prevent a runtime error if the shortcut does not point to an Outlook folder.

OutlookBarStorage Object

The OutlookBarStorage object acts as an intermediary between the OutlookBarPane object and the OutlookBarGroups collection. The OutlookBarStorage object is accessed through the Contents property of the OutlookBarPane object:

```
Dim oeExpl As Explorer
Dim ocpPanes As Panes
Dim obpPane As OutlookBarPane
Dim obsStore As OutlookBarStorage
'intervening code to instantiate oeExpl
Set ocpPanes = oeExpl.Panes
Set obpPane = ocpPanes.Item("OutlookBar")
Set obsStore = obpPane.Contents
```

The OutlookBarStorage object has no methods or events. Table 3-19 lists its properties:

Table 3-19
Properties of the OutlookBarStorage Object

Name	Description
Application	Returns the Outlook Application object.
Class	Returns the olObjectClass constant, in this case olOutlookBarStorage having a value of 64.
Groups	Returns a reference to the OutlookBarGroups collection associated with the OutlookBarStorage object.
Parent	The parent object, which is the OutlookBarPane.
Session	Returns the NameSpace object for the current session.

The Groups property fulfills the OutlookBarStorage object's role as an intermediary between the OutlookBarPane object and the OutlookBarGroups collection by permitting the OutlookBarPane object access to the OutlookBarGroups collection, as shown by the code in Listing 3-21:

Listing 3-21: Using the Groups property of the OutlookBarStorage Object

```
Dim oeExpl As Explorer
Dim ocpPanes As Panes
Dim obpPane As OutlookBarPane
Dim obsStore As OutlookBarStorage
Dim ocsBarGrps As OutlookBarGroups
'intervening code to instantiate oeExpl
Set ocpPanes = oeExpl.Panes
Set obpPane = ocpPanes.Item("OutlookBar")
Set obsStore = obpPane.Contents
Set ocsBarGrps = obsStore.Groups
```

The intermediary status of the OutlookBarStorage object is illustrated by the combination of the final two lines of code into the following statement:

```
Set ocsBarGrps = obpPane.Contents.Groups
```

OutlookBarGroups Collection

The OutlookBarGroups collection contains the OutlookBarGroup objects in the Outlook Bar. Each OutlookBarGroup object represents a group in the Outlook Bar. The Outlook Bar in Figure 3-5 has three OutlookBarGroup objects, named "Outlook Shortcuts," "My Shortcuts," and "Other Shortcuts."

Table 3-20 lists the properties of the OutlookBarGroups collection:

Table 3-20
Properties of the OutlookBarGroups Collection

Name	Description
Application	Returns the Outlook Application object.
Class	Returns the olObjectClass constant, in this case olOutlookBarGroups having a value of 65.
Count	Returns the number of objects, in this case the number of OutlookBarGroup objects in the collection.
Parent	Returns the parent object, which is the OutlookBarStorage object of the OutlookBarPane to which the collection belongs.
Session	Returns the NameSpace object for the current session.

Table 3-21 lists the methods of OutlookBarGroups collection:

Table 3-21
Methods of OutlookBarGroups Collection

Name	Description	Parameters
Add	Adds an OutlookBarGroup object to the collection.	Required: the name of the Outlook BarGroup object to be added. Optional: the one-based position where it will be added.
Item	Returns an OutlookBarGroup object to the collection.	The position or name of the Outlook BarGroup object to be returned.
Remove	Removes an OutlookBarGroup object from the collection.	The position or name of the Outlook BarGroup object to be removed.

The code in Listing 3-22 adds an OutlookBarGroup named "Top Secret Shortcuts" in the second position in the Outlook Bar:

Listing 3-22: **Using the Add method of the OutlookBarGroups Collection**

```
Dim obpPane As OutlookBarPane
Dim obsStore As OutlookBarStorage
Dim ocsBarGrps As OutlookBarGroups
Dim obgBarGrp As OutlookBarGroup
'intervening code to instantiate oeExpl
Set ocpPanes = oeExpl.Panes
Set obpPane = ocpPanes.Item("OutlookBar")
Set ocsBarGrps = obpPane.Contents.Groups
Set obgBarGrp = ocsBarGrps.Add "Top Secret Shortcuts", 2
```

The "Top Secret Shortcuts" group would be retrieved by the following statement:

```
Set obgBarGrp = ocsBarGrps.Item("Top Secret Shortcuts")
```

This group also could be retrieved by this statement:

```
Set obgBarGrp = ocsBarGrps.Item(2)
```

The Remove method requires the one-based position of the group in the collection. Unlike the Remove method for some other objects or collections, here you can't use the name of the object to be removed instead of its position. Therefore, it is necessary to iterate through the collection, using the Count property of the collection to locate the object. The code in Listing 3-23 removes the "Top Secret Shortcuts" group:

Listing 3-23: **Using the Remove method of the OutlookBarGroups Collection**

```
Dim counter As Integer
For counter = 1 To ocsBarGrps.Count
   If obgBarGrp.Name = "Top Secret Shortcuts" Then
      ocsBarGrps.Remove counter
      Exit For
   End If
Next Counter
```

Table 3-22 lists the events of the OutlookBarGroups collection:

Table 3-22
Events of OutlookBarGroups Collection

Name	Fires When ...	Cancelable?
BeforeGroupAdd	Just before OutlookBarGroup is added to the collection.	Yes
BeforeGroupRemove	Just before OutlookBarGroup is removed from the collection.	Yes
GroupAdd	Just after OutlookBarGroup is added to the collection.	No

The code in Listing 3-24 shows how to use the BeforeGroupAdd event to prevent a user from adding a new group:

Listing 3-24: **Using the BeforeGroupAdd event of the OutlookBarGroups Collection**

```
Dim obpPane As OutlookBarPane
Dim obsStore As OutlookBarStorage
Dim WithEvents ocsBarGrps As OutlookBarGroups
Dim obgBarGrp As OutlookBarGroup
'intervening code to instantiate oeExpl
Set ocpPanes = oeExpl.Panes
Set obpPane = ocpPanes.Item("OutlookBar")
Set ocsBarGrps = obpPane.Contents.Groups
Set obgBarGrp = ocsBarGrps.Add "Top Secret Shortcuts", 2

Private Sub ocsBarGrps_BeforeGroupAdd(Cancel As Boolean)

MsgBox "Addition of groups is strictly prohibited!"
Cancel = True

End Sub
```

The BeforeGroupAdd event does not "know" the group you are trying to add. Therefore, it cannot be used to prevent the addition of some groups but not others. However, the GroupAdd event does know which group is being added. While the

group has already been added, it can be removed with the Remove method. The code
in Listing 3-25 permits an added group to remain only if it has an acceptable name:

Listing 3-25: Using the GroupAdd event of the OutlookBarGroups Collection

```
Private Sub ocsBarGrps_GroupAdd( _
   ByVal NewGroup As OutlookBarGroup)

   If NewGroup.Name <> "Acceptable Name" Then
MsgBox "Name of newly added group unacceptable"
   Dim counter As Integer
   For counter = 1 To ocsBarGrps.Count
      If obgBarGrp.Name = "Top Secret Shortcuts" Then
         ocsBarGrps.Remove counter
         Exit For
      End If
   Next Counter
   End If

End Sub
```

The code to remove the shortcut is discussed above in connection with the Remove
method.

The BeforeGroupRemove event, unlike the BeforeGroupAdd event, does know the
group that is the subject of the event. Therefore, the BeforeGroupRemove event
can be used to prevent the removal of a particular group, as shown by the code in
Listing 3-26:

Listing 3-26: Using the BeforeGroupRemove event of the OutlookBarGroups Collection

```
Private Sub ocsBarGrps_BeforeGroupRemove( _
   ByVal Group As OutlookBarGroup, Cancel As Boolean)

If NewGroup.Name = "Essential group" Then
MsgBox "Removal of this group strictly prohibited!"
   Cancel = True
End If

End Sub
```

OutlookBarGroup Object

The OutlookBarGroup object represents an individual group in the Outlook Bar. It has no methods or events, but it does have properties, which are listed in Table 3-23:

<table>
<tr><td colspan="2" align="center">Table 3-23
Properties of the OutlookBarGroup Object</td></tr>
<tr><td>*Name*</td><td>*Description*</td></tr>
<tr><td>Application</td><td>Returns the Outlook Application object.</td></tr>
<tr><td>Class</td><td>Returns the olObjectClass constant, in this case olOutlookBarGroup having a value of 66.</td></tr>
<tr><td>Name</td><td>Returns a string representing the name of the object. This value is set by the Add method of the OutlookBarGroups collection.</td></tr>
<tr><td>Parent</td><td>Returns the parent object, which is the OutlookBarStorage object for the OutlookBarPane to which the OutlookBarGroup belongs.</td></tr>
<tr><td>Session</td><td>Returns the NameSpace object for the current session.</td></tr>
<tr><td>Shortcuts</td><td>Returns a reference to the OutlookBarShortcuts collection for the OutlookBarGroup. That collection, discussed in the next section, contains all the shortcuts for the group.</td></tr>
<tr><td>ViewType</td><td>Sets or returns whether the icons representing the shortcuts will be large (olLargeIcon, or 1) or small (olSmallIcon, or 2).</td></tr>
</table>

The Name property was used in preceding code examples of the OutlookBarGroups collection to determine the identity of the particular group on the Outlook Bar. The Shortcuts property is used to access the OutlookBarShortcuts collection discussed in the next section. The code in Listing 3-27 sets the OutlookBarShortcuts collection variable ocsShort to the shortcuts in the "My Shortcuts" group:

Listing 3-27: Using the Name property of the OutlookBarGroup Object

```
Dim obpPane As OutlookBarPane
Dim ocsBarGrps As OutlookBarGroups
Dim obgBarGrp As OutlookBarGroup
```

```
Dim ocsShort As OutlookBarShortcuts
'intervening code to instantiate oeExpl
Set ocpPanes = oeExpl.Panes
Set obpPane = ocpPanes.Item("OutlookBar")
Set ocsBarGrps = obpPane.Contents.Groups
Set obgBarGrp = ocsBarGrps.Item("My Shortcuts")
Set ocsShort = obgBarGrp.Shortcuts
```

OutlookBarShortcuts Collection

The OutlookBarShortcuts collection contains all of the shortcuts in a particular group on the Outlook Bar.

Properties

Table 3-24 lists the properties of the OutlookBarShortcuts collection:

Table 3-24
Properties of the OutlookBarShortcuts Collection

Name	Description
Application	Returns the Outlook Application object.
Class	Returns the olObjectClass constant, in this case olOutlookBar Shortcuts having a value of 67.
Count	Returns the number of objects, in this case the number of OutlookBarShortcut objects in the collection.
Parent	Returns the parent object, which is the OutlookBarGroup object.
Session	Returns the NameSpace object for the current session.

The Count property is useful for iterating through the shortcuts in the collection.

Methods

Table 3-25 lists the methods of the OutlookBarShortcuts collection:

Table 3-25
Methods of OutlookBarShortcuts Collection

Name	Description	Parameters
Add	Adds and returns the OutlookBarShortcut object to the collection.	See Table 3-26.
Item	Returns an OutlookBarShortcut object to the collection.	The position in the collection or name of the OutlookBarShortcut object to be returned.
Remove	Removes an OutlookBarShortcut object from the collection.	The position in the collection of the OutlookBarShortcut object to be removed.

Table 3-26
Parameters of the Add Method of the OutlookBarShortcuts Collection

Name	Data Type	Required	Description
Target	Variant	Yes	The folder, file, or URL to which the shortcut points. If a folder, a MAPIFolder object. If a system folder or file or a URL, a string with the path and file name.
Name	String	Yes	The name of the OutlookBarShortcut object to be added.
Index	Long	No, optional	The position in the collection where the OutlookBarShortcut object will be added.

The code in Listing 3-28 adds to two shortcuts to the shortcuts in the "My Shortcuts" group, a subfolder under the Inbox called "IDG" and a URL to IDG's web page:

Listing 3-28: Using the Add method of the OutlookBarShortcuts Collection

```
Dim ofFolder As MAPIFolder
Dim obpPane As OutlookBarPane
Dim ocsBarGrps As OutlookBarGroups
Dim obgBarGrp As OutlookBarGroup
```

```
Dim ocsShort As OutlookBarShortcuts
'intervening code to instantiate oeExpl
Set ocpPanes = oeExpl.Panes
Set obpPane = ocpPanes.Item("OutlookBar")
Set ocsBarGrps = obpPane.Contents.Groups
Set obgBarGrp = ocsBarGrps.Item("My Shortcuts")
Set ocsShort = obgBarGrp.Shortcuts
Set ofFolder = Application.GetNameSpace("MAPI"). _
    GetDefaultFolder(olFolderInbox).Folders("IDG")
ocsShort.Add ofFolder, "IDG"
ocsShort.Add "http://www.idgbooks.com", "IDG-WWW"
```

The following code example uses the Item method to assign to the
OutlookBarShortcut object variable osShort the "IDG-WWW" shortcut:

```
Set osShort = ocsShort.Item("IDG-WWW")
```

The Remove method requires the one-based position of the shortcut in the collection. Unlike the Remove method for some other objects or collections, here you
can't use the name of the object to be removed instead of its position. Therefore, it
is necessary to iterate through the collection, using the Count property of the collection to locate the object. The code in Listing 3-29 uses the Remove method to
remove the "IDG" subfolder:

Paths

The code example showing the second invocation of the Add method added a shortcut to
a Web page on the Internet. The first parameter was the path to the Web page. How you
specify the path varies with whether the file is on the Internet, an intranet, a local drive, or
a network drive.

If the Web page was on a local intranet in the idg directory of the server named "ntserver,"
the statement could be changed to read:

```
ocsShort.Add "http://ntserver/idg/index.html", "IDG-WWW"
```

If the same Web page was on the local drive in the idg directory instead, the statement
could be changed to read:

```
ocsShort.Add "file://c:\mydocs\idg\index.html", "IDG-WWW"
```

If the same Web page name was moved to a network drive in the idg directory of the
server named "ntserver," the statement could be changed to read:

```
ocsShort.Add "file://ntserver/mydocs/idg/index.html", _
    "IDG-WWW"
```

> **Listing 3-29: Using the Remove method of the OutlookBarShortcuts Collection**
>
> ```
> On Error Resume Next
> Dim counter As Integer
> For counter = 1 To ocsShort.Count
>    Err.Clear
>    If osShort.Target.Name = "IDG" Then
>       If Err.Number = 0 Then
>          ocsShort.Remove counter
>          Exit For
>       End If
>    End If
> Next Counter
> ```

The error handler is necessary because the code, in particular the statement `osShort.Target.Name`, expects that the target of the shortcut will have a `Name` property. The target does have this property if it is a MAPIFolder object. However, shortcuts may also point to system folders or files or URLs.

Events

Table 3-27 lists the events of the OutlookBarShortcuts collection:

Table 3-27
Events of OutlookBarShortcuts Collection

Name	Fires When ...	Cancelable?
BeforeShortcutAdd	Just before OutlookBarShortcut is added to the collection.	Yes
BeforeShortcutRemove	Just before OutlookBarShortcut is removed from the collection.	Yes
ShortcutAdd	Just after OutlookBarShortcut is added to the collection.	No

The `BeforeShortcutAdd` event can be used to prevent a user from adding a new shortcut, such as the addition of a shortcut to the IDG subfolder in Listing 3-30:

Listing 3-30: **Using the BeforeShortcutAdd event of the OutlookBarShortcuts Collection**

```
Dim ofFolder As MAPIFolder
Dim obpPane As OutlookBarPane
Dim ocsBarGrps As OutlookBarGroups
Dim obgBarGrp As OutlookBarGroup
Dim WithEvents ocsShort As OutlookBarShortcuts
'intervening code to instantiate oeExpl
Set ocpPanes = oeExpl.Panes
Set obpPane = ocpPanes.Item("OutlookBar")
Set ocsBarGrps = obpPane.Contents.Groups
Set obgBarGrp = ocsBarGrps.Item("My Shortcuts")
Set ocsShort = obgBarGrp.Shortcuts
Set ofFolder = Application.GetNameSpace("MAPI"). _
   GetDefaultFolder(olFolderInbox).Folders("IDG")
ocsShort.Add ofFolder, "IDG"

Private Sub ocsShort_BeforeShortcutAdd(Cancel As Boolean)

MsgBox "Addition of shortcuts is strictly prohibited!"
Cancel = True

End Sub
```

The BeforeShortcutAdd event does not "know" the shortcut you are trying to add any more than the BeforeGroupAdd event "knows" the group you are trying to add. Therefore, it cannot be used to prevent the addition of some but not other groups. However, the ShortcutAdd event does know which group is being added. While the group already has been added, it can be removed with the Remove method. The code in Listing 3-31 removes the addition of a shortcut to the "IDG" subfolder:

Listing 3-31: **Using the ShortcutAdd event of the OutlookBarShortcuts Collection**

```
Private Sub ocsShort _ShortcutAdd( _
   ByVal NewShortcut As OutlookBarShortcut)

On Error Resume Next
If NewShortcut.Target.Name <> "IDG" Then
MsgBox "Shortcut to IDG folder strictly prohibited"

   Dim counter As Integer
   For counter = 1 To ocsShort.Count
```

Continued

Listing 3-31 *(continued)*

```
        Err.Clear
        If osShort.Target.Name = "IDG" Then
            If Err.Number = 0 Then
                ocsShort.Remove counter
                Exit For
            End If
        End If
    Next Counter

End If

End Sub
```

The code to remove the shortcut was discussed earlier in connection with the Remove method.

The BeforeShortcutRemove event, unlike the BeforeShortcutAdd event, does know the shortcut that is the subject of the event that you are trying to add. Therefore, the BeforeShortcutRemove event can be used to prevent the removal of a particular shortcut, as shown by the code in Listing 3-32:

Listing 3-32: Using the BeforeShortcutRemove event of the OutlookBarShortcuts Collection

```
Private Sub ocsShort_BeforeGroupRemove( _
    ByVal Shortcut As OutlookBarShortcut, Cancel As Boolean)

On Error ResumeNext
If Shortcut.Target.Name = "IDG" Then
MsgBox "Removal of this shortcut strictly prohibited!"
    Cancel = True
End If

End Sub
```

OutlookBarShortcut Object

The OutlookBarShortcut object represents each shortcut in a group. The Outlook BarShortcut object is usually used to link to an Outlook folder. However, one of the new features of Outlook 2000 is that the shortcut may also link to a folder or file on a local or network drive or navigate to a URL.

The OutlookBarShortcut object has no methods or events, but it does have properties, which are listed in Table 3-28:

Table 3-28	
Properties of the OutlookBarShortcut Object	
Name	**Description**
Application	Returns the Outlook Application object.
Class	Returns the olObjectClass constant, in this case olOutlookBar Shortcut having a value of 68.
Name	Returns a string representing the name of the object. This value is set by the Add method of the OutlookBarShortcuts collection.
Parent	Returns the parent object, which is the OutlookBarGroup object.
Session	Returns the NameSpace object for the current session.
Target	Returns what the shortcut points to.

The data type of this property is a Variant. The Target may be a MAPIFolder object if the shortcut is to an Outlook folder, or it may be the path and name of a system folder or file or a URL. The TypeName function may be used to determine if the Target is a MAPIFolder:

```
If TypeName(myOlShortcut.Target) <> "MAPIFolder" Then
    'Do something
End If
```

The properties or methods of the Target can be accessed through the Target property. Several of the code examples accessed the Name property of the target:

```
MyOlShortcut.Target.Name
```

Caution   This code works fine if the target is a MAPIFolder since that object supports a Name property. However, not all potential objects that could be the target support a Name property. Trying to access the Name property of an object that does not support it will result in an error. Therefore, a judicious combination of the TypeName function (to determine if the object is a MAPIFolder) and an error handler may be advisable.

Summary

In this chapter you learned how to use the Outlook 2000 object model to navigate the Outlook folder hierarchy programmatically by using the properties, methods, and events of the Folders collection. Additionally, you learned how to add or remove folders. You also learned how to use the properties and methods of the individual folders, each a MAPIFolder object. The MAPIFolder object has its own properties and methods that also can be accessed through the object model.

The Outlook 2000 object model also provides the Explorer object to represent the window through which the user views the contents of a folder. This chapter explained how to use the properties, methods, and events of this object and its container, the Explorers collection, and how to have programmatic control over the user's view of the folders contents and the user's ability to navigate among folders and views of the folders.

Finally, this chapter analyzed the considerable portion of the object model relating to the Outlook Bar. This bar not only contains shortcuts to Outlook folders, but new with Outlook 2000, may also contain shortcuts to non-Outlook folders or files on a local or network drive or even to URLs on the World Wide Web. You learned how to use this object model to have programmatic control over the shortcut groups and individual shortcuts displayed in the Outlook Bar and the user's ability to navigate among these groups and shortcuts.

Folders are the gateway through which you access the Outlook items in the folder. The next two chapters focus on the different Outlook items and the forms through which the items are displayed for viewing and editing.

✦   ✦   ✦

Outlook Items

The Windows operating system and most applications use a file to represent data. For example, this chapter was initially written in Microsoft Word and, therefore, started life as a .doc file. Outlook, not surprisingly, is different. In this chapter we'll take a closer look at the various types of items that comprise the data in Outlook, as well as the properties, methods, and events associated with each.

What Are Items?

Outlook's data consist of various items, such as mail messages, contacts, appointments, and tasks. While these items can be saved as files, the Outlook 2000 object model does not regard them as file objects. Rather, a mail message is a MailItem object, a contact is a ContactItem object, an appointment is an AppointmentItem object, and so on.

Items are contained in folders. Items are accessed through the Items property of the MAPIFolder object. This property returns a collection of the items in a folder. This collection of items is called (not surprisingly) an Items collection. For example, the mail message items contained in the Inbox folder are members of the Items collection of that folder. The Items collection is the gateway through which the individual items in a folder are accessed.

Items are often sent to someone. The most beautifully written mail message has little value until it is sent. In the object model, each recipient of an item is a Recipient object, and all recipients of an item collectively constitute a Recipients collection.

A recipient's e-mail address is often stored and retrieved from an address book, such as the Global Address List. The Address Lists collection contains all address books, each of which is an AddressList Object. The AddressEntries Collection contains all address entries in an address book, each entry being an AddressEntry Object.

Items also often contain attachments. Each attachment is, you guessed it, an Attachment object and a member of the Attachments collection. Items also may be linked to each other, involving the Link object and the Links collection.

Each item object has its own unique properties and methods, which we will explore in depth in this chapter. However, while the item objects are different both in appearance and in function, they do have a number of properties and methods in common, and share the same events. These common properties, methods and events conveniently flatten your learning curve.

Finally, the window through which an item is viewed is an Inspector object, which is a member of the Inspectors collection. The Inspector object is to items what the Explorer object is to folders.

Items Collection

The Items collection represents all of the items in a folder and is used to access the items in that folder. The collection may be empty, when there are no items in a folder. Figure 4-1 shows the position of the Items collection and the item objects within the Outlook 2000 object hierarchy. Table 4-1 lists the properties of the Items collection:

Figure 4-1: Items collection in the Outlook object model hierarchy

	Table 4-1
	Properties of the Items Collection

Name	Description
Application	Returns the Outlook Application object.
Class	Returns the olObjectClass constant, in this case olItems having a value of 16.
Count	Returns the number of items in the collection.

Name	Description
IncludeRecurrences	Returns a Boolean value indicating whether the item has a recurrences pattern. Some items, such as an AppointmentItem, may have this pattern.
Parent	Returns the Parent object, in this case a MAPIFolder.
Session	Returns the NameSpace object through which the Items collection was accessed.

The Count property returns the number of objects contained in the collection. This property is useful to iterate through the Items collection. The code in Listing 4-1 uses the Count property to determine the number of items in the Inbox. The output was "395 items in Inbox." Obviously one of the authors needs to clean his Inbox!

Listing 4-1: Using the Count property of the Items collection

```
Sub Main()
Dim olOutlook As Outlook.Application
Dim ns As Outlook.NameSpace
Dim fld As Outlook.MAPIFolder
Dim itms As Outlook.items
Set olOutlook = New Outlook.Application
Set ns = olOutlook.GetNameSpace("MAPI")
Set fld = ns.GetDefaultFolder(olFolderInbox)
Set itms = fld.items
Debug.Print itms.Count & " items in " & fld.Name
olOutlook.Quit
Set olOutlook = Nothing
End Sub
```

Methods of the Items Collection

The Items collection has a number of methods reminiscent of a database object, including Add and Remove, GetFirst, GetNext, GetPrevious and GetLast for moving through items, Find and FindNext for finding items, and Sort for sorting. Table 4-2 lists the methods of the Items collection:

Table 4-2
Methods of the Items Collection

Name	Description	Parameter
Add	Creates and returns a new Item object of the type specified in the parameter, or, if no parameter, the default item type for the folder to which the Items collection belongs.	Optionally a valid message class or one of the olItemType constants in Table 2-8 in Chapter 2.
Find	Returns the first Item in the collection that matches the filter.	The filter, a string that will evaluate to True or False. (See Listing 4-1.).
FindNext	Called after the Find method to find and return the next Item in the collection that matches the filter used in the Find method, beginning from the Item found through the Find method. (See Listing 4-2.).	None.
GetFirst	Returns the first folder in the collection, or Nothing if no folder exists.	None.
GetLast	Returns the last folder in the collection, or Nothing if no folder exists.	None.
GetNext	Returns the next folder in the collection, or Nothing if no folder exists or at last folder.	None.
GetPrevious	Returns the previous object in the collection, or Nothing if no folder exists or at first folder.	None.
Item	Returns a folder from the collection.	Index or other identifier of folder to be accessed.
Remove	Removes folder from the collection.	Index of folder to be removed.
ResetColumns	Clears the properties that have been cached with the SetColumns method.	None.
Restrict	Applies a filter to an Items collection, returning a new collection containing all items from the original that match the filter.	The filter, a string that will evaluate to True or False.

Name	Description	Parameter
SetColumns	Allows the caching of specified properties. Permits faster access to those particular properties of an item than opening the item to access the properties. See Help for more details.	A comma-delimited list of the properties to be cached.
Sort	Sorts items in the collection by the specified property.	The property name, and optionally True to sort in descending order and False (the default value) to sort in ascending order.

The most commonly used methods of the Items collection can be categorized as follows:

✦ Searching for an Item: Find, FindNext, Restrict

✦ Navigating the collection: GetFirst, GetNext, GetPrevious, GetLast

✦ Modifying the collection: Add, Remove

✦ Ordering the collection: Sort

✦ Returning an Item: Item

The Find method locates and returns the first item that matches certain criteria, or Nothing if no item matches. Listing 4-2 prints the subject of the first mail message in the Inbox sent by one of the co-authors:

Listing 4-2: **Example of the Find method**

```
Sub Main()

Dim olOutlook As Outlook.Application
Dim ns As Outlook.NameSpace
Dim fld As Outlook.MAPIFolder
Dim itms As Outlook.items
Dim itm As Object
Set olOutlook = New Outlook.Application
Set ns = olOutlook.GetNameSpace("MAPI")
Set itms = ns.GetDefaultFolder(olFolderInbox).items
Set itm = itms.Find("[SenderName] = ""David Jung""")
If itm.Class = olMail And TypeName(itm) <> "Nothing" Then _
Debug.Print itm.Subject
End If
```

Continued

Listing 4-2 *(continued)*

```
olOutlook.Quit
Set olOutlook = Nothing

End Sub
```

The embedded quotes and brackets in the parameter to the Find method are unusual. The outside quotation marks are necessary because the parameter to the Find method is a string. The double quotation marks around the name being searched for are necessary because the name is also a string. The search criteria need not be a string. It can be another data type, such as an integer. The field name SenderName is in brackets because it is a field.

The equality operator (=) is used in Listing 4-2, but the Find method also supports the other comparison operators: >, >=, <, <=. and <>.

Listing 4-2 uses the TypeName function to test if the itm object variable points to an object because the Find method returns Nothing if there is no match for the search criteria. Testing for itm Is Nothing is an alternative to the TypeName function.

Class Property

Listing 4-2 also examines the Class property of the itm object variable. The Class property has been mentioned in connection with other objects and collections but until now has not been used in a code example. Usually an Items collection contains only one type of item, the type corresponding to the folder. For example, an item in the Inbox by default is a MailItem, an item in the Contacts folder by default is a ContactItem, an item in the Appointments folder by default is an AppointmentItem, and so on. However, a folder may contain items different from its default type. Thus, an Items collection may contain several types of items.

A MailItem property has a Subject property. However, not all Outlook items have a Subject property. Invoking this property by the statement Debug.Print itm.Subject could cause an error if the item matching the search criteria was of a type that did not support this property. Therefore, the Class property of the item matching the search criteria was checked by the itm.Class = olMail statement to determine if the item is a MailItem object. The Class property returns a constant representing the olObjectClass of an item. There are numerous constants. The following table lists the constants that correspond to the standard items.

Constant	Value
OlItems	16
OlAppointment	26
OlContact	40
OlJournal	42
OlMail	43
OlNote	44
OlTask	48
OlTaskRequest	49

The `Class` property is often used to determine the type of item (mail message, contact item, etc.) when your code is iterating through the Items collection of a folder.

The `FindNext` method finds the next item that matches the criteria that are the argument to the `Find` method. Listing 4-3, using the `FindNext` method in a loop, finds each mail message sent by one of co-authors and prints out the subject of each successive message that was sent by him:

Listing 4-3: **Example of the FindNext method**

```
Sub Main()

Dim olOutlook As Outlook.Application
Dim ns As Outlook.NameSpace
Dim fld As Outlook.MAPIFolder
Dim itms As Outlook.items
Dim itm As Object
Set olOutlook = New Outlook.Application
Set ns = olOutlook.GetNameSpace("MAPI")
Set itms = ns.GetDefaultFolder(olFolderInbox).Items
Set itm = itms.Find("[SenderName] = ""David Jung""")
Do Until itm Is Nothing
    If itm.Class = olMail Then Debug.Print itm.Subject
    Set itm = itms.FindNext
Loop
olOutlook.Quit
Set olOutlook = Nothing

End Sub
```

The condition in the `Do Until` loop `itm Is Nothing` is to test for no further matches. Otherwise there would be no end to the loop.

The `Restrict` method applies a filter to a collection and returns another collection limited to those items in the first collection that match the filter criteria. The code in Listing 4-4 performs the same function as the combination of `Find` and `FindNext` in the preceding examples. A second collection is created with only those items matching the criteria, and then the `For Each ... Next` syntax is used to iterate through the filtered collection:

Listing 4-4: **Example of the Restrict method**

```
Sub Main()

Dim olOutlook As Outlook.Application
Dim ns As Outlook.NameSpace
Dim fld As Outlook.MAPIFolder
Dim itms As Outlook.Items
Dim myRestrict As Outlook.Items
Dim itm As Object
Set olOutlook = New Outlook.Application
Set ns = olOutlook.GetNamespace("MAPI")
Set itms = ns.GetDefaultFolder(olFolderInbox).Items
Set myRestrict = itms.Restrict("[SenderName] = ""David Jung""")
For Each itm In myRestrict
    If itm.Class = olMail Then Debug.Print itm.Subject
Next
olOutlook.Quit
Set olOutlook = Nothing

End Sub
```

While the code seems simpler than the preceding examples, the `Find/FindNext` method may be faster. Using the `Restrict` method may be preferable if the filtered collection will be reused.

The `GetFirst`, `GetLast`, `GetNext` and `GetPrevious` methods have no parameters. They return the first, last, next, or previous collection item, respectively. The `Get First` method returns the first object in the collection or returns `Nothing` if no first object exists, such as if the collection is empty. The other `Get` methods work similarly. For example, the `GetPrevious` method returns the previous item in the collection, or `Nothing` if there is no previous item. The code in Listing 4-5 calls the `GetFirst` method and then loops through the items in the Inbox using the GetNext method. The loop terminates (or never begins) when one of these methods returns Nothing:

Listing 4-5: **Using the ViewSwitch event of the Explorer Object**

```
Dim onNS As Outlook.NameSpace
Dim ofFolder As Outlook.MAPIFolder
Dim oiItems As Outlook.Items
Dim anItem As Object
Set oaOutlook = New Outlook.Application
Set onNS = oaOutlook.GetNameSpace("MAPI")
Set oiItems = onNS.GetDefaultFolder(olFolderInbox).Items
Set anItem = oiItems.GetFirst
Do Until anItem Is Nothing
    If itm.Class = olMail Then Debug.Print anItem.Subject
    anItem.GetNext
Loop
```

Outlook Help suggests: "To ensure correct operation of the GetFirst, GetLast, GetNext, and GetPrevious methods in a large collection, call GetFirst before calling GetNext on that collection, and call GetLast before calling GetPrevious." This is good advice, because Outlook may contain numerous Items collections. Explicitly creating a variable that refers to the specific Items collection you're interested in ensures that you are always making the calls on the same collection.

The Add method adds a new Outlook item in the Items collection for the folder and returns the new item. If not specified, the type of the item defaults to the type of the folder, or to MailItem if the parent folder is not typed. The Outlook item type for the new item can be one of the olItemType constants listed in Table 2-8 in Chapter 2. To save you having to look back at that table, the constants are repeated here: olAppointmentItem(1), olContactItem(2), olJournalItem(4), olMailItem(0), olNoteItem(5), olPostItem(6), or olTaskItem(3). If a custom item is involved, then the second parameter may be any valid message class. This code snippet creates a contact item:

```
Set myOlApp = CreateObject("Outlook.Application")
Set myNameSpace = myOlApp.GetNameSpace("MAPI")
Set myFolder = _
    myNamespace.GetDefaultFolder(olFolderContacts)
Set myItem = myFolder.Items.Add
```

The Remove method simply removes an item by its index, which is its one-based position within the collection. Remove finds the item associated with the index (for example, an index of 3 finds the third item in the collection) and deletes it.

Sort takes two parameters. The first is the property to sort. The second, a Boolean, is optional, True for descending, False (the default) for ascending. The code in Listing 4-6 sorts contacts in the Contacts folder by company name in ascending alphabetical order.

Listing 4-6: **Example of the Sort method**

```
Set myOlApp = CreateObject("Outlook.Application")
Set myNamespace = myOlApp.GetNamespace("MAPI")
Set myFolder = _
    myNameSpace.GetDefaultFolder(olFolderContacts)
Set myItems = myFolder.Items
myItems.Sort "[CompanyName]", False
For Each myItem in myItems
    MsgBox myItem.CompanyName
Next myItem
```

The Item method returns a specific item from a collection. The code in Listing 4-7 returns the second item in the collection.

Listing 4-7: **Example of the Item method**

```
Set myOlApp = CreateObject("Outlook.Application")
Set myNameSpace = myOlApp.GetNameSpace("MAPI")
Set myFolder = _
    myNameSpace.GetDefaultFolder(olFolderInbox)
Set mySecondItem = myFolder.Items.Item(2)
```

The code in Listing 4-8 uses the For Each ... Next syntax to navigate the Items collection, in this case of the Inbox, to print out the subject of each mail message in the Inbox from one of the co-authors:

Listing 4-8: **Example of the For Each ... Next syntax**

```
Sub Main()

Dim olOutlook As Outlook.Application
Dim ns As Outlook.NameSpace
Dim fld As Outlook.MAPIFolder
```

```
Dim itms As Outlook.Items
Dim itm As Outlook.MailItem
Set olOutlook = New Outlook.Application
Set ns = olOutlook.GetNameSpace("MAPI")
Set fld = ns.GetDefaultFolder(olFolderInbox)
Set itms = fld.items
For Each itm In itms
    If itm.SenderName = "David Jung" Then
        If itm.Class = olMail Then Debug.Print itm.Subject
    End If
Next itm
olOutlook.Quit
Set olOutlook = Nothing

End Sub
```

While Items can be referred to generically, itm is declared as a specific type of Item, in this case a mail item since that is the type of item in the Inbox. A mail item has a host of properties, including SenderName, which is the display name of the sender, and Subject, which is the text on the subject line of the mail message. These specific item types will be discussed in later in this chapter.

Events of the Items Collection

Table 4-3 lists the three events of the Items collection. These events are similar to those of the Folders collection. They are not available from VBScript and also cannot be canceled.

Table 4-3	
Events of the Items Collection	
Name	**Fires When ...**
ItemAdd	Item is added to collection.
ItemChange	Item in collection is changed.
ItemRemove	Item is removed from collection.

The ItemAdd event has as a parameter the Item object that has been added, either by user action or program code:

```
Private Sub colItems_ItemAdd(ByVal Item As Object)
```

The Item parameter is declared as a generic object, rather than a particular Outlook item, because the item could be any type of Outlook item. This event could be used to check if the Item was of a particular class (using the Class property as discussed above) and, if so, use properties of the item to take an action. For example, if the item was a "New Potential Customer" form, a mail message could be sent to the sales staff with the contact item as an attachment.

The ItemChange event has as a parameter the Item object that has been changed, either by user action or program code:

```
Private Sub colItems_ItemChange(ByVal Item As Object)
```

Once again the Item parameter is declared as a generic object rather than a particular Outlook item because the item could be any type of Outlook item. This event could be used, after appropriate checks for the class of the item, to notify sales staff of changes in customer information so they can update their own personal records.

```
The ItemRemove event, unlike the other events, does not have a
parameter:Private Sub colItems_ItemRemove()
```

Notwithstanding this event's lack of a parameter, it can be used to work with other events. As with the combination of the FolderAdd and FolderRemove events in Chapter 3, the ItemRemove and ItemAdd events can complement each other. For example, if an item in a folder is deleted, it is removed from the Items collection of that folder, triggering the ItemRemove event for that collection. The deleted item is added to the Items collection of the Deleted Items folder, triggering the ItemAdd event for that collection. In the code in Listing 4-9, a deleted item is moved back from the Deleted Items folder only if the item came from the Inbox. If the folder came from another location, the folder remains in Deleted Items:

Listing 4-9: Example of ItemAdd and ItemRemove events

```
Public ns As NameSpace
Public WithEvents ocolInboxItems As Items
Public WithEvents ocolDeletedItems As Items
Public blnFromInbox As Boolean

Private Sub Application_StartUp()

    Set ns = Application.GetNameSpace("MAPI")
    Set ocolInboxItems = ns.GetDefaultFolder _
        (olInbox).Items
    Set ocolDeletedItems = ns.GetDefaultFolder _
        (olDeletedItems).Items
    blnFromInbox = False
```

```
End Sub

Private Sub ocolInboxItems_ItemRemove()

   blnFromInbox = True

End Sub

Private Sub ocolDeletedItems_ItemAdd _
   (ByVal Item As Object)

   If blnFromInbox Then
      Item.Move ns.GetDefaultFolder(olFolderInbox)
      blnFromInbox = False
   End If

End Sub
```

The ItemAdd and ItemRemove events worked together in this code example to complement each other. The ItemAdd event does not know the where the added item came from, but the ItemRemove event did because it is an event of the object variable that represents the specific Items collection from which the item was removed. The ItemRemove event uses its "knowledge" of the origin of the item to set a Boolean variable that notifies the ItemAdd event of the Deleted Items collection that the item newly added to it came from the Inbox. The ItemRemove event does not have as a parameter the item involved and therefore cannot retrieve the item. However, the item is a parameter of the ItemAdd event. Therefore, the ItemAdd event can use that parameter to return the item to the Inbox. This is essentially the same logic used for the code example in Chapter 3 in which the FolderAdd and FolderRemove events worked together.

Recipients, Attachments, and Links

Many Outlook items may be sent to recipients. All Outlook items except for Notes may contain attachments. All Outlook items may also have links to other Outlook items.

Recipients, attachments, and links each are represented by a collection and an object. The Recipients collection is a collection of recipients (each a Recipient object) of an item. The Attachments collection is a collection of the attachments (each an Attachment object) to an item. Finally, the Links collection is a collection of links (each a Link object) to an item.

Recipients

Mail messages are sent to recipients. However, a mail message is not the only Outlook item that is sent to a recipient. Meeting and task requests are also sent to recipients. Figure 4-2 shows the Recipients collection and Recipients object in the object model.

Figure 4-2: Recipients collection and Recipients object in object model

Recipients collection

Each recipient is a Recipient object. The Recipients collection is a collection of Recipient objects. For example, each recipient of a mail message is a Recipient object, and all of the recipients of the mail message would comprise a Recipients collection. The Recipients collection may be empty. For example, a new mail message, when created, has no recipients. A Recipients collection is created by the Recipients property of an Outlook item. Not all Outlook items have a Recipients property. The Outlook items that support this property are the MailItem, PostItem, AppointmentItem, MeetingItem, or TaskItem. This code example creates a Recipients collection using a MailItem object:

```
Dim oiMail As MailItem
Dim oiRecips As Recipients
Set oiMail = Application.CreateItem(olMailItem)
Set oiRecips = oiMail.Recipients
```

Table 4-4 lists the properties of the Recipients collection:

Table 4-4 Properties of the Recipients Collection	
Name	**Description**
Application	Returns the Outlook Application object.
Class	Returns the OlObjectClass constant, in this case olRecipients having a value of 17.
Count	Returns the number of objects, in this case Recipient objects, in the collection.
Parent	Returns the parent object.
Session	Returns the NameSpace object for the collection.

You can use the `Count` property to iterate through the Recipient objects in the collection.

Table 4-5 lists the methods of the Recipients collection:

<table>
<tr><td colspan="3" align="center">Table 4-5
Methods of the Recipients Collection</td></tr>
<tr><td>*Name*</td><td>*Description*</td><td>*Parameter*</td></tr>
<tr><td>Add</td><td>Creates a new Recipient object and adds it to the Recipients collection, and returns the new folder as a MAPIFolder object.</td><td>Name of recipient. Example:
`olMail.Add "Jeff Kent"`</td></tr>
<tr><td>Item</td><td>Returns a Recipient object from the collection.</td><td>Index: One-based position of Recipient object within collection.</td></tr>
<tr><td>Remove</td><td>Removes a Recipient object from collection.</td><td>Index: One-based position of Recipient object within collection.</td></tr>
<tr><td>ResolveAll</td><td>Returns True if all recipients resolved, False if one or more recipients not resolved.</td><td>None.</td></tr>
</table>

The `Add` method creates a new Recipient object and adds it to the Recipients collection. It uses the name of the recipient as a parameter.

This code example uses the `Add` method to add the co-authors to a collection of the recipients of a mail message. Note that this method does not verify that either of the co-authors has a valid e-mail address:

```
Dim oiMail As MailItem
Dim oicRecips As Recipients
Set oiMail = Application.CreateItem(olMailItem)
Set oicRecips = oiMail.Recipients
oicRecips.Add "Jeff Kent"
oicRecips.Add "David Jung"
```

The `ResolveAll` method does try to determine whether each recipient has a valid e-mail address. This method first checks if the recipient has an e-mail address in the Address Book. The Address Book collections and objects are covered later in this chapter. If the recipient is not in the Address Book, then the `ResolveAll` method checks if the recipient's name is in a valid e-mail format, such as `yourname@yourisp.com`.

The `ResolveAll` method returns True if each recipient name either is in the Address Book or is in a valid e-mail format, and False otherwise. This code example sends the e-mail message only if the `ResolveAll` method returns True:

```
Dim oiMail As MailItem
Dim oicRecips As Recipients
Set oiMail = Application.CreateItem(olMailItem)
Set oicRecips = oiMail.Recipients
oicRecips.Add "Jeff Kent"
oicRecips.Add "David Jung"
If oicRecips.ResolveAll Then oiMail.Send
```

The `ResolveAll` method is an "all or nothing" proposition. If even one of 100 recipients cannot be resolved, the method returns False. The `Resolve` method of the Recipients object, discussed next, provides more granular control.

The `Item` method, which returns a Recipient object from the collection, and the `Remove` method, which removes a Recipient object from the collection, both may take as a parameter the one-based position of the object in the collection. The `Item` method may alternatively take the name of the recipient as a parameter. The `Remove` method cannot take the name of the recipient as a parameter; attempting this will cause an error.

Recipient object

The Recipient object has a rich set of properties. Table 4-6 lists these properties.

<table>
<tr><td colspan="2" align="center">Table 4-6
Properties of the Recipient Object</td></tr>
<tr><td>*Name*</td><td>*Description*</td></tr>
<tr><td>Address</td><td>Sets (without validation) or returns the e-mail address of the current Recipient.</td></tr>
<tr><td>AddressEntry</td><td>Returns the AddressEntry object (covered later in this chapter) for the current Recipient.</td></tr>
<tr><td>Application</td><td>Returns the Outlook Application object.</td></tr>
<tr><td>AutoResponse</td><td>Sets or returns the auto response, which is an automatic reply message used while, for example, you are on vacation.</td></tr>
<tr><td>Class</td><td>The OlObjectClass constant, in this case olRecipient having a value of 4.</td></tr>
</table>

Name	Description
DisplayType	Returns one of the OlDisplayType constants listed in Table 2-8 in Chapter 2, disclosing whether a user or distribution list is involved.
EntryID	Returns the unique ID created when the Recipient object is created.
Index	The object's one-based position within the Recipients collection.
MeetingResponseStatus	Returns the status of whether the recipient has accepted, declined, responded, etc. to a meeting, with one of the following olMeetingResponse constants: olResponseNone(0) — no response status was set (default); olResponseOrganized(1) — meeting has been assigned to a task; olResponseTentative(2) — a tentative response was received; olResponseAccepted(3) — the recipient has accepted the meeting; olResponseDeclined(4) — the recipient has declined the meeting; olResponseNotResponded(5) — the recipient has not responded.
Name	The display name of the recipient.
Parent	The parent object.
Resolved	Returns True if Recipient's e-mail address is in an address book or has a valid format for an e-mail address.
Session	Returns the NameSpace object for the collection.
TrackingStatus	Sets or returns the tracking status, which pertains to the progress of the mail message, using one of the olTracking status constants: olTrackingNone(0) — no tracking set (default); olTrackingDelivered(1) — item received by recipient; olTrackingNotDelivered(2) — item not yet received by recipient; olTrackingNotRead(3) — item not yet read by recipient; olTrackingRecallFailure(4) — item cannot be retrieved from recipient; olTrackingRecallSuccess(5) — item retrieved from recipient; olTrackingRead(6) — item read by recipient; olTrackingReplied(7) — item replied to by recipient.

Continued

Table 4-6 *(continued)*	
Name	*Description*
TrackingStatusTime	Sets or returns the tracking status date and time for a recipient. This property holds the value of when the TrackingStatus property changes, such as when a recipient reads or replies to a message.
Type	Sets or returns the type of recipient, which depends on the type of item. If a JournalItem, the only choice is olAssociated Contact(1), the recipient is an associated contact. If a MailItem, olOriginator(0) — the recipient is the originator of the item; olTo(1) — the item is TO the recipient; olCC(2) — the recipient is a CC; olBCC(3) the recipient is a BCC. If a MeetingItem, olOriginator(0), the recipient is the originator of the meeting; olRequired(1) — the recipient is a required meeting participant; olOptional(2) — the recipient is an optional meeting participant; olResource(3) the recipient is a resource (e.g., a meeting room). If a TaskItem, olUpdate(2) — the task has been updated; olFinalStatus(3) — the task is in its final status.

A recipient in a message has a display name, the one you see in the TO, CC or BCC fields, and the recipient's e-mail address. The Name property contains the display name. The Address property contains the e-mail address.

The e-mail address in the Address property has not been validated. The e-mail address is validated using the Resolve method (discussed next) of the Recipient object. The method of validation is the same as with the ResolveAll method of the Recipients collection discussed above. The e-mail address is validated if it's either in the Address Book or is in proper e-mail format. If the e-mail address is validated, then the Resolved property of the Recipient object is True. This code example first uses the ResolveAll method of the Recipients collection and then states for each Recipient whether the e-mail address has been resolved by testing the Resolved property:

```
Dim oiMail As MailItem
Dim oicRecips As Recipients
Dim oiRecip As Recipient
Dim counter As Integer
Set oiMail = Application.CreateItem(olMailItem)
```

```
Set oicRecips = oiMail.Recipients
oicRecips.Add "Jeff Kent"
oicRecips.Add "David Jung"
oicRecips.ResolveAll
For counter = 1 to oicRecips.Count
   Set oiRecip = oiRecips.Item(counter)
   If oiRecip.Resolved Then
      Debug Print oiRecip.Name & " resolved."
   Else
      Debug Print oiRecip.Name & " not resolved."
   End If
Next counter
```

Further information about the recipient can be accessed through the AddressEntry property. That property returns the AddressEntry object for the recipient. The Address Entry object is discussed later in this chapter.

The Name property also can be used with the Remove method of the Recipients collection. That method, as discussed above, removes from the collection the Recipient object at a specified position. However, you may know only the name and not the position of the Recipient object to be removed. This code example uses the Count property of the collection to iterate through it, and uses the Item method of the collection to access the Recipient object at the specified position. The Name property of that Recipient object is compared to the name of the Recipient object to be removed. If there is a match, then the current value of the counter is passed to the Remove method since that value is the one-based position of the object within the collection.

```
Dim oiMail As MailItem
Dim oicRecips As Recipients
Dim counter As Integer
Set oiMail = Application.CreateItem(olMailItem)
Set oicRecips = oiMail.Recipients
oicRecips.Add "Jeff Kent"
oicRecips.Add "David Jung"
For counter = 1 to oicRecips.Count
   If oicRecips.Item(counter).Name = "David Jung" Then
      oicRecpips.Remove(counter)
      Exit For
   End If
Next counter
```

Methods of the Recipient object

As stated earlier, each recipient is a Recipient object. Table 4-7 lists the methods of the Recipient object:

Table 4-7
Methods of Recipient Object

Name	Description	Parameter
Delete	Removes the current Recipient from the Recipients collection.	None.
FreeBusy	Returns as a string a month of free/busy information for the current Recipient.	See Table 4-8.
Resolve	Returns True if recipient resolved, which is either found in address book or in correct e-mail format. False otherwise.	None.

Table 4-8
Parameters of FreeBusy Method of Recipient Object

Name	Data Type	Required?	Description
Start	Date	Yes	The start date of the period of free/busy information.
MinsPerChar	Long	Yes	The number of minutes each character represents in a free/busy string.
CompleteFormat	Boolean	No, optional	Detail of information. False (default) sets 0 to free and 1 to busy. If True then olFree(0) — recipient is free; olTentative(1) — recipient is tentative; olBusy(2) recipient is busy; olOutOfOffice(3) out of office.

The Resolve method, like its counterpart the ResolveAll method of the Recipients collection, validates a Recipient's e-mail, either if the Recipient is in the Address Book or the e-mail address is in proper e-mail format. The difference between the two methods is that the Resolve method is used on a recipient-by-recipient basis, whereas the ResolveAll method has to be used against the whole collection at one time. The code in Listing 4-10 states for each Recipient whether the e-mail address has been resolved:

Listing 4-10: **Example of the Resolve method**

```
Dim oiMail As MailItem
Dim oicRecips As Recipients
Dim oiRecip As Recipient
Dim counter As Integer
Set oiMail = Application.CreateItem(olMailItem)
Set oicRecips = oiMail.Recipients
oicRecips.Add "Jeff Kent"
oicRecips.Add "David Jung"
For counter = 1 to oicRecips.Count
    Set oiRecip = oiRecips.Item(counter)
    oiRecip.Resolve
    If oiRecip.Resolved Then
        Debug Print oiRecip.Name & " resolved."
    Else
        Debug Print oiRecip.Name & " not resolved."
    End If
Next counter
```

The `Delete` method, as its name suggests, deletes from the Recipients collection the Recipient object associated with the object variable that invokes the `Delete` method. The `Delete` method should be used with care; it is not reversible.

The default of the `FreeBusy` method is to return a string representing one month of free/busy information for the recipient. The string contains one character for each `MinPerChar` minute, up to one month of information from the specified Start date. If the optional argument `CompleteFormat` is omitted or False, then "free" is indicated by the character 0 and all other states by the character 1. If `CompleteFormat` is True, then the same length string is returned as defined above, but the characters now correspond to the **OlBusyStatus** constants described in Table 4-8 for the `CompleteFormat` parameter.

The Recipients collection has no events.

Attachments

Figure 4-3 shows the location of the Attachments collection and the Attachment object in the Outlook 2000 object model.

Figure 4-3: Attachments collection and Attachment object in object model

All Outlook item objects except the NoteItem object may contain attachments. An attachment may be either a file or a link to a file. Except for DocumentItem and ReportItem objects, attachments are displayed in the body of the item. Mail messages are sent to recipients. Each recipient is a Recipient object. The attachments of DocumentItem and ReportItem objects are seen in the Preview Pane.

The Attachments collection is a collection of Attachment objects. The collection may be empty.

An Attachment collection is created by the `Attachments` property of an Outlook item, as seen in the following code example:

```
Dim oiMail As MailItem
Dim oacAttachs As Attachments
Set oiMail = Application.CreateItem(olMailItem)
Set oacAttachs = olMail.Attachments
```

Attachments collection

Table 4-9 lists the properties of the Attachments collection:

Table 4-9
Properties of the Attachments Collection

Name	Description
Application	Returns the Outlook Application object.
Class	Returns the `olObjectClass` constant, in this case `olAttachments` having a value of 18.
Count	Returns the number of objects, in this case Attachment objects, in the collection.
Parent	Returns the parent object, the particular Outlook `Item` object containing the Attachments.
Session	Returns the NameSpace object for the collection.

The Count property is useful for iterating through the collection.

Table 4-10 lists the methods of the Attachments collection:

Table 4-10
Methods of Attachments Collection

Name	Description	Parameter
Add	Creates and returns a new Attachment object and adds it to the Attachments collection.	See Table 4-12 below.
Item	Returns an Attachment object from the collection.	Index: One-based position of Attachment object within collection.
Remove	Removes an Attachment object from collection.	Index: One-based position of Attachment object within collection.

Table 4-11 lists the parameters of the Add method of the Attachments collection:

Table 4-11
Parameters of Add Method of Attachments Collection

Name	Data Type	Required	Description
FileName	Variant	Yes	File name and path of attachment.
Type	Long	No, optional	One of the following olAttachmentType constants: olByValue(1) — copy of file or Outlook item; olByReference(4) — shortcut to file; olEmbeddedItem(5) — shortcut to Outlook item.
Position	Long	No, optional	Returns the number of characters within the body text at which the attachment is positioned (default is for the attachment to be positioned at end of the body text).
DisplayName	String	No, optional	The name of the attachment (default is file name).

The code in Listing 4-11 uses the Add method to add a copy of a file (which must exist) as an attachment to a mail message:

Listing 4-11: Example of Add method of Attachments Collection

```
Dim oiMail As MailItem
Dim ocAttachments As Attachments
Set oiMail = Application.CreateItem(olMailItem)
Set ocAttachments = oiMail.Attachments
ocAttachments.Add "c:\outlook2k\badchapter.doc", _
    olEmbeddedItem, , "Chapter XX"
```

Attachments object

Table 4-12 lists the properties of the Attachment object:

Table 4-12
Properties of the Attachment Object

Name	Description
Application	Returns the Outlook Application object.
Class	The olObjectClass constant, in this case olAttachment having a value of 4.
DisplayName	The name of the attachment in the body of the message.
FileName	The file name (without path) of the attachment.
Index	The one-based position of the Attachment object in the Attachments collection.
Parent	The parent object, which is the Outlook item containing the attachment.
PathName	The path and file name of the attachment. Corresponds to FileName parameter of Add method of Attachments collection.
Position	The number of characters within the body text the attachment is positioned. Corresponds to Position parameter of Add method of Attachments collection.
Session	Returns the NameSpace object for the collection.
Type	One of the olAttachmentType constants, Corresponds to Type parameter of Add method of Attachments collection.

The FileName property is of particular interest. It can be used to determine if the file being attached is, for example, an .exe file. If the network administrator does not want users to be attaching executables, then the BeforeAttachmentSave event of an Outlook item object can be used to prevent the executable from being sent as an attachment. This event is discussed later in this chapter.

Table 4-13 lists the methods of the Attachment object:

Table 4-13
Methods of Attachment Object

Name	Description	Parameter
Delete	Removes the current Attachment object from the Attachments collection.	None.
SaveAsFile	Saves the file to disk.	The path and file name.

The code in Listing 4-12 uses the SaveAs method to save the attachments in each message in the Inbox to the C:\Work directory (which must exist) by the file name of the attachment:

Listing 4-12: Example of SaveAs method of Attachment Object

```
Dim ofInbox As MAPIFolder
Dim oiMail As MailItem

Dim ocItems As Items
Dim ocAttachments As Attachments
Dim ooAttachment As Attachment
Dim iCount As Integer

Set ofInbox = Application.GetNameSpace("MAPI"). _
    GetDefaultFolder(olFolderInbox)
Set ocItems = ofInbox.Items
iCount = ocItems.Count
For iCount to 1 Step -1
    If ocItems(iCount).Class = olMail And _
        ocItems(iCount).Attachments.Count > 0 Then
        Set oiMail = ocItems(iCount)
        Set ocAttachments = oiMail.Attachments
        For Each ooAttachment in ocAttachments
            ooAttachment.SaveAsFile "c:\work\" & _
                ooAttachment.FileName
```

Continued

> **Listing 4-12** *(continued)*
>
> ```
>         Next
>     End If
> Next iCount
> ```

Links

Figure 4-4 shows the location in the Outlook object model of the Link object and the Links collection. A Link object is an item associated with another Outlook item. All Outlook item objects may have links. However, the only Outlook item which may be a link is a `ContactItem`.

Figure 4-4: Link collection and Link object in object model

The Links collection is a collection of Link objects. The collection may be empty. A Links collection is created by the `Links` property of an Outlook item.

```
Dim oiMail As MailItem
Dim ooLinks As Links
Set oiMail = Application.CreateItem(olMailItem)
Set ooLinks = oiMail.Links
```

Table 4-14 lists the properties of the Links collection:

	Table 4-14 Properties of the Links Collection

Name	Description
Application	Returns the Outlook Application object.
Class	The olObjectClass constant, in this case olLinks having a value of 76.
Count	The number of objects, in this case Link objects, in the collection.
Parent Links.	The parent object, the particular Outlook item object containing the Links.
Session	Returns the NameSpace object for the collection.

Table 4-15 lists the methods of the Links collection:

	Table 4-15 **Methods of Links Collection**	
Name	**Description**	**Parameter**
Add	Creates a new Link object and adds it to the Links collection.	The Outlook item (must be a ContactItem) to be linked.
Item	Returns an Attachment object from the collection.	Either Index (one-based position of Link object within collection) or Name property of Link object.
Remove	Removes an Attachment object from collection.	Index: One-based position of Link object within collection.

The Link object has no methods or events. Table 4-16 lists its properties:

	Table 4-16 **Properties of the Link Object**
Name	**Description**
Application	Returns the Outlook Application object.
Class	The olObjectClass constant, in this case olLink having a value of 75.
Item	Returns the contact item that is linked. If that item was moved or deleted after it was linked, using this property will trigger an error.
Name	The Name of the linked contact item, which is its Subject property.
Parent	The parent object.
Session	Returns the NameSpace object for the collection.
Type	Returns the olObjectClass constant of the linked item. Since only contact items may be linked, this property will return olContact or 40.

Common Outlook Item Properties, Methods, and Events

There are a number of different Outlook items. Despite their visual and functional differences, they share the same events. They also share a number of properties and methods, in addition to having their own distinct properties and methods.

Common Item Properties

Each of the Outlook items has a number of properties. Many of these properties are unique to a particular item, such as the Gender property for a contact. However, most of the Outlook items have in common several properties, listed in Table 4-17, which are important to a programmer:

Table 4-17
Important Common Outlook Item Properties

Name	*Description*
Actions	Returns the Actions collection for the item.
Attachments	Returns the Attachments collection for the item.
Class	Returns the olObjectClass constant for the item.
FormDescription	Returns the FormDescription object for the item.
GetInspector	Returns the Inspector object for the item.
Links	Returns the Links collection of the item.
MessageClass	Returns the message class of the item.
Recipients	Returns the Recipients collection of the item.
UserProperties	Returns the UserProperties collection for the item.

The Attachments, Links and Recipients properties were used earlier in this chapter to instantiate the collections of the same name. The Actions and User Properties properties also are used to instantiate collections of the same name. Those collections are covered in Chapter 5.

Preceding code examples used the Class property to determine the type of item (mail message, contact item, etc.) in an Items collection of a folder. Similarly, the MessageClass property is useful for accessing the type of form being displayed by the Inspector, which can be accessed by the GetInspector property. The Message Class property is important in dealing with custom forms, the subject of Chapter 5. The reason is that the Class property of custom forms is that of the default item on which the custom form is based and therefore cannot be used to identify the custom form.

Common Item Methods

Table 4-18 lists the methods that the Outlook items have in common:

Table 4-18
Common Item Methods

Name	Parameters	Description
Close	Optionally the Save Mode, an olInspectorClose constant, olSave(0) to save the item without prompting the user, olDiscard(1) to discard all changes to the item without prompting the user, and olPromptForSave(2) to prompt the user to save or discard changes.	Closes the display of the item (usually by an Inspector object) and optionally saves any changes to the item.
Copy	None.	Creates and returns a copy of the item.
Delete	None.	Deletes the item from the collection.
Display	Optional True to make the Inspector modal. Default is False.	Displays a new Inspector object for the item.
Move	MAPIFolder object.	Moves the item to a folder. The folder should host MailItem objects.
PrintOut	None.	Prints the item using default settings.
Save	None.	Saves the item to the current folder. For newly created items, the item is saved to theDrafts folder.
SaveAs	See Table 4-19.	Saves the item to the local hard drive.

Table 4-19
Parameters of the SaveAs Method of the Items Collection

Name	Data Type	Required?	Description
Path	String	Yes	Path and file name for new file.
Type	Long	No, optional	The type of the new file, represented by one of the following olSaveAsType constants: olTXT(0) — text (.txt) file; olRTF — rich text format (.rtf) file; olTemplate — Outlook template (.oft) file; olMSG — Outlook message (.msg) file, which is the default.

Display

The Display method displays the item, either modally or non-modally, in a new Inspector object. This object, discussed later in this chapter, is the window through which items are viewed. The opposite number of the Display method is the Close method. The Close method usually closes the Inspector object through which the item is viewed. However, the Close method also will work even if the item is not open for viewing. For example, if the content of an item is changed through code, and the SaveMode parameter is olPromptForSave, the user will still be asked whether to save changes or not.

Save

The Save method can be used before the Close method. The Save method is save the item to *a* folder. Your responsibility is to ensure that the folder is the correct one. The Save method will save the item to the current folder if there is a current folder. If there is no current folder, then the Save method will save a pre-existing item to the folder that is the default for the item. For example, a pre-existing contact item will be saved to the Contacts folder. However, if the item is newly created, then it will be saved to the Drafts folder.

SaveAs

The SaveAs method is useful if you want to save the item to a system folder on disk rather than to an Outlook folder. The olSaveAsType constants listed in Table 4-6 apply to all Outlook items. Additional constants may apply depending on the item. For example, a ContactItem may be saved as a virtual business card (vCard), which is represented by the olSaveAsType constant olVCard with the value 7.

Copy

The Copy method is useful for backups. This code example backs up all task items in the Tasks folder to the Backup folder. You can make such a backup before making changes to task information. The code in Listing 4-13 uses the Copy method to make a copy of each task item and then the Move method to move the item to the Backup folder.

Listing 4-13: Example of Copy method of Item Objects

```
Dim ns As NameSpace
Dim ofTasks As Outlook.MAPIFolder
Dim ofBackup As Outlook.MAPIFolder
Dim oiTask As TaskItem
Dim oiBackup As TaskItem
Dim counter As Integer

Set ns = Application.GetNameSpace("MAPI")
Set ofTasks = ns.GetDefaultFolder(olFolderTasks)
Set ofBackup = ns.GetDefaultFolder(olFolderTasks). _
```

```
        Folders.Item("Backup")

   For counter = 1 To ofTasks.Items.Count
      If ofTasks.Items.Item(counter).Class = olTask Then
         Set oiTask = ofTasks.Items.Item(counter)
         Set oiBackup = oiTask.Copy
         oiTask.Move ofBackup
      End If
   Next counter
```

The code uses the Count property of the Items collection to iterate through the items in the Tasks folder. The code also checks the Class property of each item in the Tasks folder so that only task items are backed up since the Tasks folder could contain items of types other than task items.

Delete

The Delete method is perhaps the easiest to use. It deletes the item that invokes the method. However, you should take care not to use the item object variable after it has called the Delete method until it has been reassigned to another item because the item it references has, after all, been deleted. The usual cautions about making sure you want to delete before you do so also apply.

Common Item Events

Table 4-20 lists the common Outlook item events:

Table 4-20			
Outlook Item Events			
Name	**Fires When ...**	**VBScript Parameter**	**VBA Parameter**
Open	User opens item or creates new item.	None	Cancel (discussed below)
Read	User selects item for editing.	None	None
Write	After user edits item and, in form view, clicks the Save, Close or Next Item button, or in list view, tabs away from item.	None	Cancel

Continued

Table 4-20 *(continued)*

Name	Fires When ...	VBScript Parameter	VBA Parameter
Close	In form view, user saves and closes item. In list view, when user tabs away from item.	None	Cancel
Send	User sends item, usually by clicking Send button or choosing File ⇨ Send menu item.	None	Cancel
Reply	User replies to item, usually by selecting item and clicking Reply button.	Response (the new item being sent in response)	Response and Cancel
Reply All	Same as Reply except Reply All button clicked.	Response	Response and Cancel
Forward	Same as Reply except Forward button clicked.	Forward (the new item being forwarded)	Forward and Cancel
BeforeCheckNames	User or program checks e-mail names.	None	Cancel
AttachmentAdd	User inserts an attachment.	Attachment (the attachment being added)	Attachment
AttachmentRead	User opens an attachment.	Attachment	Attachment
BeforeAttachmentSave	Newly inserted attachment is saved (occurs after AttachmentAdd).	Attachment	Attachment and Cancel
CustomAction	Custom action attached to Outlook form executes.	None	Cancel

The code for these events is written in the Script Editor, the Outlook development environment for writing form code. This environment is more limited than the Visual Studio development environments, but is adequate for the task. Figure 4-5 shows the Script Editor, which is opened by the Form ➪ View Code menu command while the form is in design view.

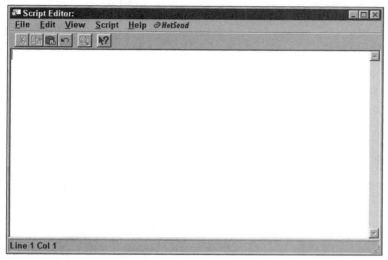

Figure 4-5: The Script Editor

The Script Editor saves you the work of writing stubs for the event handlers. Figure 4-6 shows the Insert Event Handler dialog box, which is displayed by the Event Handler command under the Script menu. You create the stub by selecting an item from the list and pressing the Add button. For example, selecting Open creates the following stub code:

```
Function Item_Open()

End Function
```

Figure 4-6: The Insert Event Handler dialog box

An Object Browser may be displayed while within the Script Editor by the menu command Object Browser under the Script menu or by the F12 shortcut key. However, this Object Browser is limited to the Outlook object model. You can access the "full" Object Browser by the F2 shortcut key while within the Visual Basic Editor, which you can access by the Alt-F11 shortcut key.

Once you finish writing your code, simply close the Script Editor. There is no Save button or command.

Tip

A good way of learning how to use the Script Editor and the Outlook item events is to insert event handlers for each of the 13 Outlook item events, and within each event handler show a message box stating that the event occurred. For example, the code for `Item_Open()` would be:

```
Function Item_Open()
MsgBox "Open event"
End Function
```

After writing the code, save the form and publish it to your Personal Forms Library, naming it `CodeTest`. You then can open the form by choosing it from the Choose Form dialog box, which you can access from the File ➪ New ➪ Choose Form menu command.

Table 4-21 lists the order of events that result from taking different Outlook item user actions:

Table 4-21
Events Triggered by Outlook Item User Actions

Action	Event(s)
Open the form from the Choose Form dialog box.	Open
In already open form, add or edit text in the message control and then click Save from the File menu.	Write
Choose Recipient from Address Box and Send.	BeforeCheckNames, Send, Write and Close
After receiving an item, double click it. –	Read and Open.
Click Reply.	Reply
Click ReplyAll.	ReplyAll
Click Forward.	Forward (may get macro warning)

Continued

Action	Event(s)
Send Item to yourself but first add attachment.	AttachmentAdd, BeforeCheck Names, Send, Write, Before AttachmentSave and Close
Open message that contains attachment.	AttachmentRead (may get warning)
Post item	Write, Close
Close item	Close

Events are useful when you need to take an action at a specific point. For example, the Write event is ideal for data validation because it occurs after a user finishes editing an item but before the editing has been saved. Therefore, you can use this event to determine if data have been entered in required fields or if a date or other data are within a valid range.

However, determining that the data entry is invalid is only half the battle. You also need to prevent the invalid data from being saved. "Canceling" the event does this. As explained in Chapter 2, when an event is canceled, the event still fires, but the consequence of the event is cancelled. For example, if the user failed to enter data in the required field LastName, the Write event can be used to warn the user and cancel the saving of the edited item, as we see in the code in Listing 4-14:

Listing 4-14: **Example of Canceling an event**

```
Function Item_Write()

If Item.LastName = "" Then
   MsgBox "Need to enter last name"
   Item_Write = False
End If

End Function
```

The consequence of the event, in this case the saving of the changes, is canceled by setting the function value to False. This is different from prior code examples, where the Cancel argument was set to True. The reason is that VBA uses a different syntax to cancel events. In VBA the event procedure contains a Cancel argument that is set to True to cancel the event. In VBScript the return value of the Function is set to False.

Since the Open event occurs before the form is displayed, it can be used to initialize the visual interface of the form, instantiate global variables, or connect to a database.

The Read event occurs when an existing item is opened, either because it was received or because it may be edited. One of its uses is to determine if the user is creating a new item or viewing an existing item.

The Write event occurs after the user has finished editing an item. Therefore, it can be used to validate data entry. If the data are invalid, or required fields have not been completed, the event can be cancelled.

Since the Close event occurs when the application is finished, it is a good place to update global variables and release memory.

The Send event occurs when the user is sending the item. The item will not be sent if the function return value is set to False. If you permit the item to be sent, you can set properties of the item. The code in Listing 4-15 requests read and delivery receipts programmatically:

Listing 4-15: **Requesting read and delivery receipts for the initial message**

```
Function Item_Send()

Item.ReadReceiptRequested = True
Item.OriginatorDeliveryReportRequested = True

End Function
```

The Reply event occurs when the user is replying to an item. No reply will occur if the function return value is set to False. If you permit the reply to occur, then you can set the properties of the Reply object. The Reply object is the parameter of the event procedure, in code example named theResponse. The code in Listing 4-16 requests read and delivery receipts programmatically for the response, just as the code in Listing 4-14 requested these receipts were requested for the initial message:

Listing 4-16: **Requesting read and delivery receipts for the response**

```
Function Item_Reply(ByVal theResponse)

theResponse.ReadReceiptRequested = True
theResponse.OriginatorDeliveryReportRequested = True

End Function
```

Note that this example does the same task as the Send event example (Listing 4-15), but in the Send event there is no parameter. The difference is that in the Send event no parameter is needed for the Item because the Item is open and being sent. In the Reply event only the Item being responded to is open; the response is not yet open.

The code in Listing 4-17 uses the ReplyAll event to check if there were more than nine recipients of the original message. If so, the user is asked if the user really wants to reply to over 10 recipients (the sender of the original message also will be a recipient). If the user responds no, then the event is canceled.

Listing 4-17: **Example of the ReplyAll event**

```
Function Item_Reply(ByVal theResponse)

If Item.Recipients.Count > 9 Then
    strMsg = "Do you really want to reply to over 10
recipients?"
    answer = MsgBox(strMsg)
End If
If myResult = 1 Then
    Item_ReplyAll = True
Else
    Item_ReplyAll = False
End If

End Function
```

The code in Listing 4-18 uses the Forward event to prevent the recipient from forwarding your message with the Forward button (though the recipient could still accomplish the same result through cut and paste):

Listing 4-18: **Example of the Item_Forward event**

```
Function Item_Forward(ByVal ForwardItem)

    MsgBox "Forwarding this message is strictly forbidden!"
    Item_Forward = False

End Function
```

The BeforeCheckNames event occurs when Outlook starts resolving the names of the recipients, either automatically or because the user manually invoked name resolution by Tools ⇨ Check Names. While we could conjure up a code example, frankly it will be unusual for you to use this event programmatically.

The AttachmentAdd event occurs when an attachment is added, and therefore is useful to determine if the size of the attachment is too large and warn the user. The code in Listing 4-19 uses the AttachmentAdd event to warn the user that the attachment exceeds 500,000 bytes:

Listing 4-19: **Example of the AttachmentAdd event**

```
Function Item_AttachmentAdd (ByVal attach)

If attach.Type = 1 Then
If Item.Size > 500000 Then
    MsgBox "Warning: Item too large: " & Item.Size & " bytes."
End If

End Function
```

Note that the Size property (number of bytes) is of the Item, not the Attachment object, which does not have a Size property. However, if the size of the Item is large, this is likely because of a large attachment.

The AttachmentAdd event cannot be cancelled. The BeforeAttachmentSave event can be cancelled. A network administrator may want to prevent the attachment of executable files. The code in Listing 4-20 accomplishes this:

Listing 4-20: **Example of the BeforeAttachmentSave event**

```
Function Item_BeforeAttachmentSave(ByVal attach)

If Instr(attach.FileName, ".exe.") Then
    MsgBox "Attaching programs is strictly forbidden!
    Item_BeforeAttachmentSave = False
End If

End Function
```

The AttachmentRead event occurs when an attachment is being opened. The code in Listing 4-21 shows how to use this event to prevent users from saving executable files they receive as attachments:

Listing 4-21: **Example of the AttachmentRead event**

```
Function Item_AttachmentRead(ByVal attach)

If Instr(attach.FileName, ".exe.") Then
    MsgBox "Attaching programs is strictly verboten!
    Attach.Delete
End If

End Function
```

Outlook Items

Outlook supports a rich set of items. Table 4-22 lists the different standard Outlook items:

Table 4-22
Outlook Items

Item Name	Description
AppointmentItem	An appointment in the Calendar folder.
ContactItem	A contact in the Contacts folder.
DistListItem	A distribution list in the Contacts folder.
DocumentItem	A document other than an Outlook item in an Outlook folder. Usually this will be an Office document but may be any type of document or executable file.
JournalItem	A journal entry in the Journal folder.
MailItem	A mail message in the Inbox folder.
MeetingItem	This item is created automatically in the Inbox folder of each recipient of an AppointmentItem object, notifying them of a meeting.
NoteItem	A note in the Notes folder.
PostItem	A post in a public folder.

Continued

Table 4-22 *(continued)*	
Item Name	*Description*
RemoteItem	A remote item in the Inbox folder. Similar to the MailItem object, but created by the system and containing only the Subject, Received Date and Time, Sender, Size, and the first 256 characters of the body of the message. Purpose is to provide remote user a basis for deciding whether to download the message.
ReportItem	A mail-delivery report in the Inbox folder. Similar to a MailItem object, but created by the system and containing a report (usually the non-delivery report) or error message from the mail transport system.
TaskItem	A task in the Tasks folder.
TaskRequestAcceptItem	Item created automatically in the Inbox of the person who delegated a task by sending a TaskRequestItem by sending the delegator an acceptance.
TaskRequestDeclineItem	Item created automatically in the Inbox of the person who delegated a task by sending a TaskRequestItem by sending the delegator a declination.
TaskRequestItem	Item created automatically in the Inbox of each person whose Tasks list is changed by the sender or another party.
TaskRequestUpdateItem	Item created automatically in the Inbox of the person who delegated a task by sending a TaskRequestItem by changing properties of the task such as its due date.

These Outlook items have unique methods in addition to the common methods discussed earlier. In the following section, the items are grouped by functionality. For example, the TaskItem, TaskRequestAcceptItem, TaskRequestDeclineItem, Task RequestItem, and TaskRequestUpdateItem objects are grouped together because they all relate to tasks.

Messages

Given the ever-increasing use of e-mail, the MailItem is the message item that you are most likely to use in your applications. The PostItem is akin to a mail message except that it is posted to a folder rather than sent to specific recipients. The RemoteItem also is becoming more important as users access their e-mail from locations other than their main offices. This item, which Outlook offers under Tools ➪ Remote Mail, permits users to download the "headers" of their messages so they can avoid downloading spam mail, messages with attachments that are huge or of a type not supported by the remote computer, or bad news from their boss. Finally, the ReportItem informs you that your message was not received, usually because of a bad address or the (hopefully) temporary unavailability of the mail server.

The RemoteItem and ReportItem objects have no methods in addition to those that all items have in common. Table 4-23 lists additional methods unique to MailItem and PostItem objects:

Name	Parameters	Description	Applies To
ClearConversationIndex	None	Clears the index of the conversation thread to start a new thread.	Both
Forward	None	Creates a new item with the body and subject of the item calling the method. Unlike with Reply and ReplyAll methods, no recipients are added.	MailItem only
Post	None	Posts the item to the current folder. Comparable to Send method of MailItem.	PostItem only
Reply	None	Creates a new item with the body and subject of the item calling the method and adds as a recipient the creator of the item being replied to.	Both

Table 4-23
Additional MailItem/PostItem Methods

Continued

		Table 4-23 *(continued)*	
Name	**Parameters**	**Description**	**Applies To**
ReplyAll	None	Creates a new item with the body and subject of the item calling the method and adds as recipients the creator and all other recipients of the item being replied to.	MailItem only
Send	None	Sends the item to the recipients. Comparable to Post method of PostItem.	MailItem only.

The ClearConversationIndex method is used for threaded discussion views, common in newsgroups. A number of Outlook items have a ConversationIndex property. Outlook uses this property to thread the messages corresponding to which messages respond to which. The ConversationIndex property of the first item has an ASCII value of 22. This value increases by five for each successive item. For example, a reply to or forward of the first item would have a ConversationIndex property of 27. The ClearConversationIndex method rests the ASCII value of the ConversationIndex property to 22.

The Forward, Reply, and ReplyAll methods are similar. Each creates a new mail message containing the body and the subject of the original item. The Body property returns the body of the original item unless the message is in HTML format, in which case the applicable property is the HTMLBody. The Subject property returns the subject line of the message.

The main difference among the Forward, Reply ,and ReplyAll methods is whether or not the recipients are automatically added to the new message. The Forward method does not add any recipients to the new message. The Reply method adds as a recipient only the sender of the message to which the new item is responding. The SenderName property returns the name of the sender of the initial message being replied to. Finally, the ReplyAll method adds as recipients the originator and all other recipients of the message to which the new item is responding.

The ReplyRecipients property returns a reference to what would be the Recipients collection if the user replied to an item. If the user does reply to the item, then the Recipients property of the reply item returns a reference to the Recipients collection of the new message.

The To property returns a semicolon-delimited string of the display names of the recipients in the To field. The CC and BCC properties are similar except that they relate to the CC and BCC fields, respectively. The ReplyRecipientsName property returns a semicolon-delimited string of the display names of the recipients.

> **Note** Another difference among the Forward, Reply and ReplyAll methods is in the prefix on the Subject line. By default, the prefix for forwarded messages is FW: whereas the prefix for reply and reply all messages is RE:. Chapter 5 explains how to change this default prefix either through the Outlook GUI using the Actions page or programmatically through the Prefix property of the Action object.

The Send method does exactly what its name suggests. It sends the item that calls the method. The one exception is if the Recipients collection of the item is empty, that is, there are no recipients in the To, CC or BCCfields. In that event, the item is not sent.

The Sent property returns True if the item already has been sent and False if it has not. The SentOn property returns the date and time when the item was sent, or the date 01/01/4501 if the item has not been sent. Obviously this property has a Year 4501 problem that hopefully will be fixed by Outlook 4500.

If the item is sent but could not be delivered to one or more of the recipients, such as if the recipient's e-mail address was wrong or no longer valid, then a ReportItem object is returned.

The Post method is comparable to the Send method except that the item is sent to a folder rather than to a recipient.

The Move method is not unique to mail message items, and has been discussed earlier under methods common to Outlook item objects. The code example there backed up all task items in the Tasks folder to the Backup folder. The Move method can also be used to move all messages meeting a certain criteria. For example, the code in Listing 4-22 uses the Move method to move all messages in the Inbox with the subject "Outlook 2000 Programming Bible" to a Book folder:

Listing 4-22: **Example of the Move method**

```
Dim ofDestFolder As MAPIFolder
Dim ofInbox As MAPIFolder
Dim oiMail As MailItem
Dim iCounter As Integer


Set ofInbox = Application.GetNameSpace _
   ("MAPI").Folders("Inbox")
```

Continued

Listing 4-22 *(continued)*

```
Set ofDestFolder = Application.GetNameSpace _
    ("MAPI").Folders("Book")
For iCounter = 1 to ofInbox.Items.Count
    If ofInbox.Items(iCounter).Class = olMail Then
        If ofInbox.Items(iCounter).Subject = _
            "Outlook 2000 Programming Bible" Then
            Set oiMail = ofInbox.Items(iCounter)
            oiMail.Move ofDestFolder
        End If
    End If
Next iCounter
```

Contacts

If you have a thriving business, you have many customers. If you follow the authors' investment advice, you have many creditors. These, as well as family, friends, and enemies, are contacts, each represented by a ContactItem object. This object holds information about the contact, such as their various addresses, telephone numbers, and e-mail addresses.

While a Contacts folder usually holds ContactItem objects, it also may hold DistList Item objects. Each of these objects is a distribution list that contains a number of contacts related in some way. For example, one of the authors is a member of his college's Space and Work Committee (you don't want to know what it does) and has a distribution list of its members so he can send all of the other committee members an e-mail simply by adding the applicable DistListItem object as a recipient.

A ContactItem can be instantiated by the `CreateItem` method of the Application object:

```
Dim oiContact as ContactItem
Set oiContact = Application.CreateItem(olContactItem)
```

A ContactItem also can be instantiated by the `Add` method of the Items collection, for instance the Items collection of the Contacts folder. The code in Listing 4-23 does this:

Listing 4-23: Example of instantiating a ContactItem object

```
Dim oiContact as ContactItem
Dim oicContactItems As Items
Set oicContactItems = Application.GetNameSpace("MAPI"). _
    GetDefaultFolder(olFolderContacts).Items
```

Set oiContact = oicContactItems.Add (olContactItem). Similarly, a DistList Item can be instantiated by the CreateItem method of the Application object:

```
Dim oiDist as DistributionListItem
Set oiDist = Application.CreateItem(olDistributionListItem)
```

A DistListItem also can be instantiated by the Add method of the Items collection of a folder that supports distribution lists, as shown by the code in Listing 4-24.

Listing 4-24: Example of instantiating a DistListItem object

```
Dim oiDist as DistributionListItem
Dim oicContactItems As Items
Set oicContactItems = Application.GetNameSpace("MAPI"). _
   GetDefaultFolder(olFolderContacts).Items
Set oiDist = oicContactItems.Add(olDistributionListItem)
```

The ContactItem object has one method in addition to the ones that all items have in common, the ForwardAsVCard method. This method sends the ContactItem, which calls the method as an attachment to a MailItem object. The attachment is a .vcf file which, when opened by the recipient, appears as a ContactItem. The term *VCard* is an acronym for virtual business card, perhaps because users often forward their own ContactItem as their business card.

The ContactItem object has well over 100 properties. Many correspond directly to fields in the Contacts form, such as FirstName, BusinessAddress, Spouse, Mistress (actually Microsoft hasn't added this one yet), etc.

The DistListItem has, in addition to the Close and Move methods shared with other items, the following unique methods listed in Table 4-24:

Table 4-24
DistListItem Object Methods

Name	Parameters	Description
AddMembers	Recipients collection	Adds Recipient objects in the Recipients collection parameter to distribution list.

Continued

Table 4-24 *(continued)*		
Name	*Parameters*	*Description*
GetMember	One-based position of recipient within distribution list position.	Returns the member of the distribution list at the specified
RemoveMembers	Recipients collection	Removes the Recipient objects in the Recipients collection parameter from distribution list.

The code in Listing 4-25 creates a distribution list and uses the AddMembers method to add the co-authors to the list:

Listing 4-25: **Example of using the AddMembers method**

```
Dim ofContacts As MAPIFolder
Dim oiDistList As DistributionList
Dim oiMail As MailItem
Dim ocRecipients As Recipients
Set ofContacts = Application.GetNameSpace _
    ("MAPI").GetDefaultFolder(olFolderContacts)
Set oiDistList = ofContacts.Items.Add _
    (olDistributionListItem)
Set oiMail = Application.CreateItem(olMailItem)
Set ocRecipients = oiMail.Recipients
ocRecipients.Add "Jeff Kent"
ocRecipients.Add "David Jung"
ocRecipients.ResolveAll
oiDistList.AddMembers ocRecipients
oiDistList.Save
```

The code in Listing 4-10 from earlier in this chapter created a collection of recipients to a MailItem by using the Recipients property of that object. However, neither a ContactItem nor a DistListItem object has a Recipients property. Creating a collection of recipients for a ContactItem or a DistListItem object is a two-step process. First, an Outlook item that has a Recipients property, such as a MailItem object, is used to create the Recipients collection. After the Add method of the Recipients collection is used to add recipients, in this example the co-authors, the second step is to pass the Recipients collection as a parameter to the AddMembers method.

A Recipients collection is also a required parameter of the RemoveMembers method, which removes from the distribution list those members who are in the Recipients collection. The following code would execute after the code in the AddMembers method code example above, and would remove one of the authors from the distribution list:

Listing 4-26: **Example of using the RemoveMembers method**

```
Dim As Recipients
Dim counter As Integer
For counter = 1 to oiDistList.MemberCount
    Set oiRecip = oiRecips.Item(counter)
    If oiRecip.Name = "David Jung" Then
        ocRemoveRecips.Add "David Jung"
        Exit For
    End If
oiDistList.RemoveMembers ocRemoveRecips
```

This code creates a second Recipients collection, ocRemoveRecips, which will hold the Recipient objects to be removed from the distribution list. The MemberCount property of the DistListItem object is used to loop through the other Recipients collection, oiRecips, which represents the members of the distribution list. The MemberCount property returns the number of members in the list. After those members of the list to be removed are added to ocRemoveRecips, that Recipients collection is passed as a parameter to the RemoveMembers method.

The GetMember method retrieves a particular member of the distribution list. This method requires the one-based position of the recipient within the list. The code in Listing 4-27 also uses the MemberCount property to loop through the list:

Listing 4-27: **Example of using the GetMember method**

```
Dim counter As Integer
For counter = 1 to oiDistList.MemberCount
    Set oiRecip = oiRecips.Item(counter)
    If oiRecip.Name = "David Jung" Then
        oiDistList.GetMember(counter)
        Exit For
    End If
Next counter
```

Appointments and Meetings

An appointment is when you have to be at a particular place at a particular time, whether for a business meeting, drinks with a friend, or going to the office of the principal of your daughter's school to discuss paying for damaged property. The AppointmentItem object, shown in Figure 4-7, holds information about the appointment.

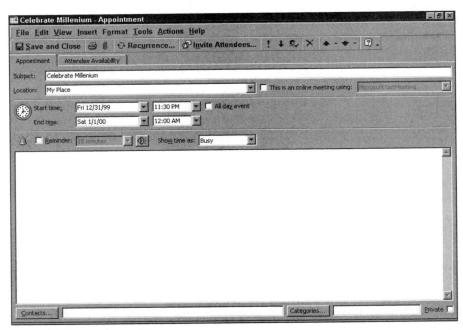

Figure 4-7: AppointmentItem

In addition to making appointments for yourself, you can invite others to an appointment by choosing Invite Attendees from the Actions menu. The invitation creates a MeetingItem object, shown in Figure 4-8. This object does not represent a meeting, but a request for a meeting.

The meeting request is sent to the Inbox of each invitee. Figure 4-9 shows the message received in the co-author's Inbox (he invited only himself to avoid rejection).

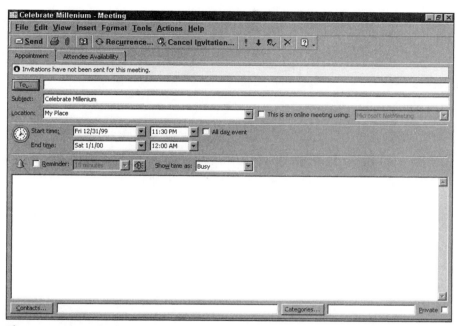

Figure 4-8: MeetingItem

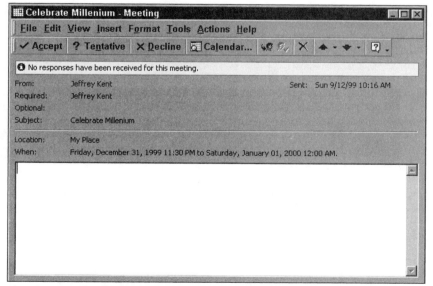

Figure 4-9: Inbox message showing request for meeting

If the request for the meeting is accepted, then an AppointmentItem object is created in the Calendar folder to represent the meeting, as shown in Figure 4-10.

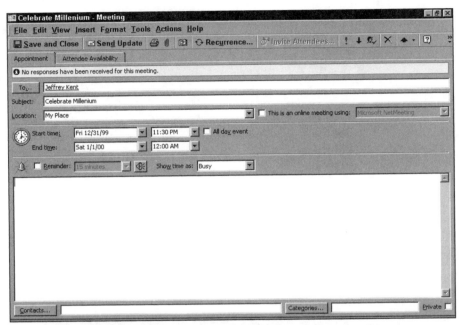

Figure 4-10: AppointmentItem representing meeting

Finally, some appointments are recurring. (Hopefully the appointment with the principal of your daughter's school isn't one of them.) For example, the meetings of the dreaded Space and Work Committee mentioned in connection with distribution lists are recurring, taking place on the first Thursday of every month. The Recurrence Pattern object holds information on how an AppointmentItem recurs. If any of the recurring items depart from the recurrence pattern—for example, one month the committee decides to meet on a Tuesday, or, better yet, not at all—this information is contained in an Exception object.

The AppointmentItem and MeetingItem objects have, in addition to the methods that all items have in common, the unique methods listed in Table 4-25:

Table 4-25
AppointmentItem Object Methods

Name	Parameters	Description
ClearRecurrencePattern	None	Sets a recurring meeting or appointment back to a single occurrence.
ForwardAsVCal	None	Returns a MailItem that has a vCal file as an attachment. The term *vCal* is short for virtual calendar. A vCal file, when opened by the recipient, contains the essential information regarding the appointment item.
GetRecurrencePattern	None	Returns the Recurrence pattern object for the current item.
Respond	See Table 4-26	Responds to originator of meeting. Causes error if used to respond to appointment.

Table 4-26
Parameters of Respond Method of AppointmentItem Object

Name	Data Type	Required?	Description
lResponse	Long	Yes	Response to meeting request, represented by one of the following olMeeting Response constants: olMeeting Tentative(2) — tentatively accepted; olMeetingAccepted(3) — accepted; olMeetingDeclined(4) — declined.
fNoUI	Boolean	No, optional	True (default), no GUI will be shown. False, GUI shown. Discussed below.
AdditionalText	Boolean	No, optional	Ignored if fNoUI parameter True. True shows dialog box discussed below, False (default) does not.

A response to a meeting request through the Outlook GUI displays the dialog box shown in Figure 4-11 asking you if you want to edit the response, send the response immediately, or cancel without sending a response. A response through code will not display the dialog box unless the fNoUI parameter is False and the AdditionalText parameter is True. Choosing Edit from the dialog box will display a Response message for editing as shown in Figure 4-12. If the fNoUI parameter is False and the AdditionalText parameter is False, then no dialog box will be displayed, and a Response message will be displayed immediately for editing.

Figure 4-11: The dialog box displayed if the fNoUI parameter is False

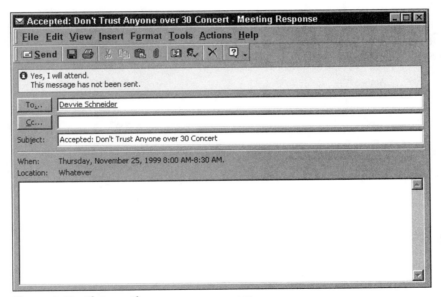

Figure 4-12: The meeting response message

You can respond to a meeting request through code as well as through the Outlook GUI. However, you should confirm that the AppointmentItem is a meeting request before calling the Respond method. The Respond method will cause an error if the AppointmentItem that calls it is not a meeting request, but instead an appointment. You can confirm that the AppointmentItem represents a meeting request by the MeetingStatus property of the AppointmentItem object. This property returns one of the olMeetingStatus constants listed in Table 4-27:

Table 4-27		
MeetingStatus Property of AppointmentItem Object		
Constant	**Value**	**Description**
OlNonMeeting	0	Item is an appointment, not a meeting.
OlMeeting	1	Item is a meeting request.
OlMeetingReceived	3	Meeting request received.
OlMeetingCanceled	5	Meeting request canceled.

The code in Listing 4-28 checks that an AppointmentItem object is a meeting request before invoking the Respond method:

Listing 4-28: **Example of using the Respond method**

```
Dim oiAppt As AppointmentItem
Dim oiMtg As MeetingItem
...
If oiAppt.MeetingStatus = olMeeting Then
Set oiMtg = oiAppt.Respond(olMeetingAccepted, True, False)
oiMtg.Send
End If
```

Outlook creates an AppointmentItem object for each MeetingItem the user receives. The MeetingItem object has one unique method, GetAssociatedAppointment. The GetAssociatedAppointment method obtains the AppointmentItem that is associated with the MeetingItem. This allows you to avoid iterating through the Calendar folder to find the AppointmentItem.

```
Dim oiMtg As MeetingItem
Dim oiAppt As AppointmentItem
...
Set oiAppt = oiMtg.GetAssociatedAppointment(False)
```

The RecurrencePattern object has only one method, `GetOccurrence`, which returns the associated AppointmentItem for the current RecurrencePattern object. This method takes one parameter, the start date and time for the AppointmentItem to be retrieved.

The Exceptions collection has only one method, the familiar `Item` method that takes as its one parameter the index number representing the one-based position of the exception within the collection. The Exception object has no methods.

Tasks

Tasks demonstrate the truism of the saying "it is better to give than to receive." In the authors' perfect world, they would delegate TaskItem objects to their minions, who would accept the tasks with TaskRequestAcceptItem objects and would not dare respond with TaskRequestDeclineItem objects. The recipients would later follow up with TaskRequestUpdateItem objects to update the status of the tasks. Alas for the authors, they are on the receiving and not the giving end of TaskItem objects.

The TaskItem object, shown in Figure 4-13, holds information about the task.

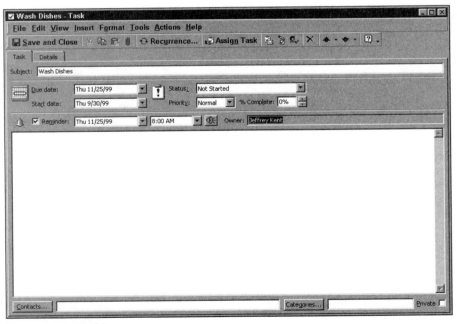

Figure 4-13: TaskItem

In addition to making tasks for yourself, you can assign the task to others by choosing Assign Task from the Actions menu. The assignment creates a TaskItem object, shown in Figure 4-14. This object does not represent a task, but an attempt to assign a task.

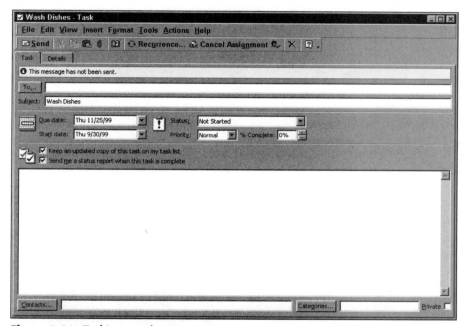

Figure 4-14: TaskItem assignment

The meeting request is sent to the Inbox of each invitee. Figure 4-15 shows the message received in one the authors' Inbox (he gets all the good tasks).

If the task assignment is accepted (and it had better be), then a TaskItem object is created in the Tasks folder to represent the task, as shown in Figure 4-16.

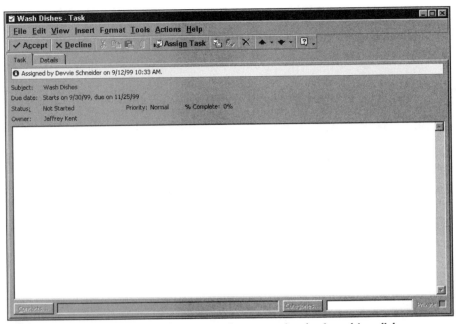

Figure 4-15: Inbox message showing assignment of task of washing dishes.

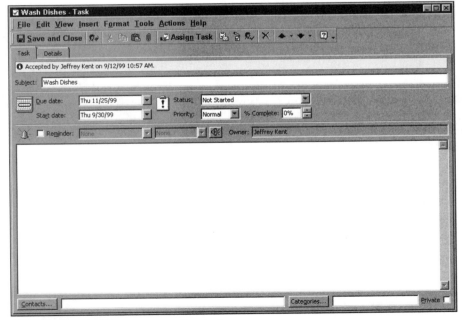

Figure 4-16: TaskItem representing task

Table 4-28 lists the unique methods of the TaskItem object:

Table 4-28 TaskItem Object Methods		
Name	**Parameters**	**Description**
Assign	None	Assigns the current TaskItem to a recipient. Need to call Send method to send TaskItem to recipient.
CancelResponseState	None	Changes a delegated task to a non-delegated task.
ClearRecurrencePattern	None	Changes a recurring task to a non-recurring one.
GetRecurrencePattern	None	Returns the Recurrence object for the current TaskItem.
MarkComplete	None	Marks the task as completed.
Respond	See Table 4-29. Similar to parameters of Respond method of AppointmentItem object	Responds to originator of task.
SkipRecurrence	None	Skips the next recurring time for the task.
StatusReport	None	Returns a mail item with the current status of the task, addressed to all recipients in the StatusUpdate Recipients property.

		Table 4-29	
	Parameters of Respond Method of TaskItem Object		
Name	*Data Type*	*Required?*	*Description*
Iresponse	Long	Yes	Response to task request, represented by one of the following olTask Response **constants:** olTask Simple(0) — task not delegated; olTaskAssign(1) — assigned recipient not responded to task; olTaskAccept(2) — task accepted; olTaskDeclined(3) — task declined.
FnoUI	Boolean	No, optional	True (default), no GUI will be shown. False, GUI shown. Discussed below.
AdditionalText	Boolean	No, optional	True shows dialog box discussed below, False (default) does not. Ignored if fNoUI parameter True.

A response to a task request through the Outlook GUI displays the dialog box shown in Figure 4-17 asking you if you want to edit the response or send the response immediately. Unlike the dialog box for the AppointmentItem object, this dialog box does not give you the option to cancel without sending a response. A response through code will not display this dialog box unless the fNoUI parameter is False and the AdditionalText parameter is True. Choosing Edit from the dialog box will display a Response message for editing as shown in Figure 4-18. If the fNoUI parameter is False and the AdditionalText parameter is False, then no dialog box will display, and a Response message will be displayed immediately for editing.

Figure 4-17: The dialog box displayed if the fNoUI parameter is False

The other task objects, TaskRequestItem, TaskRequestUpdateItem, TaskRequest AcceptItem, and TaskRequestDeclineItem, have only one unique method: Get AssociatedTask. This method returns the task item with which the request is associated. It has one required parameter, a Boolean value. True means that the task will be added to the default Tasks folder.

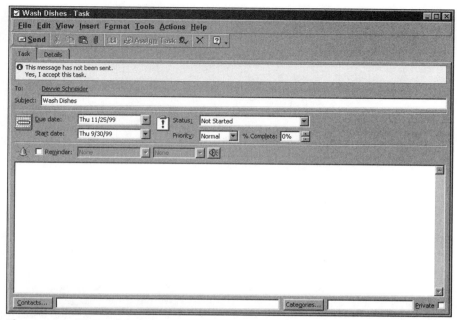

Figure 4-18: The task response message

The code in Listing 4-29 uses the Assign method of the TaskItem object to delegate tasks depending on a message's SenderName (the Subject also could be used):

Listing 4-29: **Example of using the Assign method of the TaskItem object**

```
Dim oiMail As MailItem
Dim oiTask As TaskItem
Dim ocItems As Items
Dim iCount As Integer
Dim ofInbox As MAPIFolder

Set ofInbox = Application.GetNameSpace("MAPI"). _
   GetDefaultFolder(olFolderInbox)
Set ocItems = ofInbox.Items.Restrict("[Unread] = True")
iCount = ocItems.Count
For iCount to 1 Step -1
   If ocItems(iCount).Class = olMail Then
      Set oiMail = ocItems(iCount)
      With oiMail
```

Continued

Listing 4-29 *(continued)*

```
            Set oiTask = Application.CreateItem(olTaskItem)
            oiTask.Subject = .Subject
            oiTask.Body = .Body
            Select Case .SenderName
                Case "Editor"
                    oiTask.Recipients.Add "Co-Author"
                Case "Ex-Spouse"
                    oiTask.Recipients.Add "Divorce Lawyer"
            End Select
            oiTask.Assign
            oi.Recipients.ResolveAll
            oiTask.Send
        End With
    End If
Next iCount
```

The code iterates through all unread messages in the Inbox. If the message is from the editor, then it is delegated as a task to the co-author. If the message is from an ex-spouse, it is delegated to the lawyer. This example shows the potential for automating an application. The `SenderName` property of the message could be used in an intranet helpdesk application where users are assigned to particular support personnel. The Subject property of the message could be used to route a message, as a task, to those support personnel with expertise in solving the problem.

Notes

Notes are Outlook's substitute for Post-Its, also known as sticky notes. Indeed, the message class of the NoteItem object is `IPM.StickyNote`.

There are two ways to create a NoteItem. One way is through the `CreateItem` method of the Application object:

```
Dim oiNote As NoteItem
Set oiNote = Application.CreateItem("olNoteItem")
```

The other alternative is to use the `Add` method of the Items collection of a folder that supports notes.

An existing NoteItem can be referenced by its `Subject` property:

```
Dim oiNote As NoteItem
Set oiNote = ofFolder.Items("Help!!!")
```

A NoteItem, unlike for example a MailItem, does not have a Subject line. The value of a NoteItem's `Subject` property is the body of the note up to the first carriage return.

While a note form cannot be customized, a note can be created and saved program-matically, as shown by the code in Listing 4-30:

Listing 4-30: **Example of creating a Note object**

```
Dim ofNotes As MAPIFolder
Dim oiNote As NoteItem
Set ofNotes = Application.GetNameSpace("MAPI"). _
    GetDefaultFolder(olFolderNotes)
Set oiNote = ofNotes.Items.Add(olNoteItem)
With oiNOte
    .Body = "Chapter due by Monday - or else"
    .Color = olGreen
    .Left = 250
    .Top = 250
    .Height = 250
    .Width = 250
    .Save
End With
```

The NoteItem object has no unique methods.

Journal

The JournalItem object is an electronic log of events.

There are two ways to create a JournalItem. One way is through the `CreateItem` method of the Application object:

```
Dim oiJournal As JournalItem
Set oiJournal = Application.CreateItem("olJournalItem")
```

The other alternative is to use the `Add` method of the Items collection of a folder that supports journals.

An existing NoteItem can be referenced by its `Subject` property:

```
Dim oiJournal As JournalItem
Set oiJournal = ofFolder.Items("Help!!!")
```

The JournalItem object has only two unique methods, the `StartTimer` method and the `StopTimer` method. Neither method has any parameters. The `StartTimer` method starts a timer for a journal entry, and the `StopTimer` method stops the timer.

Documents

The DocumentItem object is a file from a source other than Outlook that is stored in an Outlook folder. The file usually originates from but is not limited to another Microsoft Office application. Additionally, the file need not be a document. It can be an executable.

The DocumentItem object cannot be created by code. It can be created through the Outlook GUI by the File ➪ New ➪ Office Document menu command or the Ctrl-Shift-H shortcut key. This will display the New Office Document dialog box shown in Figure 4-19. You then can choose an Excel worksheet, Excel chart, Word document or PowerPoint presentation. Once you make that choice, you will be asked whether you want to "Post the document in this folder" or "Send the document to someone."

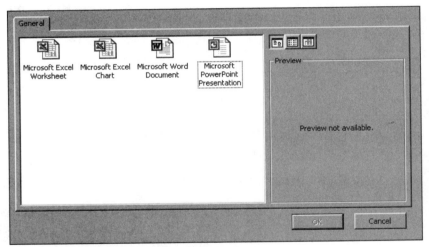

Figure 4-19: New office document dialog box

You can set a reference programmatically to an existing DocumentItem object. You can accomplish this through the Item method of the Items collection of the folder in which the DocumentItem is stored. Assuming the object variable olFolder refers to the applicable folder, the following VBA code snippet obtains a reference to the first item in the folder:

```
Dim odDoc as Outlook.DocumentItem
Set odDoc = olFolder.Items.Item(1)
```

The DocumentItem object has no unique methods.

Inspectors

Figure 4-20 shows the location of the Inspectors collection and the Inspector object in the Outlook 2000 object model. An Inspector object is an Outlook window that displays the contents of an item. The Inspectors collection contains a set of Inspector objects representing all inspectors. An inspector need not be visible to be included in the collection. This collection and object are useful to you as a programmer to determine the user's current view of an item or to set that view for the user.

Figure 4-20: Inspectors collection and Inspector object in object model

Inspectors Collection

The properties of the Inspector collection are typical of collections generally. Table 4-30 lists the properties of the Inspectors collection:

Table 4-30
Properties of Inspectors Collection

Name	Description
Application	Returns the Outlook Application object.
Class	Returns the olObjectClass constant, in this case olInspectors having a value of 61.
Count	Returns the number of items in the collection.
Parent	The Parent object, in this case the Application object.
Session	The NameSpace object through which the collection was accessed.

These collection properties should be familiar by now. They are essentially the same as the corresponding properties of Folders, Items, and Explorers.

Table 4-31 lists the methods of the Inspectors collection:

Table 4-31
Methods of Inspectors Collection

Name	Description	Parameter
Add	Creates and returns a new Inspector.	The item to display in the Inspector window
Item	Returns an Inspector from the collection.	One-based position of the Inspector to be accessed

The Add method creates and returns a new Inspector window. It has one argument, the item to display. The code in Listing 4-31 displays the first item sent by one of the co-authors in a new Inspector window:

Listing 4-31: **Example of Add method of Inspectors collection**

```
Dim olApp As Outlook. Application
Dim olItems As Outlook.Items
Dim olItem As Outlook.Item
Set olApp = New Outlook.Application
Set olItems = myOlApp.GetNamespace("MAPI") _
    .GetDefaultFolder(olFolderInbox).Items
Set olItem = olItems.Find("[SenderName] = ""David Jung""")
If TypeName(olItem0 <> "Nothing" Then
Set myInspector = olApp.Inspectors.Add(olItem)
olInspector.Activate
End If
```

The Inspectors collection's only event is NewInspector. This event fires after a new inspector window is created, either as a result of user action or through program code such as the Add method, but before it is displayed. This event is not available in VBScript. We will discuss this event in connection with the Inspector object.

Inspector object

Table 4-32 lists the properties of the Inspector object:

Table 4-32
Properties of Inspector Object

Name	Description
Application	Returns an Application object that represents the parent application (Microsoft Outlook) for an object. The `Parent` property also returns the Application object.
Caption	Returns the window caption (title-bar text) of an Inspector window.
Class	Returns the `olObjectClass` constant for this object, `olNamespace`, having a value of 1.
CommandBars	Returns a CommandBars collection object that represents all the menus and toolbars in the Inspector.
CurrentItem	Returns the current item being displayed in the Inspector, or an error if there is no currently open item.
EditorType	Returns one of the `olEditorType` constants listed in Table 4-33.
Height	Returns or sets the height in pixels of the Inspector object.
HTML Editor	Returns the HTML Document Object Model of the message being displayed. Property only applies if the `EditorType` property of the item's associated Inspector is `olEditorHTML`.
Left	Returns or sets the position (in pixels) of the left vertical edge of an inspector from the edge of the screen.
ModifiedFormPages	Returns the Pages collection that represents all the pages for the item in the inspector. You can use the `Add` method to obtain up to five customizable pages.
Parent	Returns the parent object, in this case the Application object. The `Application` property discussed above also returns the Application object.
Session	Returns the NameSpace object for the current session.
Top	Returns or sets the position (in pixels) of the top horizontal edge of an Inspector from the edge of the screen.
Width	Returns or sets the width in pixels of the Inspector object.
WindowState	Returns or sets the window state of an Explorer or Inspector window using one of the `olWindowState` constants listed in Table 3-11.
WordEditor	Returns the Word Document Object Model of the message being displayed. Property only applies if `IsWordMail` returns True and the `EditorType` is `olEditorWord`.

Table 4-33
Editor Type Constants

Editor Type	Constant	Value
Text	OlEditorText	1
HTML	OlEditorHTML	2
Rich Text Format	OlEditorRTF	3
Word	OlEditorWord	4

As discussed in detail in Chapter 5 on Outlook forms, the opening of an item is an event (Item_Open) for which you can write VBScript code. However, with the CurrentItem and Class properties you can set a reference in a VBA application to the item. This means you can use VBA rather than the more limited VBScript to deal with that item.

First, you declare object variables, with the WithEvents keyword, for the Inspector object and for each of the item types in which you are interested. For example:

```
Public WithEvents myInspector As Outlook.Inspector
Public WithEvents myMailItem As Outlook.MailItem
Public WithEvents myTaskItem As Outlook.TaskItem
```

Next, in the NewInspector event, you determine if the CurrentItem is the type of item in which you are interested, and if so, set the appropriate object variable to it. This is illustrated by the code in Listing 4-32:

Listing 4-32: **Example of NewInspector event**

```
Private Sub olInspectors_NewInspector(ByVal Insp As Inspector)

Dim objItem as Object
Set myInspector = Inspector
On Error Resume Next
Set objItem = myInspector.CurrentItem
Select Case objItem.Class
    Case olMail
        Set myMailItem = objItem
    Case olTask
        Set myTaskItem = objItem
...
End Select

End Sub
```

The error handler is necessary because the CurrentItem property will raise an error if there is no currently open item.

Note

> The Class property does not differentiate between whether the item is a default or custom item based on the default item. For example, default and custom mail items will have the same Class value, though they will have different message class values. Message classes will be discussed in Chapter 5 on Outlook forms.

While the NewInspector event is useful, it has its limitations. If Word is the e-mail editor, and the message format is either plain text or HTML (as opposed to rich text format), then the creation of a new mail message does not create an Inspector, and the NewInspector event does not fire. The EditorType property returns the particular editor in use. If the editor is Word, then the WordEditor property returns the Word application object, from which the Word object model can be accessed. Alternatively, if the editor is HTML, the HTMLEditor property returns the HTML Document object, from which that object model can be accessed.

The Left, Top, Height and Width properties can be used to specify the position and size of the Inspector object. Alternatively, the WindowState property can be used to specify the Inspector's window as maximized, minimized or normal.

The CommandBars property returns the CommandBars collection. This collection contains all of the toolbars and menus for the Inspector. The CommandBars collection is discussed in Chapter 8 on COM add-ins.

The ModifiedFormPages property returns those pages of a form that may be modified. We discuss this in detail in Chapter 5 on Outlook forms.

Table 4-34 summarizes the methods of the Inspector object:

Table 4-34 Methods of Inspector Object		
Method Name	**Action**	**Parameter**
Activate	Makes an Inspector object the active window.	None
Display	Displays an Inspector object. Only retained for backward compatibility. You should use the Activate method.	Optional True to display as modal.

Continued

Table 4-34

Method Name	Action	Parameter
Close	Closes the Inspector object.	One of the olInspectorClose constants listed in Table 4-35 indicating how the item should be saved. Property only applies if item displayed in the inspector has been changed.
ShowFormPage	Shows a particular tabbed page of the currently open item.	A string representing the name of the page
HideFormPage	Hides a particular tabbed page of the currently open item.	A string representing the name of the page
SetCurrentFormPage	Determines the particular tabbed page to show when the form is opened.	A string representing the name of the page
IsWordMailMethod	Returns True if the mail message is displayed in Microsoft Word (that is, if Word Mail is in use), the EditorType property being olEditorWord. Returns False if displayed in Outlook Inspector.	None

Table 4-35
SaveMode Constants

Description	Constant	Value
Save all changes without prompting.	OlSave	0
Discard all changes without prompting.	OlDiscard	1
Prompt to save or discard all changes.	OlPromptForSave	2

The ShowFormPage, HideFormPage and SetCurrentFormPage methods can be used to manipulate the visibility and focus of those items with multiple pages. For example, the Contacts form by default has five pages, including General, Details and All Fields.

The General page has focus by default. The code example in Listing 4-33 shows the HideFormPage method to hide the All Fields page and the SetCurrentFormPage method to place focus on the Details page as the top page:

Listing 4-33: **Example of HideFormPage and SetCurrentFormPage methods**

```
Dim ofContacts As MAPIFolder
Dim oiContact As ContactItem
Dim ocItems As Items
Dim oiInsp As Inspector
Set ofContacts = Application.GetNameSpace("MAPI"). _
    GetDefaultFolder(olFolderContacts)
Set ocItems = ofContacts.Items
If ocItems.Count > 0 Then
    Set oiContact = ocItems.GetFirst
    oiContact.Display
    Set oiInsp = Inspectors.Item(1)
    oiInsp.HideFormPage "All Fields"
    oiInsp.SetCurrentFormPage "Details"
End If
```

You use the ShowFormPage method if you want to show the All Fields page which you hid using the HideFormPage method:

```
oiInsp.ShowFormPage "All Fields"
```

The Activate, Display and Close methods are comparable to the methods of the Explorer object with the same names. Finally, the IsWordMail method is useful in determining if the current editor is Word.

Table 4-36 lists the events of the Inspector object.

Table 4-36
Events of Inspector Object

Event Name	Fires When ...
Activate	Inspector becomes the active window either through user action or programmatically.
Close	Inspector is closed, either through user action or programmatically.
Deactivate	Inspector ceases to be the active window either through user action or programmatically.

The Inspector object has only three events, `Activate`, `Close`, and `Deactivate`. These events are comparable to the corresponding events of the Explorer object.

The `Activate` event occurs when the Inspector object becomes the active window. The item being displayed can be accessed with the `CurrentItem` property. The code in Listing 4-34 hides the All Fields page if the Outlook item being displayed is a ContactItem:

Listing 4-34: **Example of CurrentItem property**

```
Dim WithEvents oiInsp As Inspector
Set oiInsp = Inspectors.Item(1)
...

Private Sub oiInsp_Activate()
    If oiInsp.CurrentItem.Class = olContact Then _
        oiInsp.HideFormPage "All Fields"
End Sub
```

The `Deactivate` event occurs when the Inspector object is no longer the active window. The `CurrentItem` property can no longer be accessed during this event. Attempting to do so will cause an error. The following code example uses the `Deactivate` event to minimize the Inspector object when it is not active:

```
Private Sub oiInsp_Deactivate()
    oiInsp.WindowState = olMinimized
End Sub
```

The `Close` event occurs when the Inspector object is closed. The `Deactivate` event is fired before the `Close` event when an Inspector object is closed. As was the case with the `Deactivate` event, the CurrentItem property can no longer be accessed during the `Close` event.

Address Books

Outlook provides users with contact items to store the e-mail addresses, phone numbers, and other contact information of family, friends and business acquaintances. This information is stored on the user's local hard drive.

Additionally, in an office intranet served by the Microsoft Exchange Server, the e-mail address of others on the office intranet, as well as other information such as their departments and phone numbers, are on the Global Address List. This information is stored on the server.

While the Contacts folder and the Global Address List are in different locations, both are AddressList objects. Figure 4-21 shows the Address Book, accessed by the Tools ➪ Address Book menu command, with the "Show Names from the" dropdown list displaying the available AddressList objects.

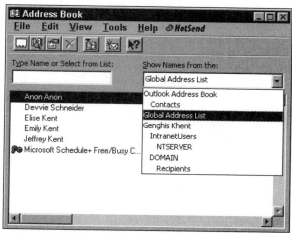

Figure 4-21: The Outlook Address Book lists the available AddressList objects

Not all of these AddressList objects displayed in Figure 4-21 contain address information. In this example, the Outlook Address Book is a folder that contains no address information. Instead, the Outlook Address Book contains the Contacts folder, which does contain address information. Nevertheless, both are AddressList objects.

All of the AddressList objects listed in the Address Book are contained in an Address Lists collection. Additionally, each AddressList object has its own AddressEntries collection. The AddressEntries collection contains all of the entries in a particular address book. All of the contact items in the Contacts folder are contained in one AddressEntries collection. All of the listings in the Global Address List are contained in another AddressEntries collection.

Each listing in an AddressEntries collection is an AddressEntry object. Thus, both an individual contact item and an entry in the Global Address List each is an Address Entry object.

Figure 4-22 shows the address book object hierarchy.

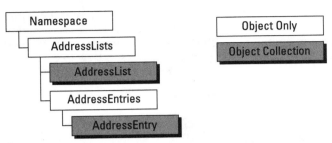

Figure 4-22: The Address Book object hierarchy

AddressLists Collection

The AddressLists collection can be accessed only through the `AddressLists` property of the NameSpace object:

```
Set myAddressLists = myNameSpace.AddressLists
```

The AddressLists collection is used to access the AddressEntry object.

Table 4-37 lists the properties of the AddressLists collection:

<table>
<tr><td colspan="2" align="center">Table 4-37
AddressLists Collection Properties</td></tr>
<tr><td>*Name*</td><td>*Description*</td></tr>
<tr><td>Application</td><td>Returns the Outlook Application object.</td></tr>
<tr><td>Class</td><td>Returns the olObjectClass constant, in this case olAddressLists having a value of 20.</td></tr>
<tr><td>Count</td><td>Returns the number of AddressList objects in the collection.</td></tr>
<tr><td>Parent</td><td>Returns the Parent object, in this case the NameSpace object.</td></tr>
<tr><td>Session</td><td>Returns the NameSpace object through which the collection was accessed.</td></tr>
</table>

The AddressLists collection has only one method, `Item`. This method returns an AddressList object. This method has one parameter, the index or other identifier of the AddressList object to be accessed. The Item method is used in a code example for the AddressList object.

Unlike other collections, the AddressLists collection does not have an Add method. Thus, an AddressList object cannot be added programmatically. You can add an AddressList object through the Outlook user interface by creating a new folder that holds contact items. Chapter 3 on Outlook forms shows how to do this.

The AddressLists collection has no events.

AddressList Object

The AddressList object is accessed through the Item method of the AddressLists collection:

```
Set myAddressList = myAddressLists.Item("Personal Address Book")
```

In this code fragment the parameter of the Item method is the unique identifier Personal Address Book. The parameter also could have been the one-based position of the AddressList object in the AddressLists collection.

Tip

As a general rule, it is preferable, where the Item method of the particular collection permits it, to use an identifier such as the name of the object instead of the number representing the object's position in the collection. Collections, unlike arrays, do not guarantee that an object's position will not change without programmer intervention. Therefore, the object's current position in the collection may not be its position later.

The AddressList object has no methods or events. Table 4-38 lists its properties:

Name	Description
	Table 4-38 **AddressList Object Properties**
Name	*Description*
AddressEntries	Returns the AddressEntries collection (covered next) for the AddressList object. Used in AddressEntries code example below.
Application	Returns the Outlook Application object.
Class	Returns the olObjectClass constant, in this case olAddressList having a value of 7.
ID	Returns a unique value that is created when the AddressList object is created.
Index	Returns the AddressList object's position (one-based) in the AddressLists collection.
Name	Returns the display name in the Address Book, such as Personal Address Book.
Parent	Returns the Parent object, in this case the AddressLists collection.

Continued

Table 4-38 (continued)	
Name	**Description**
IsReadOnly	Returns True if you cannot add or remove entries, False otherwise. Not related to ability to modify data in individual entries.
Session	Returns the NameSpace object through which the collection was accessed.

The code in Listing 4-35 displays the names of all of the AddressList objects. It uses the Count property and Item method of the AddressLists collection and the Index and Name properties of the AddressList object:

Listing 4-35: **Displaying the names of all AddressList objects**

```
Dim myOutlook As Outlook.Application
Dim myLists As Outlook.AddressLists
Dim myList As Outlook.AddressList
Dim counter As Integer
Set myOutlook = New Outlook.Application
Set myLists = myOutlook.GetNameSpace("MAPI").AddressLists
For counter = 1 To myLists.Count
    Set myList = myLists.Item(counter)
    Debug.Print myList.Name
Next
```

AddressEntries collection

The AddressEntries collection is accessed from the AddressList object. This is because the AddressEntries collection contains the entries for a particular Address List object. The AddressEntries property of the AddressList object is used to create the AddressEntries collection:

```
Set myAddressEntries = myAddressList.AddressEntries
```

Table 4-39 lists the AddressEntries collection's properties:

Table 4-39
AddressEntries Collection Properties

Name	Description
Application	Returns the Outlook Application object.
Class	Returns the olObjectClass constant, in this case olAddressEntries having a value of 21.
Count	Returns the number of AddressEntry objects in the collection.
Parent	Returns the Parent object, in this case the AddressList object whose entries the collection contains.
Session	Returns the NameSpace object through which the collection was accessed.

Table 4-40 lists the methods of the AddressEntries collection:

Table 4-40
Methods of the AddressEntries Collection

Name	Description	Parameter
Add	Creates and returns an AddressEntry object in the AddressEntries collection.	Optionally a valid message class or one of the olItem Type constants in Table 2-8 in Chapter 2
GetFirst	Returns the first AddressEntry in the collection, or Nothing if no AddressEntry exists.	None
GetLast	Returns the last AddressEntry in the collection, or Nothing if no Address Entry exists.	None
GetNext	Returns the next AddressEntry in the collection, or Nothing if no Address Entry exists.	None
GetPrevious	Returns the previous AddressEntry object in the collection, or Nothing if no AddressEntry exists.	None

Continued

Table 4-40 *(continued)*

Name	Description	Parameter
Item	Returns a specified AddressEntry object from the collection.	Index or other identifier of folder to be accessed
Sort	Sorts items in the collection by the specified property.	The property name by which the AddressEntry objects will be sorted, and one of the olSortOrder constants listed in Table 4-41

Table 4-41
Sort Order Constants

Description	Constant	Value
Default. Sort order not changed.	OlSortNone	0
Sorted in ascending order.	OlAscending	1
Sorted in descending order.	OlDescending	2

The AddressEntries collection has no events.

AddressEntry Object

The AddressEntry object can be created from the Item method of the AddressEntries collection:

```
Set myAddressEntry = myAddressEntries.Item(index)
```

The AddressEntry object also can be created by the AddressEntry property of an existing Recipient object. This object is covered in Chapter 3 on Outlook forms.

Table 4-42 lists the AddressEntry object's properties:

Table 4-42
AddressEntry Object's Properties

Name	Description
Address	Sets or returns the e-mail address.
Application	Returns the Outlook Application object.
Class	Returns the olObjectClass constant, in this case olAddressEntry having a value of 8.
DisplayType	Returns one of the olDisplayType constants listed in Table 4-43 below, disclosing whether a user or distribution list is involved.
ID	Returns the unique string value assigned to object when it is created.
Manager	Returns Manager, which is listed on the Organization tab of the properties of an AddressEntry in the Global Address List.
Members	Returns AddressEntries collection if AddressEntry object is a distribution list, or Nothing if object is a user.
Name	Returns the display name of the AddressEntry object.
Parent	Returns the Parent object, in this case the AddressEntries collection or the Recipient object, depending on how the AddressEntry object was instantiated.
Session	Returns the NameSpace object through which the collection was accessed.
Type	Sets or returns a string determining the type of entry referenced.

Table 4-43
olDisplayType Constants

The Recipient is a ...	Constant	Value
User	OlUser	0
Distribution List	OlDistList	1
Forum	OlForum	2
Agent	OlAgent	3
Organization	OlOrganization	4
Private Distribution List	OlPrivateDistList	5
Remote User	OlRemoteUser	6

Table 4-44 lists the methods of the AddressEntry object:

Table 4-44
Methods of the AddressEntry object

Name	Description	Parameter
Delete	Removes an AddressEntry object from the AddressEntries collection.	None
Details	Opens the properties dialog box for the AddressEntry object.	Optionally, the handle of the parent window. Without this parameter the properties dialog box is modal rather than a child window
GetFreeBusy	Returns free/busy time during a month for the AddressEntry object.	Listed in Table 4-45
Update	Saves changes to the AddressEntry object.	Listed in Table 4-46

Table 4-45
Parameters of GetFreeBusy Method of AddressEntry object

Name	Data Type	Required?	Description
Start	Date	Yes	Start date for information.
MinPerChar	Long	Yes	Number of minutes per free/busy time interval.
CompleteFormat	Boolean	No	False (the default) uses a 0 to indicate free and 1 to indicate busy for a time interval. True indicates out of office and tentative information.

Table 4-46
Parameters of Update Method of AddressEntry object

Name	Data Type	Required	Description
MakePermanent	Boolean	No	True (the default) commits the changes to the messaging system, False does not.
RefreshObject	Boolean	No	True reloads (refreshes) the properties for the object, False (the default) does not.

The AddressEntry object has no events.

Summary

Outlook's data consist of various items, including mail messages, contacts, appointments, and tasks. The items in an Outlook folder are part of an Items collection. The Items collection is the gateway through which the individual items in a folder are accessed. In this chapter you learned about the properties, methods and events of the Items collection.

Outlook has many different types of items to implement Outlook's diverse and powerful functionality. Outlook has a MailItem object for a mail message, a ContactItem object for a contact, an AppointmentItem object for an appointment, and so on. In this chapter you learned about the properties and methods of the different Outlook items, including a number of properties and methods that the Outlook items share.

The window through which an item is viewed is an Inspector object, which is a member of the Inspectors collection. The Inspector object is to items what the Explorer object is to folders. In this chapter you learned about the properties, methods and events of the Inspectors collection and the Inspector object.

Items often contain attachments, each of which is an Attachment object and a member of the Attachments collection. Items also may be linked to each other, involving the Link object and the Links collection.

Items are often sent to someone. In the object model, each recipient of an item is a Recipient object and a member of the Recipients collection. A recipient's e-mail address may be stored and retrieved from an address book, which is represented by two objects and two collections. In this chapter you learned about the Recipients collection and Recipient object, and the Address Book collections and objects.

✦   ✦   ✦

Outlook Forms

The form is the window to your application. This is not another trite saying like "the eyes are the windows of the soul"; the statement is literally true. Forms are the usual medium through which the user interacts with your application. Outlook is no exception, also using forms to enable its users to view and modify data. However, consistent with Outlook's duality as a development environment as well as an application, Outlook also enables you to customize its standard forms, not just cosmetically, but also functionally by, for example, adding objects such as Excel spreadsheets or changing actions such as what happens when you click a command button. Your ability to customize Outlook forms is integral to using Outlook in applications you develop.

Introduction to Outlook Forms

Outlook has several standard forms to enable its users to view and modify data. Each of these forms is designed for a particular task. For example, an Outlook user may use the mail message form to send e-mail to a customer, the contacts form to look up the customer's phone number, the appointment form to record an upcoming meeting with the customer, and the task form to record what needs to be done before the meeting.

While the standard Outlook forms are quite useful, the needs of your application may require that a form include data fields that do not appear in the default form, or that a response use a form different from the default response form. With many applications, your only recourse when you need to modify the built-in forms is to e-mail wishlist@softwarecompany.com and hope the functionality you need will be incorporated into the next version. However, Outlook enables you to customize the standard Outlook forms. The customization is not limited to changing the appearance of a form. You can add to the form new data fields or even Microsoft Office objects like Excel spreadsheets. Additionally, you can change a form's actions, such as specifying that another form appears when a user replies to your custom form.

Outlook forms may be customized either through the Outlook GUI or programmatically. Often there is a one-to-one correspondence between an Outlook GUI element and an Outlook object or collection. This is like Visual Basic, wherein you can set the property of a form or control either through the development environment or programmatically.

The extent to which you can customize Outlook forms without code, while substantial, does have its limits. This chapter and following ones will show how to use code to extend the functionality of Outlook forms. However, to the extent that you can accomplish your goals without code using the powerful tools integrated into Outlook for customizing forms, you can use the time you save for fun, travel, romance ... let's get real, to write other code. Therefore, this chapter first will cover these tools as well as their corresponding programmatic objects and collections.

Creating a Custom Form

There is a fundamental difference between form development in Outlook and in Visual Basic and Office applications. In Visual Basic and Office applications you start with a new, blank form. By contrast, in Outlook you are limited to customizing one of the Outlook standard forms.

 Note   You can further customize a custom form. However, the form that you are customizing must be descended from a standard form. In other words, the custom form need not be a child of a standard form, but it needs to be a descendant like a grandchild or great grandchild.

While the fact that a custom form must be based on a standard form in Outlook may seem limiting, it is not without its advantages. A custom form *inherits* the functionality of the standard form on which it is based. For example, clicking the Send button on a custom form based on the standard mail message form will send the custom form just as clicking Send would send a standard mail message. No programming is required because the custom form inherits the functionality of its parent form, including the functionality of the Send button.

The ability of a custom form to inherit the capabilities of a standard form is very useful. It saves you from having to write code to duplicate the functionality of a standard form. Instead, you can use Microsoft's code for that functionality, and focus your effort on changing specific features of the standard form.

Inheritance

Inheritance is the ability to define a new class that starts with the same variables, properties, methods, and events of an existing class. The new class is referred to as a child class, and the existing class on which it is based is referred to as a parent class. However, while reproduction of most species requires two parents, inheritance in most programming languages requires only one.

The child class would have no separate purpose if it remained identical to its parent class. Therefore, the child class either has additional variables, properties, methods, or events not found in its parent, or it implements differently from its parent certain of the properties, methods, or events that it inherited.

For example, an existing class called *human* would have properties for name and birth date. A new class called *student* may logically be a child of the human class because students are a subset of humans (though some teachers would dispute this). The student class, by being a child of the human class, would start out with name and birth date properties without the user needing to write any code. However, students, unlike humans generally, take courses, or at least are supposed to. Therefore, the student class may implement an additional Boolean `Resident` property to specify residency status (for tuition or state funding purposes), an `Enroll` method to sign up for classes, a `Drop` method to drop classes, and a `Flunk` event if the teacher is mean.

Inheritance furthers the development of reusable software components. Once a class is fully tested and debugged, it can be modified for use in other applications by having the modified class inherit from the tested and debugged class. The functionality of the parent class need not be reinvented or retested; only the changes need to be tested and debugged.

Getting back to Outlook, the standard mail message form has presumably been thoroughly tested and debugged by Microsoft. A custom mail message form starts out with the properties, methods, and events of the standard mail message form; none of this functionality needs to be reinvented. You can then add to or change the implementation of the properties, methods or events of the standard mail message form to customize it to the needs of your application.

Figure 5-1 shows a Contact form which has been opened for regular use with the menu commands File ⇨ New ⇨ Contact. This form, in its current state, can be used but not modified. Indeed, this is true of all of the standard forms that are opened for regular use.

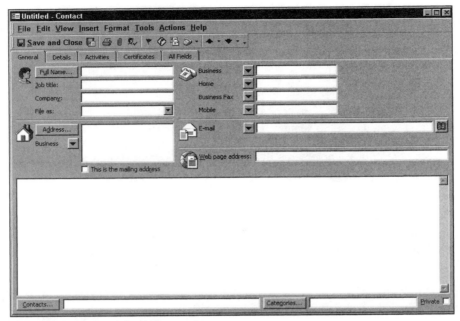

Figure 5-1: The standard Contact form

An Outlook *user* who is creating or reading messages, appointments, tasks, or contact information is using Outlook forms in *run* mode. Opening a standard form by File ➪ New opens the form in run mode. An Outlook *developer* who is customizing a form must do this work when the form is in *design* mode. The Outlook form's run and design modes are comparable to these modes in development environments such as Visual Basic.

One method of opening a form in design mode is first to open the form in run mode, using the File ➪ New menu command, and then to choose the Tools ➪ Forms ➪ Design This Form menu command.

You also can open a form in design mode by following these steps:

1. Access the Design Form dialog box shown in Figure 5-2 by the Tools ➪ Forms ➪ Design a Form menu command.

2. Access the location of the form from the Look In dropdown list. The location may be a forms library, a folder, or a template. Choose the Standard Forms Library, which contains (of course) the standard forms. We will cover other locations later in this chapter.

3. You can obtain information about any form in the location chosen from the Look In dropdown list by selecting the form and clicking the Details button. The information includes the form's description, version number, and message class.

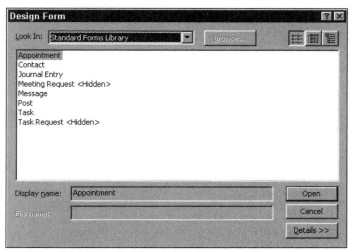

Figure 5-2: You can use the Design Form dialog box to select the form to customize

4. Open a form in design mode by either double-clicking the form name or by selecting it and clicking the Open button. Choose the Contact form.

Figure 5-3 shows the standard Contact form in design mode.

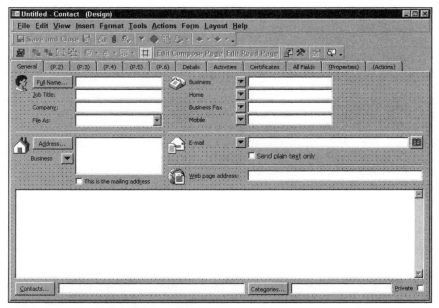

Figure 5-3: The Contact form in design mode

Tip While our intent is to cover customization of Outlook forms fully, Outlook Help does have two "books" on designing Outlook forms. In Contents, under Advanced Customization, there are book icons for Working with Forms and Customizing an Outlook Form.

Form Pages

You can customize the GUI of a form only if either the visibility of at least one of its form's pages can be changed or if one of its visible (by default) pages can be edited by changing its appearance or constituent controls (if any). Since the Notes form has only one page whose visibility cannot be changed and that cannot be edited, the GUI of the Notes form cannot be customized.

You can "add" some, though not all, form pages to a form by toggling their visibility from False to True or "delete" them by toggling their visibility from True to False. Actually, you're not adding or deleting any pages; you're only changing their visible status. Outlook does not permit you to add your own pages to a standard form or to delete an existing page. Therefore, your form always has the same number of pages.

You can use either the Outlook GUI or the Pages collection to toggle the visibility of a form page (whose visibility can be toggled) or to edit an editable form page.

Form Page Visibility and Editability Through the Outlook GUI

The standard mail message form has one page. To be more accurate, it has one page that you can see. Additionally, it has eight pages you cannot see. Figure 5-4 shows the message form in design view. The form has nine tabs. The first tab, Message, is the only one you see in run mode of the standard mail message form. The next eight tabs have names in parentheses. The parentheses indicate that those pages are hidden at run time. Conversely, a tab name without parentheses, like Message, indicates that the page is visible at run time.

Many, though not all, of the pages that by default are not visible can be made visible. You can toggle their visibility from False to True. Conversely, you can make many, though again not all, of the pages that by default are visible at run time invisible at run time by toggling their visibility from True to False.

The pages labeled "(P.2)" through "(P.6)" can be made visible at run time. Simply click the tab of the page to bring it to the front, and then choose Display This Page from the Form menu. As Figure 5-5 shows, before you click Display This Page, the area to the left of that menu item is blank, and the name of the tab is in parentheses. After you click Display This Page, as Figure 5-6 shows, a checkbox appears to the left of the Display This Page menu item, and the parentheses disappear. The checkbox and the lack of parentheses confirm that this page will be visible at run time.

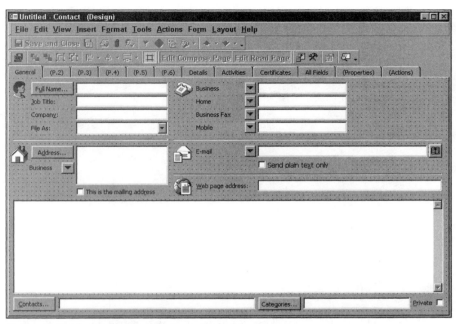

Figure 5-4: The mail message form in design view

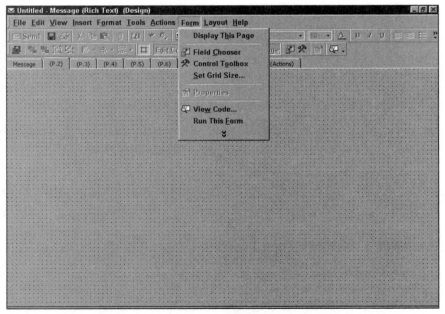

Figure 5-5: The Message page will be invisible at run time because the Display This Page menu item is unchecked and the tab name is in parentheses.

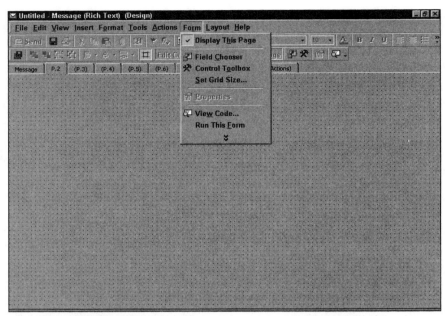

Figure 5-6: The Message page will be visible at run time because the Display This Page menu item is checked and the tab name is not in parentheses.

Note While all custom forms must be based on existing Outlook forms, a custom form may look and act totally differently from the existing form on which it is based. For example, you can hide the Message form page of the default mail message form, with the only visible pages being one or more of the extra blank pages. Additionally, you can have the controls on these extra blank pages relate only to custom fields. This scenario would be unusual, however, as the custom form would be deprived of much of the inherent functionality of its parent form.

Similarly, you can make a page like the Message page that is visible by default invisible by toggling the Display This Page menu command so that the checkbox is removed. The name Message on the tab then will be in parentheses.

Caution You can make the Message page invisible if at least one other page of the form is visible. However, if no other page has been made visible, then you will not be permitted to make the Message page invisible. Instead, you will be sternly warned: "At least one page must be visible in a form." This is logical, as how could a user use an invisible form?

Tip A page that is not visible nevertheless may be used in a custom form. You can place a control on an invisible page and controls on the visible pages will be able to use the value of that control.

Some Outlook pages can be edited. The editing may involve changing properties such as background color, or adding or deleting controls.

You can tell if you're able to edit a page or not by whether you can see a grid in design mode. First, you should enable the grid view by choosing Show Grid from the Layout menu. If the Show Grid menu item is disabled, then dots do not appear and the page is not editable. If Show Grid is enabled and the page has the grid dots, then the page can be edited.

Another method of determining if a page is editable is to click on a control. For example, on the Message page, click on the To: command button, and it is outlined. By contrast, on the All Fields page, clicking on any control will not bring about this result.

 The All Fields page is on all of the standard forms except Notes. The All Fields page is visible by default on some forms but not visible by default on others, but in all standard forms its visibility can be toggled. However, it is not editable on any of the forms. The All Fields page is used to display the values of the fields chosen in the dropdown list.

Table 5-1 summarizes the ability to edit or hide default pages or add (by toggling visibility) blank pages:

Table 5-1 Ability to Edit, Hide and Add Pages of Standard Forms			
Form	*Can Default Pages Be Edited?*	*Can Default Pages Be Hidden?*	*Can Blank, Editable Pages be made visible?*
Message	Yes	Yes	Yes
Post	Yes	Yes	Yes
Appointment	No	Yes	Yes
Meeting Request	No	Yes	Yes
Contact	Yes	Yes	Yes
Task	No	Yes	Yes
Task Request	No	Yes	Yes
Journal Entry	No	Yes	Yes
Notes	No	No	No

Compose vs. Read Mode

The mail message form for messages that you receive is similar but not identical to the mail message form for messages that you send. The mail message form that appears when you create a new mail message is a *compose* form. The mail message form that appears when you double-click a received message to view it is a *read* form.

Outlook enables you as a form designer to use a compose page that is different from a form page. To activate this feature, in design mode, select the page that you want to have separate compose and read layouts, and on the Form menu, check Separate Read Layout. At the beginning, the compose and read pages will be identical. However, you can then choose which page to modify by choosing either Edit Compose Page or Edit Read Page from the Form menu.

Sometimes you will find that extensive changes to your compose page result in your read page being "out of sync." Rather than duplicate the work you did with the compose page with the read page, you can uncheck Separate Read Layout and then check it again. This copies the existing compose page layout to the read page layout.

Pages Collection

You can access customized pages and change them programmatically through the Pages collection. This collection holds the pages that have been customized. These pages may be pages displayed by default that have been edited, such as a customized Message page in a mail message form. The Pages collection may also include any of the initially hidden blank pages that have been customized. The collection may contain the main page and up to five custom pages. Adding more pages to the collection will result in an error. The Pages collection may be empty, as it would be if no pages were customized.

Table 5-2 lists the properties of the Pages collection:

Table 5-2	
Properties of the Pages Collection	
Name	**Description**
Application	Returns the Outlook Application object.
Class	The olObjectClass constant, in this case olPages having a value of 36.
Count	The number of customized pages in the collection.
Parent	The parent object, in this case the Inspector that is displaying the Outlook item having the pages.
Session	Returns the NameSpace object for the collection.

Table 5-3 lists the methods of the Pages collection:

	Table 5-3 **Methods of Pages Collection**	
Name	*Description*	*Parameter*
Add	Creates and returns a new customizable page to the Pages collection.	The name of the page.
Item	Returns a customized page from the collection.	Either Index (one-based position of the page within the collection) or the name of the page.
Remove	Removes a customized page from collection.	Index: One-based position of page within the collection.

The following code example uses the Pages collection to add a new page named Enemies List (some presidents have found this handy) to a contact item.

```
Dim oiContact As ContactItem
Dim ocPages As Pages
Set oiContact = Application.CreateItem(olContactItem)
Set ocPages = olMail.GetInspector.ModifiedFormPages
ocPages.Add("Enemies List")
```

The ModifiedFormPages property of the Inspector object returns the Pages collection for the item displayed by the Inspector. The Add method then is used to add the customized page to the form.

Form Properties

Form properties are properties that apply to the overall form as opposed to its constituent pages. You can set these properties through the Outlook GUI via the Properties page and also programmatically through the FormDescription object.

Properties Page

You can use the Properties page of the form, as its name indicates, to view and set the form's properties. This page never is visible at run time since its sole purpose is to set properties of the form.

Figure 5-7 shows a Properties page for a mail message form. The other standard forms that can be customized also have Properties pages that are quite similar to the one shown in Figure 5-7.

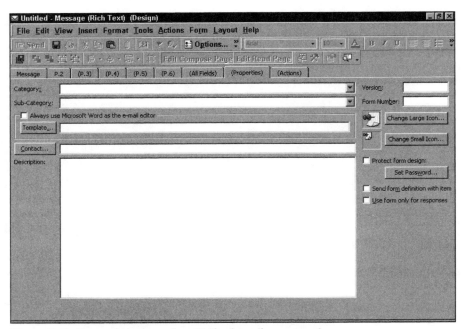

Figure 5-7: Properties page of an Outlook mail message form

Table 5-4 lists the properties on the Properties page and their purposes:

Table 5-4
Outlook Form Properties

Name	Purpose
Category	Enables you to group forms (by category of course) in the Choose Form dialog box.
Subcategory	Enables you to group forms within the existing categories of the Choose Form dialog box.
Always Use Microsoft Word as the Email Editor	Specifies the use of Microsoft Word, instead of Plain Text or HTML, as the editor in the Message control. Permits use of Word's additional formatting and tools.[1]

Name	Purpose
Template	Specifies which Microsoft Word template to use in Message control.[1]
Contact	Specifies the contact responsible for maintaining the form. The contact name appears as the contact under Details in the Choose Form dialog box and in the About dialog box of the form accessed by Help ⇨ About This Form. Not available if form definition is sent with item as discussed below.
Description	Describes the form. The description appears under Details in the Choose Form dialog box and in the About dialog box of the form.
Version	Enables you to specify version number of the form. This is a good idea when developing a form to track which revision is the most recent. The version number appears under Details in the Choose Form dialog box and in the About dialog box of the form.
Form	Enables you to specify a number for the form, which will appear in the About dialog box of the form.
Change Large Icon	Used to choose a large icon that appears in the large icon view of the folder containing the form.
Change Small Icon	Used to choose a small icon that appears in the small icon view and other views of the folder containing the form.
Protect Form Design	Enables password protection to prevent others from changing the design of your published form. This is usually prudent unless the form is of a nature that requires modification.
Set Password	Specifies password for protection of form design.
Send Form Definition With Item	Discussed in the section "Saving the Custom Form."
Use Form Only With Responses	Forms that are used not to initiate but rather to respond to communications, such as an approval form. These forms are "hidden" in that they do not appear in the Choose Form dialog box. Instead, you can only access them by responding to the initiating form.

1. The Always Use Microsoft Word as the Email Editor and the Template properties are enabled only if the standard form has a message control and the default format for outgoing messages is Microsoft Outlook Rich Text, as opposed to Plain Text or HTML. You may set the default mail format by choosing Options from the Tools menu, clicking the Mail Format tab, and selecting Microsoft Outlook Rich Text from the dropdown box labeled "Send in this message format."

Form pages also have Advanced Properties. You can use these properties to set the appearance of the form, such as its caption, its foreground and background colors, its border style, and so on. Figure 5-8 shows the Advanced Properties dialog box, which you can access by right-clicking any editable page.

Figure 5-8: The Advanced Properties dialog box

Caution   Make sure you right-click the page itself and not a control on the page. Otherwise the Advanced Properties will be for the control, not the page.

You change the value of a property by clicking it. Its value (if any) appears in the box at the top of the Advanced Properties dialog box next to the Apply button. Some of the properties, such as BorderStyle, limit you to a choice of several values. For those properties, the box next to the Apply button becomes a dropdown box listing the available choices. For other properties, such as caption, your choices are not limited, so the box next to the Apply button becomes an editable text box. In either case, you make your choice and set it using the Apply button.

FormDescription Object

You can also access the properties of a form programmatically through the FormDescription object. This object also returns several other properties, such as the MessageClass, that do not appear on the Properties page. Thus, you can use this object to create a definition for a new custom form, and its one PublishForm method can save the form definition to one of the forms libraries discussed below.

However, the ability to create a new form using the FormDescription object is limited. This object, unlike the form design tools in the Outlook GUI, does not permit you to change the GUI of the form except for its caption and icon. You cannot change the FormDescription object to change controls or the form's appearance.

The `FormDescription` property of an Outlook item creates the FormDescription object. This code snippet assumes an instantiated MailItem object variable `oiMail`:

```
Dim ooFormDescrip As FormDescription
Set ooFormDescrip = oiMail.FormDescription
```

Table 5-5 lists the properties of the FormDescription object:

<table>
<tr><td colspan="2" align="center">**Table 5-5**
Properties of the FormDescription Object</td></tr>
<tr><td>*Name*</td><td>*Description*</td></tr>
<tr><td>`Application`</td><td>Returns the Outlook Application object.</td></tr>
<tr><td>`Category`</td><td>Returns or sets the category for the form. Corresponds to the string value in the Category text box on the Properties page.</td></tr>
<tr><td>`CategorySub`</td><td>Returns or sets the subcategory for the form. Corresponds to the string value in the Sub-Category text box on the Properties page.</td></tr>
<tr><td>`Class`</td><td>Returns the `olObjectClass` constant, in this case `olFormDescription` having a value of 37.</td></tr>
<tr><td>`Comment`</td><td>Returns or sets the comment for the form. Corresponds to the string value in the Description text box on the Properties page.</td></tr>
<tr><td>`ContactName`</td><td>Returns or sets the contact person for the custom form. Corresponds to the name chosen from the Select Contact dialog box displayed by the Contact command button on the Properties page.</td></tr>
<tr><td>`DisplayName`</td><td>Returns or sets the name of the form that appears in the Choose form dialog box.</td></tr>
<tr><td>`Hidden`</td><td>True if the form can only be opened by another form, False (default) if it can be opened from the Choose Form dialog box. Corresponds to whether the "Use form only for responses" checkbox on the Properties page is checked.</td></tr>
<tr><td>`Icon`</td><td>Path and file name of the large icon for items based on the custom form. Corresponds to the file chosen from the File Open dialog box displayed by the Change Large Icon command button on the Properties page.</td></tr>
<tr><td>`Locked`</td><td>True if users are not permitted to make changes to the design of the form, False if they are. Corresponds to whether the Protect form design check box on the Properties page is checked.</td></tr>
</table>

Continued

Table 5-5 *(continued)*

Name	Description
MessageClass	The MessageClass of the form, which is the Name property appended to the MessageClass of the form on which the custom form was based.
MiniIcon	Path and file name of the small icon for items based on the custom form. Corresponds to the file chosen from the File Open dialog box displayed by the Change Small Icon command button on the Properties page.
Name	Returns or sets the name of the form which appears on its caption and is appended to its MessageClass. Corresponds to the string value when the form was saved.
Number	Returns or sets the number used to identify the form. Corresponds to the string value in the Form Number text box on the Properties page.
OneOff	True if the form is to be used only once and discarded, False (default) if it is to be retained.
Parent	The parent object.
Password	Returns or sets the password that a user has to enter in order to modify the custom form. Corresponds to the string value entered in the Password dialog box displayed by the Set Password command button on the Properties page.
ScriptText	Returns a string containing all the VBScript in the form's Script Editor.
Session	Returns the NameSpace object for the collection.
Template	Path and file name of the Word template to be used by the custom form. Corresponds to the file chosen from the File Open dialog box displayed by the Template command button on the Properties page.
UseWordMail	True if Word is the e-mail editor, False otherwise. Corresponds to whether the "Always use Microsoft Word as the e-mail" editor checkbox on the Properties page is checked.
Version	Version number for the form. Corresponds to the string value in the Version text box on the Properties page.

PublishForm is the one method of the FormDescription object. This method saves the definition of the FormDescription object in the specified form registry. It has two parameters. Its first parameter is one of the olFormRegistry constants listed in Table 5-6. Its second parameter, which is optional unless the olFormRegistry constant is olFolderRegistry, is the MAPIFolder from which the form is accessed.

Table 5-6
olFormRegistry Constants

Description	Constant	Value
Item handled without regard to its form class.	OlDefaultRegistry	0
Only the form's creator may access the form.	OlPersonalRegistry	2
All users with the requisite permissions for the folder may access the form.	OlFolderRegistry	3
All users in the organization have access to the form.	OlOrganizationRegistry	4

Forms are registered as one of three classes: Folder, Organization, or Personal. These classes correspond to the Folder Forms Library, the Organizational Forms Library and the Personal Forms Library discussed later in the section "Saving the Custom Form." The Folder form registry holds a set of forms that are only accessible from that specific folder, whether public or private. The Organization form registry holds forms that may be accessed by anyone in the organization. The Personal form registry holds forms that are accessible only to their creator. These forms libraries are also discussed later in this chapter in the section "Saving the Custom Form."

The code in Listing 5-1 creates a new custom mail message form:

Listing 5-1: **Creating a new custom mail message form**

```
Dim oiMail as MailItem
Dim ooFormDescrip as FormDescription
Set oiMail = CreateItem(olMailItem)
Set ooFormDescrip = oiMail.FormDescription
With ooFormDescrip
    .Comment = "Plea for editorial mercy"
    .Name = "MercyPlea"
    .DisplayName = "Plea for Mercy"
    .Number = "1.0"
    .Version = "1.1"
    .Locked = True
    .Password = "lousyoutlook"
    .PublishForm olPersonalRegistry
End With
```

The setting of many of these properties is optional. However, the Name property needs to be set since the form's MessageClass is based on this property.

Form Actions

A form has three default actions such as Reply, Send, and Forward. These default actions have properties. These properties can be returned, and in most cases set, either through the Outlook GUI via the Actions page or programmatically through the Actions collection and the Action object.

Actions Page

The Actions page, like the Properties page, never is visible at run time. Figure 5-9 shows the Actions page for a mail message form.

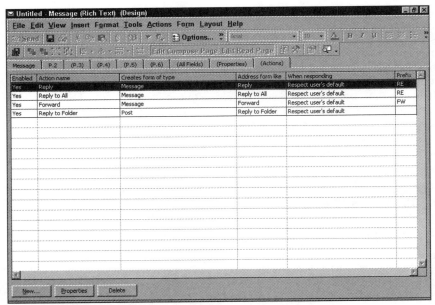

Figure 5-9: The Actions page of a mail message form

The Actions page has the following six columns:

✦ Enabled — Whether the action is enabled. The only two possible values are Yes and No.

✦ Action Name — The name of the action. The four default actions are:

  • Reply — The sender of the message being replied to is a recipient of the reply without the user's needing to select the sender's address.

  • Reply to All — All recipients of the message being replied to — not just the sender but also other recipients who were copied — are recipients of the reply without the user's needing to select their addresses.

- Forward — The message received is sent to a specified recipient.

- Post to Folder — The message being replied to was posted to a folder rather than sent to specified recipients, so the reply likewise is posted to a folder.

✦ Creates form of type — Specifies the type of form that will be used for the action. The mail message form is the default form for the Reply, Reply to All, and Forward actions, and the post form is the default form for the Forward action. However, these default forms can be changed as discussed below.

✦ Address form like — Specifies whether the form should be addressed like a Reply, a Reply to All, a Forward, or a Reply to Folder. This choice is usually dictated by the choice made in the "Creates form of type" column.

✦ When responding — The choices are:

- Do not include original message.

- Attach original message.

- Include original message text.

- Include and indent original message text.

- Prefix each line of the original message.

- Attach link to original message.

- Respect user's default (the default).

✦ Prefix — Specifies the prefix in the Subject box as RE, FW or other.

You can set these properties, among others, from the Form Action Properties dialog box. Figure 5-10 shows this dialog box, which you can display by double-clicking a row of the Actions page for one of the actions or selecting a row and clicking the Properties command button.

Figure 5-10: The Form Action Properties dialog box

Table 5-7 summarizes the fields of the dialog box:

Table 5-7		
The Fields of the Form Action Properties Dialog Box		
Property	*Control*	*Purpose*
Action Name	Text box	Read only. Value based on row selected in Action name column.
Enabled	Checkbox	Specifies whether the action is permitted.
Form Name	Dropdown list	Specifies the form to be used if the action is enabled. Choosing Forms displays the Choose Form dialog box from which any form therein can be chosen.
Message Class	Text box	Read only. Value based on form selected in Form Name dropdown box.
Characteristics of New Form When Responding	Dropdown list	See discussion above of "When responding" column.
Characteristics of New Form – Address Form Like A ...	Dropdown list	Usually read only. See discussion above of "Address form like" column.
Show Action on	Checkbox and Option group	Adds the action name to the menu or menu and toolbar of the custom form
This action will ...	Option group	If Show Action on is enabled, this specifies whether the menu (or toolbar) command that is added to your form opens the form, sends it, or prompts the user.
Subject prefix	Text box	See discussion above of "Prefix" column.

In addition to the Properties command button, the New and Delete command buttons are located at the bottom of the Properties page. The New command button creates a new action. Choosing it brings up the Form Action Properties dialog box. The Delete command button deletes the selected action.

Tip

Don't delete an action unless you are sure you won't need it again. Instead, just set the Enabled column to no. That way, if you need the action again you can simply set the Enabled column to yes. By contrast, if you delete the action and later discover you need it, you have to create it all over again.

Actions Collection and Action Object

You can also access the actions of the form programmatically through the Actions collection and the Action object. New actions, as well as the default actions such as Reply, Send, and Forward, are all Action objects. The Actions collection is a collection of the Action objects for an Outlook item.

An Actions collection is created by the Actions property of an Outlook item. The following code snippet assumes an instantiated MailItem object variable oiMail:

```
Dim ocActions As Actions
Set ocActions = oiMail.Actions
```

Table 5-8 lists the properties of the Actions collection:

Table 5-8
Properties of the Actions Collection

Name	Description
Application	Returns the Outlook Application object.
Class	Returns the OlObjectClass constant, in this case olActions having a value of 33.
Count	The number of objects, in this case Action objects, in the collection.
Parent	The parent object, the particular Outlook item object containing the Actions.
Session	Returns the NameSpace object for the collection.

Table 5-9 lists the methods of the Actions collection:

Table 5-9
Methods of Actions Collection

Name	Description	Parameter
Add	Creates a new Action object, adds it to the Actions collection and returns the new Action.	None.
Item	Returns an Action object from the collection.	Either Index (one-based position of Action object within collection) or Name property of Action object.
Remove	Removes an Action object from the collection.	Index: One-based position of Action object within collection.

Table 5-10 lists the properties of the Action object:

Table 5-10 **Properties of the Action Object**	
Name	*Description*
Application	Returns the Outlook Application object.
Class	Returns the OlObjectClass constant, in this case olAction having a value of 32.
CopyLike	Sets and returns one of the following olActionCopyLike constants indicating which attributes of the original item will be used by the new item resulting from the execution of the action: olReply (0) – originator of original item in the To line and the subject and body of the original item (default); olReplyAll (1) – originator of original item in the To line, all other recipients of original item in the CC line and the subject and body of the original item; olForward (2) –subject and body of the original item; olReplyFolder (3) – conversation, body and Post To copied from original; olRespond (4) – same as olReply except response GUI contains text prompting recipient to respond. Corresponds to the "Address form like a" dropdown box of the Form Action Properties dialog box of the Actions page.
Enabled	Returns True if the action is enabled, False if it is not.
MessageClass	Returns the message class of the item that will be created by the action. Displayed by the Message class textbox of the Form Action Properties dialog box of the Actions page.
Name	Sets and returns the displayed name of the action. Corresponds to the Action name textbox of the Form Action Properties dialog box of the Actions page.
Parent	Returns the parent object, the Outlook item to which the action belongs.
Prefix	Sets and returns the prefix (if any) that begins the Subject line of the item, such as RE: or FW:. The colon is appended automatically to the end of the Prefix and is not part of the value of this property. Corresponds to the Subject Prefix textbox of the Form Action Properties dialog box of the Actions page.

Name	Description
ReplyStyle	Sets and returns one of the following olActionReplyStyle constants indicating the formatting for the new item resulting from the execution of the action: olOmitOriginalText (0) — original text not included in reply; olEmbedOriginalItem (1) — original item included in reply as an attachment; olIncludeOriginal Text(2) — original text included in reply; olIndentOriginal Text(3) — original text included in reply and indented; olLink OriginalItem(4) — a shortcut to the original item included in reply olUserPreference (5) — original user's default reply style used; olReplyTickOriginalText(1000) — original text included in reply with a greater than sign (>) beginning each line. Corresponds to the "When responding" dropdown box of the Form Action Properties dialog box of the Actions page.
ResponseStyle	Sets and returns one of the following olActionResponseStyle constants indicating whether when the action is executed the user may edit the message before it is sent: olOpen (0) — new item opened for editing; olSend (1) — message automatically sent without the user being able to make changes; olPrompt(2) — user asked if he or she wants to edit the message before it is sent. Corresponds to the "This action will" option button group of the Form Action Properties dialog box of the Actions page.
Session	Returns the NameSpace object for the collection.
ShowOn	Sets and returns one of the following olActionShowOn constants indicating whether the action is shown on either the Actions menu or the toolbar of the item: olDontShow(0) — not shown; olMenuandToolbar(1) — show on both menu and toolbar; olMenu — just show on menu. Corresponds to the "Show action on" checkbox and option button group of the Form Action Properties dialog box of the Actions page.

Table 5-11 lists the methods of the Action object:

Table 5-11 **Methods of Action Object**		
Name	**Description**	**Parameter**
Delete	Deletes the current action object from the Actions collection.	None.
Execute	Executes the current action object and returns the new item thereby created.	None.

The code in Listing 5-2 creates and executes a new action that will be similar to a Reply, but will have the prefix FYI and will insert a greater than sign (>) before each line of the original text:

Listing 5-2: **Creating a new Action**

```
Dim oiMail as MailItem
Dim ocActions As Actions
Dim ooAction As Action
Set oiMail = Application.CreateItem(olMailItem)
Set ocActions = oiMail.Actions
Set ooAction = ocActions.Add
ooAction.Enabled = True
ooAction.Prefix = "FYI"
ooAction.ReplyStyle = olReplyTickOriginalText
ooAction.CopyLike = olReply
ooAction.Name = "FwdIncludeOriginator"
oiMail.Actions.Item("FwdIncludeOriginator").Execute
```

Form Fields

Fields in Outlook are comparable to fields in a database. Each field has a name that identifies it and a data type for the information it contains.

Outlook provides numerous built-in fields. For example, the default mail message form has From, To, CC, and BCC fields for addressing the message, a Subject field for the message's subject, and a Message field for the message and any links and attachments. Additionally, you can add new fields, through either the Outlook GUI, primarily through the Field Chooser, or programmatically through the UserProperties collection and the UserProperty object.

Field Chooser

Figure 5-11 shows the Field Chooser that appears when a form is in design mode. Figure 5-12 shows the dropdown list of the Field Chooser. This dropdown list is in essence a filter. Figure 5-13 shows the fields listed when Date/Time Fields item is chosen from the dropdown list.

Figure 5-11: Field Chooser

Figure 5-12: Field Chooser dropdown list

Figure 5-13: Fields listed after date/time fields chosen from the dropdown list

Figure 5-14 shows the Field Properties dialog box that you display by double-clicking a field in the Field Chooser, in this case the Subject field. This dialog box shows the field's name, data type, and format.

Figure 5-14: The Field Properties dialog box displays the name, type and format of a field

The Field Chooser lists the fields built into Outlook. However, you can create new fields to represent data not provided for in the built-in fields.

You start the process of creating a new field by clicking the New button of the Field Chooser. Figure 5-15 shows the resulting New Field dialog box, which looks much like the Field Properties Dialog Box. The difference between the two dialog boxes is that the Field Properties Dialog Box is read only, whereas you can write to the fields in the New Field dialog box.

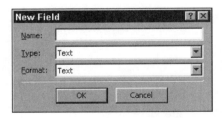

Figure 5-15: You can use the New Field dialog box to create a new field

The name of the new field may be any legal name. The data type dictates the available formats. Table 5-12 lists the available data types and the corresponding available formats.

Caution Plan carefully before you choose a data type for a custom field. Once you create the field you can no longer change the data type, only the format. If you want to change the data type for the custom field then you have to delete the field and create a new field.

Table 5-12
Data Types and Formats for Outlook Custom Fields

Data Type	Description	Formats
Combination	Combines the values of several fields or literal text into a single expression.	Not applicable.
Currency	Numbers expressed as currency.	Yes. Option whether to show cents.
Date/Time	A specific month, day, or time.	Yes. Similar to date/time display options in Microsoft Word.
Duration	Time interval.	Yes. For example, 12h or 12 hours to specify duration in hours.
Formula	Calculations based on values in fields.	Not applicable.
Integer	Whole numbers.	Yes. Standard (1,024) or computer (1 MB) notation.
Keywords	Multiple text values delimited by commas.	No. Literal text.
Number	Numbers with decimal points.	Yes. Number of digits to right of decimal. Option of scientific or computer notation (e.g., 64 MB).
Percent	Numbers expressed as percentage (17.5%).	Yes. Number of digits to right of decimal.
Text	Text, including numbers. Two hundred and fifty-five character limit.	No. Literal text.
Yes/No	Boolean (True or False).	Yes. Yes/No, On/Off, True/False or Icon.

The Combination and Formula types are not true data types. Each expresses a value based on other data and is consequently read only. The difference between the two types is that the Combination type concatenates data from several fields or literal text strings, whereas the Formula type involves a formula.

Create a Combination field as follows:

1. While a form is in design mode, open the Field Chooser and click the New command button to display the New Field dialog box.

2. Type a name for the field in the "Name:" text box.

3. Choose Combination from the "Type:" dropdown box.

4. Once you've chosen the Combination type, the label Format changes to Formula and an Edit command button appears, as shown in Figure 5-16.

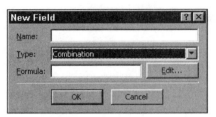

Figure 5-16: Changed New Field dialog box when combination data type chosen

5. Figure 5-17 shows the Combination Formula Field dialog box you display by clicking the Edit command button.

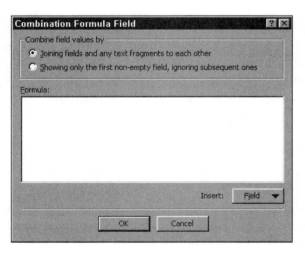

Figure 5-17: Combination Formula Field dialog box

You can type literal text into the Formula text box. Additionally, you can insert field values with the Field command button. You can tell literal text from field values in the Formula text box because field values are enclosed in brackets. You now must choose between two option buttons:

    a. Select the joining fields and any text fragments to each other—This concatenates field values chosen from the Field command button and any literal text strings.

    b. Showing only the first non-empty field, ignoring subsequent ones—This is the choice if you want to show a secondary value when the primary value is not available. For example, you might want the field to show a contact's primary phone number, which is usually a standard business number but could be a cell phone for certain occupations. You could insert, using the field command button, Business Phone, Business Phone 2, and Mobil Phone. The first field with a value would be displayed in this new field.

Create a Formula field by following these steps:

1. While a form is in design mode, open the Field Chooser and click the New command button to display the New Field dialog box.

2. Type a name for the field in the "Name:" text box.

3. Choose Formula from the "Type:" dropdown box.

4. Once you've chosen the Formula type, the label Format changes to Formula and an Edit command button appears, just as was the case with the Combination field as shown in Figure 5-16.

5. Figure 5-18 shows the Formula Field dialog box you display by clicking the Edit command button. The Formula Field dialog box differs from the Combination Formula Field dialog box shown in Figure 5-17 in that it does not have the option buttons but does have an additional Function command button.

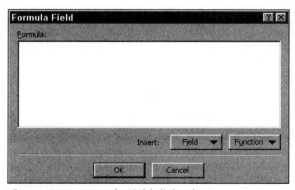

Figure 5-18: Formula Field dialog box

6. Use the Function command button to insert a function with placeholder arguments. For example, the DateAdd function returns the date resulting from your adding a specified time interval to another date. Choose the Function command button and select the DateAdd function. This displays in the Formula text box: DateAdd(interval, number, date). You then need to replace the placeholder arguments. Replace `interval` with "w" (without the quotation marks) and `number` with 1 to add one week. The final argument, `date`, could be a field value, such as `Received`. Field names are placed in brackets. Select "date" and choose the Received field with the Field command button. The Formula text box now reads `DateAdd( w , 1 , [Received]  )`. The value of the new field will be one week after the Received date.

UserProperties Collection and UserProperty Object

You can access custom fields programmatically through the UserProperties collection and the UserProperty object.

Each new field is a UserProperty object. The UserProperties collection is a collection of UserProperty objects. The collection may be empty, as would be the case if there were no user-defined fields.

A UserProperties collection is created by the `UserProperties` property of an Outlook item. The following code snippet assumes an instantiated MailItem object variable `olMail`:

```
Dim olUserProps As UserProperties
Set olUserProps = olMail.UserProperties
```

Table 5-13 lists the properties of the UserProperties collection:

Table 5-13
Properties of the UserProperties Collection

Name	Description
Application	Returns the Outlook Application object.
Class	Returns the olObjectClass constant, in this case olUserProperties having a value of 38.
Count	The number of objects, in this case Action objects, in the collection.
Parent	The parent object, the particular Outlook item object containing the UserProperties.
Session	Returns the NameSpace object for the collection.

Table 5-14 lists the methods of the UserProperties collection.

Table 5-14
Methods of the UserProperties Collection

Name	Description	Parameter
Add	Creates and returns a new UserProperty object and adds it to the UserProperties collection.	Listed in Table 5-15.
Find	Returns the UserProperty object specified by the first parameter, or Nothing if there is no user property with that name.	Required: the name of the property; Optional: True (default) if a user property, False if a system property.
Item	Returns a UserProperty object from the collection.	Either Index (one-based position of UserProperty object within collection) or Name property of UserProperty object.
Remove	Removes a UserProperty object from the collection.	Index: One-based position of UserProperty object within collection.

Table 5-15 lists the parameters of the Add method:

Table 5-15
Parameters of the Add Method of the UserProperties Collection

Parameter	Required?	Data Type	Description
Name	Yes	String	The name of the user-defined field.
Type	Yes	Long	The data type of the user-defined field, one of the olUserPropertyType constants listed in Table 5-16.
AddToFolderFields	No, optional	Boolean	True (default) if the field will be added to the folder fields so that it will be available in the form designer and as a column in an Explorer object; False otherwise.

Continued

Table 5-15 *(continued)*

Parameter	Required?	Data Type	Description
DisplayFormat	No, optional	Long	The index of the format of the specified olUserProperty Type constant.

Table 5-16
olUserPropertyType Constants

Name	Value	Data Type
olCombination	19	Variant
olCurrency	14	Currency
olDateTime	5	Date/Time
olDuration	7	Time interval
olFormula	18	Formula
olKeywords	11	Comma-delimited string of keywords
olNumber	3	Number
olPercent	12	Percentage
olText	1	Text
olYesNo	6	Boolean

Table 5-17 lists the properties of the UserProperty object:

Table 5-17
Properties of the UserProperty Object

Name	Description
Application	Returns the Outlook Application object.
Class	Returns the olObjectClass constant, in this case olUserProperty having a value of 39.
Formula	Returns or sets the formula (if any) for the user property. Corresponds to the Formula text field of the Formula Field dialog box.

Name	Description
Name	Returns the name of the object, which is the first parameter of the Add method of the UserProperties collection.
Parent	The parent object.
Session	Returns the NameSpace object for the collection.
Type	Data type. One of the olUserPropertyType constants listed in Table 5-16.
ValidationFormula	Returns or sets the validation formula. Corresponds to the string value in the Validation Formula text box on the Validation tab of the Control properties dialog box.
ValidationText	Returns or sets the message if validation fails. Corresponds to the string value in the "Display this message if the validation fails" text box on the Validation tab of the Control properties dialog box.
Value	Returns or sets the value of the custom property.

The UserProperty object has one method, Delete, which deletes the object from the UserProperties collection. The method has no parameters.

The following VBA code snippet uses the Add method to add a custom property of Boolean data type to determine if a contact is a family relation. This code snippet assumes an instantiated ContactItem object variable oiContact:

```
Dim ooUserProp As UserProperty
Set ooUserProp = oiContact.UserProperties _
    .Add("Family", olYesNo)
```

The following VBA code snippet uses the Find method to search for the custom property "Family", having a Boolean data type, to determine if a contact is a family relation. This code snippet assumes an instantiated ContactItem object variable oiContact:

```
Dim ooUserProp As UserProperty
Set ooUserProp = oiContact.UserProperties.Find("Family")
If ooUserProp Is Nothing Then
Debug.Print "No such property"
Else
Debug.Print "Property found"
End If
```

Property Events

The `PropertyChange` event occurs when the value of a standard Outlook property has been changed. The `CustomPropertyChange` event occurs when the value of a user-defined property has changed. Each event passes one parameter, the name (not value) of the property that was changed.

One example of the use of the `PropertyChange` event is that a change in the business address of a contact will automatically generate an e-mail notifying the user's secretary of the change.

Controls

Controls are usually used to read from and write to fields. For example, the General tab of the Contact form uses a text box for the company name and a checkbox to indicate whether the contact is private. Both these fields are standard Outlook fields, but you may also use controls to read from and write to Outlook custom fields.

These controls are bound to a field, or to use the parlance of Visual Basic and other programming environments, are "data bound" controls. A change in the value of the control changes the value of the field "automatically" and without code. Actually, the change does require code, but the code is already built into Outlook. You do not have to write code to update a field from a control.

Additionally, the binding of a control and a field is a two-way street. Just as a change in the value of the control changes the value of the field, a change in the value of a field changes the value of the control. For example, both Control A and Control B may be bound to the same field. A change made to the field's value in Control A will be reflected in Control B. In this scenario Control A and Control B are sometimes referred to as "shared fields," which may be a misnomer since they are controls that share a field.

A control does not have to correspond to a field. For example, on the General tab of the Contact form, the words Job Title and Company next to text boxes are label controls. These label controls are used to identify the fields to which the adjacent text box controls correspond. However, these label controls are not bound to a field.

Outlook provides a number of controls. Table 5-18 lists and provides information on these controls, which are listed by functionality rather than alphabetically.

Table 5-18
Standard Outlook Controls

Type	Bindable?	Functionality
Label	Yes	Describes adjacent controls or displays unchanging value such as a caption. Usually unbound, but can be bound for a read-only display of a field's value.
TextBox	Yes	Bound when used to read or write data in a field. Unbound to show results of a calculation.
ListBox	Yes	Displays multiple values, one value per row. If MultiSelect property is true, the user can select multiple values. Otherwise, only one value can be selected from the list.
ComboBox	Yes	Combines features of TextBox and ListBox controls. The dropdown style enables the user to add a new value to the list by typing in the TextBox portion. The Droplist style requires the user to select an existing value from the list.
CheckBox	Yes	Enables the user to set Boolean field value by checking or unchecking a box.
ToggleButton	Yes	Enables the user to set Boolean field value set toggling the status of a button.
OptionButton	Yes	Enables the user to set Boolean field value by selecting or unselecting a radio button. Differs from CheckBox and ToggleButton in that the value of one and only one of OptionButtons in a group can be True. OptionButtons can be grouped by a Frame control or by the GroupName property.
Frame	No	You can use this control to group other controls, particularly option buttons.
CommandButton	No	Click event used to run VBScript code to perform an action.
Image	Yes	Displays an image on a form. The image may be a .bmp, .cur, .gif, .ico, .jpg or .wmf file. Usually not bound to a field. However, binding would be useful if the field were, for example, an image file of a contact.
TabStrip	Yes	The tab control. The various tabbed pages are not separate forms. They have the same controls and layout. Used for consistent layout to display different data on each tabbed page.

Continued

Table 5-18 *(continued)*		
Type	*Bindable?*	*Functionality*
MutliPage	No	Every page is a separate form and therefore may have a different layout from the other pages. Used to categorize information. For example, one page might contain business information, another personal information, and another a log of recent contacts.
ScrollBar	Yes	The horizontal and vertical scroll bars we all know and love.
SpinButton	Yes	Used to increment or decrement a number.

Outlook does not limit you to these controls. You also can use ActiveX controls. However, not all ActiveX controls function properly on an Outlook form. Additionally, if other users will be using the form, they will need to have the same version of the control installed on their system.

Tip   Not that we are hawking Microsoft products, but you may want to invest in the Office 2000 Developer edition if you plan to use ActiveX controls with your custom Outlook application. This edition includes a set of ActiveX controls that work with Outlook and other Microsoft Office programs. The Developer edition also includes a Package and Deployment Wizard to prepare distribution disks that include the files necessary for these ActiveX controls to work on the users' forms.

Adding a Control to a Form

You access the standard Outlook controls from a toolbox that is essentially the same as the toolbox in the Visual Studio and VBA Integrated Development Environments (IDEs). You access the toolbox either from the Control Toolbox menu item on the Form menu or from the toolbox toolbar button. Figure 5-19 shows the Toolbox.

Figure 5-19: The Toolbox

Tip   The Toolbox can also be customized. You can add other controls to the Toolbox simply by dragging them from an Outlook form and dropping them on to the Toolbox. You can add ActiveX controls by right-clicking the Control page and choosing Custom Controls from the context menu. You can add additional pages to the Toolbox by right-clicking it and choosing New Page from the context menu.

There are two ways of adding a control to a form. The first uses the toolbox. The second is using the Field Chooser.

Using the toolbox involves dragging the control from the toolbox and dropping it onto the form. This is quite similar to what you do in the Visual Studio and VBA IDEs.

Using the Field Chooser also involves drag and drop. However, this time you are dragging a field from the Field Chooser onto the form. With this method the control's type will be chosen for you and the control will be bound to a field. For example, dragging the Company Main Phone field to a contact form will place on the form a TextBox control bound to the Company Main Phone field and an adjacent unbound label control with the caption "Company Main Phone" to identify the TextBox control.

Tip You can also click on a tool and then drag a field. This allows you to specify the type of control to be used, rather than leaving it up to Outlook.

You can access the properties of a control by right-clicking the control and choosing Properties from the context menu. This displays the Properties dialog box shown in Figure 5-20.

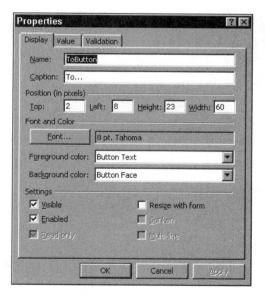

Figure 5-20: Control Properties dialog box with the Display tab shown

The Properties dialog box has three tabs: Display, Value, and Validation. The Display tab enables you to set the properties that govern the control's appearance. Which of these properties can be set depends on the control involved. The Display tab properties include the control's position, foreground and background color, its caption and font size if the control has a text display, and whether it should be resized with the form. However, the properties on the Display tab are not limited exclusively to appearance. They also include whether the control is visible, whether it's enabled, and whether it's read-only.

Figure 5-21 shows the Value tab page of the control Properties dialog box. Once again, which of the properties on this page can be set depends on the control involved.

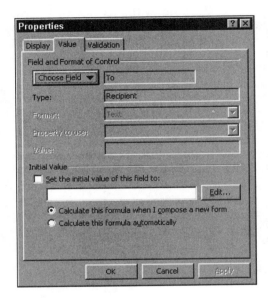

Figure 5-21: The Value tab of the control Properties dialog box

The Value page has the following controls:

    ✦ Choose Field

    ✦ New

    ✦ Type

    ✦ Format

    ✦ Property to Use

    ✦ Value

    ✦ Set the initial value of this field to

    ✦ Calculate this formula …

        • When I compose a new form

        • Automatically

Figure 5-22 shows the Validation tab page of the control Properties dialog box. Once again, which of the properties on this page can be set depends on the control involved.

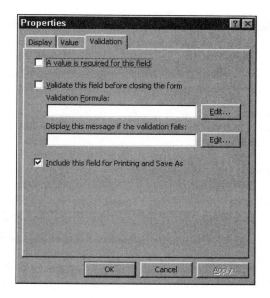

Figure 5-22: The Validation tab of the control Properties dialog box

The Validation page has the following controls:

✦ A value is required for this field

✦ Validate this field before closing this form

✦ Validation formula

✦ Display this message if the validation fails

✦ Include this field for Printing and Save As

Each control also has Advanced Properties with further settings relating to its appearance. Figure 5-23 shows the Advanced Properties dialog box, which you access by right-clicking the control and choosing advanced Properties from the context menu. The operation of this dialog box is essentially the same as the operation of the Advanced Properties dialog box for form pages discussed above.

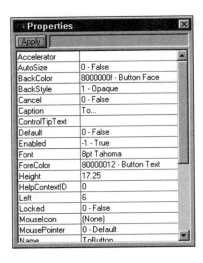

Figure 5-23: Advanced Properties dialog box

Controls Collection

All of the controls on a form page are part of a Controls collection. This collection is not part of the Outlook 2000 object library. Rather, it is part of the Microsoft Forms 2.0 Object Library. You can access this object library through the Outlook 2000 Object Browser by choosing MSForms from the library dropdown box. Visual Basic Editor Help also includes a book titled Microsoft Forms Reference that discusses this object library.

The Controls collection has no events and only one property, Count, which returns the number of controls in the collection. Table 5-19 lists the methods of the Controls collection:

Table 5-19		
Methods of Controls Collection		
Name	**Parameter**	**Description**
Add	See Table 5-20.	Adds a control to a form page and its collection of controls.
Clear	None.	Removes all controls from the collection.
Item	Index: Zero-based position of control object within collection.	Returns the specified control from the collection.

Name	Parameter	Description
Move	Two numbers, comma-delimited. For example: 25, 35.	Specifies a single-precision value, in points, that specifies the change from the current horizontal and vertical position for each control in the collection.
Remove	Either zero-based position of control object within collection or property of control.	Removes the specified control from the collection.

Table 5-20
Parameters of the Add Method of the Controls Collection

Name	Data Type	Required?	Description
ProgID	String	Yes	Programmatic identifier of control. Usually `Forms.<ControlType>.1`. A checkbox's ProgID is `Forms.CheckBox.1`.
Name	String.	No, optional	Name of control. If not specified, default name specified, such as `TextBox1`.
Visible	Boolean	No, optional	True (default) if control is visible, False if hidden.

A previous code example for the Pages collection added a new page named Enemies List to a contact item. The code in Listing 5-3 will use the Add method of the Controls collection to add a label captioned Enemies to the new page:

Listing 5-3: Using the Add Method of the Controls Collection

```
Dim oiContact As ContactItem
Dim ocPages As Pages
Dim fcLabel As Label
Set oiContact = Application.CreateItem(olContactItem)
Set olPages = oiContact.GetInspector.ModifiedFormPages
olPages.Add("Enemies List")
'Now add label and place caption on it.
Set fcLabel = ocPages("Enemies List").Controls. _
    Add("Forms.Label.1", "lblEnemiesList", True)
fcLabel.Caption = "Enemies List"
```

The One Control Event — Click

Most of the controls have a number of properties and methods. These properties and methods are not unique to Outlook, and would be familiar to programmers who use these controls for other types of applications. However, the events, or more accurately event, of these controls is unique to Outlook. Only some of the Outlook controls have even one event, Click, and then only if the control is not bound to a field.

The CommandButton, Frame and Image controls are never bound to a field and therefore always have a click event.

If a CheckBox, OptionButton or ToggleButton control is bound to a field, it does not have a Click event. You must use the PropertyChange or CustomProperty Change event discussed next. Even if these controls are not bound to a field, Microsoft recommends, as do the authors, that you use the PropertyChange or CustomPropertyChange events.

Similarly, the ComboBox and ListBox controls do not have a Click event if they are bound to a field, and you should use the PropertyChange or CustomProperty Change event in any case. However, the Click event fires for these controls when an item is selected as opposed to when the control is clicked.

You create a Click event procedure by typing the name of the control followed by an underscore, the word Click, and empty parentheses, since the procedure has no parameters. The following is an example of the Click event procedure for the CommandButton named cmdTest:

```
Sub cmdTest_Click()
    MsgBox "cmdTest clicked!"
End Sub
```

Note   The Insert Event Handler dialog box does not include the Click event. You have to type the click code manually into the Script Editor.

Tip   Outlook's Help on the Click event appears in the book "Control Reference" under Advanced Customization in Contents.

Saving the Custom Form

The next step after creating a customized form for your users is to save the form. The most common method of saving a form is to *publish* it to a *library*.

You can also save a form as a template or message, among other formats.

Much as a library contains books, a form library contains forms. Outlook offers several form libraries, which differ based on their location and whether they are connected with a particular folder:

✦ The *Organizational Forms Library* is on the Exchange Server. The forms in this library are available globally. Therefore, forms such as travel expense reports that should be available to everyone in the organization are often stored in this library.

✦ The *Folder Forms Library* is for forms connected with a specific folder. The folder may be private or public. If the form is private, then the forms library may be on a local hard drive. If the folder is public, the forms library is on the Exchange Server, like the Organizational Forms Library. However, unlike forms in the Organizational Forms Library, forms in the Folder Forms Library are not available globally. Rather, these forms are available only to users with the correct permissions for the public folder.

✦ The *Personal Forms Library* contains forms that only their creator may access. This library is a good choice for forms that are truly personal to a particular user, such as customized greeting messages. This library is also a good place to test forms before they are distributed since other users can't inadvertently use a form that has not yet been fully tested. Additionally, you can distribute a group of forms by placing them in a personal folder (.pst file) and then distributing it.

✦ The *Web Forms Library* contains HTML forms that are used by Outlook Web Access, which is covered in Chapter 4. These forms were either created using HTML or were converted to HTML by the HTML Forms Converter, which is also covered in Chapter 4.

Once you've chosen the library, you publish your form as follows:

1. When the form is in design mode, choose the Tools ➪ Forms ➪ Publish Form As menu command. This will display the Publish Form As Dialog Box shown in Figure 5-24.

2. Select the forms library where you will publish the form from the Look in dropdown list.

3. In the Display Name text box, type a name for the form. You can type in a different form name if you want. That form name is appended to the message class of form on which it was based.

4. Click Publish.

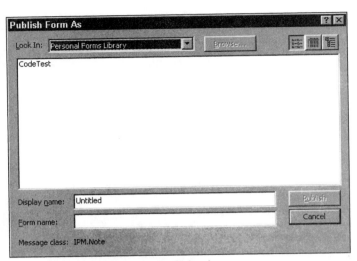

Figure 5-24: Publish Form As dialog box

You have two additional options when saving your form. One is to save the form as an Outlook template, or .oft file. You can then embed the .oft file in a mail message and send it even to users who do not have the form on their systems. Recipients can open the form like any other attachment. They can publish the form to their forms libraries. They can also fill out the form template and return it to you. You can save the form as an Outlook template as follows:

1. When the form is in design mode, choose the File ➪ Save As menu command.

2. Choose Outlook Template (*.oft) from the Save as type dropdown box.

3. Navigate to the location where you want to save the file, type a name for the file in the File name box and click the Save command button.

The other option is to save the form definition with the form. This enables users to use the form without having it on their systems. You can save the form definition with the form by checking the "Send form definition with item" checkbox on the Properties page of the form.

Saving the form definition with the item has disadvantages. One is that the form size will be larger. Another is that the item will not be automatically updated by a new version, as would be the case if the form were saved without the form definition. Additionally, the user will receive a warning message if the form includes VBScript and the form is not on the user's system, which means that you have to let users know what to do in this circumstance.

Message Classes

Outlook identifies forms by their *message class*. Each form's message class begins with IPM. IPM is an acronym for *interpersonal message*. Next, after a dot, is the type of item. For example, the message class of an Appointment form is IPM.Appointment. Table 5-21 lists the message classes of the standard forms.

Table 5-21
Message Classes of Outlook Standard Forms

Form Name	Message Class
Contact	IPM.Contact
Task	IPM.Task
Task Request	IPM.TaskRequest
Message	IPM.Note
Appointment	IPM.Appointment
Meeting Request	IPM.Schedule.Meeting.Request
Distribution List	IPM.DistList
Journal Entry	IPM.Activity
Note	IPM.StickyNote
Post	IPM.Post

Note   As Table 5-21 reflects, the message class and the form name are not always the same. The IPM class for the forms Appointments, Contacts, Tasks, and Task Requests are the form name. However, the IPM class of the mail message form is Note, and the IPM class of the Note form is StickyNote.

When you create and publish a custom form, the name of the form is added on after the name of the form on which it was based. For example, if you create a custom form called SalesCall based on the Contact form, the MessageClass value of the SalesCall custom form will be IPM.Contact.SalesCall. Piggybacking a custom form on the standard form allows the item to use the standard form in case a custom form is not available.

Outlook uses Message Classes to find the form that a user is attempting to open. Outlook searches for the desired form in the following order:

1. Is the form a standard form?

2. If not, is a form with the specified Message Class in the forms cache on the local machine?

3. If not, is a form with the specified Message Class in the forms library of the current folder?

4. If not, is a form with the specified Message Class in the user's Personal Forms Library?

5. If not, is a form with the specified Message Class in the Organizational Forms Library?

6. If not, is a form with the specified Message Class in the Web Forms Library (assuming Web Services are enabled)?

7. If not, Outlook launches the standard form that is the direct or indirect ancestor of the custom form. For example, if the custom form is for prospective customers, so it is a contact form with the message class `IPM.Contact.Sucker`, then the standard contact form is launched.

The forms cache is a folder on the user's local machine. By default, Outlook caches all custom forms into this folder. This speeds up the loading of the form. Outlook stores the definition of a custom form into the cache when the form is opened for the first time on the local machine. If the form is changed, the form definition in the forms cache will be updated automatically when the user next opens that form. This feature guarantees that the user will be using the latest version of the form.

Summary

In this chapter you learned how to customize an Outlook form. You can customize the pages, fields and controls of an Outlook form either through the Outlook GUI or programmatically. This chapter also showed you how to customize a form's properties and actions, again both through the Outlook GUI and programmatically.

✦   ✦   ✦

Outlook Applications

Building Outlook Applications

When it comes to application development, using Outlook as a development environment or a tool does not immediately come to people's minds. Most people who use Outlook use it the way Microsoft shipped it, as an e-mail client, task scheduler, newsgroup reader, address book, and so on. What a lot of people don't realize is that Outlook is really a foundation on which other contact management tools can be based. For example, one of the most overlooked functions of Outlook is the Journal folder. By using the Journal folder, you can get a summary of all the transactions that occurred between you and a particular contact. This is a very useful resource in a customer relationship management (CRM) tool.

Through the use of Outlook forms, you can create a help desk system to track problems within your enterprise by storing the information in public folders, which can act as a repository for archived problems and solutions. One of the most frequently discussed Outlook applications is the Microsoft Digital Dashboard, which provides you with immediate feedback about the health of your organization, much like to an executive information system.

There are several different means by which features and functions can be added to your Outlook environment. This chapter will cover how Visual Basic for Applications, macros, and class modules can be used to develop such features and functions. For building an Outlook application, using Visual Basic and COM objects will also be discussed.

Using Visual Basic for Applications

In previous versions, Outlook was extended through the use of VBScript. VBScript is occasionally known as Visual Basic, Scripting Edition. It is a subset of Visual Basic and it was first introduced in Microsoft Internet Explorer 3.0. It is intended to be an Internet programming language for Microsoft products, and is Microsoft's answer to Netscape's JavaScript language.

With Outlook 2000, the inclusion of Visual Basic for Applications (VBA) provides developers with a new set of programming abilities. VBA offers developers the ability to provide procedures to the entire environment rather than just embedding them within Outlook forms. This means that your application isn't bound to just one Outlook form. It also means that you can integrate any automation-enabled application into Outlook. VBA has a much richer set of programming functions than VBScript does, provided through the Outlook Object Model and accessed through the Visual Basic Editor (VBE), which is an integrated development environment (IDE) based on the one Visual Basic developers have enjoyed for years.

VBScript code is stored in the Outlook forms. VBScript code can only be run when the form that contains it is open and provides no interoperability with other forms. Another drawback is that you cannot use Windows APIs.

Any form that is designed using techniques introduced in Chapter 5, "Outlook Forms," can use VBA. Developers can access events and procedures through the Outlook Object Model and the Collaborative Data Object (CDO). CDO enables you to develop messaging and collaboration applications for the Web, as well as client-based and server-based applications. CDO also enables you to refer to address books and e-mail addresses that aren't available in the Outlook Object Model. Table 6-1 offers a quick look at comparison between the two languages.

Table 6-1 Comparison Between VBScript and VBA		
Feature	**VBScript**	**VBA**
Automation	No	Yes
Class Modules	No	Yes
Development Online Help	Yes (limited)	Yes
Events	Yes (very limited object model)	Yes (object model)
IDE (VBE)	No	Yes
Macros	No	Yes
Object Browser	No	Yes

Automation

As was discussed in Chapter 2, Automation (originally known as OLE Automation and ActiveX Automation) is a technology based on the Component Object Model (COM) that enables you to expose a set of functions that other applications can use. Applications such as spreadsheets and word processors have many features that can be useful to other applications. Mail merge and spell checking are features that are built into word processors that you might take advantage of within your own application. Rather than writing your own features, through Automation you can access a component's set of functions within your application and provide your clients with a familiar feature from another application.

Class Modules

A *class* is a definition of a custom object type containing events, methods, and properties. *Class modules* are similar to standard modules, with the exception that they are mostly used for creating your own object code. Essentially, think of class modules as blueprints for objects. Before you can start coding your class modules, you have to design them. There are a number of resources covering various object-oriented design techniques, and each technique would require a book of its own; therefore, this is just a superficial overview of what you need to consider when designing a class module.

Think of a class module as a blueprint. This blueprint can be used to make as many houses as you'd like. All the houses will look exactly alike as soon as you build them. If you modify the blueprint, all the new houses will look exactly alike, but they won't look like the earlier homes.

The first thing you need to do is identify all the data you want to work with. Don't edit your list as you write down your information because you want to make sure you capture everything. It's better to have too much information and reorganize later than to have to add elements after the object has been constructed.

You then divide the items you wrote down into entities and attributes. You can think of entities as the objects you want to work with and of attributes as the properties of the entities. For each entity you define, that is the number of class modules you will have. Each attribute becomes a property of the entity. In many ways, creating a class module is a lot like normalizing a database, which is the act of removing redundant fields from the database's table design.

Visual Basic Editor (VBE)

If you've developed applications using any of the Microsoft Office products that are VBA enabled or if you've used Visual Basic, you'll discover that the VBE has a striking resemblance to Visual Basic's IDE (Integrated Development Environment).

Visual Basic is arguably one of the most popular development languages, and Micro-soft has taken advantage of this fact by providing developers with an environment and interface that they are most likely familiar with. This familiarity empowers developers and encourages productivity.

Unlike the VBScript editor, which resembles Windows Notepad, VBE provides you with a very powerful development environment. The VBScript environment only offers you a simple editing window, access to the Outlook Object Model, and some basic events, as shown in Figure 6-1. The editor does not offer any of the testing or debugging features that you might expect from a code editor.

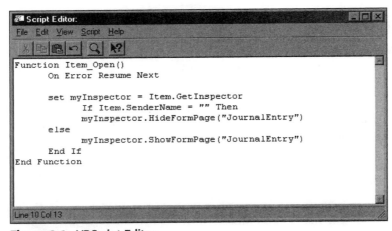

Figure 6-1: VBScript Editor

The VBE makes code writing, testing, and debugging much easier. It provides feed-back on the code you're typing by inspecting it as you go. Basic syntactical errors like forgetting to put a Then keyword at the end of an If clause will produce an error that you can correct immediately. With the VBScript editor, you would not be notified of an error until you executed the procedure.

To view the VBE, you can choose it from the Tools menu or through a keyboard shortcut. From the Tools menu, you'll find the Visual Basic Editor under the Macro menu item. The keyboard shortcut is Alt+F11. When you first open the VBE, it opens with a default Project, Project1 (VbaProject.OTM), as shown in Figure 6-2. When you open the VBE and you already have code or forms in a project, you will get a macro warning, like the dialog box shown in Figure 6-3. Click the Enable Macros button to continue. This is a security warning to help notify you by running a macro, you may introduce viruses onto your system that might not be discovered by your anti-virus software.

Note If you're not sure if the macros on your system are virus-free, you should obtain the latest version of any of the popular anti-virus programs on the market that offer the latest macro virus detection signatures and scan your system before continuing.

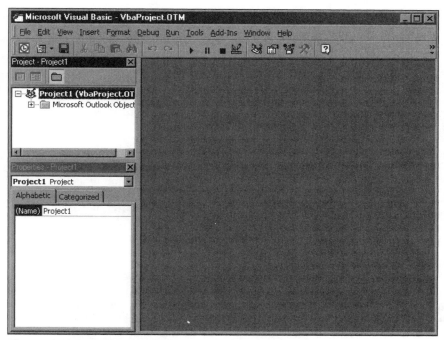

Figure 6-2: Outlook's VBE looks very similar to the Visual Basic IDE

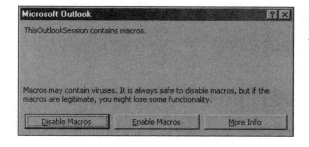

Figure 6-3: Warning dialog asking if you want to enable the macros or not

When you first open the VBE, you will see a Project Explorer and Properties window. The Project Explorer window is a container that lists all the UserForms, Modules, and Class Modules and displays them in a hierarchical manner. UserForms are windows or dialog boxes that become part of your Outlook application's user interface. In previous versions of Outlook, UserForms could only be modal forms, which meant that your users were forced to respond to a form before using any other part of the application. Starting with Outlook 2000, you can now define UserForms as modeless. Unlike a modal form that stops all code from processing and waits for input from the user, modeless forms display information, but the code continues to process with or without user intervention.

 Note   UserForms are accessible through VBA and are not to be confused with Outlook forms. Outlook forms must always be based on an existing form type and are tied to an Outlook item.

A module is a collection of procedures and functions but contains no user interface. Module-level declarations and definitions are by default Public, which means that constants, variables, and procedures declared within a standard module are by default accessible by code in other modules and UserForms.

One element that is included in every Outlook project is a folder named Microsoft Outlook Objects, which contains a special class module named ThisOutlookSession. A class module is a type of module that contains the definition of a class. The definition includes the methods and properties that are part of the class. ThisOutlook Session is a good place to put all the procedures and code initialization that should be run when Outlook starts.

ThisOutlookSession

New to Outlook 2000 is the special class module called ThisOutlookSession that contains special events that are Application-level events. You can access application-level events throughout the Outlook application. Table 6-2 lists the events that are available for the Outlook Application object and what they do.

Table 6-2 ThisOutlookSession Application-Level Events	
Event	*When it occurs*
ItemSend	When an item is sent.
NewMail	When one new message (or more) is received in the Inbox.
OptionsPageAdd	When the Options dialog box is opened from the Tools menu or when a folder's Properties dialog box is opened.
Quit	When Outlook is closing, but only after all Explorer and Inspector windows are closed.
Reminder	Before an event, like a task or an appointment, is scheduled to take place, a message box will appear notifying the user of event.
Startup	When Outlook starts up, but only after all add-in programs have been loaded.

Events

An event is something that can happen to an object and to which the object can respond. Within the Outlook Object Model, there are a number of events you can use to develop interactive applications, like the Application event, Explorer event, and OutlookBar Group event, just to name a few.

Note   Outlook has two event models that don't appear in any other Office product: Explorers and Inspectors events. Explorers are Outlook's reference name to folders (the file system folder on the computer or folders within the Outlook Folder List). Inspectors are Outlook's reference to times that are opened for display within the Outlook environment.

Macros

A macro is a set of instructions grouped together in a public procedure located in any code module. A function or a private procedure cannot be a macro. Macros also can't be located within a class or form module. Unlike standard procedures and functions, macros cannot contain passed arguments.

A feature that Office users often use when creating a macro is the Record Macro feature. Unfortunately, the Outlook development team, for whatever reason, neglected to include this feature in Outlook 2000. This means that you have to program any macro you decide to create for an Outlook application.

To view or access a macro, go to the Macro dialog box under the Tools menu or through the keyboard shortcut Alt-F8. Figure 6-4 shows the Macro dialog box. From the dialog box, you can run, step into (execute line by line), create, or delete a macro. The dialog box displays all the macros that are in your Outlook environment. To execute a macro, simply select the macro and click Run or double-click the macro name.

For more information on macros, see the "Working with Macros" section later in this chapter.

Object Browser

Each OLE and Automation application provides a list of objects, methods, and properties that are available to other developers. This list is known as the object model and it is stored in either an object library (.olb) or type library (.tlb) file. The VBE provides you with a facility that allows you to look at the object model in a hierarchical manner. This facility is called the *Object Browser*.

To view the Object Browser, you can select its button from the toolbar, choose the command from the View menu, or press F2 on the keyboard. Figure 6-5 illustrates the Object Browser highlighting some basic information about the Attachments property of the JournalItem class. The main dropdown list box contains all the object models that are part of the current project.

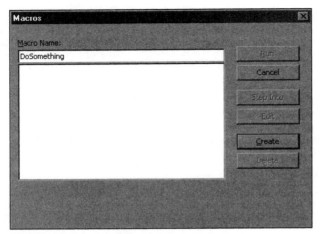

Figure 6-4: Macro dialog box

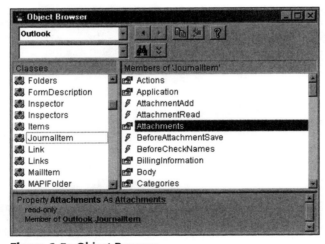

Figure 6-5: Object Browser

The left pane of the browser displays the object's classes while the right pane displays methods, functions, or properties of a chosen object. At the bottom of the browser is a description field that describes the class, method, function, or property chosen.

With so many different items in an object model, a lot of times you might not remember what object it belongs to. Under the main dropdown list box is a Search dropdown list box. Enter the name of a class, property or method you're looking for and a result window will display all the object libraries that contain the information you're looking for. To add more object models, use the References dialog box. The References dialog box is found under the Tools menu item. Figure 6-6 shows the References dialog box with the ActiveX Data Objects 2.5 Library being added to a project, which allows your Outlook applications to access database resources like a Microsoft Access or SQL Server database. By referencing new object models, you are extending the development features of the Outlook application.

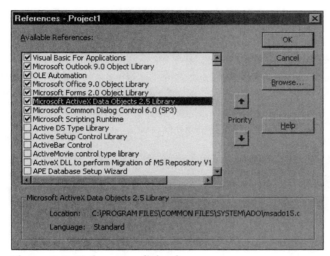

Figure 6-6: References dialog box

Working with Macros

As mentioned earlier, a macro is a set of instructions grouped together in a public procedure in any code module. It cannot be a Function or Private procedure, nor can it accept any arguments passed to it. You can execute a macro from the Macro dialog box; however, if you really want to exploit the macro you created, you can add it to your Outlook menu bar or toolbar.

Creating a Macro

To add a macro to Outlook, you will need to access the Macro dialog box. To open the dialog box, press Alt+F8 or use the Macro menu item found under the Tools menu. The dialog box lists all the procedures that meet the Macro criteria, which is a public procedure that does not allow any passed arguments.

To create a macro, determine the name you want to call the macro and enter into the Macro Name field. Don't feel that the name you use has to be perfect because you can always change it later. By entering a name into the Macro Name field, you enable the Create button on the dialog box.

Creating the world's simplest macro

In every programming book there is always some really simple example that is supposed to provide you with the profound insight to completely understand the technology you are about to embark on. This is that example! Well, not really. But it will show you how simple it is to create a macro within Outlook.

1. Enter **Hello World** into the Macro Name field and press the Create button.

2. The Visual Basic Editor will open and place you within the code editing window within the procedure you just created, as shown in Figure 6-7. If you're familiar with Visual Basic, this is similar to adding a procedure using the Add Procedure menu item.

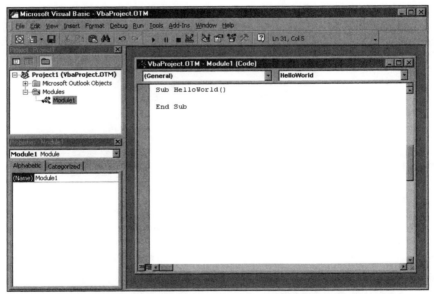

Figure 6-7: VBE showing the basic information of the Hello World macro

3. Enter the following code illustrated in bold into the HelloWorld procedure:

```
Sub HelloWorld()
    MsgBox "Hello World!"
End Sub
```

The `MsgBox` statement is a VBA command to display a message to the user. In this example the message is obviously "Hello World!"

4. Unlike with the VBScript Editor, you can immediately test the code you've just entered. This makes macro debugging more interactive within the development cycle. To test your code, press the F5 key or the Start button in the Toolbar menu. Figure 6-8 shows the result of the code you just entered.

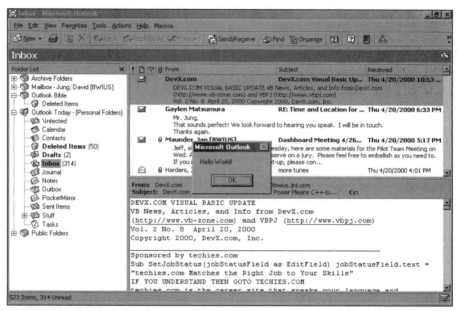

Figure 6-8: Hello World macro running within Outlook

5. Press the OK button on the message box to return control back to the VBE. Close the VBE to save the macro and return to Outlook.

6. To execute the macro from within Outlook, simply bring up the Macro dialog box, select the Hello World macro, and press the Run button.

You should now have a full understanding of how macros work and how to write them. Well, not really. You should have a clearer understanding of how to write macros, but you're probably wondering what type of macro you can write that is worth all the effort, right?

Creating a macro to display contact information

This next macro example might offer some more insight into the process. As you start using Outlook as more than just an e-mail client, you will probably start using many of the other features such as the Contact folder. The Contact folder contains detailed information about a person, assuming you have entered it in yourself or received a vCard from a correspondent. This next example will illustrate more than just a simple VBA command. A portion of Outlook's Object Model will be used to display some of the e-mail sender's information.

1. In the Macro dialog box, enter ShowSendersPhone and press the Create button.

2. In the VBE code window, enter the following code within the ShowSendersPhone procedure:

```
Sub ShowSendersPhone()
    Dim oApp As Outlook.Application
    Dim oExp As Outlook.Explorer
    Dim oSelected As Outlook.Selection
    Dim oItem As Outlook.MailItem
    Dim oNS As Outlook.NameSpace
    Dim oFldr As Outlook.MAPIFolder

    Dim x As Integer
    Dim sSenderName As String

    Set oApp = Outlook.Application
    Set oExp = oApp.ActiveExplorer
    Set oSelected = oExp.Selection

    If oSelected.Count <> 1 Then GoTo Exit_ShowSendersPhone

    Set oItem = oSelected.Item(oSelected.Count)
    sSenderName = oItem.SenderName

    Set oNS = oApp.GetNamespace("MAPI")
    Set oFldr = oNS.GetDefaultFolder(olFolderContacts)

    On Error GoTo Err_SenderNotFound

    With oFldr.Items(sSenderName)
        MsgBox .FirstName & " " & .LastName & vbCrLf _
            & .EmailAddress & vbCrLf _
            & .BusinessTelephoneNumber
    End With

Exit_ShowSendersPhone:
    Exit Sub

Err_SenderNotFound:
    MsgBox "Sender information not found", vbInformation, _
```

```
"Outlook Bible"
GoTo Exit_ShowSendersPhone

End Sub
```

3. To execute the macro, select an e-mail from the Outlook item list, open up the Macro dialog box, select the ShowSendersPhone macro, and press the Run button.

4. Assuming the person who sent the e-mail is in your Contact folder, you should see a message similar to the one in Figure 6-9.

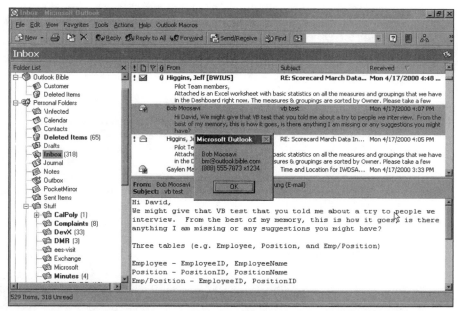

Figure 6-9: Show Sender's Phone message box displaying the sender's business phone number

The first set of declarations defines the variable names to members of the Outlook Object Model. The next set of declarations identifies the *x* variable to the Integer data type and sSenderName as the String data type.

Cross-Reference For more detailed information about the object model, refer to Chapters 2 and 3.

The Set statement instantiates the oApp object variable to the Application object member. The next Set statement assigns the oExp object variable to the ActiveExplorer object member assigned to the oApp object variable. The last Set statement assigns the oSelected object variable to the Selection object member.

The If-Then statement checks the Selection member's Count property assigned to the oSelected object variable. If the value does not equal 1, which would mean that either more than one or no e-mail message was selected, then the macro will exit the procedure. If only one e-mail is selected, the selected e-mail is assigned to the oItem object variable, which is assigned to the MailItem collection. Within the MailItem collection, the SenderName property contains the name of the sender of the e-mail you received. The sender's name is assigned to the sSenderName string variable.

The next Set statement assigns the oNS object variable to retrieve the active NameSpace using the GetNamespace method. The NameSpace is an object within Outlook object model that contain the messaging support. Then using the GetDefaultFolder method, the oFldr object variable is assigned to the Contact folder. The olFolderContacts constant is equal to 10, which is defined in the Microsoft Outlook 9.0 Object Library.

The On Error statement is used to help trap any errors that may occur from this point on. If an error does occur, the macro will jump to the Err_SenderNotFound subroutine within the macro.

Using the With statement, the macro searches through the oFldr collection for a matching value stored in the sSenderName string variable. If there is a match, the sender's information will be displayed in a message box. If there isn't a match, an error will be generated and the On Error statement will cause the procedure to execute the Err_SenderNotFound subroutine, displaying "Sender information not found" in a message box to provide the user some feedback that the sender is not in the Contact folder.

Accessing Macros

Accessing macros can be a bit cumbersome if you only access them through the Macro dialog box. A more effective way is to access the macros through the Outlook menu. Just like all Microsoft Office products, the Outlook menu is completely customizable. To customize the menu, proceed with the following steps:

1. Right-click the menu to bring up its context menu, and then select the Customize item, as shown in Figure 6-10.

Figure 6-10: Outlook menu's context popup menu

2. Select the Commands tab from the Customize dialog box.

3. To create a new menu item at the menu toolbar level, select New Menu in the Categories list box. Then in the Commands list box, click and drag the New Menu command to the Outlook menu toolbar as illustrated in Figure 6-11.

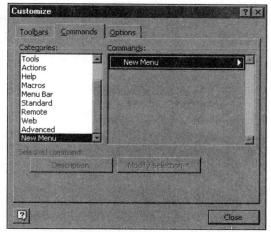

Figure 6-11: Adding a new menu to the Outlook menu toolbar

4. Once the menu has been added, its name is New Menu. To change the name to something more meaningful, right-click the newly placed menu item to bring up its context menu. Select the Name field and type in **Outlook Macros** as shown in Figure 6-12.

Figure 6-12: Context menu of new menu item

5. Select the Macros item in the Categories list box. This displays all the macros that are created in your Outlook environment. To add a macro to the "Outlook Macros" menu item, select the Project1.ShowSenderPhone macro we created in the previous section and drag it on top of the "Outlook Macros" menu item. The menu for the menu item will display, and you can drop the macro into it.

6. Changing the name of the macro is just like changing the name of the menu item. Right-click on the newly created menu item, Project1.ShowSenderPhone, and then select the Name field and change the description to **Show Sender's Phone**. You can change the icon associated with the macro, display just the name of the macro, and so on. For this example, we'll leave the properties to their default.

7. Select the Close button in the Customize dialog box to save the custom changes to the menu toolbar.

8. To run the macro, select an item in the Inbox message list and select the Show Sender's Phone macro item from the Outlook Macros menu item.

As you can see, this is a lot more efficient than selecting a message, pressing Alt-F8, selecting the macro, and pressing Run.

Rather than adding a bunch of macros to your menu bar, you can add them to an existing toolbar or create your own toolbar. To add a macro to existing toolbar, perform a step similar to step 5, but rather than placing the macro in the menu, place it on a toolbar of your choice.

To add your own toolbar to Outlook, click the main toolbar or menu bar with the right mouse button and select **Customize** from the context menu. This brings up the Customize dialog box. The Toolbar tab lists then names of all the available toolbars. Click to **New** button and provide a name for your toolbar in the New Toolbar dialog box. The newly created toolbar will appear as a floating toolbar. To add your macros to the toolbar, follow the same instructions outlined in step 5.

Understanding Macro Security

You will receive a security message every time you start the VBE once a form or module has been added to Outlook. This can be quite annoying for developers because it appears each time; however, you can change the VBA security setting. Select the Security submenu item within the Macro menu item under the Tools menu. By default, Macro Security is set to Medium, as shown in Figure 6-13. This setting lets users know that unsigned macros are contained within the Outlook environment.

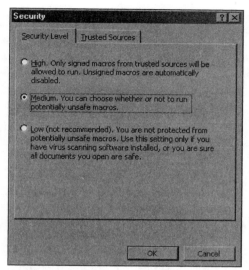

Figure 6-13: Outlook's Macro Security set to Medium by default

The High security level will only allow macros from trusted sources to be executed. You can use the Trusted Sources tab in the Security dialog box to add and delete trusted sources. The project or COM add-in that is added from a trusted source must be signed with a Digital ID. A Digital ID is a digital certificate that guarantees users that your macro project or COM Add-in came from a trusted source. There are several sources from which you can obtain digital certificates. To create a personal digital certificate, there's a program included on the Office 2000 CD-ROM called self-cert.exe. This allows you to certify your own macro code yourself. Your organization might have its own internal certification authority division that uses a product like Microsoft Certificate Server. This allows you create in-house digital certificates for your entire organization. Lastly, you can obtain commercial-class digital certificates from outside vendors, like Thawte or VeriSign. For up-to-date providers, check out Microsoft's Security Partners Web site at http://backoffice.Microsoft.com/securitypartners/default.asp.

The Low security level is not a recommended setting, simply because there are so many macro viruses floating around. It's not a good idea to leave your system unprotected. Microsoft only recommends using this setting if you have an anti-virus software that can scan your e-mail environment, but since new viruses are being created every day, there's no way to guarantee you're fully protected even if you have the latest virus pattern signatures.

Note   At the time this book was published, the ILOVEYOU virus had struck and infected millions of systems across the world. It was one of the fastest moving viruses to affect users since 1988 when Robert Morris, Jr. unleashed his Internet virus to the world. However, contrary to popular belief, the ILOVEYOU virus was not a VBA macro virus like its cousin, the Melissa virus. The virus was in fact a Windows Scripting Host (WSH) virus.

Due to all the potential hazards of macro viruses, you need to be very careful with your security settings. When receiving files from someone, don't assume they are virus free, even if they come from a reliable source. Sometimes it's good to be paranoid. As a developer, if you plan to distribute your Outlook macros, you may wish to consider obtaining the Digital ID or personal digital certificate.

Working with Class Modules

A class is a group of templates that can be created, commonly referred to as instantiated, into objects that fit a certain profile. Unlike UserForm modules, class modules do not support any user interface features. Class modules are similar to standard modules in that they support functions and procedures more suited to tasks that don't require any interface, such as performing calculations, access database information and so on, but that's where the similarities end.

The class module acts as a container that exposes code and selected variables inside it the same way you would access any function, method, or property within an object. You invoke class procedures and assign values to variables using the same syntax used for the properties and methods of objects. To use the code within a class module, you do not have to know anything about how it works. Also, since class modules expose properties, methods, and events like other objects do, any VBA developer or application that supports automation can use them.

A class module defines what interface the object presents to other objects and to you as the developer. The interface is the set of properties and methods for an object. The class also defines whether the object is public, and when it can be created. This is done through the class module's Instancing property. Unlike the Class module in Visual Basic, Microsoft Office's Class modules only contain two possible properties, Private and PublicNotCreateable, explained in greater detail in Table 6-3.

Additionally, class modules have two built-in events, `Initialize` and `Terminate`, that enable operations that need to take place at the opening and closing of a class instance. Standard modules do not have these events. They are private events that are visible only from within the class module.

Methods, which are procedures that the object performs, are the Function and Sub procedures. Just as in the standard module, they are declared as `Public`, but they can also be declared as Friend. Public methods can be used anywhere your class is visible. Friend methods can only be used within your project.

Table 6-3 Instancing Properties for the Class Module	
Property	Description
Private	Other applications are not allowed access to type library information about the class and cannot create instances of it. Private objects are only for use within your component.
PublicNotCreateable	Other applications can use objects of this class only if your component creates the objects first. Other applications cannot use the CreateObject function or the New keyword to create objects from the class.

In order to use a class module, you must first instantiate the object. This is the act of creating an object based on a class. An object is an instance of a class, the physical incarnation of the class. An object gets instantiated when you access a method or property, or when you create a new instance of that class using the New keyword.

```
Sub InstantiateObject()

    Dim oJobTicket As TroubleCall

    Set oJobTicket = New TroubleCall

    oJobTicket.FName = "Bruce"
    oJobTicket.Subject = "Can't run Windows"

End Sub
```

In the above example, the object is called TroubleCall and it assigned to object variable oJobTicket. From what you can see, it has at least two properties, FirstName and Subject.

Properties

Just like properties of an Outlook Control in the VBE toolbox, object properties are placeholders for data about a particular object. The properties are defined by the class to be used by each individual object instantiated by that class. Properties can either be made public or private, which is different from making the entire class public or private. When a property is public, it is exposed for use by other objects or code within the application. Private properties are only accessible to the object itself.

Methods

Methods are procedures or functions defined within a class. They can only be invoked through a corresponding object that's created as that type of class. They are typically used to change something about the object or tell the object to perform a certain action.

Class Module Creation

To add a class module to your Outlook application, select the Class Module item from the Insert menu in the VBE. After creating a class module shell, you can populate it with procedures and declarations, which equip it with custom properties and methods. In the following we'll take a look at how to create a simple class module.

Using the TroubleCall object as the example, use the following steps to create a new class.

1. Go into the VBE and insert a new Class Module to the default project.

2. Press F4 to set focus to the Properties window, and then set the Name property to **TroubleCall**.

3. Add the following Private data variables to the Class module in the General Declaration section:

   ```
   Private mlTroubleCallID As Long
   Private msFirstName As String
   Private msLastName As String
   Private msSubject As String
   Private msDesc As String
   Private mnResponseTime As Integer
   ```

   By defining these variables as Private, you are preventing them from being read or written to by any routine outside of this class module.

4. So to enable other modules within the project to read those private data variables, you need to add multiple Property Get procedures to the class module. Add the following Property Get procedures to the TroubleCall class.

   ```
   Property Get TroubleCallID() As Long
       TroubleCallID = mlTroubleCallID
   End Property

   Property Get FName() As String
       FName = msFirstName
   End Property

   Property Get LName() As String
       LName = msLName
   End Property
   ```

```
Property Get Subject() As String
    Subject = msSubject
End Property

Property Get Desc() As String
    Desc = msDesc
End Property

Property Get ResponseTime() As Integer
    ResponseTime = mnResponseTime
End Property
```

A `Property Get` procedure is similar to a function in that it returns a value to the procedure that calls it. To return a value from a function, you need to set the function name equal to the value it's supposed to return.

5. So that other modules can write values into the private data values, you need to use the `Property Let` procedure. A `Property Let` procedure is a routine that accepts one argument, the value to set. It should have the same name as the `Property Get` procedure. Add the following procedures to the class module.

```
Property Let TroubleCallID(ByVal lTroubleCallID As Long)
    mlTroubleCallID = lTroubleCallID
End Property

Property Let FName(ByVal sFName As String)
    msFName = sFName
End Property

Property Let LName(ByVal sLName As String)
    msLName = sLName
End Property

Property Let Subject(ByVal sSubject As String)
    msSubject = sSubject
End Property

Property Let Desc(ByVal sDesc As String)
    msDesc = sDesc
End Property

Property Let ResponseTime(ByVal nResponseTime As Integer)
    mnResponseTime = nResponseTime
End Property
```

Tip

You can use the Add Procedure dialog box, found under the Insert menu of the VBE, to add a new procedure to a module. It will create the basic `Property Get` and `Property Let` procedures in the module so you don't have to remember to type both in; however, all the data types are defined as Variant data types. If you change the data types from Variant to a different data type, make sure you change the data types in both the `Property Get` and `Property Let` procedures.

6. When a class module is first instantiated as an object, all the private variables are initialized to the default values appropriate for their respective data type. String data types are initialized as blank and numeric data types are set to 0. There may be instances where you would want the data type to be set to a specific value each time the object is instantiated. You can set these values in the Class_Initialize event.

```
Private Sub Class_Initialize()
    mlTroubleCallID = 1000
    mnResponseTime = 4
End Sub
```

In the above code, the TroubleCallID is seeded to start at 1,000 and the response time is set to 4, which represents four hours.

7. Now we need to create a form that will use the class module. Add a new UserForm to the Outlook project. Add the following controls and properties as outlined in Table 6-4. The result should look similar to Figure 6-14.

Table 6-4
Controls and Properties for the Trouble Call UserForm

Control	Property	Setting
UserForm	Name	frmTroubleCall
	Caption	Trouble Call
Label	Name	lblFName
	Caption	"First Name:"
Label	Name	lblLName
	Caption	"Last Name:"
Label	Name	lblSubject
	Caption	"Subject:"
Label	Name	lblDesc
	Caption	"Problem Description:"
TextBox	Name	txtFName
TextBox	Name	txtLName
TextBox	Name	txtSubject
TextBox	Name	txtDesc
	MultiLine	True
CommandButton	Name	cmdOK
	Caption	"OK"
CommandButton	Name	cmdCancel
	Caption	"Cancel"

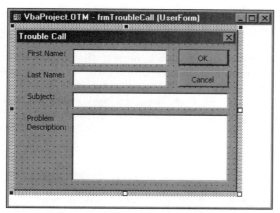

Figure 6-14: The Trouble Call UserForm at design time

8. Add the following code to the cmdOK command button's click event. In this procedure, it will instantiate the TroubleCall object, put data into the object, and display information to the user in a message box.

```
Private Sub cmdOK_Click()
    Dim oTroubleCall As TroubleCall
    Dim sMsg As String

    Set oTroubleCall = New TroubleCall

    oTroubleCall.FName = txtFName
    oTroubleCall.LName = txtLName
    oTroubleCall.Subject = txtSubject
    oTroubleCall.Desc = txtDesc

    sMsg = oTroubleCall.TroubleCallID & vbCrLf
    sMsg = sMsg & oTroubleCall.LName & ", "
    sMsg = sMsg & oTroubleCall.FName & vbCrLf
    sMsg = sMsg & "Subject: " & oTroubleCall.Subject & vbCrLf
    sMsg = sMsg & "Problem: " & oTroubleCall.Desc & vbCrLf
    sMsg = sMsg & "Response Time: " &
oTroubleCall.ResponseTime
    MsgBox sMsg, vbInformation, "Trouble Calls - " _
        & "Outlook Prog Bible"

End Sub
```

9. Add the following code to the cmdCancel command button's Click event to close the form when this button is pressed.

```
Private Sub cmdCancel_Click()
    Unload Me
End Sub
```

Save your work and you are now ready to try it. Enter information into the text box fields and press the OK button. The information you entered will be displayed in a message box, similar to the one shown in Figure 6-15. One way to see how everything works is to place a breakpoint on one of the lines in the cmdOK command button's `Click` event and then step through the procedure. To set a breakpoint within the code, place the cursor on the line of code you want to stop on and press the F9 key and the line will be highlighted. By default, breakpoints are highlighted in red. To remove the breakpoint, place the cursor on the line with the existing breakpoint and press F9 key. Stepping through your code is the process of watching each line of code execute by pressing the F8 key. Each time you press F8, the VBE will execute the next line of code.

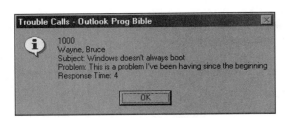

Figure 6-15: Message box displaying information entered in the Trouble Call UserForm

Developing Outlook Applications

A macro is the simplest form of building applications and expanding Outlook's capabilities. By using Outlook as a foundation for your application you can create a complete customer relationship management (CRM) and sales force automation (SFA) system.

For example, say you have an SFA system from Moss Software (http://www.mosssoftware.com) or Siebel Systems (http://www.siebel.com) that has an integrated Web interface for customers to enter contact information into. The data that is captured from the Web site goes into a Microsoft SQL Server database table. All your sales personnel use Outlook as their contact manager and e-mail client. You can develop an Outlook application that retrieves new contact information from the database and creates a new contact, task, and journal entry. These entries notify the sales personnel that they need to make contact with the person who requested information about their product or service. This can all happen in real time as long as your sales representative is connected to the network directly or through a remote connection. Imagine the potential increase in sales and customer contact your company can realize by being able to respond to potential customers even before they leave your Web site.

The following section will cover using elements of the VBE to develop components that could potentially be integrated into a full Outlook Application solution.

Change the Area Code

As you fill your Contacts folder with your personal and professional contacts, you will probably at one point have to change some information across all your contacts. You're probably wondering what type of massive change would warrant an application for just changing elements of a contact, right? An increase in cellular phones and pagers in the workforce and in the home means that area codes change very frequently. That's the kind of change that might make you want an application for changing contact elements.

Since Outlook only provides a Find feature, doing a traditional find and replace is out of the question; therefore, in order to perform such a task, you need to develop a small application to do it for you.

1. Go into the VBE and insert a new UserForm to the default project.

2. Using the controls in the toolbox, place the controls and adjust their properties as listed in Table 6-5 on the UserForm. The UserForm should look similar to Figure 6-16 when you're done.

	Table 6-5	
Controls and Properties for the frmChangeArea UserForm		
Control	*Property*	*Setting*
UserForm	Caption	Change Area Code
	Name	frmChangeArea
Label	Caption	Old Area Code:
	Name	lblOldAC
Label	Caption	New Area Code:
Name	lblNewAC	
TextBox	Name	txtOldAC
	MaxLength	3
TextBox	Name	txtNewAC
	MaxLength	3
CommandButton	Caption	OK
	Default	True
	Name	cmdOK
CommandButton	Caption	Cancel
	Cancel	True
	Name	cmdCancel

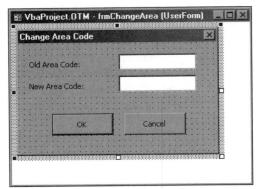

Figure 6-16: UserForm frmChangeArea at design time

3. Open the code window and enter the following code behind the cmdOK command button. To open the code window, either double-click the cmdOK command button or select it with the right mouse button and select View Code from the context menu. This code scans all the contacts within your Contacts folder and changes the area code of the contact's business telephone number, provided the phone number meets the Old Area Code search criterion. If you want to change the area codes of all the contact's telephone numbers that meet the search criterion, you would add the additional Replace functions with all the telephone properties.

```
Private Sub cmdOK_Click()

  On Error GoTo Err_cmdOK

  Me.MousePointer = fmMousePointerHourGlass

  If IsNumeric(txtOldZip) And IsNumeric(txtNewZip) Then
    Dim oApp As Outlook.Application
    Dim oNS As Outlook.NameSpace
    Dim oFldr As Outlook.MAPIFolder
    Dim oContact As Outlook.ContactItem
    Dim rc

    Set oApp = Outlook.Application
    Set oNS = oApp.GetNamespace("MAPI")
    Set oFldr = oNS.GetDefaultFolder(olFolderContacts)

    For Each oContact In oFldr.Items
      If InStr(oContact.BusinessTelephoneNumber, _
            txtOldZip) = 2 Then
        rc = Replace(oContact.BusinessTelephoneNumber, _
            txtOldZip, txtNewZip, 1, 1)
      End If
```

```
      Next
   End If

Exit_cmdOK:
   Me.MousePointer = fmMousePointerDefault
   txtOldZip = ""
   txtNewZip = ""

   Exit Sub

Err_cmdOK:
   GoTo Exit_cmdOK
End Sub
```

   4. Enter the following code in the cmdCancel command button's `Click` event. The code is used to close the form when you're done with the application.

```
Private Sub cmdCancel_Click()
    Unload Me
End Sub
```

   5. In order to access the application, you need an event that loads and displays the UserForm. In the Macro dialog box, create a macro called ChangeAreaCodes and enter the following code within the procedure. The procedure will show the form as Modal, which means that Outlook's focus is on the Change Area Codes application and no other Outlook function can be accessed as long as the UserForm is loaded.

```
Sub ChangeAreaCodes()
    frmChangeZip.Show vbModal
End Sub
```

When you execute the application, the frmChangeArea form is displayed. Type in the area code you're looking to replace in the Old Area Code textbox and enter the area code you want to replace it with in the New Area Code textbox. Then press the OK button to execute the find and replace.

First, the procedure checks to see if the values entered into the text boxes are numeric. If they are, then the application instantiates the Outlook Application and its subsequent object models to their respected object variables.

The `For Each` statement loops through all the items within the Contacts folder collection. The Instr function searches for the Old Area Code value within each contact's business phone number. If the value is found starting at the second position within the phone number, the Old Area Code value was found where the area code should be, not within the phone number itself. You can use the Replace function to replace the old area code with the new area code.

Access Data using ADO

When it comes to developing Outlook applications, you will often want to work with data that does not reside within the Outlook environment. In a customer relationship management program, some of the data you will want to work with probably resides in a database management system like Oracle or SQL Server. In order to access the information, you will have to use a Microsoft Data Access Component (MDAC) such as DAO (Data Access Object), RDO (Remote Data Object), or ADO (ActiveX Data Object).

ADO is the latest database connectivity method from Microsoft. It is designed to provide a universal high-level data access method and is a collection of COM (Component Object Model) objects that can retrieve, update, and create records using any OLE DB data provider rather than using ODBC. OLE DB is a native driver layer that replaces ODBC. It came about because Microsoft discovered that developers weren't just accessing data from databases, but through other sources such as spreadsheets, documents, and e-mail. These sources are also known as OLE DB data providers. Application programs that access data by way of OLE DB interfaces are called OLE DB data consumers.

In the following example, we are going to use ADO to access an Access database and display the results in on a form.

1. Go into the VBE and insert a new UserForm to the default project.

2. Using the controls in the toolbox, place the controls and adjust their properties as listed in Table 6-6 on the UserForm. The UserForm should look similar to Figure 6-17 when you're done.

Table 6-6
Controls and Properties for the frmADO UserForm

Control	Property	Setting
UserForm	Name Caption	frmADO Biblio Authors
Label	Caption Name	Authors: lblAuthors
ListBox	Name	lstAuthors
CommandButton	Caption Name	All Authors cmdAllAuthors
CommandButton	Caption Name	Top 10 Authors cmdTopAuthors
CommandButton	Caption Name	Cancel cmdCancel

Figure 6-17: Outlook displaying an ADO resultset in a custom UserForm

3. Add the following code to the cmdAllAuthors command button Click event. The mouse pointer will change to an hourglass while the procedure is being executed. It then calls the procedure DisplayAuthors and passes the name of the listbox control to the procedure. Before the procedure is exited, the mouse pointer is set back to the default pointer.

```
Private Sub cmdAllAuthors_Click()
    Me.MousePointer = fmMousePointerHourGlass
    Call DisplayAuthors(lstAuthors)
    Me.MousePointer = fmMousePointerDefault
End Sub
```

4. Add the following code to the cmdTopAuthors command button Click event. The mouse pointer will change to an hourglass while the procedure is being executed. It then calls the procedure DisplayAuthors and passes the name of the listbox control to the procedure. In addition, the second parameter is a switch for the DisplayAuthors procedure that will be described in greater detail in step 7. Before the procedure is exited, the mouse pointer is set back to the default pointer.

```
Private Sub cmdTopAuthors_Click()
    Me.MousePointer = fmMousePointerHourGlass
    Call DisplayAuthors(lstAuthors, True)
    Me.MousePointer = fmMousePointerDefault
End Sub
```

5. Add the following code to the cmdCancel command button's Click event. This will close the UserForm and unload it from memory.

```
Private Sub cmdCancel_Click()
    Unload Me
End Sub
```

6. Before you continue, since we know that we are going to use ADO as our database access model, we need to reference the ADO object model within our project. To add the reference to the ADO object model, select References from the Tools menu. In the References dialog box, scroll until you find the Microsoft ActiveX Data Object object library and mark the check box, as shown in Figure 6-18.

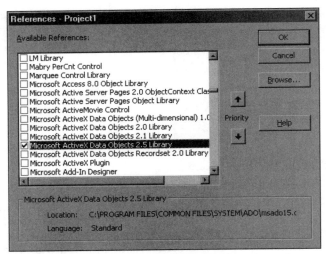

Figure 6-18: Reference dialog box with the Microsoft ActiveX Data Object 2.5 object model selected

Note

The latest ADO object model is version 2.5. This object model comes installed with Microsoft Windows 2000, Microsoft Internet Explorer 5.5, or you can download it from the Microsoft Universal Data Access Web site at http://www.microsoft.com/data. You don't need the latest object model for this example; therefore, you can use ADO object model that is installed on your system.

7. If there isn't already one, add a new Module to the project. In the module, add the DisplayAuthor procedure. This procedure accepts two arguments, a control variable and a Boolean variable. The control argument is used to determine the control the ADO resultset will populate. The second argument, the Boolean argument, is optional and by default is set to False. This argument is used to determine which query should be used against the data source: Should the entire set of authors be retrieved or only the top 10 authors?

To connect to the Access database, the procedure is using a DSN-less connection string. A DSN (data source name) provides your Windows environment with the information necessary to connect to a data source. Defining a DSN in the ODBC administrator allows you create a single connection path that more than one application can use. For this example, we are using a DSN-less connection that means that we are defining all the connection parameters with our application.

Note

That database connection string assigned to the sConn string variable assumes that your copy of the biblio.mdb resides in the Visual Studio directory. If your copy resides anywhere else, change the connection path in the DBQ parameter accordingly.

Once the connection to the data source has been made, the control is cleared and the query is executed, based on the Boolean argument. If the EOF (end-of-file) flag is true, then that means that no information was returned by the query. If data was returned, the Do While statement will iterate through the result set until the EOF flag is reached. Each record that is returned is added to the control that was passed to the procedure.

```
Sub DisplayAuthors(ctrl As Control, _
    Optional bSubset As Boolean = False)

    Dim cn As ADODB.Connection
    Dim rs As ADODB.Recordset

    Dim sConn As String
    Dim sSQL As String

    sConn = "Driver={Microsoft Access Driver (*.mdb)}; " _
        & "DBQ=c:\progra~1\micros~2\VB98\biblio.mdb;" _
        & "UID=Admin;PWD=;"

    Set cn = New ADODB.Connection
    cn.Open sConn

    ctrl.Clear

    If bSubset = False Then
        sSQL = "SELECT * FROM AUTHORS "
    Else
        sSQL = "SELECT TOP 10 * FROM AUTHORS"
    End If

    Set rs = New ADODB.Recordset
    rs.Open sSQL, cn
    Do While Not rs.EOF
        ctrl.AddItem rs(1)
        rs.MoveNext
    Loop
    rs.Close
    Set rs = Nothing

End Sub
```

8. In order to access the application, you need an event that loads and displays the UserForm. In the Macro dialog box, create a macro called DisplayAuthors and enter the following code within the procedure. The procedure will show the form as Modal, which means that Outlook's focus is on the Display Authors application and no other Outlook function can be accessed as long as the UserForm is loaded.

```
Sub DisplayAuthors()
    frmADO.Show vbModal
End Sub
```

When you execute the application, the frmADO form appears. Press either the All Authors or Top 10 Authors command button. If you press the All Authors buttons, the application returns all the names of the authors within the biblio.mdb file. If you press the Top 10 Authors command button, the application will return the first 10 records in the biblio.mdb file.

Showing just the top ten records within the entire table doesn't offer a lot of information. If the biblio.mdb file contained more information like the Pubs database that comes with Microsoft SQL Server, you could write a more sophisticated query that returned the top 10 authors' names based on revenues generated, number of books sold, and so on.

The examples shown in the chapter merely touch the surface of what you can do with macros, VBA, UserForms, and so on. If you're developing any applications that require contact or e-mail capabilities, using Outlook as part of your application solution can definitely help you shorten your development lifecycle. As you will see in Chapter 7, Outlook can be integrated with other Microsoft Office applications as well as any application that supports VBA.

One of the biggest hurdles you will have to overcome as an Outlook application developer is that the Outlook Object Model is very sophisticated in the way it is broken down. On one side of the coin, it offers a very rich set of methods and collections to choose from that make it very flexible. However, its flexibility is also one of its faults. If you plan to get information based on one folder, the development path is very straightforward, but if you need to get information from a folder based on information received from another folder, the different branches of the object model become your worst nightmare. Essentially what you have to do is take the information that you have, go up the Object Model hierarchy to the top of the model, and then go back down into the branch of information you were trying for.

Don't let that hurdle stop you from trying to develop applications using Outlook. Since many companies are using Outlook as their e-mail and contact management software, integrating applications like a help desk, SFA, CRM, or digital dashboard with Outlook will aid in reducing the amount of time to train employees on new software. A company can reduce its total cost of ownership (TCO) because its employees already know their way around Outlook; also, using Outlook technology to deploy an application with a similar look and feel as Outlook helps reduce the amount of training needed as well as software deployment and maintenance costs.

Categorizing E-Mail

One of the features that Outlook offers is the ability to group your contacts by a category or categories. Rather than trying to make a distribution list, it can be just as efficient to send an e-mail to your contacts who are grouped by specific category.

To assign a category to a contact, open an existing contact or new contact and press the Categories button in the lower right-hand corner of the Contact form as illustrated in Figure 6-19. When you click on the button, the Categories dialog box lists all the categories you have defined on your system. The categories in the list-box are stored on your computer within a System Registry entry and are referred to as the Master Category List. When you click on the Master Category List button, you can add, modify or remove any category. If you don't want a category to be part of the master list, simply enter any category you wish. When you look at the category list, the category the contact is assigned to will be depicted as **not in Master Category List**, as shown in Figure 6-20.

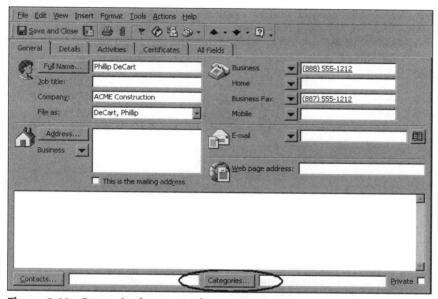

Figure 6-19: Categories button on the Contact form

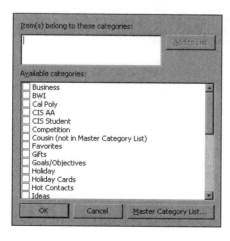

Figure 6-20: Categories dialog box with a Category not in the Master Category List

Within Outlook, if you want to send an e-mail to all contacts based on their category, the only way you can do this is by viewing all your contacts by category and selecting and dragging the category onto the Inbox folder. The following application will help automate the process.

In the following example, we are going to create the application that will display all the Master categories and allow you to send a mass mailing to your contacts based on the category selected.

1. Go into the VBE and insert a new UserForm to the default project.

2. This project is going to require an ActiveX Control that's not part of the standard toolbox. First, you need to have a UserForm displaying in the VBE. To add the control, select the Additional Controls menu item from the Tools menu. From the Additional Controls dialog box, as shown in Figure 6-21, mark the following control to add to the toolbox: Microsoft Common Dialog Control, version 6.0.

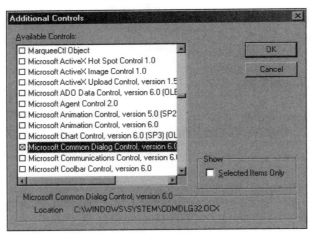

Figure 6-21: Additional Controls dialog box to add ActiveX controls to the project

3. Using the controls in the toolbox, place the controls and adjust their properties as listed in Table 6-7 on the UserForm. The UserForm should look similar to Figure 6-22 when you're done.

Table 6-7
Controls and Properties for the frmMailByCat UserForm

Control	Property	Setting
UserForm	Name	FrmEmailByCat
	Caption	"E-Mail By Category"
OptionButton	Name	OptTo
	Caption	"To:"
	Accelerator	T
	GroupName	GrpSend
OptionButton	Name	optCC
	Caption	"CC:"
	Accelerator	c
	GroupName	grpSend
OptionButton	Name	optBCC
	Caption	"BCC:"
	Accelerator	b
	GroupName	grpSend
Label	Name	lblMasterCatList
	Caption	"Master Category List"
ListBox	Name	lstMasterCatList
CommandButton	Name	cmdSend
	Caption	"Send"
	Default	True
CommandButton	Name	cmdCancel
	Caption	"Cancel"
Label	Name	lblSubject
	Caption	"Subject:"
TextBox	Name	txtSubject
TextBox	Name	txtMessage
	MultiLine	True
Label	Name	lblAttachedFile
	Caption	"Attached File:"
	Accelerator	A
TextBox	Name	txtAttachedFile
CommandButton	Name	cmdAttachedFile
	Caption	"..."
CommonDialog	Name	dlgAttachedFile
	DialogTitle	"Attached File"

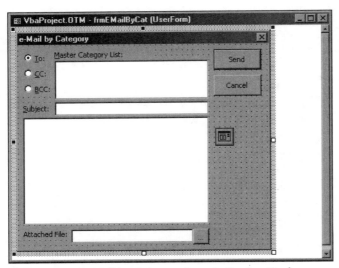

Figure 6-22: E-Mail by Category form in Design Mode

The way you groupoption buttons in VBA applications are different then the way you would group them in a Visual Basic applications. The GroupName property allows you to group option buttons by the same name. In VB, and older editions of VBA, you would have to group option buttons by placing them within a Frame control. You can still group them this way; however, screen design is more cumbersome because you first have to draw the frame, and then make sure you draw the option buttons within the frame, not just on top of it. Later, if you decide to remove the frame, you have to select all the option buttons within the frame, cut them to the clipboard and paste them outside of the frame. If you were just to delete the frame, the option buttons would go with it.

The Accelerator property provides keyboard accelerators to fields. In VB and older editions of VBA, you would place an ampersand (&) before the character you wanted to use as the keyboard accelerator, and the resulting caption would have an underscore under the letter.

4. To populate the Master Category List listbox, we need to extract that information from the Windows Registry. The categories are stored in the Registry as one continuous string. Within the Do loop, each category is extracted from the string and placed in a variant array. The result is then sent to the FillControl function that will be described in detail in the next step.

```
Private Sub UserForm_Initialize()

    Dim sCatFromReg As String
    Dim nCatLen As Integer
    Dim nPrevComma As Integer
    Dim nNextComma As Integer
```

```
Dim nCtr As Integer
Dim vValues() As Variant

nPrevComma = 1
sCatFromReg = GetOutlookCategories
nCatLen = Len(sCatFromReg)

Do Until nPrevComma > nCatLen
    ReDim Preserve vValues(nCtr)
    nNextComma = InStr(nPrevComma, sCatFromReg, ";")
    vValues(nCtr) = Mid(sCatFromReg, nPrevComma, _
        nNextComma - nPrevComma)
    nCtr = nCtr + 1
    nPrevComma = nNextComma + 1
Loop

Call FillControl(lstMasterCatList, vValues)

End Sub
```

5. Add the following code to the UserForm. The FillControl procedure will fill the control specified in the **cntl** Control variable using the values in the array that is passed to the control.

```
Sub FillControl(cntl As Control, sArray())

    On Error GoTo Handler
    Dim i As Long
    cntl.Clear
    If IsArray(sArray) Then
        For i = 0 To UBound(sArray)
            cntl.AddItem sArray(i)
        Next
    End If
    Exit Sub
Handler:
    Select Case Err.Number
        Case 13:
            Resume Next
    End Select

End Sub
```

6. Add the following code to the cmdAttachedFile command button's `Click` event. When a user clicks on this button, the common dialog box will display to allow them to select a file they wish to attach to the message. The file name and its path with are stored in the txtAttachedFile textbox.

```
Private Sub cmdAttachedFile_Click()

    dlgAttachedFile.Action = 1
    txtAttachedFile = dlgAttachedFile.FileName

End Sub
```

7. Add the following code to the cmdSend command button's `Click` event. First it checks to make sure the Subject and Message textboxes contain material. Then it determines how the message is to be sent. The last thing that is checked is if a category has been selected. If all the conditions pass, the message is sent.

```
Private Sub cmdSend_Click()

    Dim x As Integer
    Dim y As Integer
    Dim nSendType As Integer
    Dim cntl
    Dim rc as Integer

    ' Check the Subject and Message text boxes
    If txtSubject.Text = "" Or _
        txtMessage.Text = "" Then
        MsgBox "Subject and/or Message fields cannot be " _
            & "left blank.", vbCritical, _
                "E-Mail by Category - Outlook Prog Bible"
        Exit Sub
    End If

    frmEMailByCat.MousePointer = fmMousePointerHourGlass

    ' Determine which Send option is chosen
    If optTo.Value = True Then
        nSendType = olTo
    ElseIf optCC.Value = True Then
        nSendType = olCC
    Else
        nSendType = olBCC
    End If

    ' Check to see if a category is selected
    ' If so, then send send to category
    For x = 0 To lstMasterCatList.ListCount - 1
        If lstMasterCatList.Selected(x) = True Then
            rc = SendMailToCat(lstMasterCatList.List(x), _
                nSendType)
        End If
    Next

    ' Reset form
    If rc Then
        optTo.Value = True
        lstMasterCatList.ListIndex = -1
        txtSubject.Text = ""
        txtMessage.Text = ""
    Else
        MsgBox "No Category was selected", vbInformation, _
                "E-Mail By Category - Outlook Prog Bible"
```

```
        End If

        frmEMailByCat.MousePointer = fmMousePointerDefault

    End Sub
```

8. Add the following code to the cmdCancel command button's `Click` event. When the button is pressed, the form will unload from memory, terminating the application.

```
Private Sub cmdCancel_Click()

    Unload Me

End Sub
```

9. Add a Standard Module to the project and add the following code to the General Declaration section. The following is code for the program to use Windows API (application programming interface) functions to retrieve information from the Windows Registry.

```
' Declare Public variables.
' ----Begin Get 32 Bit Registry Entry Value Declarations----
Const HKEY_CURRENT_USER = &H80000001
Const ERROR_SUCCESS = 0&
Const REG_DWORD = 4
Const REG_BINARY = 3
Const REG_SZ = 1
Const REG_EXPAND_SZ = 2 ' Unicode nul terminated string
Const ERROR_NONE = 0
Const ERROR_BADDB = 1
Const ERROR_BADKEY = 2
Const ERROR_CANTOPEN = 3
Const ERROR_CANTREAD = 4
Const ERROR_CANTWRITE = 5
Const ERROR_OUTOFMEMORY = 6
Const ERROR_ARENA_TRASHED = 7
Const ERROR_ACCESS_DENIED = 8
Const ERROR_INVALID_PARAMETERS = 87
Const ERROR_NO_MORE_ITEMS = 259
Const KEY_ALL_ACCESS = &H3F
Const REG_OPTION_NON_VOLATILE = 0

Declare Function RegOpenKeyEx Lib "advapi32.dll" _
    Alias "RegOpenKeyExA" (ByVal hKey As Long, _
    ByVal lpSubKey As String, ByVal ulOptions As Long, _
    ByVal samDesired As Long, phkResult As Long) As Long
Declare Function RegCloseKey Lib "advapi32.dll" _
    (ByVal hKey As Long) As Long
Declare Function RegQueryValueExString Lib "advapi32.dll" _
    Alias "RegQueryValueExA" (ByVal hKey As Long, _
    ByVal lpValueName As String, ByVal lpReserved As Long, _
```

```
        lpType As Long, ByVal lpData As String, _
        lpcbData As Long) As Long
Declare Function RegQueryValueExLong Lib "advapi32.dll" _
    Alias "RegQueryValueExA" (ByVal hKey As Long, _
    ByVal lpValueName As String, ByVal lpReserved As Long, _
    lpType As Long, lpData As Long, lpcbData As Long) As Long
Declare Function RegQueryValueExNULL Lib "advapi32.dll" _
    Alias "RegQueryValueExA" (ByVal hKey As Long, _
    ByVal lpValueName As String, ByVal lpReserved As Long, _
    lpType As Long, ByVal lpData As Long, lpcbData As Long) _
    As Long
Declare Function RegQueryValueEx Lib "advapi32.dll" Alias _
    "RegQueryValueExA" (ByVal hKey As Long, _
    ByVal lpValueName As String, ByVal lpReserved As Long, _
    lpType As Long, lpData As Any, lpcbData As Long) As Long
```

10. Add the following function to the module. The GetOutlookCategories will
    retrieve Windows Registry data for Outlook's Master Category list. The key
    is found in the HKEY_CURRENT_USER hive.

```
Function GetOutlookCategories() As String

    Dim sKey As String
    Dim sVal As String
    Dim sCategories As Variant

    ' Set Key and Value to lookup.
    sKey = "Software\Microsoft\Office\9.0\Outlook\Categories"
    sVal = "masterlist"

    ' Check for user specified Start-Up Path.
    sCategories = QueryValue(sKey, sVal)

    GetOutlookCategories = sCategories

End Function
```

11. Add the following function, QueryValue, to retrieve the specified Registry
    entry passed in its arguments.

```
Public Function QueryValue(sKeyName As String, _
    sValueName As String)

    ' This function, in conjunction with the QueryValueEx
    ' Function will return a specified registry entry.

    Dim rc As Long        ' Result of the API functions.
    Dim hKey As Long      ' Handle of opened key.
    Dim vValue As Variant ' Setting of queried value.

    rc = RegOpenKeyEx(HKEY_CURRENT_USER, sKeyName, 0, _
        KEY_ALL_ACCESS, hKey)
```

```
        rc = QueryValueEx(hKey, sValueName, vValue)
        QueryValue = vValue
        RegCloseKey (hKey)

    End Function
```

12. Add the following function, QueryValueEx, which will use help obtain the Registry value passed from the QueryValue function.

```
Function QueryValueEx(ByVal lhKey As Long, _
    ByVal szValueName As String, vValue As Variant) _
    As Long

    ' This function, in conjunction with the
    ' QueryValue Function will return a specified
    ' registry entry.

    Dim cch As Long
    Dim rc As Long
    Dim lType As Long
    Dim lValue As Long
    Dim sValue As String

    On Error GoTo Err_QueryValueEx

    ' Determine the size and type of data to be read
    rc = RegQueryValueExNULL(lhKey, szValueName, 0&, _
            lType, 0&, cch)
    If rc <> ERROR_NONE Then Error 5
    Select Case lType
        ' For strings
        Case REG_SZ:
            sValue = String(cch, 0)
            rc = RegQueryValueExString(lhKey, szValueName, _
                0&, lType, sValue, cch)
            If rc = ERROR_NONE Then
                vValue = Left$(sValue, cch - 1)
            Else
                vValue = Empty
            End If
        Case REG_EXPAND_SZ:
            sValue = String(cch, 0)
            rc = RegQueryValueExString(lhKey, szValueName, _
                0&, lType, sValue, cch)
            If rc = ERROR_NONE Then
                vValue = Left$(sValue, cch - 1)
            Else
                vValue = Empty
            End If
        Case REG_DWORD:
            rc = RegQueryValueExLong(lhKey, szValueName, _
```

```
                           0&, lType, lValue, cch)
                 If rc = ERROR_NONE Then vValue = lValue
            Case Else
                'all other data types not supported
                rc = -1
        End Select

    Exit_QueryValueEx:
        QueryValueEx = rc
        Exit Function
    Err_QueryValueEx:
        Resume QueryValueExExit
    End Function
```

13. Add the following function, SendMailToCat, to the module. This function is will create the new mail item to be sent to all contacts that match the category that was selected on the UserForm.

```
Function SendMailToCat(sCategory As String, _
    nSendField As Integer) As Integer

    Dim oApp As Outlook.Application
    Dim oNS As Outlook.NameSpace
    Dim newMail As Outlook.MailItem
    Dim oContactFldr As Outlook.MAPIFolder
    Dim oContact As Outlook.ContactItem
    Dim oItems As Outlook.Items

    Dim sFilter As String
    Dim bAddrFilled As Boolean

    ' Return a reference to the Outlook application
    ' and MAPI layer.
    Set oApp = Outlook.Application
    Set oNS = oApp.GetNamespace("MAPI")

    ' Create a new mail message item.
    Set newMail = oApp.CreateItem(olMailItem)
    With newMail
        ' Add the subject of the mail message.
        .Subject = frmEMailByCat.txtSubject.Text
        ' Create some body text.
        .Body = frmEMailByCat.txtMessage.Text

        ' Add a recipient and test to make sure that the
        ' address is valid using the Restrict method.
        Set oContactFldr = oNS.GetDefaultFolder _
            (olFolderContacts)
        Set oItems = oContactFldr.Items
        ' Put only contacts in the collection
        sFilter = "[MessageClass] = 'IPM.Contact'"
        Set oItems = oItems.Restrict(sFilter)
```

```vb
        ' Iterate through each contact
        For Each oContact In oItems
            If InStr(oContact.Categories, sCategory) Then
                bAddrFilled = True
                With .Recipients.Add(oContact.EmailAddress)
                    .Type = nSendField
                    If Not .Resolve Then
                        MsgBox "Unable to resolve address.", _
                            vbInformation
                        Exit Sub
                    End If
                End With
            End If
        Next

        ' Attach a file as a link with an icon.
        If Len(frmEMailByCat.txtAttachedFile) Then
            Dim nBackSlashPos As Integer
            Dim nFileNameLen As Integer
            With .Attachments.Add _
                (frmEMailByCat.txtAttachedFile.Text, _
                    olByReference)
                ' Get the filename to be displayed
                ' under the icon
                nBackSlashPos = InStrRev _
                    (frmEMailByCat.txtAttachedFile, "\") + 1
                nFileNameLen = Len _
                    (frmEMailByCat.txtAttachedFile)
                .DisplayName = Mid _
                    (frmEMailByCat.txtAttachedFile, _
                        nBackSlashPos, nFileNameLen)
            End With
        End If

        If bAddrFilled Then
            'Send the mail message.
            .Send

            MsgBox "Message sent!", vbInformation, _
                "E-Mail by Category - Outlook Prog Bible"
        Else
            MsgBox "There are no Contacts that match " _
                & "the category, " & sCategory, _
                vbInformation, _
                "E-Mail by Category - Outlook Prog Bible"
        End If
    End With

    ' Release references
    Set oApp = Nothing
    Set oNS = Nothing
```

```
    Set newMail = Nothing

    SendMailToCat = True

End Sub
```

In previous versions of Outlook, distribution lists were not stored within the Contacts folders. They were part of your personal address book and stored within the PAB file. As you can guess, Microsoft has changed that by now, and stores them in the Contacts folder. This causes a problem when you use statements like the following:

```
Dim oContact As Outlook.ContactItems
...
For Each oContact In oContactFolder.Items
```

The items in the oContactFolder.Items collection contain more than just contact information now. A "type mismatch" run-time error will occur when you try to process any oContact item because it is expecting contact information, not distribution list information. The remedy for this is to use the Restrict method to only include items in the collection whose MessageClass property is set to IPM.Contact.

At this point, save your work and give it a try. When you run it, select where you want the addresses to go (To, CC, or BCC). Then select the category you wish to send the message to. Type in the subject and message, attach a file if you'd like, and then press the Send button. Obviously, in order for this to work, one or more of your contacts need to be associated with the category you selected.

Distributing Outlook VBA Projects

You just created an Outlook application solution for your organization and you want to distribute it to your user base. Unfortunately, unlike other Microsoft Office applications, Outlook can only support one VBA project at a time. The project, Project1, is available and associated with Outlook at all times. It is not possible to add another project file to the VBE, regardless of what you call the project.

Outlook's project file is called VbaProject.OTM, even if you change the project name within the VBE. On a system using Windows 9x, the location of the file is typically found in the following directory:

```
<drive letter>:\Windows\Application Data\Microsoft\Outlook
```

The <drive letter> depends on which drive your Windows operating system is installed on. On systems that have user profiles enabled, the file is located in the following directory:

```
<drive letter>:\Windows\Profiles\<name>\Application Data\
Microsoft\Outlook
```

The <name> is the name of the user profile. On Windows NT, the Windows directory is usually named WinNT.

When it comes time to distribute your application, it's best if you rename the file to something descriptive so you and your users know what file they are receiving. The user will need to rename the file VbaProject.OTM in order to use it with their Outlook client. Obviously if you just copy your VbaProject.OTM over an existing one, all code and forms contained within it will be lost; therefore, be mindful of where you copy the file to.

Another method to distribute your application would be to export all the modules within the Outlook project, package them, and copy them to your users. Once your users receive them, the files can be imported into the user's VbaProject.OTM.

Working with COM

In Chapter 8, you will learn about a new technology for adding functionality to Outlook 2000, called COM-Ins. This section has nothing to do with that, other than the fact that they share part of the same name — COM. COM stands for Component Object Model. It is a general architecture that lays the foundation on which OLE and ActiveX are based. It establishes a common model for interaction among software, like applications, library modules, system software, and more. Therefore, COM can be implemented with almost any kind of software technology using the guideline layout.

Understanding OLE and ActiveX

Now for a quick overview of what OLE and ActiveX technologies are, just in case you missed out on the past Microsoft technology years of renaming and reinventing. Prior to Microsoft Windows, in order to share the information of one application with another, you had to save data to a file and then import it into the target application. This technique was very time-consuming and not very efficient.

As the Windows operating system matured, so did its application data interchange. Microsoft introduced the ability of *dynamic data exchange (DDE)*. DDE was the means of communication between Microsoft Windows applications. It acts as a conduit for the exchange of data between connected applications. The data exchanged may either be information copied from one application to another or commands or keystrokes from the other application to process.

As with all technology, there was room for improvement. Microsoft later introduced *object linking and embedding (OLE)*. OLE gave your application the power to directly use and manipulate another Windows application's data in its native format. If the other application supported OLE automation, you might also have been able to use its objects, properties, and methods just as you would with a Visual Basic control.

OLE automation, later to be known as just *Automation*, was introduced in Visual Basic 3.0 and was one of the most important additions to Windows; it served as the basis for creating a true object-oriented environment. Applications like spreadsheets and word processors have a lot of features that can be useful to other applications. Mail merge and spellchecking features built into a word processor that you might take advantage of within your application, and by using Automation, you can integrate those features into your applicaiton.

In 1996, in Microsoft's rush to establish its Internet presence, it introduced a new term to the world of developers: *ActiveX*. When ActiveX was first introduced, it was believed to be a variation of OLE, and its technology was for Internet and Internet-based applications. As the technology became more defined and the dust started to settle, the development world soon realized that wasn't just a variation of OLE; it was OLE itself, only redefined. ActiveX included the OLE implementation but also improved on it by extending capabilities to take advantage of the Internet. The original OLE design did not include any Internet specifications.

After all the hoops and learning curves Microsoft put developers through, it decided that OLE and ActiveX were two different sets of technology after all. OLE remained the technology that referred to working with compound documents. Custom controls became know as ActiveX controls, in-process servers became ActiveX DLLs and out-of-process servers became ActiveX EXEs.

When it comes to Microsoft technology, Microsoft writes Microsoft history. It will claim that no matter what technology was introduced first, building component-based applications has always been its goal. OLE and ActiveX were just introduced first because the technology was mature enough. The component-based architecture that Microsoft has always been trying to promote has been COM. A COM object is made up of a standard interface of methods and properties that define the functions and store data. Methods for the Customer interface may include CreditCheck, to check the customer's credit, and GetBalance, to calculate and retrieve the customer's current balance. Properties of the Customer interface might include name, address, and phone number. COM objects are each assigned a *globally unique identifier*, more commonly known as GUID (pronounced GOOid) at the time the component is compiled, which is a meansof differentiating one COM object from another. By using GUIDs, a calling program can be certain that the COM object it is communicating with is the correct one. Once a COM object has been defined and published, any program that uses the object is relying on this consistency.

Given all this, you might be asking yourself "What does this have to do with Outlook development?" As a matter of fact, COM has a lot to do with Outlook development. Many of the objects that Outlook interacts with are built with COM objects. For example, in one of the previous examples we used ADO, which is a COM object.

Referencing COM Objects

Before you can use the events, methods, and properties of a COM component, you must first instantiate, or create an instance of, the component. To do this, you must declare a local object variable to hold a reference to the component, and then assign a reference to the component to the local object variable. You can use two methods to do this: *early binding* and *late binding*.

Early binding

Early binding is the most efficient method of accessing a COM component, also referred to as an object. Early binding is more efficient than late binding because it directly references the type library of the object before the project is compiled. This gives you access to all the events, methods, and properties, and loads the object within the same memory space as the instantiating application. To provide early binding for an object, you must use the References dialog box to add a reference to the object to your project. Once the object is referenced, you can instantiate the object by one of two methods:

```
Dim oObjBinding As New ObjectName.Class
```

or

```
Dim oObjBinding as ObjectName.Class
Set oObjBinding = New ObjectName.Class
```

Either method is acceptable, but the latter is the more efficient method for instantiating objects. The purpose of binding is to instantiate an object and declare an object variable. By using the first method, you create an instance of the object as soon as the object variable is declared. The problem with this is that the object is in memory the entire time the host application is running. If the user never chooses the option or function that uses the object, you've wasted quite a number of resources that could have been used by other processes or programs. The latter method declares the object to an object variable and the Set statement instantiates the object when the object is needed. This also provides you with a method of controlling when an object is loaded into memory or not, thus maintaining control over the object and the resources it may use.

Late binding

In cases where the object you are trying to reference doesn't provide a type library, or when you're not sure at design time precisely which object you might need to reference, you can simply declare an object variable as *Object*, rather than using the name of the object. The CreateObject function is used to instantiate the object for use. The following code is an example:

```
Dim oObjBinding As Object
Set oObjBinding = CreateObject("ObjectName.Class")
```

Visually, you might think there is no difference between using the New keyword and the CreateObject function with the exception of explicitly stating which object you plan to instantiate. In reality, that is the difference. Late binding causes your code to execute slower as well as making your development process slower. It executes more slowly because the application does not "bind" to the object's interface until after it executes. This means that the object's events, methods, or properties aren't available to you during development. The VBE IntelliSense Auto List Member/statement completion feature won't assist you in creating your application because it doesn't know anything about the object. If you're not familiar with the Auto List Member, it's a feature that lists the methods and properties that relate to an object or the list of objects you can reference in a dropdown list box. Figure 6-23 illustrates the dropdown list box after the user has typed just five letters.

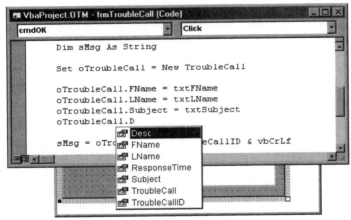

Figure 6-23: Auto List Member showing referenced object starting with "d"

By using the Auto List Member during development you get immediate feedback about the objects you can reference and their properties and methods. There are developers out there who remember all the properties and methods of an object, but for those who don't, this feature saves time spent looking them up in the online help file or manual. If you attempt to reference a property or method that is not in the dropdown list box, you can almost certainly bet that it doesn't exist.

Building COM

A lot of what you've already seen in this chapter provides you with an opportunity to interact with COM components. The real power of COM comes from the fact that any COM-enabled application can use the component. As you saw in the section

"Working with Class Modules," that object can only be used within Outlook. Also, as Outlook application, there can only be one VbaProject.OTM running at a time. If you distribute your VbaProject.OTM to everyone in your organization, then you have to redistribute the file to everyone every time you make a change. If the user has made any additions or modifications to the VbaProject.OTM file, they will be lost if you just blindly replace the file. The solution is to determine if any of the features can be placed within a reusable COM object that resides outside the Outlook environment.

You can build a COM component with any COM-compliant programming tool, including Visual Basic, Visual C++, Delphi, and even assembly language. This means that you can leverage your knowledge of a programming language rather than having to learn C or C++ and Exchange Client Extensions.

For this exercise, you're going to need a copy of Visual Basic to create the COM component and it's going to be in the form of an ActiveX DLL. The COM component is going to be based on the Class module we made earlier.

1. Launch Microsoft Visual Basic and from the New Project dialog box, select ActiveX DLL. When it creates the project, the VB's IDE (interactive development environment) will display a project with a Class module identified.

2. In the Project window, select the project, Project1. Press F4 to bring up the Properties window and name the project HelpDesk.

Note

If you did the Class module exercise before and saved the project in your VbaProject.OTM, you can save yourself a lot of typing by exporting the TroubleCall class module and adding the file to the VB project. If you do this, change the Class module's `Instancing` property to `5 – MultiUse` and proceed to Step 8.

3. In the Project window, select the Class1 class module, and then press F4 to display the Properties window of the class module, and set the `Name` property to **TroubleCall**. Unlike Outlook, Visual Basic's class modules have more properties associated with them. In order to make this object available to other applications, you need to set the `Instancing` property to `5 – MultiUse`.

4. Add the following Private data variables to the Class module in the General Declaration section:

```
Private mlTroubleCallID As Long
Private msFirstName As String
Private msLastName As String
Private msSubject As String
Private msDesc As String
Private mnResponseTime As Integer
```

By defining these variables as Private, you are preventing them from being read or written to by any routine outside of this class module.

5. In order for other modules within the project to read private data variables, we need to add multiple Property Get procedures to the class module. Add the following Property Get procedures to the TroubleCall class.

```
Property Get TroubleCallID() As Long
    TroubleCallID = mlTroubleCallID
End Property

Property Get FName() As String
    FName = msFirstName
End Property

Property Get LName() As String
    LName = msLName
End Property

Property Get Subject() As String
    Subject = msSubject
End Property

Property Get Desc() As String
    Desc = msDesc
End Property

Property Get ResponseTime() As Integer
    ResponseTime = mnResponseTime
End Property
```

A Property Get procedure is similar to a function in that it returns a value to the procedure that calls it. To return a value from a function, you need to set the function name equal to the value it's supposed to return.

6. For other modules to write values into the private data values in the class module, you need to the Property Let procedure. A Property Let procedure is a routine that accepts one argument, the value to set. It should have the same name as the Property Get procedure. Add the following procedures to the class module.

```
Property Let TroubleCall(ByVal lTroubleCall As Long)
    mlTroubleCall = lTroubleCall
End Property

Property Let FName(ByVal sFName As String)
    msFName = sFName
End Property

Property Let LName(ByVal sLName As String)
    msLName = sLName
End Property

Property Let Subject(ByVal sSubject As String)
    msSubject = sSubject
End Property
```

```
Property Let Desc(ByVal sDesc As String)
    msDesc = sDesc
End Property

Property Let ResponseTime(ByVal nResponseTime As Integer)
    mnResponseTime = nResponseTime
End Property
```

Note You can use the Add Procedure dialog box found under the Insert menu of the VBE to create the basic `Property Get` and `Property Let` procedures; however, all the data types are defined as Variant data types.

7. When a class module is first instantiated as an object, all the private variables are initialized to the default values appropriate for their respective data types. String data types are initialized as blank and numeric data types are initialized to 0. There may be instances where you would want the data type to be set to a specific value each time the object is instantiated. You can do this in the `Class_Initialize` event.

```
Private Sub Class_Initialize()
    mlTroubleCallID = 1000
    mnResponseTime = 4
End Sub
```

In the above code, the TroubleCallID is seeded to start at 1,000 and the response time is set to 4, which represents four hours.

8. Press the F5 key to execute the project. The first time you do this, you will be prompted to determine how you want to the project to be executed, as shown in Figure 6-24. This is because other programs usually invoke ActiveX DLLs, in this case Microsoft Outlook, and this tells the component how to act when instantiated.

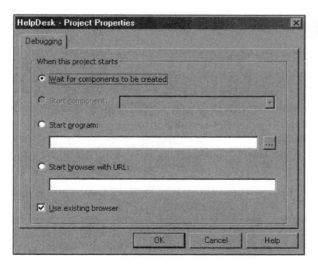

Figure 6-24: Debugging property settings the first time the COM Component is executed within the VB IDE

You can change the behavior at any time by selecting the Debugging tab from the Project Properties dialog box.

9. Go back to Outlook's VBE and create the user interface that will use the COM component. Add a new UserForm the Outlook project or use the form you created when you did the Class module exercise. If you're using the form created earlier, you can bypass this step. Add the following controls and properties as outlined in Table 6-8. The result should look similar to Figure 6-25.

Table 6-8
Controls and Properties for the Trouble Call UserForm

Control	Property	Setting
UserForm	Name	frmTroubleCall
	Caption	Trouble Call
Label	Name	lblFName
	Caption	"First Name:"
Label	Name	lblLName
	Caption	"Last Name:"
Label	Name	lblSubject
	Caption	"Subject:"
Label	Name	lblDesc
	Caption	"Problem Description:"
TextBox	Name	txtFName
TextBox	Name	txtLName
TextBox	Name	txtSubject
TextBox	Name	txtDesc
	MultiLine	True
CommandButton	Name	cmdOK
	Caption	"OK"
CommandButton	Name	cmdCancel
	Caption	"Cancel"

10. In order to use the COM component you created in VB, you need to reference it in the References dialog box. Select Tools ⇨ References to display the dialog box. Scroll down the list of references until you see HelpDesk on the list, like the References dialog box in Figure 6-26.

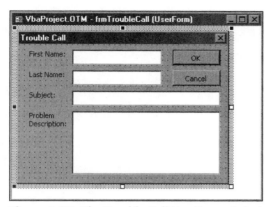

Figure 6-25: The Trouble Call UserForm at design time

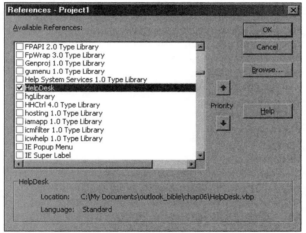

Figure 6-26: References dialog box with the HelpDesk you created highlighted

11. Add the following code to the cmdOK command button's Click event. In this procedure, it will instantiate the TroubleCall object, put data into the object, and display information to the user in a message box. This is the exact same code used in the previous Class module exercise with the exceptions highlighted in bold.

```
Private Sub cmdOK_Click()

    Dim oTroubleCall As HelpDesk.TroubleCall
    Dim sMsg As String

    Set oTroubleCall = New HelpDesk.TroubleCall
```

```
oTroubleCall.FName = txtFName
oTroubleCall.LName = txtLName
oTroubleCall.Subject = txtSubject
oTroubleCall.Desc = txtDesc

sMsg = oTroubleCall.TroubleCallID & vbCrLf
sMsg = sMsg & oTroubleCall.LName & ", "
sMsg = sMsg & oTroubleCall.FName & vbCrLf
sMsg = sMsg & "Subject: " & oTroubleCall.Subject & vbCrLf
sMsg = sMsg & "Problem: " & oTroubleCall.Desc & vbCrLf
sMsg = sMsg & "Response Time: " &
oTroubleCall.ResponseTime
MsgBox sMsg, vbInformation, "Trouble Calls - " _
    & "Outlook Prog Bible"

End Sub
```

The first part of the object declaration defines the name of the COM component and the second part is the name of the object model you wish to reference within the component.

12. Add the following code to the cmdCancel command button's `Click` event to close the form when this button is pressed.

```
Private Sub cmdCancel_Click()
    Unload Me
End Sub
```

Save your work and you are now ready to try it. Enter information into the text box fields and press the OK command button. The information you entered will be displayed in a message box.

Now what you need to do is create the ActiveX DLL as a standalone component. To do this, toggle back to the VB IDE. Select File ➪ Make HelpDesk.dll, which will invoke the Make Project dialog box. For this exercise, simply press the OK button. The IDE will generate a GUID for the COM component and register the component into your Windows Registry.

Part of the Windows Registry entry of the COM Component is the location where the component is installed. If you plan to move the file on your system, the best thing to do is remove the Registry entry using REGSVR32.EXE. To do that, type the following at a DOS prompt:

```
regsvr32 /u helpdesk.dll
```

Move the file to where you want it and reregister the component. In a DOS prompt, change to the directory where you moved the file and use the following command:

```
regsvr32 helpdesk.dll
```

When you deploy this COM component to your users, it's best that you include it within a distribution package using either Visual Studio's Package and Deployment Windows, Windows Installer, or a third-party installer like InstallShield or Wise InstallMaster. You want to deploy COM components this way because you never know if the target system has all the necessary or up-to-date support files that the component may rely on.

This section's exercise showed how to access the COM component through early binding techniques. Rather than having to worry about deploying the COM component to every user, you can use the late binding technique and store the COM component on a shared server. This way more than one type of application can use the component, you don't need to ensure that all the users have the latest copy of the component for any of their applications that use it to work, and if the component needs to be updated, you only need to update one source component.

In order to use the late binding technique, you only need to change two lines of code. And they're the two lines of code that were set in bold.

```
Dim oTroubleCall As Object

Set oTroubleCall = CreateObject("HelpDesk.TroubleCall", _
    "\\batcomputer\sharedres\")
```

What changed is that the object variable is defined as the Object data type, and you need to use the CreateObject function to instantiate the object, HelpDesk. TroubleCall. Also, because the component is stored on a file server, you need to tell the CreateObject function where on the network the component is stored. In this instance, the server's name is Batcomputer and the directory it resides in is called Sharedres. You would need to change this argument depending on your network environment.

Summary

One of the most significant improvements Microsoft has included in Outlook 2000 is finally including VBA for developers and general users alike to extend the capabilities of Outlook. You can create a simple macro to very sophisticated Outlook applications that access database information, COM components, and the like. The one drawback of all of this is that you are limited to only one VbaProject.OTM file at a time. Either you incorporate all your projects into one VbaProject.OTM file, or you rename and switch files when you need them, but that can be pretty frustrating over time.

When working with COM components in a multi-user environment, it would make more sense to centralize their location so that everyone could access the same component from his or her Outlook applications. The caveat is that if the user is not connected to the network and if he or she is required to use the Outlook application in a disconnected fashion, you will run into problems.

Learning how to create Outlook applications isn't very difficult to do since VBA is included with the software. There are a number of good books on the subject of using VBA to develop application with Office products, and if you've done any macro development with any of the other Office products like Word or Excel, you're already familiar with how it works. All of this means that you can be on your way to productivity in very little time.

✦   ✦   ✦

Integrating Outlook 2000 with Microsoft Office

◆ ◆ ◆ ◆

In This Chapter

Automation Primer

Office Automation

Outlook and
Visual Basic

◆ ◆ ◆ ◆

Long before Microsoft had come up with their first version of the graphical user interface we know today as the Windows operating system, software companies tried to offer integrated suites of word processor/spreadsheet/database programs, such as Microsoft Works, Lotus Symphony, and WordPerfect Executive. Sadly, no matter how much software companies tried, the integrated programs were never as good and full-featured as the standalone, non-integrated counterparts. Integration with other standalone applications was a very costly process because programs were "closed" environments, which meant that they only talked to programs that were made by the same company, and even then there was no guarantee of integration. Early on, even Microsoft programs were closed systems. It was difficult for one application to work with another one.

Automation Primer

With Windows 3.0, Microsoft introduced the concept of Dynamic Data Exchange (DDE). This was their first attempt to allow applications to talk to one another without having to completely understand how each worked. In a DDE conversation, the application that creates the link is known as the *destination* application, and the application that responds is known as a *source* application. (These terms used to be referred to as *client* and *server*, respectively). Any application that supports DDE can serve as either a source or a destination. One application can serve as both a destination and a source with several other applications at the same time.

Later, seeing that the world of software development was becoming more object-oriented, Microsoft and several other independent software vendors, or ISVs, created an open design specification that enabled applications to communicate with one another in a more integrated fashion. The specification also defined a programming interface that would enable an application to use another application's objects. This design specification was known as OLE, which stands for Object Linking and Embedding. Microsoft preached the virtues of OLE to developers with the claim that OLE was a major technology for modern applications. In its infancy, OLE represented the capability to link and embed documents from one application to another. Over time, OLE grew into several standards for interprocess communication, object storage, and object reuse.

Although both OLE and DDE enable you to share data and issue commands between two different applications, there are fundamental differences in how they do it and in how thoroughly the link is implemented. To discuss these differences, we must define two terms. The *originating application* is the application program that is providing services (data or functionality). The *container application* is the application that presents the information or functionality provided by the originating application. Any of the Microsoft Office products can be either an originating or container application.

OLE

Before you start looking at all the major technologies that make up OLE, study a few OLE terms to make the discussion more meaningful:

✦ Compound documents — documents that contain data from more than one application.

✦ OLE object — stores data in the object or links to a compound document that the data is stored in, such as a spreadsheet, a word-processing document, or a sound file.

✦ Automation — this makes it possible for one application to manipulate objects implemented in another application, or to *expose* objects so they can be manipulated.

✦ Visual editing — allows objects to be edited within the host application without switching to another application.

Compound documents

Prior to OLE, you would have to cut and paste any relevant information from one document to another when any information changed, you would have cut and paste again. Through OLE, the information is as up to date as the sources — that is, the compound documents — because all the information from the other sources is linked to the main document.

OLE object

An OLE object can be a receptacle that data is stored in itself or linked to within a compound document. Linking lets you use another application's data while leaving the data available for other programs to work with. The data remains on the disk as a separate file, stored in its normal, native format. It is available for editing by the original application or any other application that can read it. If the source file's information is updated, any container application that is linked to the information will also reflect the updated information.

Embedding lets you completely control the data. No other application can directly access the information. The object in your container application contains the actual data, as well as an image of what the data looks like for display within your document. If the data embedded in the container application came from an external source like a spreadsheet or database, any changes to the external source will not be realized by an embedded object.

Automation

Automation (technology formerly known as OLE Automation and ActiveX Automation) is a component of an OLE application that allows you to expose a set of functions that other applications can use. Applications like spreadsheets and word processors have a lot of features that can be useful to other applications. Mail merge and spellchecking are features built into a word processor that you might want to take advantage of from within your application.

Visual editing

Almost all OLE-complaint applications have their own menu and toolbar systems. Visual editing is a term that relates to a client application inheriting the menu and toolbar system of the server application. Figure 7-1 provides an example of Visual editing. In this example, the container application is Microsoft Word and the originating application is Microsoft Excel. You will note that although the container application is Microsoft Word, the menu and toolbar systems belong to Microsoft Excel. The menu and toolbar systems will stay that way as long as the chart has been activated for editing. Visual editing allows the server application, in this example Microsoft Excel, to execute within Microsoft Word. Without visual editing, you would have to run Microsoft Excel independent from Microsoft Word to edit the information.

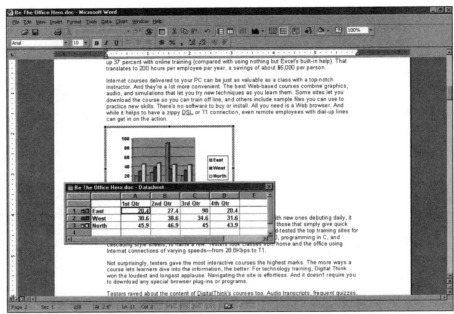

Figure 7-1: Example of visual editing with Microsoft Word and Microsoft Excel

ActiveX

So how does ActiveX technology fit into all this? In 1996, as part of its drive to establish an Internet presence, Microsoft introduced a new term to the development world: *ActiveX*. When ActiveX was first defined, Microsoft gave developers the impression that it was a variation of OLE. As it turned out, ActiveX technology included, but it was not limited to, OLE.

Component Object Model

In order to understand where OLE and ActiveX came from, where they are now, and where they are going, you need to understand a Microsoft model for building objects. This model is called the *Component Object Model*, better known by its acronym, COM. It is a general architecture that lays the foundation on which OLE and ActiveX are based. It establishes a common model for interaction among software, like applications, library modules, systems software, and more. Therefore, COM can be implemented with any kind of software technology using its guidelines.

Cross-Reference See Chapter 6, "Referencing COM Objects," for more information on working with COM objects in your application.

Objects and Collections

To use Automation you need an understanding of *objects* and *collections*. Automation clients and servers consist of objects that represent different parts of an application. For example, Outlook has an Application object that represents the Outlook application itself, a NameSpace object that represents the root of the Outlook folders, a Folder object that represents particular Outlook folders such as the Inbox, and Item objects that represent, depending on the type of item, mail messages, task requests, appointments, or contact information.

For example, say you needed to write an application that would help publishers notify authors of their status on receiving royalties for books sold. The application would access Outlook through Outlook's Application object to provide the publisher with contact information about their authors. However, accessing Outlook is not enough. The book royalty application also needs to create an Outlook mail item, add a message to the item, and direct the message to recipients. It does so through the *properties*, *methods,* and *events* of objects.

A property is a characteristic of an object. For example, a MailItem object has a Body property whose value is the text of the mail message, such as "No royalties, you owe us." This property can be used to *return* the value of the text in the subject line so you can programmatically read this value. You could use the ability to return the value of the Body property to find, among all mail messages in the Inbox, those containing particular text, such as the word "royalties."

The Body property can also be *set*, which means that you can programmatically assign the text of the message. This would be useful in, for example, automated mass e-mailings. However, some properties are *read-only*, which means they can return but not set a value. For example, a MailItem object's ReceivedTime property, which indicates when a mail message was received, is read-only since when an item was received is an objective fact that should not be altered through code.

A method is an action that the object may take. For example, a MailItem object has a Send method that sends the mail message. This method accomplishes programmatically that which the user may do repeatedly by clicking the Send button.

A method may have one or more parameters. A parameter is information that the method needs to perform its action. Some methods do not require parameters. For example, the Send method sends the MailItem object that calls that method; no further information is required. Other methods do require parameters. For example, the Move method moves a MailItem object to a different folder. This method requires as a parameter the Folder object to which the MailItem object is to be moved.

An event tells an object that something is happening to it. Perhaps the most commonly used event is a CommandButton object's Click event. You can write code in the CommandButton object's Click event procedure, and this code will run when the button is clicked.

Objects in Microsoft Office 2000 applications also have events. For example, a Mail Item object has a Send event that occurs when the item is sent, either by the user clicking the Send button or by code in which the item's Send method is called. This relationship between the Send method and the Send event is not unusual between methods and events. Often a method will cause a corresponding event to occur, or "fire." While a method enables an object to do something, an event tells the object that something is happening to it. Events also can be used to prevent a method from completing. For example, you can write code in the Send event procedure to cancel the sending of a message if the user did not fill out certain required fields.

Applications often contain more than one of a given object. For example, Outlook has several Folder objects, for the Inbox, Outbox, Contacts, Tasks, and so on. These Folder objects are part of a Folders collection. Similarly, the Inbox may contain numerous MailItem objects. These objects are part of the Items collection belonging to the Inbox folder, which belongs to the Folders collection.

A collection is a container for objects, usually the same kind of object. The MailItem object just discussed may be one of many mail messages in an Inbox or other folder. Each Folder object has an Items collection, which contains all of the MailItems and any other Item objects in the folder. Additionally, the mail message about book royalties has three recipients, the two co-authors and their literary agent. Each is a Recipient object, and these three Recipient objects are contained in the Recipients collection of the MailItem object. Further, the mail message may have attachments, such as an Excel spreadsheet showing the royalty calculation. Each attachment is an Attachment object, and the attachments are contained in the Attachments collection of the MailItem object.

A collection may have its own properties, methods, and events. For example, the Items collection has a Count property whose value is the number of objects in the collection, an Add method to add items to the collection, a Remove method to remove objects from the collection, and an ItemRemove event that fires when an item is removed from the collection.

Object Models

The objects and collections of an Office application are contained in its *Object Model*. Whether you use Visual Basic to write an application that automates Office applications, or VBA to automate an Office application from inside another Office application or create a COM Add-In, you will need to access the Object Models of the Office applications.

 Cross-Reference   See Chapter 2, "The Gateway Objects — Application and NameSpace," for more information on object models.

Each Microsoft Office application has an object model. That object model consists of the public collections, objects, properties, methods, and events. Each Office application may also have private collections, objects, properties, methods, and events, but since these cannot be accessed programmatically, except perhaps by Microsoft, they are not considered part of the object model.

The object models of Microsoft Office applications have a hierarchical structure typical of applications that support Automation. This hierarchy of objects is comparable to Windows Explorer, in which the first level is the computer, the second level is the drives, the third level is the top-level directories of a drive, the fourth level is the subdirectories, and so on down to the files of a directory or subdirectory.

Using Outlook as an example, the top-level object in the Outlook object model is the Application object. This object is comparable to the computer in Windows Explorer. A next-level object is the NameSpace. This object is the root of the Outlook folders, and is comparable to a drive in Windows Explorer, the difference being that a computer has many drives whereas Outlook has only one NameSpace object. The NameSpace object contains folders such as Personal Folders or Public Folders that themselves usually contain other folders. These top-level folders are comparable to the top-level directories in Windows Explorer. You can use the top-level folders to access the folders they contain, such as the Inbox and Outbox. These contained folders are comparable to subdirectories (or subfolders) in Windows Explorer. Finally, folders contain Item objects, whether mail messages, task requests, appointments, or contact information. These Item objects are comparable to individual files in Windows Explorer.

In Windows Explorer, one method of accessing a file is "drilling down" through drives, directories, and subdirectories until you reach the file. Similarly, in Outlook, you can use the top-level Application object to access the second-level NameSpace object, which you can use to access the Folders collection, which in turn you can use to access individual MAPIFolder objects, each of which has an Items collection, which contains the folder's items, whether they are mail messages, contacts, appointments or other item types.

Consistent with the different functionality of the Microsoft Office applications, there are differences among their respective object models. However, the object models are also quite similar, so the example above with Outlook would not be that different from the others.

Referencing the Office Application

The first step in automating an Office application is to reference the application you want to automate. This reference makes the objects exposed by the Office application visible to your application.

You reference an Office application by setting a reference to the application's type library in the References dialog box. A type library is a file, usually with a .tlb extension though sometimes with a .dll or .exe extension, that provides information about a code component. The purpose of a type library is to be accessed by other applications seeking information about the object that is the subject of the type library, such as the object's properties and methods. Not all applications have a type library. Microsoft Schedule+ 95 is an example of an application without a type library. However, the Microsoft Office applications all have type libraries.

You open the References dialog box by clicking References on the Tools menu in the Visual Basic Editor. Several boxes pertaining to Visual Basic are checked automatically. You then check the box pertaining to the Microsoft Office application you wish to automate. For example, if you want to automate Outlook 2000, you will need to set a reference to the Microsoft Outlook 9.0 Object Library. Figure 7-2 shows the aftermath of setting references to several Office applications.

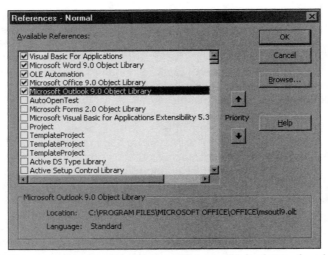

Figure 7-2: References dialog window with both Word and Outlook's object models selected

Note   You can check as many boxes as you want in the References dialog box. However, including unnecessary references will increase both the time it takes for your application to load and the memory used by your application.

Office Automation

With that out of the way, let's get busy. In Chapter 6 you learned that VBA is now part of Outlook 2000, which enables you to work with methods and properties contained not only within Outlook itself but within other applications as well. To work with the object models of other applications, there are three different methods you can use: New, CreateObject, or GetObject.

✦ New — Use the New keyword to create a new object as defined by its class. You can use New to create instances of forms, class modules, collections, or applications.

✦ CreateObject — Use the CreateObject function to create and return a reference to an object.

✦ GetObject — Use the GetObject function to return a reference to an object or create an instance of an application based on a file association.

In the following code fragment, an Application object variable is declared with the programmatic identifier for Word, which is Word.Application, and a new instance of Word is created with the Set statement and the New keyword.

```
Dim oWordApp As Word.Application
Set oWordApp = New Word.Application
```

Using the same programmatic identifier for Word, you can create a new instance of Word by using the CreateObject function. You can use the CreateObject function to provide early and late binding for development.

```
Dim oWordApp As Word.Application
Set oWordApp = CreateObject("Word.Application")
```

You can use the CreateObject function, unlike the New keyword, to instantiate an object that resides on a remote system as well.

```
Dim oWordApp As Word.Application
Set oWordApp = CreateObject("Word.Application", _
    "\\batcomputer\sandbox")
```

The GetObject function is similar to the CreateObject function in that it is used to return a reference to an instantiated object, but that's where the similarities end. Unlike the CreateObject function, the GetObject function also instantiates an object associated with an application by referencing a data file. In the following example, Visio will be instantiated because one of its data files is referenced.

```
Dim oVisio As Object
Set oVisio = GetObject("c:\mydocu~1\drawings\hq.vsd")
```

The GetObject function cannot be used to reference objects on a remote system and it cannot instantiate a new object by using the programmatic identifier. If you use the programmatic identifier and the object has not been instantiated, you will receive an error.

> **Tip** Use the `GetObject` function when there is a current instance of the object or if
> you want to create the object with a file already loaded. If there is no current
> instance, and you don't want the object started with a file loaded, use the
> `CreateObject` function.

Single-Instance vs. Multi-Instance Applications

Unlike the other Office 2000 applications, Outlook and PowerPoint are single-instance
applications. If an instance of either application is running and you use the `New` keyword or the `CreateObject` or `GetObject` function to instantiate an object variable,
that object will point to the currently running instance of the application. This single
instance of the Application object can contain any number of objects.

Freeing References to Objects

Every time you instantiate an instance of an object, it uses memory and system
resources. If the object you instantiate is a multi-instance application, every time
you invoke the `New` keyword or `CreateObject` function, additional resources are
used. It's a good programming practice to release the resources you instantiated
when you no longer need them. To unload a reference to an object variable, use the
`Nothing` keyword and assign it to the object variable by using the `Set` statement.

```
Set oOutlook = Nothing
```

Unfortunately, some applications don't release memory and resources completely,
thus causing what's known as memory and resource leaks. To illustrate, imagine your
computer is a wading pool, your computer's resources are the water in the pool, and
the objects that get instantiated are towels that get dropped into the pool. The more
towels you drop into the pool, the more the amount of available water decreases.
When you're done with the object, in this example the towels, you start freeing up
resources by setting them to `Nothing`. That is to say, you remove the towels and try
to squeeze out all the water they soaked up. When you've removed all the towels, you
will find that there is not as much water in the pool as when you started. That's what
happens with memory leaks. Therefore, don't use more resources than you should,
but also don't instantiate an object, use it once, release it, instantiate it, use it, release
it, and so on.

Using Automation with an Outlook Form

You can use Outlook forms for automation between applications that allow it. However, it won't be as easy to do because Outlook forms are limited to using VBScript
rather than VBA. Because VBScript and the Outlook object model do not support any
methods of running programs other than using `CreateObject` and `GetObject` methods, you are limited to these for instantiating objects. Listing 7-1 is an example of VBA
code to open an instance of Internet Explorer from within an Outlook form.

Listing 7-1: Automation code to open an instance of Internet Explorer from within an Outlook form

```
Sub Item_Open()
    Set oApp = Item.Application
    Set oWeb = oApp.CreateObject _
        ("InternetExplorer.Application")
    oWeb.Visible = True
    oWeb.Navigate "www.idgbooks.com"
End Sub
```

First, the Set statement creates space in memory for the object that is going to be instantiated. The next Set statement instantiates the object, which in this example happens to be Microsoft's Internet Explorer. Internet Explorer's Visible property is set to True so the user can see the browser load. The Navigate property is set to IDG's Web site URL.

Creating a new Contact with Automation

Since the word processor was first created, programmers have attempted to improve upon the mail merge feature. With Microsoft Word, performing a mail merge is very easy with data coming from a Microsoft Access database or Microsoft Outlook.

By using Microsoft Outlook as a contact manager, it's easy to perform a mail merge with information contained within the Contacts folder; however, this assumes that people you wish to have in the mail merge exist within your Contacts folder. Through the use of Automation, you can easily add the ability for any Office application to add a contact to Outlook's Contacts folder. For the following example, you will be adding this feature to Microsoft Word and adding an icon on Word's toolbar that will be used to access the feature.

First, you need to open Word. Once it's loaded, open its Visual Basic Editor (VBE) by selecting Tools ➪ Macros ➪ Visual Basic Editor or by pressing F11. Once the VBE is loaded, in the Project window, the default project entitled **Normal** is loaded. Then add a module for your code to be placed in by selecting Insert ➪ Module from the VBE menu. Add the Reference to the Outlook object model by selecting Tools ➪ References. In the References dialog window, select the Microsoft Outlook 9.0 Object Library. Listing 7-2 shows the code for the function that will allow you create a contact.

Listing 7-2: **CreateContact VBA code**

```
Function CreateContact()
    On Error GoTo Err_CreateContact

    Dim oOutlook As Outlook.Application
    Dim oContact As Outlook.ContactItem

    ' Create object
    Set oOutlook = New Outlook.Application

    ' Create and open a new contact form
    Set oContact = oOutlook.CreateItem(olContactItem)
    oContact.Display

    CreateContact = True

    ' Release Outlook object variable
    Set oOutlook = Nothing

Exit_CreateContact:
    Exit Function

Err_CreateContact:
    MsgBox Err.Number & " " & Err.Description
    CreateContact = False
    GoTo Exit_CreateContact

End Function
```

This function is fairly straightforward. First, it declares two object variables for Outlook classes, Application and ContactItem. Use the Set statement to create an instance of Outlook if one doesn't already exist. The next Set statement, using the instance of Outlook that has just been referenced, uses the CreateItem method to create a new contact item. The constant olContactItem is the reference for a Contact item. Table 7-1 lists all the possible constants that can then be used with the CreateItem method.

Table 7-1
Constants and Their Values for CreateItem Method

Constant	Value	Description
OlMailItem	0	Mail
OlAppointmentItem	1	Appointment item
OlContactItem	2	Contact item

Constant	Value	Description
OlTask	3	Task
OlJournalItem	4	Journal
OlNoteItem	5	Note
OlPostItem	6	Post

Next, the oContact object variable uses the Display method to open a new contact form in which you can enter a person's information. Assuming there are no errors during the function's execution, the return value of the function is set to True and control is returned to whatever procedure called the function. If an error occurs, the On Error routine will be activated and the error number and message will be displayed to the user. The return value will be set to False to notify the calling procedure that something didn't go right.

This function would be most accessible from a toolbar button. To add it to the toolbar, you first need to create a Word macro. To create a macro, bring up the Macro dialog window by selecting Tools ➪ Macros ➪ Macros. Press the Create button and the VBE will open back up. Enter the code in Listing 7-3 to create the macro that will call the CreateContact function.

Listing 7-3: **Macro code to call the CreateContact function**

```
Sub AddContact()

    Dim rc As Variant
    rc = CreateContact

End Sub
```

Change the name of the Macro module in the Project window to **macOutlookBible**, close the VBE and select Tools ➪ Customize from Word's menu bar. This will display the Customize dialog box. On the Commands tab, select Macros from the Categories list. In the Commands list, find the Normal.macOutlookBible.AddContact macro, and select the item with the left mouse button. The pointer will change so that there is a small bar at the tip and a small box at the base, as illustrated in Figure 7-3. Drag the selected item from the Standard toolbar and place it somewhere in the area next to Microsoft Drawing icon.

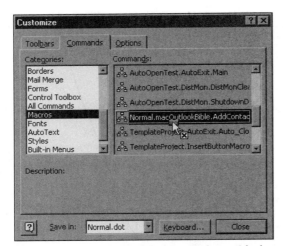

Figure 7-3: Customized dialog window with the mouse pointer showing the macro selected to be placed somewhere

At first, the name of the macro will be placed on the toolbar. To change that, while the Customize dialog window is still activated, select the macro name with the right mouse button. Its context menu will appear and you can change the name of the item in the Name property. Change it to "Add Contact." Also select the property Default Style and then select Change Button Icon to change the icon the macro is using on the toolbar. Since this macro is used to create a contact, select the icon that looks like an open phone book. Once you have done that, close the Customize dialog window, and your toolbar should resemble Figure 7-4.

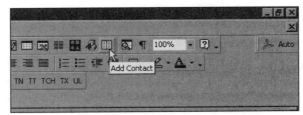

Figure 7-4: Placing the macro on the Standard toolbar

Making an Appointment through Automation

You or your company has chosen Outlook as a standard because it provides a lot of useful features other than just e-mail creation and retrieval. Among these features is the calendar, which is very useful for scheduling appointments. This next example will demonstrate how you can use Outlook's appointment feature within an Access application.

For this exercise, you will need to create a database using the schema provided in Table 7-2.

Table 7-2			
tblAppointments Table Schema			
Field Name	**Data Type**	**Size/Format**	**Required**
Appt*	Text	50	Yes
ApptDt*	Date/Time	ShortDate	Yes
ApptTm*	Date/Time	Medium Time	Yes
ApptLength	Number	Long Integer	Yes
ApptNotes	Memo	n/a	No
ApptReminder	Yes/No	n/a	No
ReminderMinutes	Number	Long Integer	No
AddedToOutlook	Yes/No	n/a	No

* denotes primary key

1. In Access's Database Object window, create a new form using the Columnar form wizard and base it on the tblAppointments table you just created. For readability, select each control and add the naming convention "txt" to the control name for textboxes and "chk" to the control name for checkboxes. Save the form as frmAppointments.

2. Open the form in Design view mode. Select the Form Header bar to give it focus in the Properties window. If the Properties window is not displayed, click anywhere on the open form with the right mouse button and select Properties from the context menu. Change the Form Header's Height property to .5 inches. Move the checkbox control, chkAddedToOutlook, to the Form Header area and set the Enabled property to False.

3. Draw a command button in the Form Header area. Use the properties denoted in Table 7-3.

Table 7-3
Properties for the Command Button in the Form Header

Control	Property	Value
Command Button	Name	cmdAddAppt
	Caption	"Send To Outlook"

When complete, your Access form should resemble Figure 7-5.

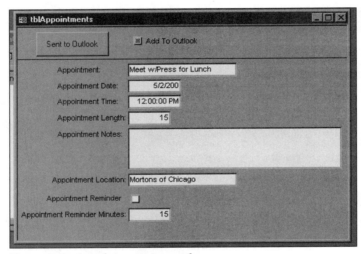

Figure 7-5: Appointment Access form

4. Add the reference to the Outlook 9.0 Object Library to the project. Then add the code in Listing 7-4 to the cmdAddAppt command button's Click event.

Listing 7-4: **Code for cmdAddAppt's Click event**

```
Private Sub cmdAddAppt_Click()

    On Error GoTo Err_cmdAddAppt_Click

    ' Save Record first to be sure required fields
    ' are filled in
    DoCmd.RunCommand acCmdSaveRecord
```

```
' Exit the proc if the appointment has already been
' added to Outlook
If chkAddToOutlook Then
    MsgBox "This appointment has already " & _
        "been added to Outlook."
    GoTo Exit_cmdAddAppt_Click
' Add a new appointment
Else
    Dim oOutlook As Outlook.Application
    Dim oAppt As Outlook.AppointmentItem
    Set oOutlook = New Outlook.Application
    Set oAppt = oOutlook.CreateItem(olAppointmentItem)
    With oAppt
        .Start = txtApptDt & " " & txtApptTm
        .Duration = txtApptLength
        .Subject = txtAppt
        If Not IsNull(txtApptNotes) Then
            .Body = txtApptNotes
        End If
        If Not IsNull(txtApptLocation) Then
            .Location = txtApptLocation
        End If
        If txtApptReminder Then
            .ReminderMinutesBeforeStart = _
                txtApptReminderMinutes
            .ReminderSet = True
        End If
        .Save
    End With
End If

' Release Outlook object variable
Set oOutlook = Nothing
' Set the AddedToOutlook flag, save the record, and
' display a message.
chkAddToOutlook = True
DoCmd.RunCommand acCmdSaveRecord
MsgBox "Appointment has been added."

Exit_cmdAddAppt_Click:
    Exit Sub

Err_cmdAddAppt_Click:
    MsgBox "Error: " & Err.Number & vbCrLf & Err.Description
    GoTo Exit_cmdAddAppt_Click

End Sub
```

Processing Folders and Messages

It's obvious that Outlook is good for handling e-mail to and from individuals. What happens if you're a small business and you receive a lot of e-mail monthly from Web site visitors who want to be on your e-mail newsletter? What about customers who have purchased items from your on-line store? Say you want to send out a mass e-mailing letting your current customer-base know that you just released a new program as well as updated your entire product line? Do you really want all of these customers and "looky-lous" in your Contacts folder? Not really, because you want to resource this folder for people that you correspond with on a very frequent basis, and you don't want to them to be mixed up.

The answer is get all the e-mail addresses that are stored in the e-mail message and place them in their respective database stored in Microsoft Access database. When it comes time to sending a bulk e-mail to either party, customers and/or newsletter recipients, you can use an Access form to create your message, the e-mail addresses would come from the database table you select, customer or newsletter, and the message would be sent out through Outlook.

There are third party programs that do this for you like MailKing, but for each customer entry, you have to key the person's information into the database by hand. That's fine if you only have a few entries a day or week. What happens if you go out of town and no one enters in the information? You will be spending a lot time doing data entry. Is that really time well spent?

Through automation and VBA, this task becomes very easy. You can write procedures that go through unread e-mail, line by line, and parse out the desired information and place it into their respective database field.

When organizing your folders, you might not have a folder hierarchy that's several levels deep before you get to the information you wish to process, but this example will use one to show how its done. Figure 7-6 is the example of the hierarchy used for this exercise. The personal folder is called "Outlook Bible". Underneath that is a folder called "Groups" which contains two folders: "PIBMUG" and "VB2Java". The folders that contain the information that needs processing are in the VB2Java folder.

In order to get to the folder you want, you will need to use the Folders object. It allows you to reference any folder that is visible within the Outlook folder list. In order to get to the folder you ultimately want to work with, you have to start at the topmost folder and work your way down. It's important to know that folder names are case sensitive and must exactly match the names as they appear in the Outlook folder list. Figure 7-7 offers an illustration of how to iterate through the Folders collection to get the desired folder. Use the following steps to complete this exercise.

1. Two tables need to be created for this exercise. One table is for the customers and the other for the people who wish to receive your e-mail newsletter. Use Table 7-4 for the attributes for the two tables you need to add the Access database you're going to use for this exercise.

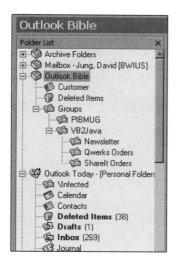

Figure 7-6: Outlook Folder List – Outlook Bible hierarchy tree

Figure 7-7: Illustration of iteration through the Folders collection

Table 7-4
Table schemas for Bulk E-Mail exercise

Table Name	Field Name	Data Type	Size/Format	Required
TblCustomers	ID*	Autonumber		Yes
	emailaddr	Text	50	
TblNewsletter	ID*	Autonumber		Yes
	emailaddr	Text	50	

* denotes Primary Key

2. In the Database Objects windows, add a form that is going to be used as your data entry form to send e-mail to people in your database. This form is also going to be used to launch the process that is going to retrieve the e-mail address from any unread e-mail from the folder hierarchy described above.

Use Table 7-5 for the properties and values of the objects you will be placing on the project's form. Try to make the layout of your form match Figure 7-8.

	Table 7-5 Objects and Properties for this Project's Form	
Object	**Property**	**Value**
Form	Caption	"Bulk Email"
	Default View	Single Form
	Views Allowed	Form
	Scroll Bars	No
	Navigation Buttons	No
Option Group	Name	fraEmailType
	Caption	"Email Type"
	Default Value	2
Option Button	Name	optNewsletter
	Option Value	1
Option Button's Label	Name	lblNewsletter
	Caption	"Newsletter"
Option Button	Name	optCustomer
	Option Value	2
Option Button's Label	Name	lblCustomers
	Caption	"Customers"
Text Box	Name	txtSubject
Text Box's Label	Caption	"Subject:"
Text Box	Name	txtMsg
Text Box's Label	Caption	"Message:"
Text Box	Name	txtAttachPath
Text Box's Label	Caption	"Attachment:"
Command Button	Name	cmdSendMsg
	Caption	"Send Message"
Command Button	Name	cmdGetEmailAddr
	Caption	"Get Email Address"
Command Button	Name	cmdExit
	Caption	"Close Form"

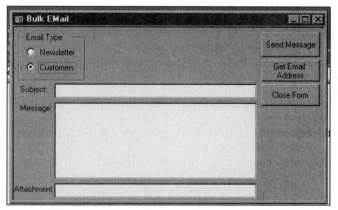

Figure 7-8: Bulk e-mail form at run time

3. Add the code shown in Listing 7-5 to the `Click` event of the cmdGetEmailAddr command button.

Listing 7-5: **Get e-mail addresses from the body of messages received from specific folders**

```
Private Sub cmdGetEmailAddr_Click()

    Dim oOutlook As Outlook.Application
    Dim oMapi As Outlook.NameSpace
    Dim ofMainFolder As Outlook.MAPIFolder
    Dim ofGroups As Outlook.MAPIFolder
    Dim ofVB2Java As Outlook.MAPIFolder
    Dim ofSection As Outlook.MAPIFolder
    Dim ofItem As Outlook.Items

    Dim cn As ADODB.Connection
    Dim rs As ADODB.Recordset
    Dim sConn As String

    Dim nItems As Integer
    Dim sMsg As String
    Dim nLoc As Integer
    Dim nLen As Integer
    Dim sEMailAddr As String
    Dim x As Integer

    ' Bind the object variables to Outlook and its
    ' object model
```

Continued

Listing 7-5 *(continued)*

```
Set oMapi = oOutlook.GetNamespace("MAPI")
Set ofMainFolder = oMapi.Folders("Personal Folders")
Set ofGroups = ofMainFolder.Folders("Groups")
Set ofVB2Java = ofGroups.Folders("VB2Java")
' Work with the Newsletter or Customers folder
If fraEmailType.Value = 1 Then
    Set ofSection = ofVB2Java.Folders("Newsletter")
Else
    Set ofSection = ofVB2Java.Folders("Qwerks Orders")
End If

' Obtain the number of item in the given folder
nItems = ofSection.Items.Count
Set ofItem = ofSection.Items

' Create ADO connection to the database
Set cn = New ADODB.Connection
sConn = "Driver={Microsoft Access Driver (*.mdb)}; "
sConn = sConn & _
    "dbq=c:\mydocu~1\outloo~1\chap7\Outloo~1.mdb;"
sConn = sConn & "UID=Admin;PWD="
cn.Open sConn

' Create ADO recordset
Set rs = New ADODB.Recordset
rs.CursorType = adOpenKeyset
rs.LockType = adLockOptimistic

' Open the Newsletter or Customer database table
If fraEmailType.Value = 1 Then
    rs.Open "tblNewsletter", cn, , , adCmdTable
Else
    rs.Open "tblCustomers", cn, , , adCmdTable
End If

For x = 1 To nItems
    ' If the message has not been read, then
    ' process the message, add the address to
    ' the database, and mark the message as read
    If ofItem(x).UnRead Then
        sMsg = ofItem(x).Body
        nLoc = InStr(sMsg, "email:") + 6
        nLen = Len(sMsg)
        sEMailAddr = Trim(Mid(sMsg, nLoc, nLen))
        rs.AddNew
        rs!emailaddr = sEMailAddr
        rs.Update
        ofItem(x).UnRead = False
```

```
        End If
    Next

    ' Close the ADO Recordset and Connection
    rs.Close
    cn.Close

    ' Release the object variables
    Set rs = Nothing
    Set cn = Nothing
    Set oOutlook = Nothing

End Sub
```

4. Add the code shown in Listing 7-6 to the Click event of the cmdSendMsg command button.

Listing 7-6: **Send a message using Outlook's MailItem object**

```
Private Sub cmdSendMsg_Click()

    Dim oOutlook As Outlook.Application
    Dim oOlMsg As Outlook.MailItem
    Dim oOlRecip As Outlook.Recipient
    Dim oOlAttach As Outlook.Attachment

    Dim sMsg As String

    ' Create the Outlook Session
    Set oOutlook = New Outlook.Application

    ' Create the messsgae
    Set oOlMsg = oOutlook.CreateItem(olMailItem)

    With oOlMsg
        ' Add to the BCC to suppress the list of addresses
        Set oOlRecip = .Recipients.Add(sEmailRecip)
        oOlRecip.Type = olBCC

        ' Set the Subject and Body
        .Subject = txtSubject
        .Body = txtMsg

        If Not IsMissing(AttachmentPath) Then
            Set oOlAttach = .Attachments.Add(txtAttachPath)
        End If
```

Continued

Listing 7-6 *(continued)*

```
        ' Resolve each Recipient's Name
        For Each oOlRecip In .Recipients
            oOlRecip.Resolve
        Next

        ' Should the message be displayed before sending?
        If DisplayMsg Then
            .Display
        Else
            .Save
            .Send
        End If
    End With

    ' Clean up after yourself
    Set oOutlook = Nothing

End Sub
```

5. Add the code shown in Listing 7-7 to the Click event of the cmdExit command button. This code will close the form.

Listing 7-7: Close the form

```
Private Sub cmdExit_Click()

    DoCmd.Close

End Sub
```

Outlook and Visual Basic

Like all Microsoft Office products, Microsoft Outlook has an object model that can be accessed through Automation. You might be wondering why you would use automation rather than MAPI (Messaging API), right? MAPI is really only good for sending and receiving messages. If you want to get tasks, calendar events, contact information, and more, Outlook's object model enables you to do it. The advantage of using MAPI is that you don't create an instance of Outlook the way you do through automation. However, if you want to do more than just send a message, you will need to use Outlook's object model.

VBA and VBScript are subsets of Microsoft Visual Basic. Visual Basic is a full-featured development environment. Applications and solutions that are created within VB's IDE (integrated development environment) can be deployed as standalone applications. Solutions you create within Outlook or within an Office product require the target user to have the entire product installed on his or her system. The one stipulation for using VB with an automation solution with Outlook or any other product is this: the product you are automating with needs to be installed on the target system. The exercises prior to the following example will require both Word and Outlook or Access and Outlook to be installed on the target user's system. If you create a solution that uses an Access database and Visual Basic for access the e-mail features of Outlook using automation, you can deploy your VB application, which is an executable, with the Access database (MDB file) and just have the target user have Outlook installed. The following example is an application that is written using Visual Basic and using automation to access information contained in Outlook.

Now that we've seen how to open and close Outlook, let's see how you can incorporate some of that knowledge into a program. One of the features of Microsoft Outlook is a summary page called Outlook Today. This feature provides you with a preview of your day's events such as appointments for the next few days, outstanding tasks and how many new e-mail messages you have. Using Visual Basic and automation, you can access Outlook's object model and display similar information with your own application.

Unlike the previous exercises, this project is going to use the late binding technique to access Outlook's object model. This means that you don't need to use the References dialog window and select the Outlook 9.0 Object Library.

1. Start a new project, Standard Exe. The default form may be the startup form. Before adding any controls to the form, add the Microsoft Windows Common Controls to the project. This project is going to use the TabStrip control. Add the controls shown in Figure 7-9, setting the properties as shown in Table 7-6. Once you've finished adding the controls and modifying its properties, save the form as Outlook.Frm.

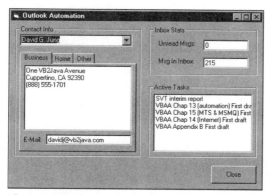

Figure 7-9: The Outlook Automation project at run time

Table 7-6
The Form's Objects and Properties

Object	Property	Setting
Form	Name Caption Height Width	FrmMain Outlook Automation 4980 6855
Frame	Name Caption	fraContact Contact Info
ComboBox	Name	cboContacts
TabStrip	Name Tab – Index Tab – Caption Tab – Index Tab – Caption Tab – Index Tab – Caption	tabAddress 1 Business 2 Home 3 Other
TextBox	Name Index	txtAddress 0
TextBox	Name Index Visible	txtAddress 1 False
TextBox	Name Index Visible	txtAddress 2 False
Label	Name Caption	lblEMail E-Mail:
TextBox	Name Index Locked	txtEMail 0 True
TextBox	Name Index Locked Visible	txtEMail 1 True False
TextBox	Name Index Locked Visible	txtEMail 2 True False

Object	Property	Setting
Frame	Name	fraInBox
	Caption	Inbox Stats
Label	Name	lblUnread
	Caption	Unread Msgs:
TextBox	Name	txtUnread
	Locked	True
Label	Name	lblInbox
	Caption	Msgs in Inbox:
TextBox	Name	txtInbox
	Locked	True
Frame	Name	fraTasks
	Caption	Active Tasks
ListBox	Name	lstTasks
CommandButton	Name	cmdClose
	Caption	Close

2. Add the following code to the Load event procedure of the form. The Move method for the form is going to center the form on the screen. The Show method is used to display the form immediately and the Refresh method is used to refresh the form on the screen. If you just used the Show method, the background of the form would display on the screen but the areas of the frame and other controls wouldn't materialize until after the all the information was loaded. From a user-interface standpoint, this is not acceptable. The Refresh method forces windows to display the entire form before anything else happens. The FillCtrlWithOutlookContacts procedure is used to fill the cboContacts ComboBox with all of the names in Outlook's Contact folder. The GetInboxStats function is used to retrieve either the total number of messages in the Inbox folder or the number of unread messages in the Inbox folder. The GetActiveTasks procedure is used to retrieve all the active tasks found in the Task folder and fills the lstTasks ListBox.

```
Private Sub Form_Load()
    Me.Move ((Screen.Width - Me.Width) / 2), _
        ((Screen.Height - Me.Height) / 2)
    Me.Show
    Me.Refresh
    Call FillCtrlWithOutlookContacts(cboContacts)
    txtInbox = GetInboxStats(gInboxMsgs)
    txtUnread = GetInboxStats(gUnreadMsgs)
    Call GetActiveTasks(lstTasks)
End Sub
```

3. Add the following code to the form's Unload procedure. The procedure will first call the Outlook_Close procedure, which will be described in greater detail in Step 7. Briefly, this procedure is used to close the instance of Outlook used by this application and remove its reference from memory.

```
Private Sub Form_Unload(Cancel As Integer)
    Call Outlook_Close
    End
End Sub
```

4. Add the following code to the cboContacts' Click event. This procedure calls several functions for several different controls. The GetContactInfo and GetContactEMail functions will be described in greater detail later in this exercise. In a nutshell, when the user selects a contact name from the cboContacts ComboBox, the contact's mailing information and e-mail address are retrieved from the Contact folder and placed in the respected TextBox controls.

```
Private Sub cboContacts_Click()
    txtAddress(0) = GetContactInfo _
        & (cboContacts.Text, gBusContact)
    txtEMail(0) = GetContactEMail _
        & (cboContacts.Text, gBusContact)
    txtAddress(1) = GetContactInfo _
        & (cboContacts.Text, gHomeContact)
    txtEMail(1) = GetContactEMail _
        & (cboContacts.Text, gHomeContact)
    txtAddress(2) = GetContactInfo _
        (cboContacts.Text, gOtherContact)
    txtEMail(2) = GetContactEMail _
        (cboContacts.Text, gOtherContact)
End Sub
```

5. Add the following code to the Click event procedure of the TabStrip control's tabAddress procedure. This is used to display specific txtAddress and txtEMail text box controls based on which tab was pressed. The two text boxes' Visible properties that correspond with the correct tab are set to True while all the others are set to False.

```
Private Sub tabAddress_Click()
    Dim i As Integer
    For i = 0 To tabAddress.Tabs.Count - 1
        If i = tabAddress.SelectedItem.Index - 1 Then
            txtAddress(i).Visible = True
            txtEMail(i).Visible = True
        Else
            txtAddress(i).Visible = False
            txtEMail(i).Visible = False
        End If
    Next

End Sub
```

6. Add a Module to the project by selecting Add Module from the Project menu. The default properties of the module are acceptable; save the file as Outlook. Bas. In the General Declaration section of the module, add the following code to set up public variables and establish constant variables.

```
Option Explicit
Public objOutlook As Object
Public objNamespace As Object
Public mFolder As Object
Public bOutlookRunning As Boolean
Public Const ErrCreatingOutlookObject$ = _
    "Could not create the Microsoft Outlook " _
    & "automation object. Check to make sure " _
    & "that Microsoft Outlook is properly installed."
Const olFolderCalendar = 9
Const olFolderContacts = 10
Const olFolderDeletedItems = 3
Const olFolderInbox = 6
Const olFolderJournal = 11
Const olFolderNotes = 12
Const olFolderOutBox = 4
Const olFolderSentMail = 5
Const olFolderTasks = 13

Public Const gBusContact = 0
Public Const gHomeContact = 1
Public Const gOtherContact = 2
Public Const gInboxMsgs = 0
Public Const gUnreadMsgs = 1
```

First, define the object variables needed for the next two functions. The variables are defined as Object to show this example using the late binding technique. If you want to use early binding, you need to reference the Microsoft Outlook 9.0 Object Library object model using the References dialog window. If you do this, reference the object variables as follows:

```
Public objOutlook As Outlook.Application
Public objNamespace As Outlook.Namesapce
Public mFolder As Outlook.MAPIFolder
```

Also, if you decide to use the early binding technique, you don't need to define any of the Outlook constants like olFolderSentMail because they are defined as part of Outlook's object model.

The ErrCreatingOutlookObject$ constant contains an error message that displays if the Outlook object can't be loaded or is installed on the target system.

7. Add the Outlook_Open function and the Outlook_Close procedure to the module.

```
Public Function OutLook_Open() As Boolean

    On Error Resume Next
```

```
        bOutlookRunning = False

        ' Check to see if Excel is already loaded
        Set objOutlook = GetObject(, "Outlook.Application")

        If objOutlook Is Nothing Then
            ' Create a new instance of it
            Set objOutlook = CreateObject("Outlook.Application")

            ' Check to make sure it worked
            If objOutlook Is Nothing Then
                MsgBox ErrCreatingOutlookObject
                GoTo Err_Outlook_Open
            End If

        End If

        Set objNamespace = objOutlook.GetNamespace("MAPI")
        bOutlookRunning = True
        OutLook_Open = True

Exit_Outlook_Open:
        Exit Function

Err_Outlook_Open:
        OutLook_Open = False
        MsgBox "Error: " & Err.Number & " " & Err.Description
        GoTo Exit_Outlook_Open
End Function
```

This function is designed to determine if Outlook is already loaded. If it is, then you don't need a new instance of Outlook to be loaded because the automation application will use the existing instance of Outlook. If it is not loaded, then a new instance of Outlook is loaded into memory. If everything within the function works, the function returns True to the procedure that called it.

The GetObject method is used to determine if an instance of the application specified is loaded in memory. The argument, Outlook.Application, is the class name of object that consists of the application's name and the object type. In this case, the application name is Outlook and the object type in which the objOutlook object variable is looking for is the Application.

If the value of the objOutlook object variable is Nothing, that means that an instance of the Outlook object is not loaded in memory yet. If this is the case, then the CreateObject function attempts to instantiate an instance of Outlook and is assigned to object variable objOutlook.

If the objOutlook object variable is still set to Nothing, then that means the application is having problems instantiating Outlook, which usually means that Outlook is not installed on the system. If this is the case, a message box displays an error message and then the error subroutine is called.

If the function gets this far, the `objNamespace` object variable is assigned to the Outlook NameSpace object using the GetNameSpace object. The bOutlook Running Boolean variable is set to True and the function is also set to True.

The `Exit_Outlook_Open` subroutine is used to exit the function. If the procedure is directed to go the `Err_Outlook_Open` subroutine, it means that something went wrong during the execution of the function. The function's return value is set to False and a message box displays the error number and description.

```
Public Sub Outlook_Close()

    On Error Resume Next

    If Not objOutlook Is Nothing Then
        objOutlook.Close
    End If

    ' If Outlook was not running before the
    ' app use it, then close it. Otherwise
    ' leave it open.
    If Not bOutlookRunning Then
        objOutlook.Quit
    End If

    ' Release the application
    Set objOutlook = Nothing

End Sub
```

If the objOutlook object variable is not set to Nothing, then it means that an instance of Outlook was opened by the Outlook_Open function. If so, then the instance of Outlook that was open is closed.

If Outlook was not running before this application used it, the bOutlookRunning Boolean value would be False. If Outlook was not running before, then the procedure would close it; otherwise Outlook will remain open. It is not good programming practice to close an application on users if they are still using it. Setting the object variable objOutlook to Nothing releases the object from memory.

8. Add the `FillCtrlWithOutlookContracts` procedure to the module. The argument variable for this procedure accepts the name of a control. This procedure uses the late binding technique to interact with Outlook. First the procedure checks to make sure that Outlook can be started. If so, then the object variables are assigned to their hierarchical object reference. If you've used Outlook, you know that everything is stored in folders. The folder that is going to be used for this procedure is the Contact folder; therefore the `objFolder` object variable is assigned to the Contact folder. The `For Each` statement is used to loop through the collection of contact names. If the `FullName` property is not blank, then the value is added to the control that was designed in the argument parameter. After all the names in the collection have been processed, the ListIndex value of the control is set to −1 so that no item will be selected in the control.

```
Sub FillCtrlWithOutlookContacts(ctrl As Control)

    Dim objFolder As Object
    Dim objAllContacts As Object
    Dim Contact As Object

    Screen.MousePointer = vbHourglass

    If OutLook_Open Then
        ' Set the default Contacts folder
        Set objFolder = _
            objNamespace.GetDefaultFolder(olFolderContacts)
        ' Set objAllContacts = the collection of all contacts
        Set objAllContacts = objFolder.Items
        ' Set the Contact object to ContactItem
        ' Collection of Outlook
        Set Contact = objOutlook.ContactItem
        ' Loop through each contact
        For Each Contact In objAllContacts
            ' Display the Fullname field for the contact
            If Len(Trim(Contact.FullName)) <> 0 Then
                ctrl.AddItem Contact.FullName
            End If
        Next
    End If
    ctrl.ListIndex = -1
    Screen.MousePointer = vbDefault

End Sub
```

9. Add the following two functions, GetContactInfo and GetContactEMail, to the module. The purpose of these functions is to get the contact's mailing information and e-mail address of a given person. The function accepts two parameters, the sContactName string variable and the ContactType integer variable. The sContactName variable contains the name of the person we are looking for. The ContactType variable is used to denote what type of contact information we should be looking for — business, home, or other. The objFolder object variable is assigned to Outlook's Contact folder in order to search that folder for the contact information we are looking for. Depending on the numeric value in the ContactType, the business, home, or other information will be retrieved from the Contact folder and returned to the procedure that called it.

```
Function GetContactInfo(sContactName As String, _
    ContactType As Integer) As String

    Dim objFolder As Object
    Dim sContact As String

    ' olFolderContacts = Contacts Folder
    Set objFolder = _
        objNamespace.GetDefaultFolder(olFolderContacts)

    With objFolder.Items(sContactName)
        Select Case ContactType
            Case gBusContact
```

```
                        sContact = .BusinessAddress & vbCrLf
                        sContact = sContact &
    .BusinessTelephoneNumber
              Case gHomeContact
                        sContact = .HomeAddress & vbCrLf
                        sContact = sContact & .HomeTelephoneNumber
              Case gOtherContact
                        sContact = .OtherAddress & vbCrLf
                        sContact = sContact & .OtherTelephoneNumber
          End Select
      End With

      GetContactInfo = sContact
      Set objFolder = Nothing

  End Function

  Function GetContactEMail(ContactName As String, _
      ContactType As String) As String

      Dim objFolder As Object
      Dim sEMail As String

      ' olFolderContacts = Contacts Folder
      Set objFolder = _
        objNamespace.GetDefaultFolder(olFolderContacts)

      With objFolder.Items(ContactName)
          Select Case ContactType
              Case gBusContact
                  sEMail = .Email1Address
              Case gHomeContact
                  sEMail = .Email2Address
              Case gOtherContact
                  sEMail = .Email3Address
          End Select
      End With

      GetContactEMail = sEMail
      Set objFolder = Nothing

  End Function
```

10. Add the following procedure, `GetActiveTasks`, to the module. This procedure will get all the active tasks from the Tasks folder and display them in the control designated in the procedure argument. In order to determine if the task is still active, you check the task's property, Complete. If the property is set to True, then the task is complete and it is not added to the control.

```
Sub GetActiveTasks(ctrl As Control)

    Dim objFolder As Object
    Dim objTasks As Object
    Dim sTask As Object
```

```
Set objFolder = _
  objNamespace.GetDefaultFolder(olFolderTasks)

Set objTasks = objFolder.Items
' Loop through each task and
' display only incomplete tasks
For Each sTask In objTasks
    If Not sTask.Complete Then
        ctrl.AddItem sTask.Subject
    End If
Next

Set objFolder = Nothing

End Sub
```

11. Add the GetInboxStatus function to the module. This function will return either the total number of messages in the Inbox folder or the number of unread messages in the Inbox. The objFolder folder variable is the Inbox folder. The `Count` property returns the total number of messages in the Inbox folder and the `UnReadItemCount` property returns the total number of unread messages in the Inbox folder.

```
Function GetInboxStats(InboxStats As Integer) As Integer

    Dim objFolder As Object

    Set objFolder =
objNamespace.GetDefaultFolder(olFolderInbox)
    Select Case InboxStats
        Case gInboxMsgs
            GetInboxStats = objFolder.Items.Count
        Case gUnreadMsgs
            GetInboxStats = objFolder.UnReadItemCount
    End Select

    Set objFolder = Nothing

End Function
```

Unless you're just using Outlook as an Internet mail client and not using it with a corporate e-mail system, you will be prompted by Outlook to either connect to your e-mail server or work offline. Regardless of how you're using Outlook, when you run the application, an instance of Outlook in loaded in memory but is not visible. It will take about a minute for your application to gather all the contact names, e-mail totals and active tasks. You can select any name from the Contact Info's combobox and the contact's corresponding information will be retrieved and displayed.

This only takes a snapshot of the information stored in Outlook. If you want the form to update regularly, you can add the Timer control to the form, set the interval to 60,000, and add the GetInboxStats function for both the total of messages in the Inbox and unread messages in the Timer's `Timer` procedure. The problem with using the Timer control is that the highest value you can set is 65,535, which is slightly over one minute. Some people might consider that too frequent. A way around using the Timer control would be to add a Refresh button that allowed the user to refresh the information whenever he or she desired.

Summary

As you conclude your work in this chapter, you should start to see that Automation is the heart of what makes integration with other applications possible. The exercises in this chapter might have been specific to working a host application like Microsoft Word or Access, but nothing should stop you from using these examples within other applications that support Automation, such as Visio or AutoCAD. Automation isn't restricted to Visual Basic or any of the development tools within Visual Studio—it can be used with other development languages like Delphi. Obviously the key words to enable automation with other development languages are going to be a bit different, but the properties, methods, and functions with which you access the object models are going to be the same.

✦   ✦   ✦

COM Add-Ins

Office 97, including Outlook 98, had substantial built-in functionality. However, developers often want to extend the built-in features of the Microsoft Office applications as part of a customized solution. In this chapter we will see how you can use Outlook 2000's COM Add-Ins to increase Outlook's functionality across all Office applications.

Extending Outlook's Functionality

You could extend Outlook 98 with templates to standardize forms and macros to automate repetitive tasks. You also could extend the GUI of Outlook 98 for viewing and modifying data relatively easily by adding custom forms. However, you faced a far more difficult task if you wanted to extend the GUI of the Outlook application itself by, for example, adding custom tool-bars and dialog boxes. This meant writing Exchange Client Extensions. An Exchange Client Extension was a specially designed DLL that allowed developers to modify the Outlook user interface and access its object model. Exchange Client Extensions had to be authored in C or C++ and conform to the particular requirements of its design. Writing these extensions involved a long and steep learning curve.

Office 2000, including Outlook 2000, added an important tool to the developer's arsenal: COM Add-Ins. A COM Add-In is an ActiveX DLL (dynamic-link library) that implements a prede-fined interface and is specially registered so that it can be recognized and loaded by *all* Office 2000 applications. This means that a *single* COM Add-In, if it uses an object such as the CommandBar that is common to the object libraries of all Office 2000 applications, can be used to customize *all* Office 2000 applications: Word, Excel, Access, PowerPoint, Outlook, or FrontPage.

Additionally, even if your COM Add-In is only used in one of the Office applications, you can reuse much of its code in other Office applications. For example, you may decide that your custom command bar for Outlook will be different from your custom command bar for Word. However, much of the code will be common to both command bars. Therefore, you can author modules that are shared between the COM Add-Ins for Outlook and Word.

You can build a COM Add-In with any COM-compliant programming tool, including Visual Basic, Visual C++, or Visual J++. This means you can leverage your knowledge of a programming language rather than having to learn C or C++ and Exchange Client Extensions.

Additionally, you have tools that make your job even easier. Visual Basic 6.0 supports *add-in designers* that simplify the task of registering a COM Add-In for use by Office 2000 applications. In turn, the Microsoft Office 2000 Developer edition provides a COM Add-In template. This template includes an Office 2000 add-in designer and a reference to the IDTExtensibility2 library that supplies the events that make up the COM Add-In interface.

COM Add-Ins, in addition to simplifying your task of writing code by writing some of the code for you, also ease your task of distribution and installation because a COM Add-In is a compiled DLL. Additionally, both Visual Basic 6.0 and Office 2000 Developer provide the Package and Deployment wizard, which automates the tasks required to prepare your COM Add-In for distribution and installation.

If you are not convinced of the advantages of COM Add-Ins, Outlook 2000 does continue Outlook's support of Exchange Client Extensions, primarily for the sake of backward compatibility. However, COM Add-Ins are easier to author than Exchange Client Extensions and provide greater functionality. Therefore, you likely would not be using Exchange Client Extensions unless you had to support earlier versions of Outlook (time for the users to upgrade), feel bad about abandoning the extensions you put so much time into writing (time to let go), or are masochistic (time to get help).

Note   A COM Add-In can also be an ActiveX.exe file. This chapter focuses on creating COM Add-Ins as DLLs because they generally provide better performance than .exe files do.

Understanding the COM Add-In Object Model

The object model for COM Add-Ins consists of a COMAddIns collection and a COMAddIn object. Each COM Add-In is a COMAddIn object. The ComAddIns collection is the collection of the COM Add-Ins registered for use in the host Office 2000 application.

Figure 8-1 shows the Outlook 2000 COM Add-Ins dialog box, which graphically displays the loaded COM Add-Ins.

1. Choose the Tools ➪ Options menu command.

2. Choose the Other tab, shown in Figure 8-2.

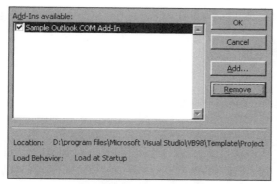

Figure 8-1: COM Add-Ins dialog box

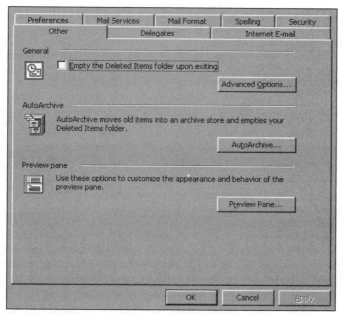

Figure 8-2: Other tab of Options dialog box

You access the COM Add-Ins dialog box by the following steps:

   3. Click the Advanced Options button, which displays the Advanced Options dialog box shown in Figure 8-3.

   4. Click the COM Add-Ins button to display the COM Add-Ins dialog box.

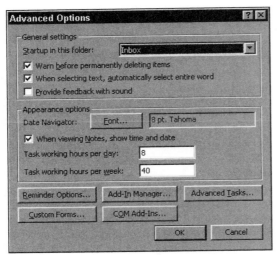

Figure 8-3: Advanced Options dialog box

COMAddIns Collection

The ComAddIns collection is the collection of the COM Add-Ins loaded in the host Office 2000 application. You can access this collection by the COMAddIns property of the Application object:

```
Dim ocComAdds As COMAddIns
Set ocComAdds = Application.COMAddIns
```

Table 8-1 lists the properties of the ComAddIns collection:

Table 8-1
Properties of the ComAddIns Collection

Name	Description
Application	Returns a reference to the Application object of the Office 2000 application that accessed the collection. The Parent property below returns the same value.
Count	The number of add-ins registered for the host Office 2000 application.
Creator	Returns a four-character code for the application in which the specified object was created. This property only appears relevant to the (boo, hiss) Macintosh.
Parent	Returns a reference to the application object of the Office 2000 application that accessed the collection. The Application property above returns the same value.

The Count property is useful for iterating through the COM add-ins registered for the host Office 2000 application.

Table 8-2 lists the methods of the ComAddIns collection:

Table 8-2		
Methods of the ComAddIns Collection		
Name	**Description**	**Parameters**
Item	Returns a member of the COMAddIns collection.	The COM Add-In's one-based position within the collection or the string representing its ProgID (discussed in Table 8-3).
Update	Refreshes the contents of the COMAddIns collection from the add-ins listed in the Windows registry.	None.

The ComAddIns collection has no events.

COMAddIn Object

The ComAddIn object represents a COM Add-In loaded in the host Office 2000 application. You can access the ComAddIn object by the Item method of the COMAddIns collection:

```
Dim ocComAdds As COMAddIns
Dim oComAdd As COMAddIn
Set ocComAdds = Application.COMAddIns
Set oComAdd = ocComAdds.Item(1)
```

Table 8-3 lists the properties of the ComAddIn object. The COMAddIn object has no methods or events.

Table 8-3	
Properties of the ComAddIn Object	
Name	**Description**
Application	Returns a reference to the Application object of the Office 2000 application that accessed the collection. The Parent property below returns the same value.

Continued

	Table 8-3 *(continued)*
Name	**Description**
Connect	Returns True if the add-in is registered and connected, False if the add-in is registered but not connected.
Creator	Returns a four-character code for the application in which the specified object was created. This property only appears relevant to the Macintosh.
Description	Returns or sets the name which will appear in the COM Add-Ins dialog box in Outlook for the current COMAddIn object. This name also will be the value of the COM Add-In's FriendlyName key in the Windows Registry.
GUID	Returns the globally unique class identifier (GUID) for the current COMAddIn object.
Object	Sets or returns the object that is the host for the current COMAddIn.
Parent	Returns a reference to the application object of the Office 2000 application that accessed the collection. The Application property above returns the same value.
ProgID	Returns the programmatic identifier (ProgID) for the current COMAddIn.

You will often use the Connect and ProgID properties. The Connect property, when set to True, loads a registered COM Add-In, and when set to False, unloads it. You use the ProgID property to uniquely identify a COM Add-In. The value of the property will be the project name and the class name separated by a period. For example, if the Visual Basic project name is "SampleAddIn" and the class module name is "SampleClass" then the ProgID property is SampleAddIn.SampleClass.

While the object model helps you understand COM Add-Ins, the best way to learn COM Add-Ins is to write them. Let's start by creating a COM Add-In template!

Creating a COM Add-In Template

You can make the task of creating an Outlook 2000 COM Add-In much easier if you use the Microsoft Office 2000 Developer. If you have not previously installed the Microsoft Office 2000 Developer, run the installation program and install the Office Developer Tools. Once you have installed the Office Developer Tools, you are ready to create a COM Add-In template to which you can add the specific code for your purpose.

Using the Add-In Designer

The Microsoft Office 2000 Developer has Office 2000 COM Add-In templates for Visual Basic, Visual C++, and Visual J++ on the Microsoft Office 2000 Developer CD in the ..\ODETools\V9\Samples\Unsupprt\mkaddin directory. If you think the folder name Unsupprt means unsupported, you're right. However, don't let that scare you. It only means that while Microsoft is willing to assist developers with free sample code; its generosity does not extend to providing free technical support.

This example will use Visual Basic 6. However, you could also use Visual C++, Visual J++, or any other COM-compliant development tool.

Before starting Visual Basic, copy the files in the VB subfolder under the ..\ODETools\ V9\Samples\Unsupprt\mkaddin directory to the Visual Basic project template folder. This directory is by default located in ..\ \Microsoft Visual Studio\VB98\Template\ Projects. Figure 8-4 shows the resulting "OfficeAddIn" project that appears as a choice in the New Project dialog box displayed with the menu command File⇨New Project.

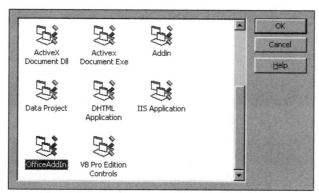

Figure 8-4: OfficeAddIn project as choice in the New Project dialog box

Choose OfficeAddIn from the New Project dialog box to open an OfficeAddIn project. This creates an ActiveX DLL project with one form and one Designer. Figure 8-5 shows the Project Explorer for the OfficeAddIn project. Figure 8-6 shows the project's properties dialog box.

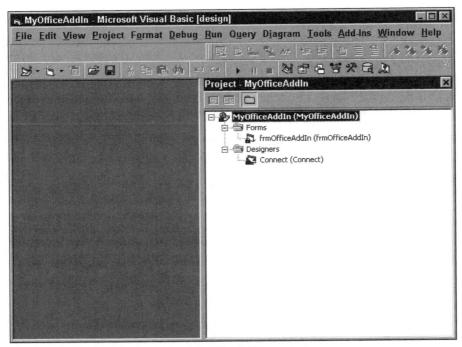

Figure 8-5: Project Explorer view of OfficeAddIn project

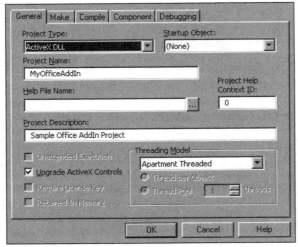

Figure 8-6: Properties of OfficeAddIn project

The COM Add-In also requires references to the Microsoft Office 9.0 Object Library, the Microsoft Outlook 9.0 Object Library, and the Microsoft Add-In Designer. The OfficeAddIn project already has references to all but the Microsoft Outlook 9.0 Object Library. It does not have this reference because it is a template for COM Add-Ins for Office 2000 generally rather than Outlook 2000 specifically. Add the reference to the Microsoft Outlook 9.0 Object Library so that your References dialog box, accessed by the Project ⇨ References menu command, appears as in Figure 8-7.

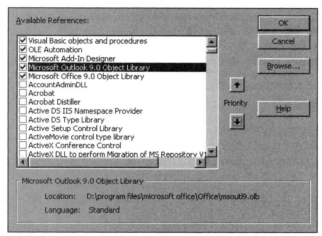

Figure 8-7: References for COM Add-In

Since the OfficeAddIn project is a template for COM Add-Ins for Office 2000 generally rather than Outlook 2000 specifically, you need to modify it. The form is unnecessary. Remove the form by right-clicking it in Project Explorer and choosing Remove from the context menu. That leaves the object Connect under Designers.

The object Connect is similar to but not the same as a class module in an ActiveX DLL project. The primary difference is that the designer Connect has a visual interface, the Add-In Designer dialog box. Figure 8-8 shows the Add-In Designer dialog box, which you can display by right-clicking Connect in Project Explorer and choosing View Object from the context menu.

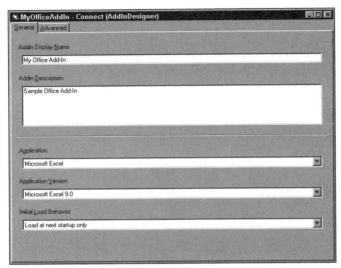

Figure 8-8: Add-In Designer dialog box

The Add-In Designer dialog enables you to set properties of the COM Add-In through a graphical user interface. Table 8-4 lists the settings on the General tab:

Table 8-4
Add-In Designer Dialog Box — General Tab Settings

Setting Name	Description
Addin Display Name	The name that will appear in the COM Add-Ins dialog box in Outlook. This name also will be the value of the Description property of the COM Add-In object and the FriendlyName key in the Windows registry.
Addin Description	This name is the value of the Description key in the Windows Registry. There is no comparable property of the COM Add-In object.
Application	The application in which the COM Add-In will run. The dropdown list includes all Office 2000 applications plus Visual Basic, VBA, and the Microsoft Development Environment.
Application Version	The version of the application in which the COM Add-In will run. When Microsoft Outlook is the application, the only choice is 9.0, because Outlook 2000 is the only version of Outlook that hosts COM Add-Ins.
Initial Load Behavior	How the COM Add-In loads in the hosting application. The value is value of the LoadBehavior key in the Windows registry. Table 8-5 lists the different load behaviors.

Table 8-5
Load Behaviors

Load Behavior	Value	Description
None	0	COM Add-In is not loaded when Outlook starts. You may load it later through the COM Add-Ins dialog box or programmatically by setting the `Connect` property of the COMAddIn object to True.
Startup	2	COM Add-In is loaded when Outlook starts.
Load on demand	8	COM Add-In is not loaded when Outlook starts. You may load it later by clicking a button or menu item or programmatically by setting the `Connect` property of the COMAddIn object to True.
Load at next startup	16	The first time after the COM Add-In is registered, the COM Add-In is loaded when Outlook starts and creates a button or menu item for itself. The next time Outlook starts, the COM Add-In is loaded on demand, i.e., by the user clicking the button or selecting the menu item. This value assumes the COM Add-In modifies the user interface by creating the button or menu item.

After the COM Add-In is registered and loaded, the `LoadBehavior` value is combined with either 0 if the COM Add-In is disconnected or 1 if the COM Add-In is connected. Therefore, a value of 9 means the `LoadBehavior` is Load on demand and the COM Add-In is connected.

The example being developed in this chapter uses the following values in the General page:

✦ Addin Display Name — Sample Outlook COM Add-In.

✦ Addin Description — Sample Outlook COM Add-In for Outlook 2000 Programming Bible.

✦ Application — Microsoft Outlook.

✦ Application Version — Microsoft Outlook 9.0.

✦ Initial Load Behavior — Startup.

Figure 8-9 shows the Advanced tab of the Add-In Designer. This page permits you to specify a file containing localized resource information for the COM Add-In and to specify additional Registry data. Its use is relatively specialized and it will not be used in this example.

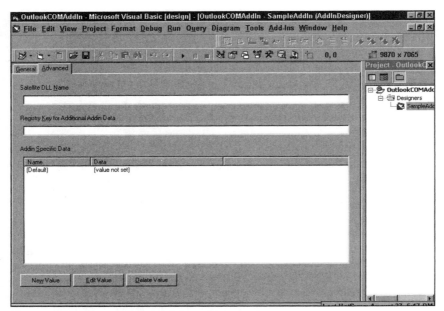

Figure 8-9: Advanced page of the Add-In Designer

Tip   Set the project name and the name of Connect to names that you want to use for the `ProgID` property of the COM Add-In. As we discussed earlier, the value of this property will be the project name and the class name separated by a period. Not changing the defaults could result in a `ProgID` of Project1.Connect that is not very descriptive. This example uses a project name of OutlookCOMAddIn and a class name of SampleAddIn for a ProgID of OutlookCOMAddIn.SampleAddIn.

No code has been written so far. However, the class module supplied by the Office Add-In template project is full of code. The beginning of this code has the statement:

```
Implements IDTExtensibility2
```

The code then contains a number of strange procedures such as `IDTExtensibility2_ OnAddInsUpdate`. This involves the next step of this sample project, the implementation of something called the IDTExtensibility2 interface.

Implementing the IDTExtensibility2 interface

When authoring a COM Add-In, you need to know when to initialize variables that concern objects of the host Office 2000 application. A COM Add-In for Outlook will probably need references to the Application, NameSpace, and other Outlook objects. However, your COM Add-In needs to connect to an instance of Outlook before it can refer to the objects of that Outlook instance. How do you know when that connection occurs?

Interface

An interface, in essence, is a group of related function prototypes. For those readers who are C++ programmers, an interface is analogous to a pure virtual base class in C++ programming. An interface *defines* its member functions by name, return type, and number and type of its parameters. However, the interface does not *implement* the functions. The functions are "empty" between the function's header and its end.

Each object that uses the interface implements the interface's functions. One object's implementation of the functions may be different from another's. However, each object that uses the interface is referring to the same function names, return types, and numbers and types of parameters.

The analogy of plugging an electrical appliance into an electrical outlet may be helpful in explaining the purpose of an interface. The electrical outlet is an interface, which defines a Plug function. The appliance implements the function by having a plug whose prongs fit the outlet. When you plug the appliance into the outlet, something behind the outlet that you cannot see supplies the appliance with electricity. You do not need to know what that something is behind the outlet or how that something supplies power to your appliance. Thus, the interface is a gateway through which you can easily access the functionality of a far more complex object.

Applying this analogy to the IDTExtensibility2 interface and COM Add-Ins, the interface supplies an OnConnection method that is called automatically when your COM Add-In connects to the host Office 2000 application. Behind the interface, hidden from you, is far more complex code that determines when your COM Add-In has connected to the host application. However, you do not need to know *how* this code determines when this connection has taken place. You only need to know that the OnConnection method is called when the hidden code determines that the connection has occurred.

If your COM Add-In loads when the host application starts up, as opposed to being loaded at some later point either by user action or code, it should not interact with the application, such as by having the application display a custom toolbar, until the host application has completed its own initialization. How do you know when the host application has completed its own initialization?

These issues are not limited to starting up your COM Add-In. Your COM Add-In, when it disconnects from the host application, needs to "clean up after itself" by dereferencing the object variables it created when it connected to the host application. Otherwise, memory leaks may occur. For example, if your COM Add-In created a global reference to the Outlook application object and did not release that reference when the COM Add-In unloaded, then Outlook may stay in memory even after the user exits and logs off the application. Thus, you need to know when the COM Add-In has disconnected from the application so you can dereference the object variables you created when it connected to the host application. How do you know when the COM Add-In has disconnected from the application?

Events are the mechanism by which you know when an occurrence, such as your COM Add-In connecting to the host application, has taken place. The events that correspond to when the COM Add-In has connected to or disconnected from the host application or when the host application has completed its own initialization are defined in an interface named IDTExtensibility2.

COM Add-Ins must implement the IDTExtensibility2 interface to work with Office 2000. The IDTExtensibility2 interface provides the five methods that are listed in Table 8-6 to tell you when your COM Add-In has connected to or disconnected from the host application, whether the host application has completed its initialization or has started to unload, or when other COM Add-Ins have been loaded. These are methods, but they behave like events in that they are called automatically when their precondition occurs.

Table 8-6
IDTExtensibility2 interface Methods

Event Procedure	Called when ...
OnConnection	The add-in is connected to the host application.
OnAddInsUpdate	There has been a change to the collection of add-ins in the Add-In Manager.
OnStartupComplete	The startup of the host application is complete.
OnBeginShutdown	The host application is about to begin its unloading process.
OnDisconnection	The add-in is disconnected from the host application, either programmatically or through the Add-In Manager.

The OfficeAddIn template implements the IDTExtensibility2 interface for you. However, if you do not have access to this template (because you do not have the Microsoft Office 2000 Developer), you can easily implement the IDTExtensibility2 interface.

1. For example, start with an ActiveX DLL project, which by default has one class module. As Figure 8-10 shows, at this point the Object dropdown box for this class module just lists "(General)" and "Class."

2. Under General Declarations type:

```
Implements IDTExtensibility2
```

That's all you need to do. Figure 8-11 shows that IDTExtensibility2 now has been added to the Object dropdown box. Additionally, as Figure 8-12 shows, the methods of IDTExtensibility2 have been added to the Procedure dropdown box.

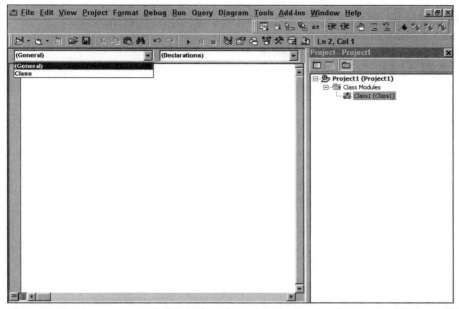

Figure 8-10: Appearance of object dropdown box before implementing IDTExtensibility2 interface

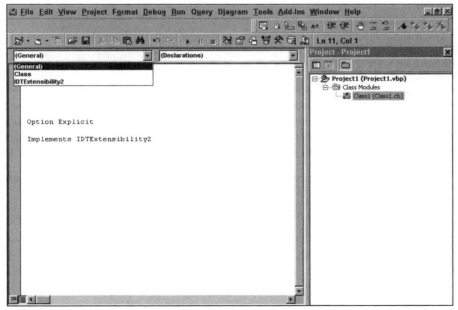

Figure 8-11: Object dropdown box includes IDTExtensibility2

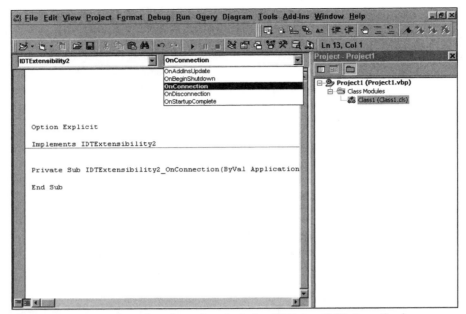

Figure 8-12: Procedure dropdown box includes IDTExtensibility2 methods

An object that implements an interface is required to implement each procedure of the interface. Returning to our plug analogy, the prongs of the electrical appliance's plug have to fit the holes in the outlet. Therefore, you need to implement each of the five methods of the IDTExtensibility2 interface. This is not as hard as it sounds. All your code needs to contain to implement a procedure is the procedure's stub. Choose a method from the Procedure dropdown box and Visual Basic will add the method's procedure stubs for you. Figure 8-13 shows the aftermath of choosing each event from the Procedure dropdown box.

Tip

You do not need to write code in any of the event procedures (though as a practical matter you will have to in at least some or your COM Add-In won't do anything). However, the compiler has a bad habit of removing empty procedures. If one of the event procedures is removed, then your COM Add-In won't work because it will have violated the rule that an object that implements an interface is required to implement each procedure of the interface. Therefore, you should put at least a comment (apostrophe) inside each event procedure for which you will not be writing code.

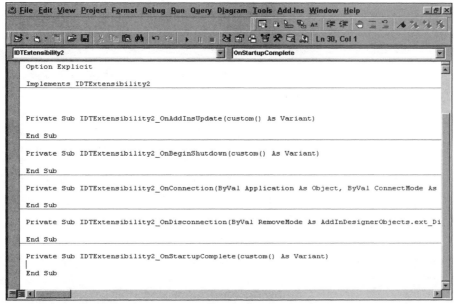

Figure 8-13: All IDTExtensibility2 methods have been implemented

Understanding IDTExtensibility2 Methods

You still haven't written any code, but you're getting closer. However, before writing code, it is helpful first to understand the syntax and rather unusual parameters of the methods of the IDTExtensibility2 interface. They are listed here in the order in which they generally occur.

OnConnection

The OnConnection method is called when the COM Add-In is loaded. Its syntax is:

```
Sub IDTExtensibility2_OnConnection _
    (ByVal Application As Object, _
    ByVal ConnectMode As _
    AddInDesignerObjects.ext_ConnectMode, _
    ByVal AddInInst As Object, custom() As Variant)
```

Table 8-7 describes the parameters of the `OnConnection` method:

Name	Description
	Table 8-7 **Parameters of the OnConnection Method**
Name	*Description*
Application	Reference to Outlook Application object.
ConnectMode	One of the `ext_ConnectMode` constants, described in Table 8-8, which indicate how the add-in was loaded.
AddInInst	Reference to current COM Add-In.
custom	Array holding user-defined data. This parameter is usually ignored for Office 2000 add-ins.

Constant	Value	How Add-In is Loaded
		Table 8-8 **ConnectMode Values for OnConnection Method**
Constant	*Value*	*How Add-In is Loaded*
ext_cm_AfterStartup	0	User checks checkbox next to Add-In in the COM Add-Ins dialog box or Connect property was set to True
ext_cm_Startup	1	Add-In is specified to load when Outlook starts; Outlook starts.

In essence, the `ext_cm_Startup` value is used if the COM Add-In loads *when* Outlook starts, and the `ext_cm_AfterStartup` value is used if the COM Add-In loads *after* Outlook starts.

The `OnConnection` event is a good place to instantiate object variables. For example, given the following declaration in General Declarations:

```
Dim WithEvents oApp As Outlook.Application
```

You would instantiate the object variable `oApp` in the `OnConnection` method using the `Application` parameter of the method:

```
Set oApp = Application
```

You then could use the instantiated object variable `oApp` to instantiate additional Outlook object variables such as the NameSpace object.

OnStartupComplete

The OnStartupComplete method is called when Outlook completes its startup, if the add-in's LoadBehavior is to load at startup. Otherwise, this method is not called. Therefore, the method will not be called if it is loaded by the user selecting it from the COM Add-Ins dialog box.

The syntax of the OnStartupComplete method is:

```
Sub IDTExtensibility2_OnStartupComplete(custom() As Variant)
```

As with the OnConnection method, the custom parameter is an array holding user-defined data and is ignored in Office 2000 applications.

The OnStartupComplete method is a good place to initialize variables or running code that relates to the user interface, such as displaying a dialog box or changing the toolbars and menu items of the host application, since such interaction with the user interface should not take place until Outlook is finished loading.

OnAddInsUpdate

The OnAddInsUpdate method is called when the collection of loaded add-ins changes, such as with the loading of another add-in or the unloading of a loaded add-in. Its syntax is:

```
Sub IDTExtensibility2_OnAddInsUpdate(custom() As Variant)
```

As with the other methods, the custom parameter is an array holding user-defined data and is ignored in Office 2000 applications.

The OnAddInsUpdate method is useful when one COM Add-In depends on another. For example, if a COM Add-In is unloaded, a COM Add-In dependent on another add-in can check to see if the add-in on which it relies was just unloaded.

OnBeginShutdown

The OnBeginShutdown method is called when Outlook starts to shut down if the add-in still is loaded. This method is not called if the add-in is not loaded, such as when it was previously unloaded by the user or through code. Its syntax is:

```
Sub IDTExtensibility2_OnBeginShutdown(custom() As Variant)
```

At the risk of sounding like a broken record, the custom parameter is an array holding user-defined data and is ignored in Office 2000 applications.

The OnBeginShutdown method is a good place to save any changes.

OnDisconnection

The OnDisconnection method is called when the COM Add-In is unloaded. If this method is called because Outlook has started to shut down, the OnBeginShutdown method is called first. The syntax for OnDisconnection is:

```
Sub IDTExtensibility2_OnDisconnection _
(ByVal RemoveMode As _
AddInDesignerObjects.ext_DisconnectMode, _
    custom() As Variant)
```

Table 8-9 describes the parameters of the OnDisconnection method:

Table 8-9
Parameters of the OnDisconnection Method

Name	*Description*
Application	Reference to Outlook Application object.
RemoveMode	One of the ext_DisconnectMode constants, described in Table 8-10, which indicate how the add-in was unloaded.
custom	Array holding user-defined data. This parameter is usually ignored for Office 2000 add-ins.

Table 8-10
DisconnectMode Values for OnDisconnection Method

ConnectMode	*Value*	*Unloaded When...*
ext_dm_HostShutdown	0	Outlook closes.
ext_dm_UserShutdown	1	User clears checkbox next to Add-In in the COM Add-Ins dialog box or Connect property set to False.

The OnDisconnection method is useful for destroying object variables and other cleanup. You can use the RemoveMode argument to determine whether to remove an add-in's customization of the command bar or menu. In essence, the ext_dm_HostShutdown value is used if the COM Add-In unloads because Outlook unloads. By contrast, the ext_dm_UserShutdown value is used if the COM Add-In unloads without Outlook unloading. If the user disconnected the add-in, and Outlook remains running, then you may want the OnDisconnection method to contain code that removes the customization. However, if the add-in was unloaded because Outlook was shutting down, you may want to retain the customization so it can be displayed when Outlook is next started. In that scenario, the add-in would be loaded (demand loading) when the user first clicks on the customized command bar or menu item.

Registering the COM Add-In

In order to work with Outlook, or other Office 2000 applications for that matter, the add-in DLL must be registered. The DLL's class ID is registered beneath the \HKEY_ CLASSES_ROOT subtree in the Registry. Figure 8-14 shows the registration of the example add-in. The value, SampleComAddIn.clsSampleAddIn, is the ProgID of the add-in.

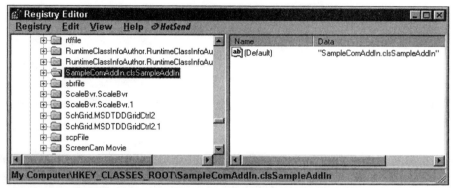

Figure 8-14: Registration of Add-In in \HKEY_CLASSES_ROOT

However, other Registry entries also are necessary. COM Add-In technology relies heavily on the system Registry to determine which add-ins are available for the different Office products. The Registry also tells the Office application how to load the add-in. For example, if you put certain configuration information into the registry, an add-in can always be loaded at the startup of the Office application. The Registry entry in \HKEY_CLASSES_ROOT does not, and is not intended to, convey this information.

Beyond holding this configuration information for add-ins, the Registry specifies the users for whom the add-in should load. This is useful if your users use different machines throughout the office. You can place the information for your add-in in the registry so that your add-in travels with the user. Also, by placing your registration in a different part of the Registry, you can force every user on a machine to use your add-in and prevent the users from uninstalling the add-in from the machine.

The two registry locations are:

✦ \ HKEY_LOCAL_MACHINE\Software\Microsoft\Office\Outlook\AddIns

✦ \ HKEY_CURRENT_USER\Software\Microsoft\Office\Outlook\AddIns

Registering the add-in under HKEY_LOCAL_MACHINE makes it available to every user on the machine. This allows developers to install an add-in on a machine once and not have to repeat the process for each user who logs onto the machine. As Figure 8-15 shows, the VBA add-in for Outlook 2000 is registered under HKEY_LOCAL_MACHINE. This is logical because it enables every user on the machine to access the add-in.

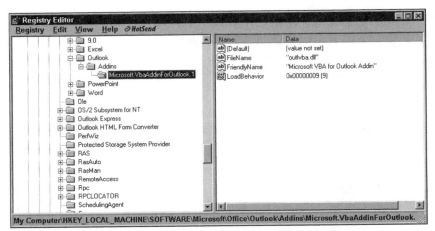

Figure 8-15: Registration of Add-in in \ HKEY_LOCAL_MACHINE

Registering the add-in under HKEY_CURRENT_USER makes it available only to the current user of the system. This is a logical choice when the add-in is suited only for certain users on a multi-user system. As Figure 8-16 shows, the sample add-in is registered under HKEY_CURRENT_USER.

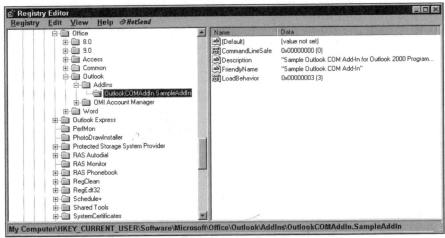

Figure 8-16: Registration of Add-in in \HKEY_CURRENT_USER

Table 8-11 lists the three values you need to write to the registry for your add-in: FriendlyName, Description, and LoadBehavior.

Table 8-11
COM Add-In Properties to Be Written to the Registry

Name	Type	Description
FriendlyName	String	The name that will appear in the COM Add-Ins dialog box in Outlook. This name also will be the value of the Description property of the COM Add-In object. It can be set from the Add-In Display Name in the Add-In Designer dialog box.
Description	String	The name that will appear at the bottom of the Add-In Manager when a user selects the add-in. It can be set from the Add-In Description in the Add-In Designer dialog box.
LoadBehavior	DWORD	This DWORD value specifies the way the COM Add-In should be loaded. It can be set from the Initial Load Behavior drop-down list in the Add-In Designer dialog box. Table 8-12 lists the alternatives.

Table 8-12
Load Behaviors

Load Behavior	Description	DWORD Value Not Connected	DWORD Value Connected
None	COM Add-In is not loaded when Outlook starts. You may load it later through the COM Add-Ins dialog box or programmatically by setting the Connect property of the COMAddIn object to True.	0×00	0×01
Startup	COM Add-In is loaded when Outlook starts.	0×02	0×03
Load on demand	COM Add-In is not loaded when Outlook starts. You may load it later by clicking a button or menu item or programmatically by setting the Connect property of the COMAddIn object to True.	0×08	0×09

Continued

Table 8-12 *(continued)*			
Load Behavior	**Description**	**DWORD Value Not Connected**	**DWORD Value Connected**
Load at next startup	The first time after the COM Add-In is registered, the COM Add-In is loaded when Outlook starts and creates a button or menu item for itself. The next time Outlook starts, the COM Add-In is loaded on demand, i.e., by the user clicking the button or selecting the menu item. This value assumes the COM Add-In modifies the user interface by creating the button or menu item.	0×16	Not applicable. Value returns to 0×09 when Outlook is reloaded.

As discussed previously, after the COM Add-In is registered and loaded, the Load Behavior value is combined with either 0 if the COM Add-In is disconnected or 1 if the COM Add-In is connected. Therefore, a value of 9 means the LoadBehavior is Load on demand and the COM Add-In is connected.

Now that you know the information that needs to be in the Registry, the question is how to get that information there. It's easy if you use Microsoft Visual Basic 6.0 or Office 2000 Developer to design your COM Add-In. The add-in designer will register the COM Add-In for you. All you need to do is compile the DLL from the File ➪ Make filename.dll menu command.

Even if you do not have use Microsoft Visual Basic 6.0 or Office 2000 Developer to design your COM Add-In, you may use a Registry editor (.reg) file to import the required information into the Registry. The following is a sample Registry editor file:

```
REGEDIT4
[HKEY_CURRENT_USER\Software\Microsoft\Office\Outlook\Addins\
SampleComAddIn.clsSampleAddIn]
"FriendlyName"="Sample Add-in"
"Description"="Sample Outlook Add-In"
"LoadBehavior"=dword:00000008
```

Once the Registry file is created, you need only double-click it in Windows Explorer. Alternatively, in the Registry Editor, which you can access with the command regedit from the Start ➪ Run menu, you can import the Registry file with the Registry ➪ Import Registry File menu command. Figure 8-17 shows you the dialog that is displayed confirming that the information has been successfully imported into the Registry.

Figure 8-17: Dialog confirming successful entry of information into the Registry

This completes the creation of the COM Add-In template. However, this is just a template. The COM Add-In has no functionality yet. The next step is to change the code in the template to give the COM Add-In specific functionality.

Creating a Command Bar COM Add-In

Both the Explorer object and the Inspector object have a `CommandBars` property. This property returns a collection of all the command bars in Outlook. Command bars in Outlook, and in Office 2000 applications generally, contain menu bars, toolbars, and shortcut menus.

The Explorer object has, in addition to its menu bar, the following four built-in toolbars that you can access with the View ➪ Toolbars menu command:

- ✦ Standard
- ✦ Advanced
- ✦ Remote
- ✦ Web

The Inspector object also has, in addition to its menu bar, the following four built-in toolbars that you can access with an item's View ➪ Toolbars menu command:

- ✦ Standard
- ✦ Formatting
- ✦ Form Design
- ✦ Clipboard

However, you are not limited to Outlook's built-in menu bar and toolbars. You can modify the built-in menu bar and toolbars or even create your own, and load and unload these custom menu bars and toolbars dynamically. COM Add-Ins are often written to load custom menus and toolbars. The code example in this section will load a custom menu and toolbar in the Explorer window. While analyzing this code we will also explore the command bar collections and objects.

Project Description

Figure 8-18 shows the custom menu. The new menu bar, imaginatively named New Menu, replaces the standard Outlook menu bar.

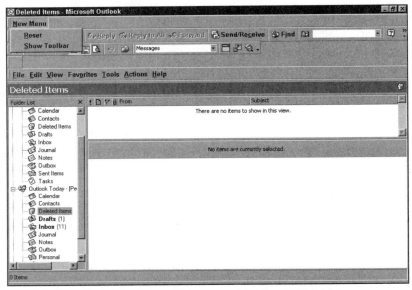

Figure 8-18: The custom menu bar created by the COM Add-In

The new menu bar has two menu items with the following functionality:

✦ Reset — This menu command hides the new menu bar and displays the standard Outlook menu bar, as shown in Figure 8-19.

✦ Show Toolbar — This menu command toggles the visibility of a custom toolbar as shown in Figure 8-20.

The custom toolbar, with the similarly imaginative name of Custom Toolbar, has three buttons with the following functionality:

✦ Ascending — This button, labeled A ↓ Z, displays messages in the Inbox in ascending order based on the Received field. As shown in Figure 8-21, the earlier the date on which the message was received, the higher it is on the list.

✦ Descending — This button, labeled Z ↓ A, displays messages in the Inbox in descending order based on the Received field, as shown in Figure 8-22.

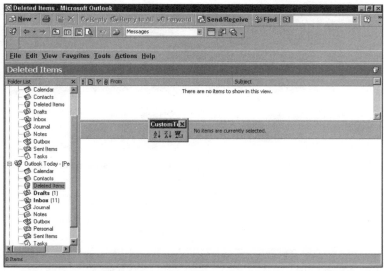

Figure 8-19: The Outlook GUI after the reset menu command is executed

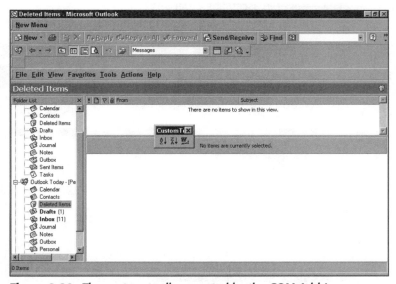

Figure 8-20: The custom toolbar created by the COM Add-In

✦ WordMail — This button, labeled with a Microsoft Word icon and an envelope, creates a new mail item using Microsoft Word as the editor. As Figure 8-23 shows, the menu commands of Microsoft Word are incorporated into the menu for the mail item.

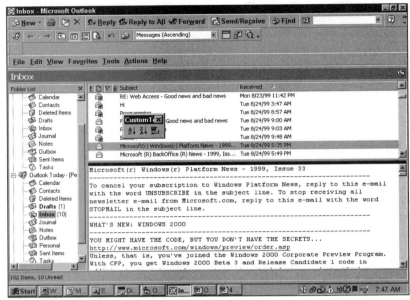

Figure 8-21: Messages in ascending order

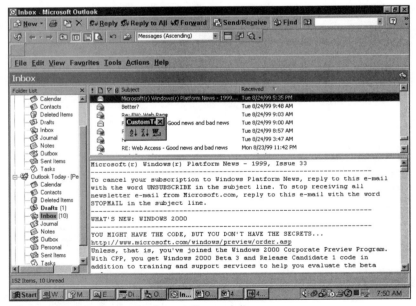

Figure 8-22: Messages in descending order

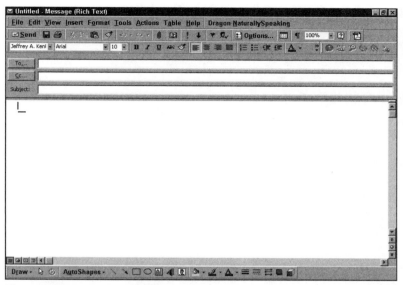

Figure 8-23: New WordMail messages

Creating a Custom View

You can also access the functionality of two of the three buttons on the custom toolbar through the Outlook GUI. You may access the WordMail editor through the Outlook GUI by the following steps:

1. Choose the Tools ➪ Options menu command to open the Options dialog box.

2. Choose the Mail Format tab to display the page shown in Figure 8-24.

3. Check the checkbox labeled "Use Microsoft Word to edit e-mail messages."

Through the Outlook GUI, you can also access the view of Inbox messages by descending received date. This view is a built-in view, named Messages, accessed by the View ➪ Current View menu command as shown in Figure 8-25.

However, you cannot access through the default Outlook GUI the view of Inbox messages by ascending received date. Indeed, the Ascending toolbar button requires a defined view that displays messages by ascending received date. By comparison, Messages is a predefined view that displays messages by descending received date. You can create this view, which is shown as Messages (Ascending) in Figure 8-25, by following these steps:

1. Select the Inbox to display its contents.

2. Choose the View ➪ Current View menu command to display the submenu shown in Figure 8-25, and choose the Define Views to open the Define Views for "Inbox" dialog box shown in Figure 8-26.

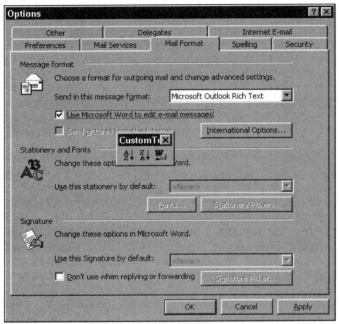

Figure 8-24: Mail format page of options dialog box

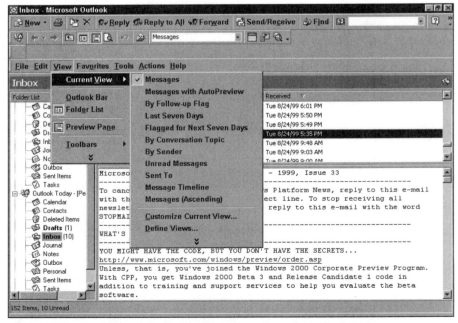

Figure 8-25: Accessing default messages view through Outlook GUI

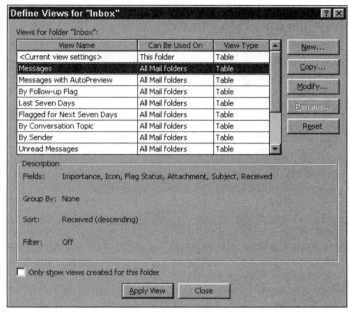

Figure 8-26: Define Views for Inbox dialog box

3. Choose Messages from the list of views and click the Copy button to display the Copy View dialog box shown in Figure 8-27. Type the name Messages (Ascending) in the "Name of new view" text box and click OK to return to the Define Views for Inbox dialog box.

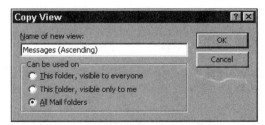

Figure 8-27: Copy View dialog box

4. Scroll to the bottom of the Define Views for Inbox dialog box until you see the "Messages (Ascending)" view and select it. As Figure 8-28 shows, the bottom of the dialog box displays a description of the view. The sort is described as descending based on the Received field because this view was copied from the built-in Messages view, which sorts by descending date. The next step is to change the sort to ascending date.

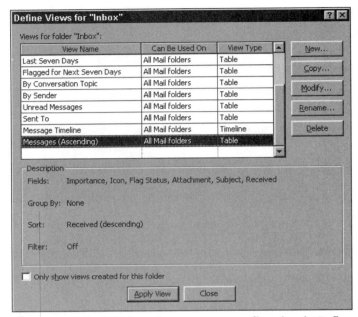

Figure 8-28: Description of messages ascending view in Define Views for Inbox dialog box

5. Click the Modify button with Messages (Ascending) view selected in the Define Views for Inbox to display the View Summary dialog box. As Figure 8-29 shows, the summary also states that the sort is descending based on the Received field.

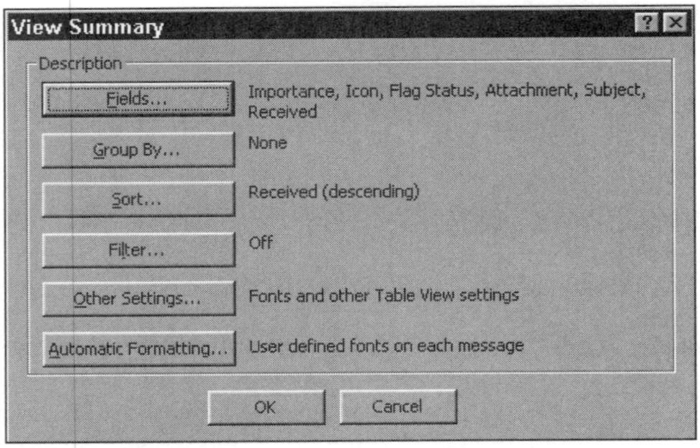

Figure 8-29: View Summary dialog box

6. Click the Sort button in the View Summary dialog box to display the Sort dialog box shown in Figure 8-30.

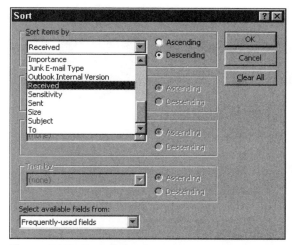

Figure 8-30: Sort dialog box

7. The "Sort Items by" dropdown box lists the fields on which to sort. Retain Received as the field. The radio buttons provide a choice between Ascending and Descending. Change the choice from Descending to Ascending. Click OK to return to the View Summary dialog box. As Figure 8-31 shows, the View Summary dialog box now shows that the sort is ascending based on the received field.

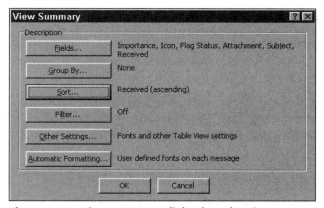

Figure 8-31: View Summary dialog box showing sort now by ascending received date

8. Click OK in the View Summary Dialog Box. You will now return to the Define Views for Inbox dialog box. As Figure 8-32 shows, the description at the bottom of the dialog box now describes the sort as ascending based on the Received field.

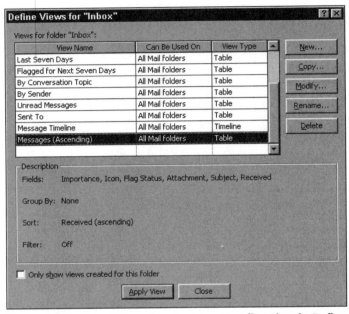

Figure 8-32: Description of messages ascending view in Define Views for Inbox dialog box

9. You're done! Well, you're done with defining the new view, not with creating the COM Add-In. Click the Close button in the Define Views for Inbox dialog box. Choose the View ➪ Current View and, as shown in Figure 8-25, you will now see the new view, Messages (Ascending), listed among the available views.

Project Code

The code for adding the custom menu and toolbar is reproduced in full in Listing 8-1. Use this code to replace the code in the OfficeAddIn template.

Listing 8-1: **Custom menu bar and toolbar code**

```
'General Declarations
Option Explicit

Implements IDTExtensibility2
```

```
Dim oApp As Outlook.Application
Dim ocCmdBars As Office.CommandBars
Dim cbMenuBar As CommandBar
Dim cbToolBar As CommandBar
Dim oExplorer As Explorer
Dim WithEvents cbToggleToolBar As CommandBarButton
Dim WithEvents cbReset As CommandBarButton
Dim WithEvents cbBarBtnAscend As CommandBarButton
Dim WithEvents cbBarBtnDescend As CommandBarButton
Dim WithEvents cbBarBtnWordMail As CommandBarButton

Private Sub cbBarBtnAscend_Click _
   (ByVal Ctrl As Office.CommandBarButton, _
   CancelDefault As Boolean)
     NavigateItems Ctrl.Parameter
End Sub


Private Sub cbBarBtnDescend_Click _
   (ByVal Ctrl As Office.CommandBarButton, _
   CancelDefault As Boolean)
     NavigateItems Ctrl.Parameter
End Sub

Private Sub cbBarBtnWordMail_Click _
   (ByVal Ctrl As Office.CommandBarButton, _
   CancelDefault As Boolean)

   Dim oiWordMail As Outlook.MailItem
   Dim oFrmDesc As Outlook.FormDescription
   Set oiWordMail = oApp.CreateItem(olMailItem)
   Set oFrmDesc = oiWordMail.FormDescription
   oFrmDesc.UseWordMail = True
   oiWordMail.Display

End Sub

Private Sub IDTExtensibility2_OnAddInsUpdate( _
      custom() As Variant)

   ' Not used in this application

End Sub

Private Sub IDTExtensibility2_OnBeginShutdown( _
   custom() As Variant)

   'no code here

End Sub

Private Sub IDTExtensibility2_OnConnection( _
```

Continued

Listing 8-1 *(continued)*

```
    ByVal Application As Object, ByVal ConnectMode As _
    AddInDesignerObjects.ext_ConnectMode, _
    ByVal AddInInst As Object, custom() As Variant)

    Set oApp = Application

End Sub

Private Sub IDTExtensibility2_OnDisconnection _
    (ByVal RemoveMode As _
    AddInDesignerObjects.ext_DisconnectMode, _
    custom() As Variant)

    On Error Resume Next

    Set cbToggleToolBar = Nothing
    Set cbReset = Nothing
    Set cbBarBtnAscend = Nothing
    Set cbBarBtnDescend = Nothing
    Set cbBarBtnWordMail = Nothing
    Set cbMenuBar = Nothing
    Set cbToolBar = Nothing
    Set ocCmdBars = Nothing
    Set oApp = Nothing

End Sub

Private Sub IDTExtensibility2_OnStartupComplete( _
    custom() As Variant)

    Dim oExplorer As Explorer
    Set oExplorer = oApp.ActiveExplorer
    If oApp Is Nothing Then
        Debug.Print "No Active Explorer"
        Exit Sub
    End If
    Set ocCmdBars = oApp.ActiveExplorer.CommandBars

    Set cbMenuBar = ocCmdBars.Add _
        ("CustomMenu", msoBarTop, True, True)

    Set cbToolBar = ocCmdBars.Add _
        (Name:="CustomToolBar", Position:=msoBarFloating)

    cbMenuBar.Visible = True
    cbToolBar.Visible = False

    Dim cbTopMenu As CommandBarPopup
```

```
        Set cbTopMenu = _
            cbMenuBar.Controls.Add(msoControlPopup, , , , True)
        Set cbReset = cbTopMenu.Controls.Add( _
            Type:=msoControlButton, temporary:=True)
        Set cbToggleToolBar = cbTopMenu.Controls.Add( _
            Type:=msoControlButton, temporary:=True)

        cbTopMenu.Caption = "&New Menu"
        cbReset.Caption = "&Reset"
        cbReset.Enabled = True
        cbToggleToolBar.Caption = "&Show Toolbar"
        cbToggleToolBar.Enabled = True

        Set cbBarBtnAscend = cbToolBar.Controls.Add _
            (Type: =msoControlButton)
        Set cbBarBtnDescend = cbToolBar.Controls.Add _
            (Type: =msoControlButton)
        Set cbBarBtnWordMail = cbToolBar.Controls.Add _
            (Type: =msoControlButton)

        With cbBarBtnAscend
            .FaceId = 210
            .Style = msoButtonIcon
            .ToolTipText = "Sort Earliest to Latest"
            .Parameter = "Ascend"
            .Enabled = True
            .Visible = True
        End With

        With cbBarBtnDescend
            .FaceId = 211
            .Style = msoButtonIcon
            .ToolTipText = "Sort Latest to Earliest"
            .Parameter = "Descend"
            .Enabled = True
            .Visible = True
        End With

        With cbBarBtnWordMail
            .FaceId = 626
            .Style = msoButtonIcon
            .ToolTipText = "New WordMail Item"
            '.OnAction = "CreateWordMailItem"
            .Enabled = True
            .Visible = True
        End With

End Sub

Private Sub cbToggleToolBar_Click( _
```

Continued

Listing 8-1 *(continued)*

```
        ByVal Ctrl As Office.CommandBarButton, _
        CancelDefault As Boolean)

        cbToolBar.Visible = Not cbToolBar.Visible

    End Sub

    Private Sub cbReset_Click( _
        ByVal Ctrl As Office.CommandBarButton, _
        CancelDefault As Boolean)

        cbMenuBar.Delete

    End Sub

    Public Sub NavigateItems(param As String)

        On Error Resume Next
        Dim oExp As Outlook.Explorer
        Set oExp = oApp.ActiveExplorer
        Select Case param
        Case "Ascend"
            oExp.CurrentView = ("Messages (Ascending)")
        Case "Descend"
            oExp.CurrentView = ("Messages")
        End Select

    End Sub
```

Finishing the Project

Once the code is written, only a few steps remain before you have a functioning COM Add-In:

1. In Visual Basic, choose the File ➪ Make `filename.dll menu` command. This will compile the COM Add-In. If you are using Microsoft Office 2000 Developer, the compilation of the COM Add-In also will register the add-in. Otherwise, you can use a registry editor (.reg) file as discussed in the section "Registering the COM Add-In."

2. Start Outlook. The new menu should display as shown earlier in Figure 8-18.

If the menu does not appear, try the following steps:

1. Activate the COM Add-Ins dialog box displayed in Figure 8-1 by following the steps outlined earlier in this chapter in the section "Understanding the COM Add-In Object Model."

2. Choose the Add button to display the Add Add-In dialog box and navigate to your COM Add-In, as shown in Figure 8-33.

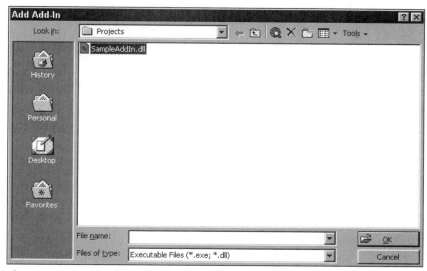

Figure 8-33: Add Add-In dialog box

3. Click OK to dismiss the Add Add-In dialog box and return to the Com Add-Ins dialog box. The COM Add-In should now be displayed in the list of COM Add-Ins as shown in Figure 8-34.

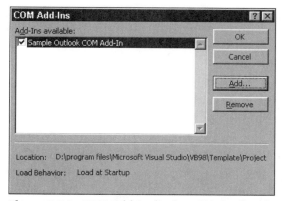

Figure 8-34: COM Add-In displayed in the list of COM Add-Ins in the COM Add-In dialog box

Analyzing Code Through the Command Bar Object Model

Since the code in Listing 8-1 uses the Command Bar object model, we will analyze the code in the context of a tour of that object model.

Command bars have their own object model. This object model is not specific to Outlook. Rather, it is part of the Microsoft Office 9.0 Object Library. The command bar collections and objects consist of:

✦ CommandBars collection—You use the `CommandBars` property to return a reference to this collection. This is a collection of CommandBar objects.

✦ CommandBar object—This object is a menu bar, submenu, shortcut menu, or toolbar. Thus, the CommandBars collection contains all of the menu bars, submenus, shortcut menus, and toolbars in the instance of the Office application, in this case Outlook. Each CommandBar object has a CommandBarControls collection.

✦ CommandBarControls collection—This is a collection of CommandBar Control objects.

✦ CommandBarControl object—This is a particular control on a menu bar, submenu, shortcut menu, or toolbar. Thus, the CommandBarControls collection contains all of the controls on a particular menu bar, submenu, shortcut menu or toolbar.

The Command Bar object model is graphically depicted in Figure 8-35.

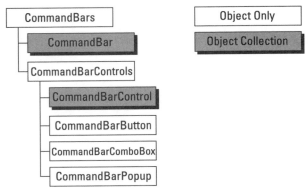

Figure 8-35: Command Bar Object Model

You use these collections and objects, and their properties and methods, to create the COM Add-In. Therefore, understanding these collections and objects is useful if you're analyzing the code for the COM Add-In.

CommandBars Collection

Each Explorer and Inspector object has a CommandBars collection, which is a collection of CommandBar objects. Menu bars, toolbars, and shortcut menus are CommandBar objects.

The code accesses the CommandBars collection through the following sequence.

1. The Application object is accessed through the Application parameter of the OnConnection method.

```
'General Declarations
Dim oApp as Outlook.Application

Private Sub IDTExtensibility2_OnConnection( _
    ByVal Application As Object, ByVal ConnectMode As _
    AddInDesignerObjects.ext_ConnectMode, _
    ByVal AddInInst As Object, custom() As Variant)

    Set oApp = Application

End Sub
```

2. The code example uses the Explorer object. You access the current Explorer through the Application object's ActiveExplorer method. You also can access the Explorer through the Application object's ActiveWindow method. The code does not use the Inspector object, but if it did, you would access that object through the Application object's ActiveInspector or Active Window methods.

```
'General Declarations
Dim oExplorer As Explorer
'OnStartUpComplete Event
Set oExplorer = oApp.ActiveExplorer
```

3. The code example checks to make sure there is an active Explorer object, because if there isn't, using the object variable to instantiate a CommandBars collection will cause an error:

```
If oApp Is Nothing Then
    Debug.Print "No Active Explorer"
    Exit Sub
End If
```

4. Access the CommandBars collection of the current Explorer or Inspector object through that object's CommandBars property.

```
'General Declarations
Dim ocCmdBars As Office.CommandBars
'OnStartUpComplete Event
Set ocCmdBars = oApp.ActiveExplorer.CommandBars
```

This example instantiates the CommandBars collection object in the `OnStartUp Complete` event but could also have done so in the `OnConnection` event.

Once you have instantiated a CommandBars collection object, you can use its properties, its methods, and its one event. Table 8-13 describes those properties of the CommandBars collection that are of primary use to the programmer:

Table 8-13
Selected Properties of the CommandBars Collection

Name	Description
ActionControl	Returns the CommandBarControl object whose `OnAction` property is set to the running procedure. The `OnAction` property is discussed in Table 8-22.
ActiveMenuBar	Returns a CommandBar object that represents the active menu bar.
AdaptiveMenus	Returns True if the command bar displays adaptive menus, False if it does not. An adaptive menu displays a subset of the menu items you use most often, with the remainder accessible through two chevrons pointing outward at the end of the menu.
Count	The number of CommandBar objects in the CommandBars collection.
Item	Returns a CommandBar object from the CommandBars collection by either its one-based position or its name.

The `ActiveControl` property is coupled with the `OnAction` property of the CommandBarControl object. The `OnAction` property is a string that is the name of a procedure that runs when the control is activated, such as by clicking it. You can use the `ActiveControl` property to return the control in the collection of controls was activated:

```
Dim cbcCtl As CommandBarControl
Set cbcCtl = oApp.ActiveExplorer.CommandBars.ActiveControl
```

The `ActiveMenuBar` property is useful in determining which of the menu bars currently has focus. It is analogous to the `ActiveControl` property but concerns menu bars instead of controls.

The `AdaptiveMenus` property is useful when the menu has many items and therefore would take up an undue amount of screen space if shown in its entirety.

The Count property is useful, as usual, for iterating through the collection of CommandBars.

The Item property is used to return an item, in this case a CommandBar, from the collection. This code retrieves a command bar with the common name Godzilla:

```
Dim cbBar As CommandBar
Set cbBar = oApp.ActiveExplorer.CommandBars.Item("Godzilla")
```

The Item property is the default property so the following statement also would work:

```
Set cbBar = oApp.ActiveExplorer.CommandBars("Godzilla")
```

The Item property also can be used to search for a CommandBar object. The Set statement above would raise a trappable error if there were no CommandBar object named Godzilla. You could use the trappable error to determine that no CommandBar object met the search criteria.

Table 8-14 lists the methods of the CommandBars collection:

Table 8-14
Methods of the CommandBars Collection

Name	Description	Parameters
Add	Creates a new command bar, adds it to the collection of command bars, and returns a CommandBar object.	Four optional parameters described in Table 8-15.
FindControl	Returns a CommandBarControl object that fits the criteria specified in the parameters, or Nothing if no object fits the specified criteria.	All optional. See Table 8-17.
FindControls	Returns a CommandBarControls collection of CommandBar objects that fit the criteria specified in the parameters, or Nothing if no object fits the specified criteria.	All optional. See Table 8-17.
ReleaseFocus	Releases the focus in the user interface from all command bars.	None.

Table 8-15
Parameters of Add Method of the CommandBars Collection

Name	Description
Name	The name of the new command bar, or if omitted, a default name.
Position	One of the msoBarPosition constants listed in Table 8-16 indicating the position or type of the new command bar.
MenuBar	True to replace the active menu bar with the new command bar, False (the default) to create an additional menu bar.
Temporary	True to make the new command bar "temporary" so that it is deleted when Outlook closes. The default value is False.

Table 8-16
Position Parameter of Add Method of the CommandBars Collection

Constant	Value	Description
msoBarLeft	0	The new command bar will be docked at the left of the Outlook window.
msoBarTop	1	The new command bar will be docked at the top of the Outlook window (default).
msoBarRight	2	The new command bar will be docked at the right of the Outlook window.
msoBarBottom	3	The new command bar will be docked at the bottom of the Outlook window.
msoBarFloating	4	The new command bar will not be docked.
msoBarPopup	5	The new command bar will be a shortcut menu.

You add a custom menu bar or toolbar to the current Explorer or Inspector object by using the Add method of the object's CommandBars collection. The syntax of the Add method is:

```
objectvariable.Add(Name, Position, MenuBar, Temporary)
```

The example has two CommandBar objects: cbMenuBar and cbToolBar, representing the new menu and toolbar, respectively. These objects are instantiated in the OnStartupComplete event:

```
Set cbMenuBar = ocCmdBars.Add _
    ("CustomMenu", msoBarTop, True, True)
```

```
Set cbToolBar = ocCmdBars.Add _
    (Name:="CustomToolBar", Position:=msoBarFloating)
```

The above implementations of the Add method show two different ways of passing parameters. The menu bar, named CustomMenu, will be positioned at the top of the Outlook window. The third parameter, being set to True, means that this custom menu bar will replace the standard menu bar. The standard menu bar will be restored as discussed later. The fourth parameter, also being set to True, means that this custom menu will be deleted when Outlook closes. The toolbar, named CustomToolBar, will be a floating toolbar.

Table 8-17 lists the parameters of the FindControl and FindControls methods:

Table 8-17
Parameters of FindControl and FindControls Method of the CommandBars Collection

Name	Description
Type	One of the msoControlType constants listed in Table 8-21 indicating the type of control.
ID	An identifier.
Tag	A tag value that can be used to contain additional information about the control.
Visible	True means the search is limited to visible controls. The default is False.
Recursive	True means the search extends to submenus and subtoolbars. The default is False. This is a parameter only for the FindControl method.
	The CommandBars collection has one event, OnUpdate. This event takes no parameters. The event is triggered by *any* change, and we do mean any change, to a command bar. For example, the OnUpdate event occurs when a user changes the selection in an Office document. The reason is that this event needs to be aware of any change to an Office document that may affect the state of any visible command bar or command bar control. Thus, you can use this event to change the availability or state of command bars or command bar controls in response to actions taken by the user. However, since many OnUpdate events can occur during normal usage, this event should be used sparingly to avoid adversely affecting the performance of your application. Microsoft suggests in the Outlook Visual Basic Reference Help file, and we concur, that the OnUpdate event be used primarily for checking that a custom command bar has been added or removed by a COMAddIn.

CommandBar Object

The next step is to add items to the menu bar and buttons to the toolbar. This means using the properties and methods of the CommandBar object. This object has no events.

Table 8-18 describes those properties of the CommandBar object that are of primary use to the programmer:

	Table 8-18
	Selected Properties of the CommandBar Object

Name	Description
AdaptiveMenus	Returns True if the command bar displays adaptive menus, False if it does not. An adaptive menu displays a subset of the menu items you use most often, with the remainder accessible through two chevrons pointing outward at the end of the menu.
BuiltIn	Returns True if the command bar is a built-in command bar of Outlook, False if it is a custom command bar.
Controls	Returns a CommandBarControls collection of all the CommandBarControl objects on the command bar.
Enabled	Sets or returns a True or False value indicating whether the command bar will appear in the list of available command bars.
Height	Returns the height in pixels of the command bar.
Index	Returns the one-based position of the command bar within the CommandBars collection.
Left	Sets or returns the distance in pixels from the left edge of the command bar to the left edge of the screen. For docked command bars, this property sets or returns the distance from the command bar to the left side of the docking area.
Name	Sets or returns the name of the command bar.
Position	Sets or returns the position of the command bar using one of the msoBarPosition constants described in Table 8-16.

Name	Description
Protection	Sets or returns one of the `msoBarProtection` constants (whose names are relatively self-explanatory) indicating the extent to which a command bar is protected from user customization: `msoBarNo Protection, msoBarNoCustomize, msoBarNoResize, msoBar NoMove, msoBarNoChangeVisible, msoBarNoChangeDock, msoBarNoVerticalDock`, or `msoBarNoHorizontalDock`.
Top	Sets or returns the distance in pixels from the left edge of the command bar to the top of the screen. For docked command bars, this property sets or returns the distance from the command bar to the top of the docking area.
Type	Returns one of the following `msoBarType` constants indicating the type of command bar: `msoBarTypeNormal, msoBarTypeMenuBar`, or `msoBarTypePopup`.
Visible	Sets or returns a True or False value indicating whether the command bar is visible. The `Enabled` property for a command bar must be set to True before the visible property is set to True.
Width	Returns the width in pixels of the command bar.

We discussed the `AdaptiveMenu` property above in connection with the Command Bars collection. The `BuiltIn` property is useful when you're iterating through the CommandBars collection to determine if the command bar is built-in or custom. Built-in command bars may be modified but they cannot be deleted, and they can be restored using the `Reset` method described in Table 8-19. By contrast, custom command bars can be deleted with the `Delete` method described in Table 8-19.

The `Controls` property is useful in obtaining the collection of CommandBar Controls belonging to the command bar.

You can use the Type property when iterating through the CommandBars collection to determine whether the command bar is a menu bar or a toolbar.

The `Visible` property of the custom menu bar is set to True:

```
cbMenuBar.Visible = True
```

The `Visible` property of the custom toolbar later will be set to True programmatically from the custom menu bar.

Table 8-19 describes the methods of the CommandBar object:

	Table 8-19 **Methods of the CommandBar Object**	
Name	*Description*	*Parameters*
Delete	Deletes the command bar. Cannot be used to delete a built-in command bar.	None.
FindControl	Returns a CommandBarControl object that fits the criteria specified in the parameters, or Nothing if no object fits the specified criteria.	See Table 8-17.
Reset	Resets a built-in command bar to its default configuration.	None.
ShowPopup	Displays a command bar as a shortcut menu at the specified coordinates or at the current pointer coordinates.	Two optional arguments, the x and y coordinates, respectively, for the location of the shortcut menu. The omission of either argument results in the current x and y coordinate, respectively, of the mouse pointer.

As discussed above, the Reset method restores the default configuration of a built-in command bar. The Delete method deletes custom command bars.

The FindControl method works the same as the identically named method of the CommandBars collection.

The ShowPopup method works only with shortcut menus. It will not work with a standard menu bar or toolbar.

The next step is to add items to the custom menu bar and buttons to the custom toolbar. Each item and button is a control or CommandBarControl object. As discussed earlier, CommandBar object's Controls property returns the controls that belong to it. Those controls comprise the CommandBarControls collection.

CommandBarControls Collection

The CommandBarControls collection has two important properties, Count and Item:

✦ Count, as with other collections, returns the number of items in the collection, in this case the controls on the command bar. Therefore, this property is useful for iterating through the controls on a command bar.

✦ Item returns a CommandBarControl object based on the one-based position or name of the object.

The CommandBarControls collection has one method, Add. Table 8-20 describes its parameters, all of which are optional:

Table 8-20
Parameters of Add Method of the
CommandBarControls Collection

Name	Description
Type	One of the msoControlType constants described in Table 8-21 that describes the type of control to be added to the command bar.
Id	An integer that specifies a built-in control. If the value of this argument is 1, or if this argument is omitted, a blank custom control of the specified type will be added to the command bar.
Parameter	For built-in controls, this argument is used by the container application to run the command. For custom controls, you can use this argument to send information to Visual Basic procedures, or you can use it to store information about the control.
Before	A number that indicates the position of the new control on the command bar. The new control will be inserted before the control at this position. If this argument is omitted, the control is added at the end of the specified command bar.
Temporary	True to make the new control "temporary" so that it is deleted when Outlook closes. The default value is False.

The Type parameter refers to the type of control. By contrast, the Type parameter of the Add method of the CommandBars collection refers to the type of command bar. Table 8-21 summarizes the msoControlType constants referring to the different types of controls:

Table 8-21 msoControlType **Constants**	
Constant	*Description*
MsoControlButton	A button on a toolbar or a menu item that runs a command when it is clicked. Both may be displayed as an icon and a caption or as a caption only. Additionally, a toolbar button may be displayed as an icon only.
MsoControlComboBox	A combo box on a menu or toolbar.
MsoControlDropdown	A dropdown list box on a menu or toolbar.
MsoControlEdit	An edit box on a menu or toolbar.
MsoControlPopup	A control on a menu bar or toolbar that either displays a menu or submenu when it is clicked or displays a submenu when the pointer is positioned over it.

The CommandBarControls collection has no events.

The code to build the custom menu bar uses the following object variables declared in General Declarations:

```
'General Declarations
Dim WithEvents cbToggleToolBar As CommandBarButton
Dim WithEvents cbReset As CommandBarButton
```

The two menu items are not declared as CommandBarControl objects even though they are CommandBarControl objects. This is because the CommandBarControl object is a generic control that encompasses several specific controls. The Command BarButton object is one of these controls. The CommandBarPopup and CommandBar ComboBox are the other two. Since the menu items to toggle the visibility of the toolbar and reset the standard menu are buttons as opposed to popups or combo boxes, it is logical to declare them specifically as CommandBarButton objects rather than generically as CommandBarControl objects. However, there are situations, such as when you're using the FindControl or FindControls method to locate particular controls, where you should use the generic CommandBarControl object since the toolbar may contain different types of controls.

You can declare the two menu items with the WithEvents keyword since they will need to "know" when they are clicked.

Next, the menu is built in the `OnStartUpComplete` event:

```
'OnStartUpComplete Event
Dim cbTopMenu As CommandBarPopup
Set cbTopMenu = cbMenuBar.Controls.Add _
    (msoControlPopup, , , , True)
Set cbReset = cbTopMenu.Controls.Add( _
    Type:=msoControlButton, Temporary:=True)
Set cbToggleToolBar = cbTopMenu.Controls.Add( _
    Type:=msoControlButton, Temporary:=True)
```

The object variable `cbTopMenu` is the top menu item, similar to File, Edit, View, and so on, on the standard menu bar. Clicking it does not run an action. Rather, clicking it displays the other menu items. Therefore, it is declared as a CommandBarPopup object, and the `Type` parameter of the Add method adding it is `msoControlPopup`. Additionally, the variable is declared locally as it only is used here to build the menu.

Because the other two menu items are CommandBarButton objects, add them to the menu with the `Type` parameter `msoControlButton`.

The toolbar is built similarly. The following object variables are declared in General Declarations:

```
'General Declarations
Dim WithEvents cbBarBtnAscend As CommandBarButton
Dim WithEvents cbBarBtnDescend As CommandBarButton
Dim WithEvents cbBarBtnWordMail As CommandBarButton
```

Next, the toolbar is built in the `OnStartUpComplete` event:

```
'OnStartUpComplete Event
Set cbBarBtnAscend =
cbToolBar.Controls.Add(Type:=msoControlButton)
Set cbBarBtnDescend =
cbToolBar.Controls.Add(Type:=msoControlButton)
Set cbBarBtnWordMail =
cbToolBar.Controls.Add(Type:=msoControlButton)
```

While the menu and toolbar have been built, the characteristics of their constituent items have yet to be defined. You will do this with the properties and methods of the CommandBarControl object and the specific CommandBarButton, CommandBar ComboBox, and CommandBarPopup objects.

CommandBarControl Object

Table 8-22 describes those properties of the CommandBar object that are of primary use to the programmer:

Table 8-22	
Selected Properties of the CommandBarControl Object	
Name	**Description**
BuiltIn	Returns True if the control is a built-in control of Outlook, False if it is a custom control or if it is a built-in control whose OnAction property has been set.
Caption	Sets or returns the caption of the control.
Enabled	Sets or returns a True or False value indicating whether the control is enabled.
Height	Sets or returns the height in pixels of the control.
Index	Returns the one-based position of the command bar within the CommandBars collection.
Left	Sets or returns the distance in pixels from the left edge of the control to the left edge of the screen.
OnAction	Sets or returns the name of the procedure that will run when the user clicks or changes the value of the control.
Parameter	Sets or returns a string that an application can use to execute a command.
Tag	Returns or sets information about the control, such as data that can be used as an argument in procedures, or information that identifies the control.
ToolTipText	Returns or sets the text displayed in a command bar control's ScreenTip.
Top	Sets or returns the distance in pixels from the left edge of the control to the top of the screen.
ToolTipText	Returns or sets the text displayed in a command bar control's ScreenTip.
Type	Corresponds to the msoControlType constants described in Table 8-21.
Visible	Sets or returns a True or False value indicating whether the command bar is visible. The Enabled property for a command bar must be set to True before the visible property is set to True.
Width	Returns the width in pixels of the control.

These Caption and Enabled properties are used to define the menu items:

```
cbTopMenu.Caption = "&New Menu"
cbReset.Caption = "&Reset"
cbReset.Enabled = True
cbToggleToolBar.Caption = "&Show Toolbar"
cbToggleToolBar.Enabled = True
```

The definition of the toolbar is more complicated. The CommandBarButton has a Style property. The code in Listing 8-2 will use the style msoButtonIcon, which as the name suggests is a button with an icon on it. The FaceID property is an integer that corresponds to an image on an image map. The value 210 is the image for ascending, 211 for descending, and 626 for WordMail. The ToolTipText property is described in Table 8-22 above. The code sets the Enabled and Visible properties to True so that the buttons can be seen and accessed. Finally, the code in Listing 8-2 uses the Parameter property to distinguish whether the Ascending or Descending toolbar button was clicked.

Listing 8-2: **Code to build the toolbar**

```
With cbBarBtnAscend
    .FaceId = 210
    .Style = msoButtonIcon
    .ToolTipText = "Sort Earliest to Latest"
    .Parameter = "Ascend"
    .Enabled = True
    .Visible = True
End With

With cbBarBtnDescend
    .FaceId = 211
    .Style = msoButtonIcon
    .ToolTipText = "Sort Latest to Earliest"
    .Parameter = "Descend"
    .Enabled = True
    .Visible = True
End With

With cbBarBtnWordMail
    .FaceId = 626
    .Style = msoButtonIcon
    .ToolTipText = "New WordMail Item"
    .OnAction = "CreateWordMailItem"
    .Enabled = True
    .Visible = True
End With
```

Face ID

The code in Listing 8-2 uses FaceID numbers of 210, 211, and 626 to obtain the icons for the toolbars. Where do these numbers come from, and how do you learn which numbers correspond to which images?

The images retrieved by the FaceID property are on an image map. There are literally thousands of images. Each image has a corresponding number, but not all of the numbers have corresponding images, especially the higher numbers.

The following procedure will create a toolbar that displays the images whose numbers are between the two parameters of the procedure. Each image has a tooltip that indicates its corresponding number:

```
Function CBShowButtonFaceIDs _
    (lngIDStart As Long, lngIDStop As Long)

    Dim intCntr As Integer

    'If the toolbar exists then delete it.
    On Error Resume Next
    ocCmdBars("ShowFaceIds").Delete
    'Create the toolbar.
    'cbrNewToolbar should be declared in this procedure
    'or in General Declarations

    Set cbrNewToolbar = ocCmdBars.Add _
        (Name:="ShowFaceIds", temporary:=True)


    'Create a new button
    'Image will match FaceId property value
    'indicated by intCntr.
     For intCntr = lngIDStart To lngIDStop
        ' cmdNewButton should be declared in this procedure
        'or in General Declarations
        Set cmdNewButton = cbrNewToolbar.Controls.Add
           _(Type:=msoControlButton)
        With cmdNewButton
           .FaceId = intCntr
           .ToolTipText = "FaceId = " & intCntr
           .Style = msoButtonIcon
           .Visible = True
        End With
    Next intCntr


    ' Show the images on the toolbar.
    With cbrNewToolbar
       .Width = 600
```

```
            .Left = 100
            .Top = 200
            .Enabled = True
            .Visible = True
        End With

    End Function
```

The code was adapted from code on the Microsoft Office 2000 Developer CD. We say *adapted* because we had to tweak the code had to make it work. You can then call the function from the COM Add-In in this chapter's code example with the statement:

```
Call CBShowButtonFaceIDs(1, 200)
```

As the comments indicate, you need to declare two object variables, `cbrNewToolbar`, a CommandBar object, and `cmdNewButton`, a CommandButton object, either in the procedure or in General Declarations. Additionally, unless you have a very fast machine with a wheelbarrow full of RAM, you might want to keep the range of the parameter to 200 images at a time.

Table 8-23 describes the methods of the CommandBarControl object:

Table 8-23
Methods of the CommandBarControl Object

Name	Description	Parameters
Copy	Copies the control to a command bar.	Two optional: The destination command bar (if omitted this will be the command bar where the control already is located), and the one-based position before which the control should be placed (if omitted the control will be placed at the end of the command bar).
Delete	Deletes the custom control.	One optional: True to delete the control for the current session only, in which case the application will display the control again in the next session.
Execute	Runs the built-in command assigned to a built-in control. Custom controls use the `OnAction` property to specify the procedure to be run.	None.

Continued

	Table 8-23 *(continued)*	
Name	**Description**	**Parameters**
Move	Moves the control to a command bar.	Two optional: the command bar to which the control will move (default is the command bar the control is on), and the one-based position on the command bar (default is end of command bar).
Reset	Resets the control to its initial configuration.	None.
SetFocus	Moves the keyboard focus to the specified control, which must be enabled and visible.	None.

The generic CommandBarControl object has no events. However, the Command BarButton object has a Click event, and the CommadBarComboBox object has a Change event.

The Reset menu item restores the default menu bar by using the Delete method of the CommandBar object:

```
Private Sub cbReset_Click( _
    ByVal Ctrl As Office.CommandBarButton, _
    CancelDefault As Boolean)

    cbMenuBar.Delete

End Sub
```

The Reset menu item and other CommandBarControl objects declared WithEvents, are listed in the Object dropdown list in the Code window, and their corresponding events, if any, is listed in the Procedures drop down list.

The Toggle Toolbar menu item toggles the visibility of the custom toolbar using the Not operator:

```
Private Sub cbToggleToolBar_Click( _
    ByVal Ctrl As Office.CommandBarButton, _
    CancelDefault As Boolean)

    cbToolBar.Visible = Not cbToolBar.Visible

End Sub
```

The Ascending toolbar button and the Descending toolbar button both call the same procedure, NavigateItems. The parameter of this procedure is the value of the Parameter property of the toolbar button that was clicked.

```
Private Sub cbBarBtnAscend_Click _
    (ByVal Ctrl As Office.CommandBarButton, _
    CancelDefault As Boolean)
      NavigateItems Ctrl.Parameter
End Sub

Private Sub cbBarBtnDescend_Click _
    (ByVal Ctrl As Office.CommandBarButton, _
    CancelDefault As Boolean)
      NavigateItems Ctrl.Parameter
End Sub
```

The NavigateItems method sets the view by ascending or descending date depending on the value of the parameter passed to it:

```
Public Sub NavigateItems(param As String)

    On Error Resume Next
    Dim oExp As Outlook.Explorer
    Set oExp = oApp.ActiveExplorer
    Select Case param
    Case "Ascend"
        oExp.CurrentView = ("Messages (Ascending)")
    Case "Descend"
        oExp.CurrentView = ("Messages")
    End Select

End Sub
```

The CurrentView property of the Explorer object sets one of the available views. The views that are available are listed by the View ➪ CurrentView menu command. The Messages view lists messages in descending date order — that is, latest date first. We created another view, Messages (Ascending), through the Outlook GUI, as discussed earlier in "Creating a Custom View." Currently a new view cannot be created programmatically through the Outlook object model. The Messages (Ascending) view differs from the Messages view only in that the messages are listed in ascending date order.

The procedure distinguishes between the two views by the value of param in its argument. The Ascending and Descending toolbar buttons each had a Parameter property, set to Ascending and Descending, respectively. The Click event of each button passed this value when it called the NavigateItems procedure.

Clicking the WordMail toolbar button creates a new mail message using WordMail:

```
Private Sub cbBarBtnWordMail_Click _
    (ByVal Ctrl As Office.CommandBarButton, _
    CancelDefault As Boolean)

    Dim oiWordMail As Outlook.MailItem
    Dim oFrmDesc As Outlook.FormDescription
    Set oiWordMail = oApp.CreateItem(olMailItem)
    Set oFrmDesc = oiWordMail.FormDescription
    oFrmDesc.UseWordMail = True
    oiWordMail.Display

End Sub
```

The `CreateItem` method of the Application object creates the new mail item. You use the FormDescription object to activate the WordMail feature by setting the object's `UseWordMail` property to True.

Finally, in the OnDisconnection event, the instantiated object variables are set to `Nothing` to release the previously allocated memory:

```
Private Sub IDTExtensibility2_OnDisconnection _
    (ByVal RemoveMode As _
    AddInDesignerObjects.ext_DisconnectMode, _
    custom() As Variant)

On Error Resume Next

Set oExplorer = Nothing
Set cbToggleToolBar = Nothing
Set cbReset = Nothing
Set cbBarBtnAscend = Nothing
Set cbBarBtnDescend = Nothing
Set cbBarBtnWordMail = Nothing
Set cbMenuBar = Nothing
Set cbToolBar = Nothing
Set ocCmdBars = Nothing
Set oApp = Nothing

End Sub
```

The `Set objectvariable = Nothing` statements are necessary not just to release the memory previously allocated to the object variables; they also may be necessary to release Outlook itself from memory. Otherwise, Outlook may remain in memory even after the user logs off.

Summary

One of the important new features of Office 2000 is the ability to create COM Add-Ins for Office 2000 applications, including Outlook 2000. A COM Add-In is an ActiveX DLL (dynamic-link library) that implements a predefined interface and is specially registered so that it can be recognized and loaded by *all* Office 2000 applications. In this chapter you learned about the COMAddIn object model, how to implement its IDTExtensibility2 interface, and how to register it so it can be used by Office 2000 applications.

You also learned about and then used tools that simplify your task of developing COM Add-Ins. Visual Basic 6.0 supports add-in designers that simplify the task of registering a COM Add-In for use by Office 2000 applications. In turn, the Microsoft Office 2000 Developer edition provides a COM Add-In template. In this chapter, you created a COM Add-In template using the add-in designer.

COM Add-Ins are often used to create custom menu bars and toolbars. Menu bars and toolbars are command bars. In this chapter, you learned about the Command Bar Object Model. You then modified the COM Add-In template to create a custom COM Add-In that added a custom menu bar and toolbar to Outlook 2000.

✦   ✦   ✦

Web Enabling Outlook

Outlook Web Components

In 1991, the creation of the World Wide Web (aka "the Web") revolutionized how data are displayed. Just as the Macintosh computer changed the computer's user interface with icons and other user-friendly graphical elements, the Web changed how users view information with hypertext technology. Previously, in an era of print media, information was presented in a linear manner. Hypertext technology permitted information to be linked, so that users could jump from topic to topic with relative ease. Additionally, the manner of linkage could enable users to view information on a general, overall level and then "drill down" in increasing levels of specificity to more detailed information. For example, at the IDG Books Web site, www. idgbooks.com, you can choose among the online bookstore, jobs, investor information or, the favorite of authors and developers, "Free and Downloadable." The "Free and Downloadable" category gives you further choices, such as audio, utilities, and games. Choosing games provides you with further choices of particular games or books about games.

In a similar way, the previous versions of Microsoft e-mail client, Microsoft Mail, Microsoft Exchange Client, and Microsoft Outlook 97, essentially supported only a linear view of your e-mail information. Information was arranged into categories such as Inbox, Outbox, Sent Items, and so on. However, there was no effective means of linking related information or drilling down from the general to the specific.

This all changed with the release of Outlook 98, when Microsoft first introduced a hypertext summary page of important information within Outlook. This summary page, which you can think of as "Outlook at a glance," was (and still is) called *Outlook Today*. Through a Web-style interface, Outlook Today provides a quick look at the number of your unread messages, your scheduled appointments for the next five days, and any open tasks you have defined.

Outlook 2000 takes the "at a glance" concept to the next level by providing you with the ability to view "at a glance" summarized information contained within folders. This format is called a Folder Home Page. A Folder Home Page enables you to link an HTML page to any folder or set of folders in Outlook. Folder Home Pages also support offline view capabilities, which enable you to have Outlook synchronize an HTML file associated with the folder offline when a user synchronizes the folder. This ensures that your HTML page is available whether the user is working online or offline.

Microsoft also has provided a COM component called the Outlook View Control that enables you to quickly look at your Outlook information. This component is an ActiveX wrapper around the Outlook views, such as the Table, Calendar, Card, and Timeline views. It can be used within a Web application, such as an Active Server Page application, or inside a Folder Home Page.

Outlook Today

Outlook Today allows users to view information in one HTML window, as illustrated in Figure 9-1. This enables users to view Outlook information in an "at a glance" format, that provides a summarization of information from multiple Outlook folders on one page rather than having to look through individual folders for the same information.

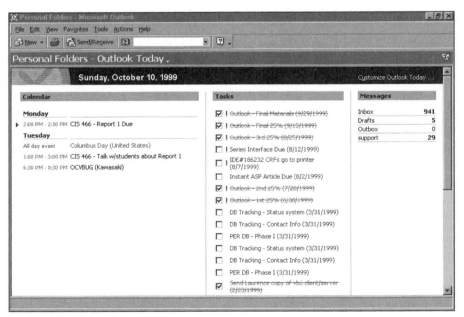

Figure 9-1: Outlook Today

Outlook Today uses a technology in Microsoft Internet Explorer called data binding, which allows Outlook to quickly display the user interface for the Outlook Today page while asynchronously downloading data to the Outlook client from the data source, usually an Exchange Server. An important advantage of this technology is that the user can modify data within Outlook Today without the need for additional calls to the Exchange Server or other data sources.

By default, Outlook Today has three data binding tables, for your Calendar, Tasks, and Mail, respectively. Correspondingly, Outlook Today displays three separate columns of information: calendar of events for the next five days, assigned tasks, and summary of unread mail for specified folders. Each item is a hyperlink to the corresponding Outlook folder, so you can easily drill down to more specific information. For example, clicking on Mail will take you to your Inbox where you can review your unread messages.

Customizing Outlook Today

You can customize Outlook Today either through the Outlook User Interface (UI) or through code. The tradeoff between the two options is the usual one. Customizing through the Outlook UI is easier than customizing through code, but the degree of customization is more limited.

Customizing through the Outlook UI

You can customize Outlook Today through the Outlook UI by selecting the Customize Outlook Today... button in the upper right-hand corner of the Outlook Today page as shown in Figure 9-2.

Figure 9-2: Customize Outlook Today

The Customize Outlook Today screen is organized into five sections:

✦ Startup — If you mark the checkbox, the Outlook Today page will launch each time the Outlook client is started.

✦ Messages — In this section, you can choose which Outlook message folders you would like to summarize on the Outlook Today page. You can select any folder that contains information, but it only displays a value if there are unread messages.

✦ Calendar — This option allows you to change the number of days you want to view events for, ranging from one to seven days.

✦ Tasks — This section allows you define the tasks you would like to see on your Outlook Today page. You can view all the tasks or just the current day's. You can also determine how you would like the information to be sorted.

✦ Styles — There are five predefined styles: standard, standard (two column), standard (one column), Summer, and Winter. Standard displays the summary information in three columns. Standard (two column) displays the summary information in two columns. Standard (one column) displays the summary information in one column. Summer displays the information in two columns but changes the color scheme from a white background with gray highlighted titles to a yellow background with tan highlighted titles. Winter also displays the information in two columns with the color scheme of a white background with soft blue highlighted titles. Figure 9-3 illustrates the layout scheme of Winter.

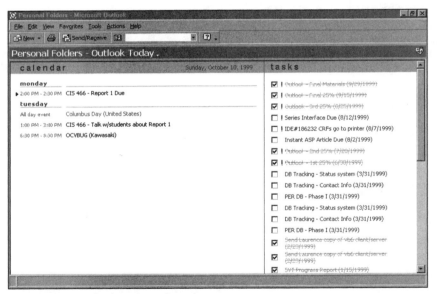

Figure 9-3: Outlook Today Winter layout

Customizing Outlook Today through code

Since Outlook Today displays information in HTML, developers can customize Outlook Today to an even greater extent than with the Customize Outlook Today feature. For example, you can add a bulletin of corporate news and a stock ticker synchronized with real-time market data taken from the Web.

Messages section

As described earlier, a user can choose which folder to show in the Messages section. System administrators can also preconfigure this section by changing settings in the Windows Registry.

By default, the Messages section is linked to the Inbox, Drafts, and Outbox folders at the location used by your Outlook client. For example, if you leave your information in public folders on an Exchange Server, Outlook Today will reflect the information in those public folders. If you store your information in personal folders on your local drive, Outlook Today will reflect the information in your personal folders on your local drive.

The names and locations of the folders pointed to by the Messages section in Outlook Today are recorded as string values in the Registry. The Registry subkey is:

```
HKEY_CURRENT_USER\Software\Microsoft\Office\9.0\Outlook\Today\Folders
```

You can have the Messages section point to a new folder by adding to the Registry subkey a numbered value entry and setting that entry's value to the folder's URL (uniform resource locator). For example, to have the Messages section link to the Inbox folder, Drafts folder, Outbox folder, and a Group Support public folder, navigate to the Registry subkey and enter the values stated in Table 9-1.

Table 9-1 Registry Setting for Custom Folders	
Value Name	**Value Data**
0	\\Personal Folder\inbox
1	\\Personal Folder\draft
2	\\Personal Folder\outbox
3	\\Public Folder\Groups\VB2Java\support

Figure 9-4 displays the Registry subkey after you add these entries.

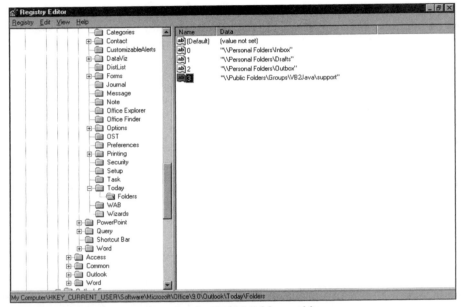

Figure 9-4: Windows Registry for the Today\Folders subkey

Calendar and Tasks section

By default, and like the Messages section, the Calendar and Tasks section in the Outlook Today home page obtains its information from the place in which your Outlook client stores it, whether it be a public folder on an Exchange Server or a personal folder on your local drive. You can, however, change the location of the folders to which the Calendar and Tasks section links by specifying a new folder path to which the Outlook Today data binding controls may link. However, unlike the Messages section, you do not achieve this by editing the Registry.

Both the Calendar and Tasks use ActiveX controls to obtain the location of the folders to which they link. You can find the references to these Active X controls within the Outlook Today HTML source file by searching for the `<object>` tag. By default these tags simply refer to the object's ID, its ClassID or GUID (Globally Unique Identifier), and its basic parameter settings. The ID provides the object with a unique name within the CSS, the ClassID provides the ActiveX control's unique identifier within the Windows Registry, and the `<param>` tag is used to allow a list of named property values to be represented. The `Name` attribute defines the property to be set and the `Value` attribute defines the property value.

You can change the folder from which Outlook Today obtains its information by adding a `<param>` tag to the control object that specifies the folder path you wish to use. For example, in the following HTML snippet the `<param>` tag in bold designates the new path on the server from which you want to obtain calendar information:

```
<OBJECT ID="CalList"
 CLASSID="CLSID:0468C085-CA5B-11D0-AF08-00609797F0E0">
<PARAM NAME="Module" VALUE="Calendar">
<PARAM NAME="path"
 VALUE="\\Public Folder\Summation\Calendar">
</OBJECT>
```

To have Outlook Today obtain Tasks information from another location, add the `<param>` tag to the TaskList object tag. For example, the following `<param>` tag denoted in bold will have Outlook Today reference the server for Tasks information.

```
<OBJECT ID="TaskList"
 CLASSID="CLSID:0468C085-CA5B-11D0-AF08-00609797F0E0">
<PARAM NAME="Module" VALUE="Tasks">
<PARAM NAME="path"
 VALUE="\\Public Folder\DevCycle\MainTasks">
</OBJECT>
```

Note   When the Value of the `<param>` tag starts with a double backslash (\\), it means the path is stored on the server where your Exchange server resides. If you omit them, Outlook Today will assume that the path resides on your local hard drive.

Outlook Today style

Each of the predefined Outlook Today styles (Standard with 1–3 columns, Summer, and Winter) corresponds to a different HTML page. The selected style is stored in the Registry under the CustomURL Value Name subkey. Table 9-2 shows the correspondence between the HTML pages and the predefined styles.

Table 9-2
CustomURL Value Data Settings

Value Data	Description
Outlook.htm	Standard 3 column Outlook Today
Outlook1.htm	Standard 2 column Outlook Today
Outlook2.htm	Standard 1 column Outlook Today
Outlook3.htm	Summer Outlook Today style
Outlook4.htm	Winter Outlook Today style

You are not limited to the predefined styles. You can create your own custom style. To accomplish this, create your own HTML page and then edit the Registry's sub-key so it points to the new HTML page.

The first step is to create your custom HTML page. You could create the custom HTML page by editing (and saving as a new page) one of the HTML pages that reflect a preexisting style. However, if you scan your system's hard drive, you will not find any of the five predefined HTML files described in Table 9-2. That's because they are a byproduct of a resource dynamic link library (DLL), `outlwvw.dll`. This does not mean that you have to bang your head against the wall trying to figure out how these styles were designed. You can obtain the HTML source files by displaying the Outlook Today page in your Web browser rather than through the Outlook client.

You change the Registry by adding a new Value Name to the HKEY_CURRENT_USER\Software\Microsoft\Office\9.0\Outlook\Today subkey. This new subkey is the **URL** string value. If you add this entry and its value, the Outlook client will use that URL as the Outlook Today page. If there is an entry in both the **CustomURL** and **URL**, the Outlook client will use the **URL** Value Name. In Figure 9-5, the **URL** Value Name is set to VB2Java.Com's Intranet portal.

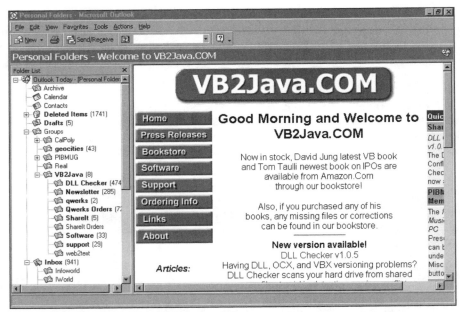

Figure 9-5: Outlook Today pointing to the company's intranet portal

The following steps describe how you can obtain the source HTML files using your Web browser.

1. In the Web browser's address box, to obtain the source file for the Standard Outlook Today page, type the following URL:

```
res://c:\Program Files\Microsoft Office\
Office\1033\outlwvw.dll/outlook.htm
```

Note Although the above line is shown as two lines, it should be typed as one line. It also assumes that Outlook was installed on the C: drive, in the Program Files folder, and so on. In order to ensure you have the correct resource line, it would be best if you scanned all your local hard drives for the DLL, outlwvw.dll.

2. In the status bar of your browser, you might receive a message stating "Error on Page." Don't be alarmed, since this is expected. The resource file is normally invoked within the Outlook client where it can obtain folder information. Figure 9-6 displays the Outlook Today page viewed using Microsoft Internet Explorer (IE).

Figure 9-6: Viewing Outlook Today outside the Outlook client

3. From the browser's View menu, select Source to display the HTML contents of the page. It will be displayed in Windows Notepad. Save the file to a working directory that you'll remember so you can edit it later.

4. To obtain the source documents for the other layouts, replace outlook.html with the names found in the Value Data column in Table 9-2.

Now that you have the source HTML for the Outlook Today layouts, you can customize them in any way that you like. These HTML files are broken down into three distinct sections: cascading style sheet (CSS) setting, standard HTML tags, and JavaScript functions. The cascading style sheet settings allow you to assign specific design styles to specific text in your Outlook Today document. The JavaScript functions provide additional functionality to your Outlook Today document such as opening up your calendar, displaying events that you click on, and so forth.

Tip Many of the links displayed on your Outlook Today may look and act like regular HTML links, but they are invoked by JavaScript functions behind the scenes. Although there are a lot of WYSIWYG (What You See Is What You Get) HTML editors on the market, including Microsoft FrontPage 2000, you might not want to use them to customize your Outlook Today pages, because these pages contain special formatting and tags that will make the file appear incorrectly. Many editors don't know how to read the formatting, and may in fact strip out the tags from the document thinking that they are illegal tags. You're really better off using an HTML editor like Windows Notepad, Allaire's Homesite, or Microsoft Visual InterDev.

Changing colors and font styles

You can change the colors and fonts that are displayed in your Outlook Today home page by changing the (CSS) definitions at the beginning of the Outlook Today HTML source file. The information is stored within the `<style>` tag. If you're not familiar with CSS, think of CSS as style templates that you might use in your word processing document so that section headers, table captions, and so on all look uniformed and so that you don't have to format each paragraph individually.

An example of a change you might want to make is the font used to display the number of messages in the Inbox folder. You may want to make that number stand out even more. By default, the CSS definition looks like the following:

```
.InboxCount      {font-weight:bold;}
```

You can change the font to Tahoma and the color to red by adding the settings that are in bold to the InboxCount setting:

```
.InboxCount      {font-family:tahoma;font-weight:bold;color:red}
```

Cross-Reference There are a number of books on changing colors and font styles, but one of the best sources is Wired Magazine's WebMonkey Web site (http://www.hotwired.com/webmonkey). Refer to their Stylesheet Guide under Quick Reference.

Adding additional ActiveX controls

You can add additional ActiveX controls to the Outlook Today page, just as you can with any HTML page. ActiveX control compatibility isn't an issue the way it is when you write regular HTML pages for the Internet because the Outlook client is built upon Internet Explorer (IE), which is an ActiveX-enabled browser. However, you need to take into account that the IE security safeguards for ActiveX controls have been disabled in Outlook Today. This means that you need to be very careful that the ActiveX controls you are using are trustworthy controls. They don't necessarily need to be signed controls, but you should make sure that you know where they came from. Otherwise, you may create a very big security hole.

Now that you've been warned, you can add an ActiveX control to your Outlook Today page simply by finding the control you wish to add and inserting the Object tag information into the page. However, this sounds easier than it really is. Unless you're using an HTML editor that's ActiveX enabled, you will have to search the Registry for suitable controls.

If you're using an editor like Allaire's Homesite, Microsoft Visual InterDev, or Microsoft ActiveX Control Pad, adding an ActiveX control is a snap. First, place the cursor in the HTML editor window where you want the control to be placed. Next, select the menu item to insert an ActiveX control, select the control from the control list box, and press the OK button. This places the control in your Outlook Today home page. Figure 9-7 shows an example of inserting the Microsoft Calendar control into the Outlook Today source page using Allaire's Homesite.

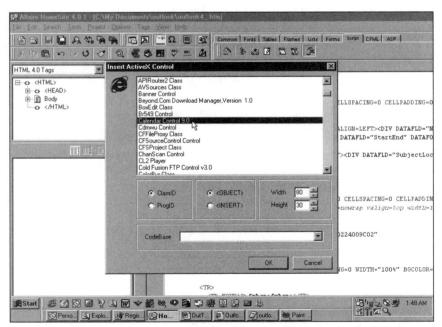

Figure 9-7: Inserting the Microsoft Calendar control into the Outlook Today source page

Inserting the Calendar control in this manner inserts the following code in the Outlook Today source page:

```
<OBJECT ID="CalControl"
 CLASSID="CLSID:8E27C92b-1264-101C-8A2F-040224009C02"
 WIDTH=320
 HEIGHT=320>
</OBJECT>
```

As you can see, without an HTML editor that's ActiveX-enabled, unless you know the ClassID of the ActiveX control you want to insert, you can't insert an ActiveX control in your Outlook Today home page. Figure 9-8 shows what your Outlook Today home page looks like after you have inserted the calendar control.

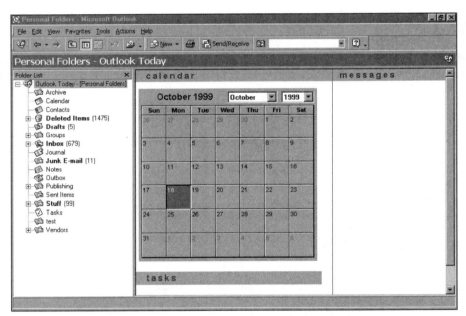

Figure 9-8: Calendar control viewed within the Outlook Today home page

The calendar control is a bit overwhelming, but it provides an excellent example of the type of ActiveX control you might want on your Outlook Today home page. Another ActiveX control people might want on their Outlook Today home page is a stock ticker (for all those day-traders you have in your office). Of course, you need to keep in mind that a real-time control like a stock ticker can absorb a lot of your network bandwidth.

Adding text and graphics

Using standard HTML and CSS properties, you can add new text or images, such as a corporate logo, to your Outlook Today home page. To format newly added text, you can use standard HTML formatting tags such as `<B>...</B>` for bold, `<I>...</I>` for italic, and so on. You can also assign text to be formatted using CSS properties.

You use one of three different protocols to add images to your page:

✦ file://—Use this protocol if the image you're using resides on your local hard drive or a mapped drive (file://c:\inetpub\wwwroot\lmp\lmp.gif).

✦ http://—Use this protocol if the image you're using resides on the Internet (`http://lastminuteproductions.hypermart.net/logo.gif`).

✦ res://—Use this protocol if the image resides within a resource file, like an ActiveX DLL. (res://c:\corporate\outlkres.dll/logo.gif).

Adding hypertext links

Another item you may want to add to your Outlook Today home page is commonly used hypertext links. You can either define these links to launch a new instance of your default Web browser or you can display them within the Outlook client, much like what was illustrated in Figure 9-5, where the Outlook Today home page was directed to the company's intranet portal site. There is a caveat you should be aware of if you load a Web page within the Outlook client: just as when you instantiate an ActiveX control within the Outlook client, the IE security model is deactivated when a Web page is loaded within the Outlook client. Therefore, unless you trust the source, you should launch a new instance of the default Web browser rather than display the link within the Outlook client.

To add a link to a Web page from within your Outlook Today page, simply add the HTML hypertext link to your source document. For example:

```
<A HREF="http://www.idgbooks.com">IDG Books</A>
```

To avoid having the Web page load within the Outlook client, use the `<A HREF>` tag's `target` property with the `_new` value, shown below in bold:

```
<A HREF="http://www.idgbooks.com" target="_new">IDG Books</A>
```

The `target` property denotes the location where the Web page is supposed to load. The `_new` property tells the `target` property to launch a new instance of the default Web browser and displays the Web page within it.

Accessing Outlook functions from Outlook Today

We've seen how Outlook Today can be used as a summary page and to display commonly used Internet links. However, you can also add functionality to Outlook Today, such as being able to create new contact items or messages. As we discussed in previous chapters, you can use the Outlook object model to create, for example, new messages or contact items. You can access the Outlook object model from within the Outlook Today page by using JavaScript. For example, this JavaScript function creates a new message when a button is clicked:

```
<A HREF="" onclick="var vItem =
 window.external.OutlookApplication.CreateItem(0);
 vItem.Display();window.event.returnValue=false;">
 New Message</A>
```

First, the `onclick` method assigns the variable, `vItem`, to the external object, Outlook Application. This references the Outlook object model the similar to the way you would in Visual Basic using the `CreateObject` method.

```
Set vItem = CreateObject("Outlook.Application")
```

The `CreateItem` method instructs Outlook to create item 0, which is a new message. Table 9-3 lists the item values and the corresponding Outlook items.

Table 9-3 CreateItem Parameters	
CreateItem value	**Outlook entry**
0	Message
1	Appointment
2	Contact
3	Task
4	Journal entry
5	Note
6	Discussion
7	Distribution List

Adding "Find a contact" to Outlook Today

In Outlook 98, Outlook Today included a feature that enabled you to find a person in your Contact folder. For whatever reason, Microsoft decided not to include this feature in Outlook Today in Outlook 2000. This is unfortunate, as the feature was quite useful if you needed to find someone and you didn't want to have to go into the Folder List and look through each Contact entry. Fortunately, you can add this feature to Outlook Today yourself.

Just as with the Calendar and Tasks folder, there needs to be an object entry that references the Contacts folder.

```
<OBJECT ID="Contacts"
 CLASSID="CLSID:0468C085-CA5B-11D0-AF08-00609797F0E0">
<PARAM NAME="Module" VALUE="Contacts">
</OBJECT>

<INPUT TYPE=TEXTBOX ID="ContactName"
 style="margin-left:5px; margin-right:3px; width:90px; " >
<span id="GoButton"
 onclick="window.external.FindPerson(ContactName.value);"
 class="link" style="cursor:hand; font-family:times;
 font-style:italic; font-weight:bold; font-
size:13pt;color:black;">
 search</span>
```

The `<input>` tag is used to identify a field whose contents may be edited or acti-vated by a user. The type attribute defines the type of data field that will be dis-played in the Outlook Today page. In this example, the attribute is set to a text box. The style attribute defines how the text box will be displayed on the page.

The `<span>` tag applies a style to text that doesn't play any structural role, or where use of standard HTML elements is not desirable. It can be used within text blocks to apply a style as defined in a stylesheet, according to a Class or ID attribute, or the Style can be specified within the `<span>` attribute. The text "search," which is denoted as bold within the `<span>` tag, is pressed by the user and the `onclick` method is invoked. Using the value entered in the `<input>` tag text box, the **Find Person** method of the Outlook Object model is invoked and value is scanned for within the Contacts folder.

The following JavaScript function monitors the text being keyed into the `<input>` tag. If the user presses the Enter key, it invokes the `FindPerson` method of the Outlook object model and the value entered in the text box is scanned from within the contacts folder.

```
<script defer language=javascript event=onkeypress
for=ContactName>
  if(window.event.keyCode == 13)
  {
   window.external.FindPerson(ContactName.value);
  }
</script>
```

In either case, whether the word "search" was pressed or the Enter key was pressed while the cursor was in the text box, if a match is found, it will display in the form of a Contact entry. If there are multiple matches, the results will show up in dialog box so you can select which entry you wish to view.

Assigning your custom Outlook Today as the default page

After modifying your Outlook Today home page, you'll need to test it within Outlook and eventually use it as the default page. In order to do that, you will need to modify the Registry. As discussed earlier, you will need to change the URL Value Data in the HKEY_CURRENT_USER\Software\Microsoft\Office\9.0\Outlook\Today subkey. Assuming your personalized Outlook Today home page is in your My Documents folder on the C: drive and is named myoutlook.htm, your URL Value Data setting should be:

```
file://c:\My Documents\myoutlook.htm
```

Limitations of Outlook Today

As versatile as Outlook Today may be to modify, there are some limitations you should be aware of.

Outlook Today is meant to provide you with a mechanism to glance into your Outlook world. Its sole purpose is to provide you with summarized information and a launching point into more detailed information. While this is what makes Outlook Today such a valuable tool, don't think of it as way to bypass the other folders.

You can only view the Outlook Today page from within the Outlook client. Don't be fooled by the fact that you can use an editor outside of the Outlook client to customize it. An ActiveX control referenced within the Outlook Today HTML source file will not work outside the Outlook client.

The ActiveX control security safeguards within Outlook have been enabled. This means that you should only use ActiveX controls that you know are safe. If you allow people in your organization to customize their Outlook Today pages, you should make sure that any ActiveX controls they use are trustworthy. Otherwise the ActiveX control could become a portal for a hacker. The final comment is about an issue Microsoft is often notorious for, backwards compatibility, or perhaps more accurately, the lack thereof. All the effort you put into customizing Outlook Today may be for naught in the next release of Outlook. Therefore, when modifying Outlook Today, keep the KISS (Keep It Simple, Stupid) philosophy in mind.

Outlook Folder Home Pages

You don't have to be looking at the Outlook Today home page to see Outlook in an "at a glance" manner. By not resting on their laurels and by extending their commitment to collaborative products, Microsoft has introduced Folder Home Pages. Much like Outlook Today, Folder Home Pages provide a Web-like look and feel to Outlook-based applications. Since Outlook's object model is available for Web page scripting, it's easy to give users access to summarized Outlook information.

When you use Folder Home Pages, you are providing the user with an HTML page that displays summarized information. Since Folder Home Pages are based on HTML, they can use client-side scripting to access the Outlook object model, perform calculations, and so on. You can also have the page access information from other data sources like Microsoft SQL Server or Oracle. You can also include ActiveX controls to help extend the HTML interface.

Folder Home Pages are promiscuous. This is not a comment on their morals. Rather, it means that Folder Home Pages don't care where data are coming from. Users can view information from a corporate intranet, extranet, database server, and so on, and to them it appears that the data are coming from one source. You can build scripts that filter out information so that only privileged users have access to the data. This way you ensure that the information the users can view is the information you want them to see.

Designing Folder Home Pages

You have a number of tools you can use in order to develop Folder Home Pages. Just as with Outlook Today, you can use an HTML editor to create and design a Folder Home Page. You might not want to use a WYSIWYG editor for all your Folder Home page development. WYSIWYG editors are good for obtaining a general idea of what the page will look like, but they aren't very useful if you plan to do any scripting or use ActiveX controls with the page. Many WYSIWYG editors don't provide a way for adding scripting or ActiveX controls into the HTML source document.

The following example shows a Folder Home Page designed for an order and support person who is responsible for managing the orders and support questions for BoguSystem's BoguStub product. Figure 9-9 shows the Folder Home Page. Figure 9-10 shows the page's source information within Windows Notepad.

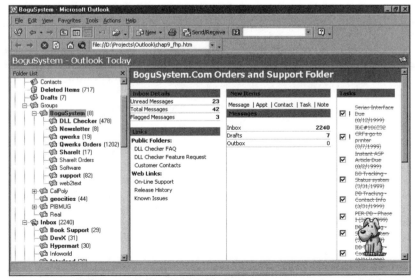

Figure 9-9: Folder Home Page for BoguSystem's order and support personnel

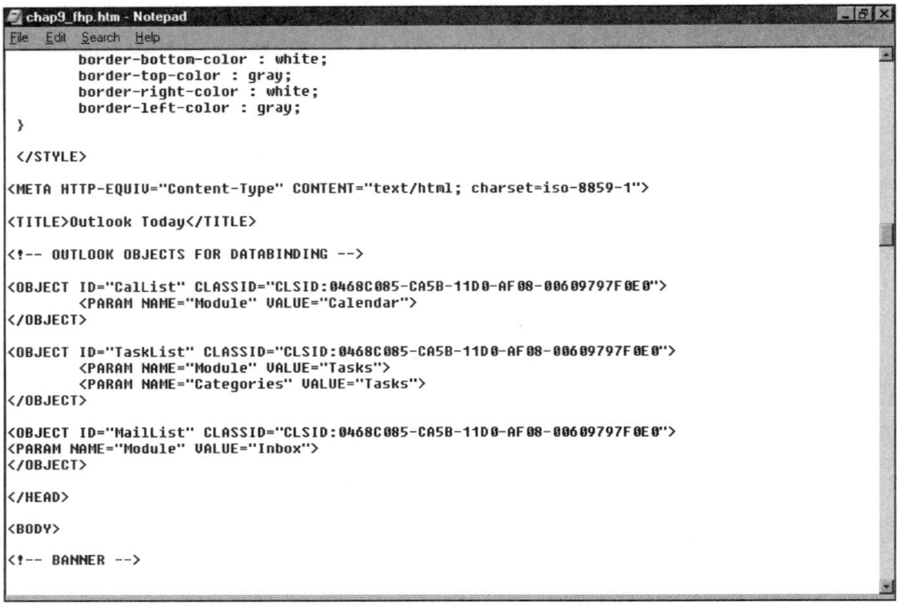

Figure 9-10: Some of the source information of the Folder Home Page in Windows Notepad

Since the Folder Home Page is based on the same technology as the Outlook Home Page, you can take advantage of cascading style sheets within the source document of the Folder Home Page you are designing. By using cascading style sheets, you can design your Outlook Home Page and Folder Home Pages to look consistent, such as by using your company colors, a standard page layout, and so on.

When planning the layout of the Folder Home Page, you want to arrange the information in a logical manner to provide easy navigation of the summarized information. In order to do this, you will need to be familiar with the Outlook Object Model and how to write JavaScript, VBScript, or both using the object model. Through scripting, you can obtain information from Exchange Server as well as information contained within the user's Outlook client.

In the BoguSystem Order and Support Folder Home page example, the left side of the page contains summarized information about how many unread order and support messages are stored in the Order mail folder and Support mail folder. It displays the total number of messages in each, and how many messages have been flagged for a follow-up response. There are links to Exchange Server's public folder so the user can get more information, and there are links to the organization's intranet site.

In the center of the page, there are links to Outlook's functions, such as creating a new message, creating an appointment, creating a contact person, and so on. Along the right-hand side, the column displays all the outstanding tasks that are assigned to the user of the Folder Home Page.

A carefully designed Folder Home Page can allow users to access folder contents through a Web browser without requiring the user to launch Outlook (although Outlook must be installed on the user's computer). This is especially useful for implementing solutions based on Outlook that do not expose all of Outlook's capabilities (such as e-mail). Of course, access by script to the Outlook object model is subject to the browser's security restrictions, so Web pages designed to access Outlook through a browser must be designed to work around this limitation. When a Web page is displayed in Outlook as a Folder Home Page, however, it is not subject to browser security restrictions when the Web page accesses the Outlook object model.

Adding a Folder Home Page to a Folder

You can add a Folder Home Page to an Outlook folder by the following steps:

1. In the Outlook Folder list, right-click the folder, and then click Properties.

2. In the Properties dialog box, click the Home Page tab.

3. Specify the path to the home page, using the Browse button if necessary. You can also specify that the home page be displayed by default for the folder.

You can distribute a solution based on Folder Home Pages. In the case of a public folder, all you need to do is to publish the home page on a Web server and then use the public folder's Properties dialog box to link the folder to the home page. If you want to assign a home page to an individual user's folder, you can send a message containing VBScript that sets the WebViewURL property of the folder to point to the home page. Alternatively, you can add script to the home page that sets this property and mail to the user a link to the home page itself.

Security for Outlook Folder Home Pages

In Microsoft Outlook 2000, you can associate a Web page with any personal or public folder. These Folder Home Pages use one of the following security modes:

✦ Use zone security and allow script access to Outlook object model

✦ Use zone security only

Use zone security and allow script access to Outlook object model is the default mode for Outlook 2000. This mode allows scripts on a Web page to access the Outlook object model and also ensures that the Outlook Today ActiveX control runs continually. The appropriate Microsoft Internet Explorer zone security settings are used in all other aspects of the Web page. For example, if the Internet Explorer zone security settings specify that ActiveX controls are not allowed to run, then no ActiveX controls can run on a Folder Home Page except for the Outlook Today ActiveX control.

The primary security implication of this mode is that it allows anyone who creates a public folder for a home page to include scripts that can manipulate data in user mailboxes. It provides you with the opportunity to create powerful public folder applications; however, the exposure to the object model opens up potential security risks.

You can activate *Use zone security only* directly through the Windows Registry or indirectly through a system policy. Scripts on the Web page do not have access to the Outlook object mode in this mode, and the Outlook Today ActiveX control is subject to the same Internet Explorer zone security settings as all other ActiveX controls. For example, if the Internet Explorer zone security settings specify that ActiveX controls are not allowed to run, then the Outlook Today ActiveX control will not be able to run on the system.

Tip   To set up system policies for Folder Home Pages, you will modify the Microsoft Outlook 2000\Miscellaneous\Folder Home Pages for Outlook special folders category. To disable Folder Home Pages, select Disable Folder Home Pages policy and then select Disable Folder Home Pages for all folders in the Settings for Disable Folder Home Pages area.

Limitations to Outlook Folder Home Pages

Aside from the security limitations, Outlook Folder Home Pages can only be used within the Outlook client. They can't be used within Outlook Web Access. Outlook Web Access allows users to access their private mailboxes from any browser that supports frames.

Outlook View Control

The Outlook View Control is an ActiveX control in the form of an ActiveX DLL, named `outlctlx.dll`, that allows you to display the contents of an Outlook folder from within your application. The ActiveX DLL can be instantiated from within an Outlook application, Web page, or Visual Studio application. The folder that the control accesses has full control over the Outlook Folder object model through it's own methods and properties, like any other ActiveX control. Through it, you can create, delete, open, and print items from the folder. You also have access to the folder's context menu through the context menu mouse button during run time. When the control is used with a Folder Home Page, it can also open the Outlook Address Book.

Since this is an ActiveX control, it can also be used within an HTML page on a Web site, assuming the user is using Internet Explorer. If the control is used within an HTML page, the control does not offer all the same features that it would if used within a Folder Home Page. For security purposes, it does not expose any user data or have access to the full Outlook object model. It does, however, provide access to a light, safe Outlook object model.

In order to use the Outlook View Control, you must have Outlook 2000 installed on the system where the control is going to be used for both development and deployment. It is possible to install the control onto any system, but if you try to use the control with any version of Outlook other than 2000, you will receive a system error. This is because the control is merely a "wrapper" around Outlook 2000 itself.

Note   This control does not come with any version of Outlook 2000 or Office 2000 product. You can download it from the Microsoft Web site at either `http://www.microsoft.com/exchange` or `http://officeupdate.microsoft.com/outlook`.

Like all ActiveX controls, the Outlook View Control has a set of properties and methods. Table 9-4 lists the properties of the control and Table 9-5 lists the primary methods.

Table 9-4
Outlook View Control's Properties

Property	Description
ActiveFolder	Returns the folder that is displayed in the control. If the control is not on an Outlook Home Page, the value returned is Nothing. This is a read-only property.
DeferUpdate	Returns or sets whether the user can change the folder displayed in the control or not. If the property is set to True, the user cannot change the control's properties.
Folder	Returns or sets the path of the folder to displayed in the control.
Namespace	Returns or sets the NameSpace property of the control.
OutlookApplication	Returns or sets the object that represents the container object of the control.
Restriction	Provides a filter for displaying only those items that match the search criteria.
View	Returns or sets the name of the view in the control.

Table 9-5
Outlook View Control's Primary Methods

Method	Description
AddressBook	Displays the Outlook address book in a dialog window.
AdvancedFind	Displays the Advanced Find dialog box that is found within Outlook.
CustomizeView	Displays the Outlook View Summary dialog box to enable you to customize the current view in the control.
Delete	Allows a user to delete groups or items displayed through the control. If one or more groups are selected, the groups and all items in the groups will be deleted.
GoToToday	Sets the day displayed in the control to the current day. This method only applies if the control is displaying the Timeline and Day/Week/Month views.
NewAppointment, NewContact, NewMessage, and NewTask	Creates and displays a new entry in Outlook.
Open and OpenSharedDefaultFolder	Open displays an item or items currently selected in the control. OpenSharedDefaultFolder displays a specified user's default folder.
PrintItem	Prints the items selected within the control. If a group is selected, the items in the group are selected and printed.
Reply, ReplyAll and ReplyInFolder	Performs the respective reply feature within Outlook.
SendAndReceive	Sends messages in the Outlook Outbox and checks services for new messages.

Using the Outlook View Control

You use the Outlook View Control by inserting it into your project just like any other ActiveX control. Assuming you're using FrontPage 2000, select Advanced from the Insert menu item and then select ActiveX Control. In the dialog window, as shown in Figure 9-11, select Microsoft Outlook View Control and click OK. If the control does not appear in the dialog window, click Customize to get the complete list of ActiveX controls installed on your system, as in Figure 9-12.

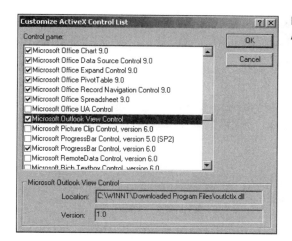

Figure 9-11: FrontPage 2000 ActiveX Control dialog window

Figure 9-12: ActiveX controls installed on the system

When you insert the control into your document, the control points to the Outlook Inbox by default. In order to change the location the control points to, you can either use the ActiveX control properties dialog window or the HTML tags.

To view an ActiveX control's properties, first select the control, and then choose Properties from the Format menu. This brings up the object's Properties dialog window. It contains two tabs, Object and Parameter. The Object tab (Figure 9-13) enables you to name the control, set the height and width of the control, and so on. The Parameter tab (Figure 9-14) tells the control which Outlook folder to display. To change the folder the control views, select the Folder property and select the Modify command button. Then the Edit Object Parameter dialog window appears, as illustrated in Figure 9-15. In the Data field, enter the Outlook folder you wish to have the control view. For example, if you want to view the Journal, type in Journal in the text field. If you want to view a private folder, enter the entire folder hierarchy. If the folder BoguSystem is a subfolder of SoftwareSupport, the Data value would be SoftwareSupport\BoguSystem.

Note   This is a very basic control and it is very much a ".0" release. You may change a value of the control through the Properties dialog window, but don't expect it to reload the values when you bring the Properties dialog window again. For whatever reason, the Data property will be reset to blank; therefore the control again will look at the Inbox folder.

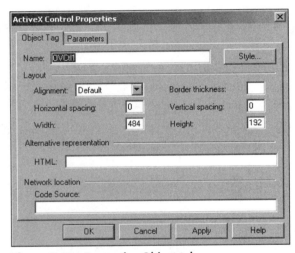

Figure 9-13: Properties Object tab

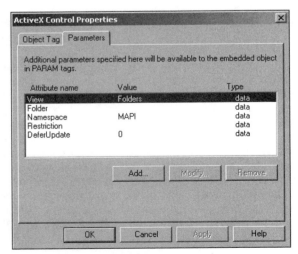

Figure 9-14: Properties Parameter tab

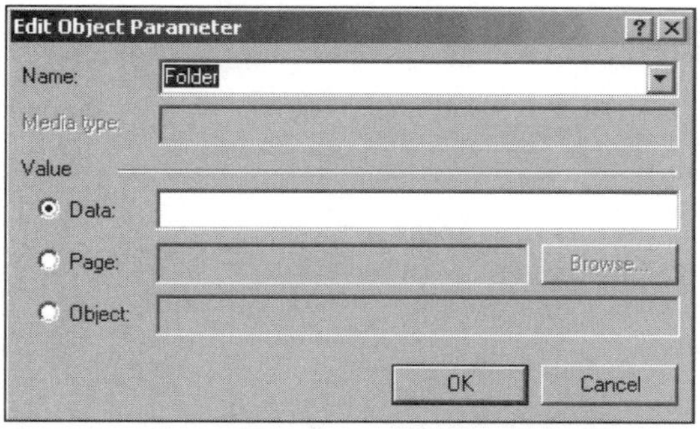

Figure 9-15: The Edit Object Parameter dialog window

Despite all the frustration you might encounter with the control's user interface deficiencies, you will find that using FrontPage's Normal editing pane to place the control is a lot more efficient than using the HTML editing pane to add it to the user interface. To insert the control using HTML, you will need to know the control's CLSID (Class ID), that is, its 38-character GUID (Globally Unique Identifier) as well as all its <PARAM NAME> information. The following code is the basic information you would need to know in order to add the control through HTML.

```
<object
  classid="clsid:0006F063-0000-0000-C000-000000000046"
  id="OVCtl1" width="484" height="192">
  <param name="View" value="Folders">
  <param name="Folder" value="Groups/BoguSystem">
  <param name="Namespace" value="MAPI">
  <param name="Restriction" value>
  <param name="DeferUpdate" value="0">
</object>
```

You can also use the Outlook View Control as part of a Visual Studio application. The following are steps to at the Outlook View Control a Visual Basic project. Just as you would with any ActiveX control, select Components from the Project menu item. This will bring up the Components dialog window. You won't find the control within the Controls tab, because the Visual Studio considers Outlook View Control to be an *Insertable Object*. An Insertable Object is an ActiveX DLL that provides automation support to the application server product the DLL is linked to. Regarding the Outlook View Control, the DLL contains access to several features of the Outlook 2000, such as viewing the Journal, Inbox, and Outbox folder. The Outlook View Control is listed as outlctlx 1.0 Type Library within the Insertable Objects tab, as show in Figure 9-16.

Once you have included the control as part of your project, it will be part of your Toolbox in the form of plain-looking document, as shown in Figure 9-17. You add the control to your form as you would add any other control, by first selecting it from the Toolbox and then drawing it onto the form. Just as on a FrontPage document, the control defaults to viewing the Inbox folder.

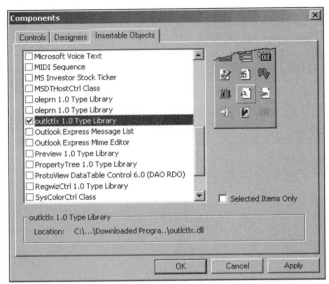

Figure 9-16: Outlook View Control within the Insertable Objects tab

Deploying the Outlook View Control

When deploying an Outlook solution that contains the Outlook View Control, Outlook 2000 itself needs to be installed in the target system as well as the ActiveX control, `outlctlx.dll`. The Outlook View Control may seem like a light control, but it's really a wrapper around the entire Outlook 2000 executable. Once instantiated, Outlook 2000 is loaded as a background process. If you're using Windows NT/2000, you can see outlook.exe running within Process tab of the Task Manager.

You can't use the Outlook View Control with the Web Outlook feature of Exchange Server.

Summary

Outlook has followed the lead of the Web in enabling users to view information in hypertext format and "drill down" in increasing levels of specificity from summarized general information to more detailed information.

Outlook Today enables you to view through a Web-style interface a summary of information, such as the number of your unread messages, your scheduled appointments for the next five days, and any open tasks you have defined.

Folder Home Pages enable you to view, at a glance, summarized information contained within folders, by linking an HTML page to any folder in Outlook. Folder Home Pages also support offline view capabilities, through which Outlook synchronizes an HTML file associated with the folder offline when a user synchronizes the folder, assuring that the HTML page will be available whether you're working online or offline.

The Outlook View Control is an ActiveX wrapper around the Outlook views, such as the Table, Calendar, Card and Timeline views, that enables you to look at Outlook information quickly. You can use this COM component within a Web application, such as an Active Server Page application, or inside a Folder Home Page.

✦　　✦　　✦

Outlook Web Access and Forms

The ever-increasing importance of the Internet is affecting the user interface of traditional Windows applications, and even Windows itself. (Case in point, the Active Desktop feature of Internet Explorer 4.) Outlook 2000 is no exception. As we saw in Chapter 9, Outlook Today and Folder Home Pages give Outlook 2000 a Web look and feel.

The Internet also has affected the traditional method of running applications from the client machine. One of the promises of the Internet is to enable even the most minimal client machine to access and run applications from a Web server, via either the Internet or an intranet.

A collaborative application based on Outlook would seem to be an excellent candidate for a Web application. However, before you fill your head with visions of making your Outlook application available to the masses — or at least the masses that access your Internet site — reality intrudes. Applications built on Outlook require the Outlook client on the user's machine, and despite Microsoft's best efforts, not everyone has Outlook.

Many advances in programming begin with the question "Why not?" In this case, why not build an application that looks and works like Outlook but runs off a Web server? Microsoft's answer is Outlook Web Access, which Microsoft provides with Exchange Server version 5.5. Microsoft also provides the HTML Form Converter to convert Outlook forms to HTML forms that can be viewed by the Web browsers accessing Outlook Web Access.

Introduction to Outlook Web Access

The user interface of Outlook Web Access looks much like the user interface of the Outlook client. Figure 10-1 shows the user interface of Outlook Web Access. Notice that the Outlook Bar in Outlook Web Access is quite similar to the one in the Outlook client.

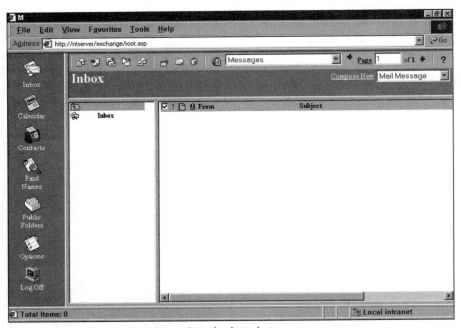

Figure 10-1: The user interface of Outlook Web Access

Outlook Web Access also performs the same types of tasks as the Outlook client. Outlook Web Access provides basic e-mail services, public folder access, and calendaring that can be accessed over an intranet, extranet, or the Internet. While these services are more limited than those provided by the Outlook client, the advantage of Outlook Web Access is that the client machine does not need Outlook. In fact, the client machine does not need to be running the Windows operating system. The client machine only needs a Web browser that supports frames, JavaScript, and cookies. Microsoft Internet Explorer version 3.0 and later and Netscape Navigator version 2.0 and later will work just fine.

The minimal client requirements of Outlook Web Access make this application very attractive, particularly to organizations that are not awash in money and whose base of workstations is, to put it kindly, elderly and diverse. There are many older workstations whose memory and hard drive space falls short of the requirements of Outlook but are perfectly adequate to run a Web browser. Outlook client licenses also cost money, whereas browsers are given away free. Additionally, organizations that did not standardize their computer procurement find themselves with a Star Wars bar scene of exotic operating systems, some of which are not supported by the Outlook client. However, browsers are available for virtually all operating systems used by businesses, organizations, and consumers.

Another attractive quality of Outlook Web Access is that it works "out of the box." No programming is required. The Exchange administrator needs only to install and configure Outlook Web Access and it is ready to use. However, an added attraction of Outlook Web Access is that it is, to use one of Microsoft's favorite words, "extensible" — that is, the forms used by Outlook Web Access can be customized.

With Outlook Web Access, you can customize more than forms. Its code also can be customized to enhance its functionality. Microsoft laudably has made the source code of Outlook Web Access open. Outlook Web Access is an Active Server Pages (ASP) application that uses Collaboration Data Objects (CDO). Thus, an ASP/CDO programmer can tailor Outlook Web Access the to the particular needs of the organization. Additionally, since ASP and CDO, the subjects of the next chapter, also are the building blocks for the even more advanced applications discussed elsewhere in this book, analyzing the code of Outlook Web Access is an excellent way to learn the basics of ASP and CDO.

While we have spent several paragraphs extolling the virtues of Outlook Web Access, it does have a dark side (not to overuse the references to *Star Wars*). As mentioned above, the e-mail and other services Outlook Web Access provides are more limited than those provided by the Outlook client. Additionally, while Outlook Web Access places a light burden on the client machine, it places a heavy burden on the server. Nevertheless, for many organizations this is an acceptable trade-off.

In the next section you will learn how to install and configure Outlook Web Access and use its features. This book is about programming, not administration. Nevertheless, you first have to get Outlook Web Access to work before you can program it. Additionally, it is difficult to write programs for an application without a solid understanding of how the application works. You also will be able to leverage your knowledge of the interplay between Outlook Web Access and Exchange Server to applications that integrate the Outlook client with Exchange Server.

Let's get started!

Installation

Outlook Web Access requires Internet Information Server (IIS) and Exchange Server. You will need version 3.0, and preferably version 4.0, of IIS and version 5.5 of Exchange Server with Service Pack 1.

Note   This book will discuss Exchange Server, IIS, and Windows NT. For an in-depth treatment, please refer to *Exchange Server 5.5 Secrets*, the *IIS 4 Administrator's Handbook*, and the *Windows NT Server 4.0 Administrator's Bible*, all published by IDG Books Worldwide.

Additionally, IIS and Exchange Server require Service Pack 4 or better of Windows NT Server 4.0.

Note   Service Packs, like medicine, sometimes have side effects. A number of articles have been written on problems that, in the article writers' opinions, were caused by Service Pack 4. The code in this book was tested with Service Pack 4. However, if you are content with Service Pack 3 and believe Service Pack 4 is a cure that is worse than the disease, then you can proceed with Service Pack 3 provided you install certain hot fixes. The hot fix files can be found at `ftp://ftp.microsoft.com/bussys/winnt/winnt-public/fixes/usa/nt40/hotfixes-postsp3/roll-up`.

You may install Outlook Web Access at the same time as Exchange Server or later. However, you must install Windows NT Server 4.0 Service Pack 4 and IIS before you install Outlook Web Access.

You are almost ready to install Outlook Web Access. However, you have another decision to make: Whether to install Outlook Web Access on the same server as Exchange Server or not. While Outlook Web Access needs Exchange Server, it does not have to be installed on the same server as Exchange Server.

There are two advantages to installing Outlook Web Access on the same server as Exchange Server. The obvious advantage is the savings in cost from not having to buy another server. The other and less obvious advantage, discussed in more detail in connection with security later in this chapter, is that you may be able to use Windows NT Challenge/Response as an authentication method.

The downside of installing Outlook Web Access on the same server as Exchange Server is performance cost. Each authenticated user is, in essence, a separate instance running on the Outlook Web Access server. This burden adds to the other burdens of the Exchange Server.

The examples in this book assume that Outlook Web Access is installed on the same server as Exchange Server. This is because the authors tested all the code in this book on their computers and are too, well, thrifty to buy an extra server for Outlook Web Access. Additionally, having both Exchange Server and Outlook Web Access on the same server is common, particularly in smaller organizations.

Now you are finally ready to install Outlook Web Access! If you are installing Outlook Web Access with Exchange Server, you can choose the Complete/Custom option when installing Exchange Server version 5.5. Figure 10-2 shows the Complete/Custom dialog box that displays when you choose the Complete/Custom option. If you have already installed Exchange Server, version 5.5, select Add/Remove Components, which also brings up the Complete/Custom dialog box. In either case, make sure the checkbox for Outlook Web Access is checked.

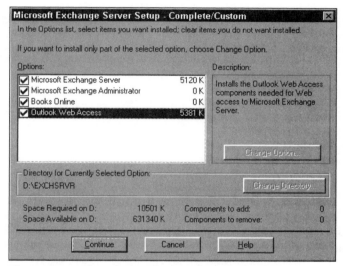

Figure 10-2: Choosing Outlook Web Access in the Complete/Custom dialog box

Once you have selected Outlook Web Access for installation, the setup program will prompt you for the name of an Exchange Server to which Outlook Web Access should connect. Once the installation is complete, you should install Exchange Server Service Pack 1 or preferably Service Pack 2.

You should test your installation of Outlook Web Access pointing your browser to the URL http://*ServerName*/exchange, replacing *ServerName* with the name of your Outlook Web Access server. Figure 10-3 shows the log-on page that should appear, which confirms that Outlook Web Access was successfully installed.

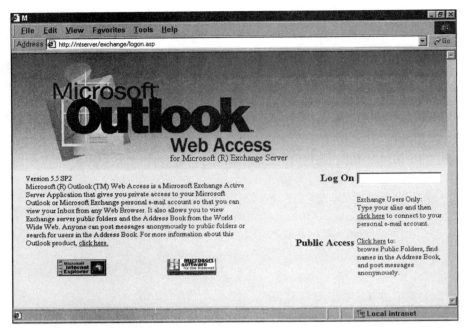

Figure 10-3: The Outlook Web Access Log On page

Security

Once you have installed Outlook Web Access successfully, you can access the log-on page. The log-on page provides you with two ways of logging on. One way is to type your user name in the text box next to the label "Log On." The other is to click the hyperlink "Click here" next to the label "Public Access."

First, click the hyperlink "Click here" next to the label "Public Access." You may get a dialog box warning you "Unable to render folder. There are no published folders." You can click OK to dismiss the dialog box; we will publish folders later. Figure 10-4 shows the Outlook Web Access user interface that will appear.

Figure 10-1 showed an Outlook Bar with a number of icons. However, as Figure 10-4 shows, with Public Access the Outlook Bar has only two icons, Public Folders and Log Off. The reason is that Figure 10-4 shows the result of entering Outlook Web Access through the door for the general public. Figure 10-1 shows the result of entering the door reserved for "club members," through which we will now go.

At the log-on page, shown in Figure 10-3, log on by typing your alias in the text box next to the label "Log On." You use an alias not because you need to disguise your identity, though after a botched programming job that might not be a bad idea; rather, the alias identifies your Exchange mailbox. Figure 10-5 shows the Exchange Mailbox properties for one of the authors, a disgruntled computer science professor who has cleverly disguised his identity with the alias "Jeff." Remember that you log on with your Exchange alias, not your NT user name.

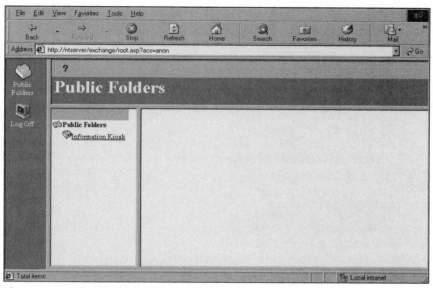

Figure 10-4: The Outlook Web Access user interface for public access

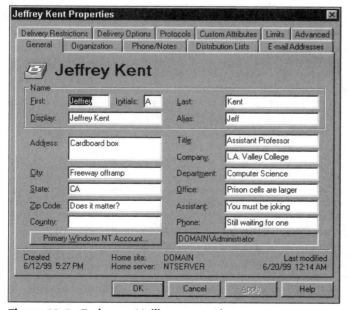

Figure 10-5: Exchange Mailbox properties

After you have logged on with your Exchange alias, a dialog box will prompt you for your username and password, which you should enter and then click OK. Figure 10-6 shows this dialog box. This time the name you enter is your NT user name, not your Exchange alias.

Note   In a small organization you could consider making NT user names the same as Exchange aliases. However, this does raise security concerns since Exchange aliases usually are quite easy to guess.

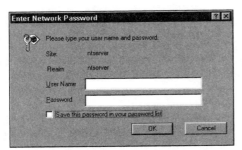

Figure 10-6: The User Name and Password dialog box

Your user name and password should be validated and your browser will display the Outlook Web Access user interface. This is the interface shown in Figure 10-1, with seven icons, Inbox, Calendar, Contacts, Find Names, Public Folders, Options, and Log Off. By contrast, as Figure 10-4 shows, entering via Public Access exposes only the Public Folders and Log Off. This difference in treatment is logical. The public should only be allowed access to those features intended for the public. The other features are reserved for those whose identities can be authenticated.

While the Outlook Web Access user interface is different for Public Access and for Exchange Users, under either method of access you would never get past the log-on page and see the user interface at all unless you were *authenticated*. Authentication is essential to security. Programmers too often dismiss security as a concern of paranoid network administrators. However, security is an essential component of ASP applications, and Outlook Web Access is an ASP application.

While security often is viewed as keeping users out, in ASP applications security rights let a user in, or to use the correct terminology, *authenticate* a user. Authentication in NT parlance is the process that determines whether a user has a valid Windows NT user account with the necessary *permissions* for accessing a particular directory or file.

Configuring security is a three-step process. First, you need to choose the authentication methods. Second, you need to configure user accounts or user groups to use these methods. Third, you need to set permissions for directories and files.

Authentication Methods

The most common methods of authentication, in order of least to most restrictive, are: Anonymous Access, Basic Authentication, and Windows NT Challenge/Response authentication. These alternatives are not mutually exclusive. Indeed, most implementations of Outlook Web Access use more than one authentication method. For example, you may use Anonymous Access security for public folders containing general information that you would want to be accessible to the general public, and use a more restrictive method of authentication for information that you would want to be accessible only to a select group. The type of security selected is not just a concern of that paranoid network administrator. The security choices also will affect the code you write.

✦ *Anonymous Access* does not authenticate the *individual* user. This is why no user name and password is requested. Instead, the only check is whether Anonymous Access is permitted.

✦ *Basic Authentication*, in contrast to Anonymous Access, does authenticate users. The user types his or her user name and password in a dialog box. Outlook Web Access then checks if the user is among the Windows NT users with rights to that directory or file, or if the user belongs to a Windows NT user group with these rights.

✦ *Windows NT Challenge/Response* also authenticates users. However, it does not prompt users for a user name and password. Instead, it uses the Windows NT security credentials of the Web user currently logged on to the server.

Since Anonymous Access does not authenticate the individual user, the only check being whether Anonymous Access is permitted, it only is appropriate for those portions of Outlook Web Access that anyone can access. A "public information" folder might be a good candidate for Anonymous Access.

There are tradeoffs between the two methods that do authenticate the individual user, Basic Authentication and Windows NT Challenge/Response. The main advantage of Basic Authentication is that it supported by most browsers, in particular Netscape Navigator. By contrast, the only browser that supports Windows NT Challenge/Response authentication is Internet Explorer.

Note   Netscape browser users can use Windows NT Challenge/Response if the Microsoft Authentication Proxy for Netscape Navigator (MAPN) is installed. You can download MAPN from `http://www.microsoft.com/msdownload/proxynet scape.htm`.

A disadvantage of Basic Authentication is that it is relatively insecure. The Windows NT user names and passwords are transmitted without encryption, as clear text. Someone trying to compromise your system's security could intercept the passwords.

Caution   This is not a trivial concern. While the government, financial institutions, and large companies may be the main targets of hackers, even small companies are not immune. As the authors remind co-workers who scoff at their security concerns, just because you're paranoid doesn't mean that they're not out to get you.

You can address this encryption problem by implementing Secure Socket Layer (SSL), which is supported by most browsers. SSL is not an authentication mechanism but rather encrypts the transferred data. However, SSL has two costs. The first is money. You have to buy a certificate from VeriSign or another vendor. The second is performance. Encryption and decryption involve substantial overhead.

Another disadvantage of Basic Authentication, with or without SSL, is that it requires an authentication dialog box. This can be confusing to users who already have logged in to the network. More importantly, hackers can "spoof" these dialog boxes to obtain user names and passwords.

Windows NT Challenge/Response is very secure. Unlike Basic Authentication, under Windows NT Challenge/Response a user name and password are not sent from the Web browser to the Web server. Indeed, Windows NT Challenge/Response does not even prompt the user for a name and password. Instead, the Windows NT security credentials of the Web user currently logged on are sent to IIS. This communication is encrypted. The result of the encryption is that the password text is converted into a 128-bit value that is recognized by the Windows NT Domain controller. Only a valid password can generate a valid 128-bit value. However, it is thought to be impossible to reverse-engineer the encryption to determine the password from the 128-bit value.

Since Windows NT Challenge/Response encrypts the password into a 128-bit value, IIS does not know the user's password, only that the user has been authenticated. This is both the good news and the bad news. The good news is that it's very secure. The bad news is that if IIS attempts to access a resource on another machine, which then prompts IIS for user credentials, IIS does not have the password. For this reason, you cannot use the Windows NT Challenge/Response method if you installed Outlook Web Access on a different server than Exchange Server, or over proxy connections. This may change in the future. However, for now, if you need to access Exchange resources that are on a different computer than IIS, you should use Basic Authentication, which in another case of the bad news also being the good news, provides IIS with the user's password.

Windows NT Challenge/Response is used most often in an intranet where the system administrator has control over the number of users, their domains, and their browser type. However, the examples in this book will use Basic Authentication, not

Windows NT Challenge/Response, as the authentication method, and will permit Anonymous Access to some resources, as this is the most common scenario.

Configuration of Authentication Methods

The installation of IIS creates a WWW (World Wide Web, as if you didn't know) service. The Web site for that service has the highly original name Default Web Site. You should rename it. In this example it was renamed NTServerWebsite.

1. In Internet Service Manager (the Microsoft Management Console snap in), right-click on NTServerWebsite and choose Properties from the context menu. Figure 10-7 shows the resulting tabbed dialog box, titled NTServerWebsite Properties.

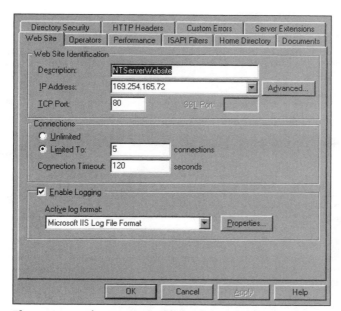

Figure 10-7: The Properties dialog box for the IIS WWW service

2. Click the Directory Security tab to display a dialog with three panels, as shown in Figure 10-8. The top panel is labeled Anonymous Access and Authentication Control. Click the edit button in that panel. Figure 10-9 shows the resulting Authentication Methods dialog box. The Allow Anonymous Access and Basic Authentication checkboxes should be checked. The Windows NT Challenge/ Response checkbox will not be checked because, as explained earlier, the examples in this book will not use this authentication method.

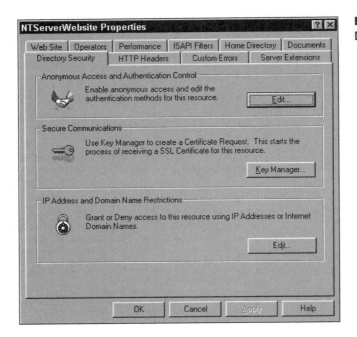

Figure 10-8: The Directory Security tab

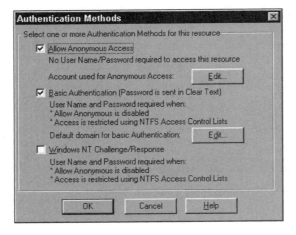

Figure 10-9: The Authentication Methods dialog box

If Basic Authentication was not checked before, when you check it you will be warned, as shown in Figure 10-10, that this method of authentication results in passwords being transmitted unencrypted over the network, with the consequence that some devious soul (read hacker) could intercept the password. This issue was discussed in the section "Authentication Methods." Accept the warning by clicking OK.

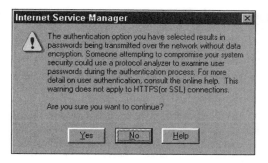

Figure 10-10: You have been warned!

3. When you apply these changes, you will be asked, as shown in Figure 10-11, whether to apply the changes you made to the IIS WWW Service's Authentication Methods to any of the listed child nodes of the WWW Service. The listed child node is called Exchange. This is Outlook Web Access. Select Exchange if it is not selected already and click Yes.

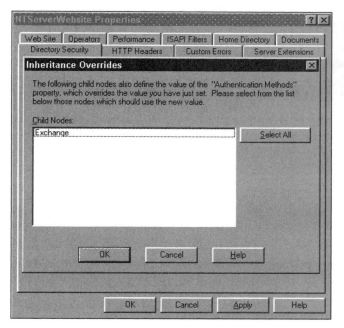

Figure 10-11: Applying the IIS WWW Service's Authentication Methods to Outlook Web Access

The Inheritance Overrides prompt in Figure 10-11 appears because, before the change, the respective Authentication Method properties of the WWW Service and Exchange subdirectory were the same, but after the change they were different.

It is not unusual for different subdirectories of the WWW Service to use different Authentication Method properties. For example, some public folders may permit Anonymous Access while others may not. Therefore, IIS does not assume that you want to propagate the change to the Authentication Method of the WWW Service to its subdirectories. On the other hand, you may want to propagate the changes. Therefore, IIS lets you decide.

Alternatively, you can configure the Exchange node directly as you did the WWW Service. Right-click on Exchange, choose Properties from the context menu, click the Directory Security tab in the resulting Exchange Properties tabbed dialog box, click the Edit button in the Anonymous Access and Authentication Control panel, and check the Allow Anonymous Access and Basic Authentication checkboxes (but not Windows NT Challenge/Response) in the Authentication Methods dialog box.

User and Group Accounts

Each user of a program that runs under Windows NT must have an account. Each *user account* is a member of a *user group* and has, either individually or as a member of a group, certain *rights* to access folders and files. Since IIS (through which Outlook Web Access operates) runs under NT, Outlook Web Access can be accessed only through a user account that has the necessary rights, no matter whether the authentication method is Anonymous Access, Basic Authentication, or Windows NT Challenge/Response.

The installation of IIS creates a user account for Anonymous Access that is assigned the necessary rights and placed in the appropriate user groups. That account is IUSR_*ComputerName*, *ComputerName* being the computer name of the server on which IIS is installed. For the examples in this book, the IUSR_*ComputerName* account name is IUSR_JEFF, the computer name being Jeff in honor of the co-author who paid for that particular computer.

Note   The installation of IIS also creates the user account IWAM_*ComputerName*. This account is used by Microsoft Transaction Server (MTS).

While IIS creates the IUSR_*ComputerName* account for Anonymous Authentication, it does not create any accounts for Basic Authentication or Windows NT/Challenge Response. You may use existing user accounts or create new ones for any user who will use either of these two authentication methods by performing the following steps:

1. Start User Manager for Domains. This is the configuration tool for users and groups. It is one of the Administrative Tools of Windows NT 4.0 Server, which you can access by clicking Start ➪ Programs ➪ Administrative Tools (Common). Figure 10-12 shows the opening screen of User Manager, which lists users, including IUSR_JEFF. Note that the Full Name of IUSR_JEFF is Internet Guest Account and the Description is Internet Server Anonymous Access. This account should not be confused with the user account IWAM_*ComputerName* that you also created when you installed IIS.

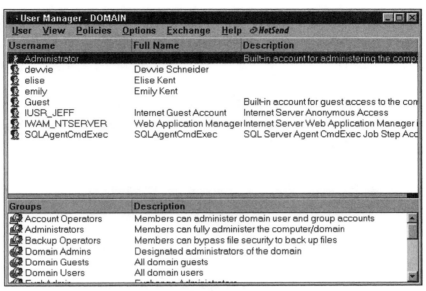

Figure 10-12: Users listed in User Manager for Domains.

2. Double-click the IUSR_JEFF account. Figure 10-13 shows the resulting User Properties dialog box. The User Cannot Change Password and Password Never Expires checkboxes should be checked and the Account Disabled checkbox should not be checked. The user's password should never expire or have to be changed because the user cannot renew or change his or her password via Outlook Web Access.

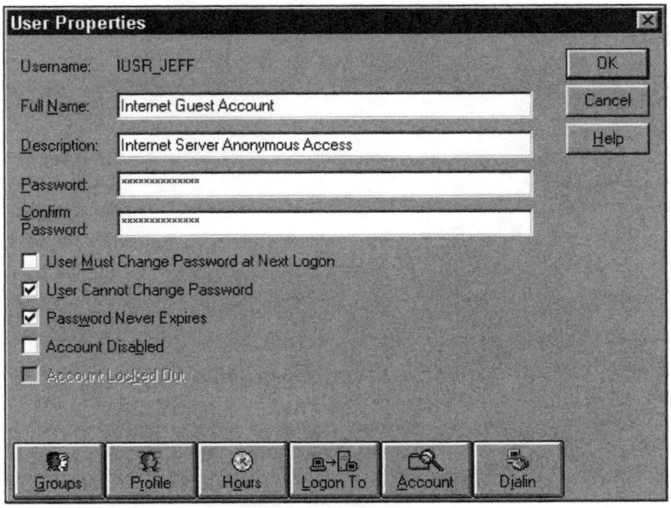

Figure 10-13: User Properties dialog

3. Click the Groups button. This brings up the Group Memberships dialog as shown in Figure 10-14. Verify that the account is a member of Domain Users. If not, use the Add button to make this account a Domain Users member. Click OK.

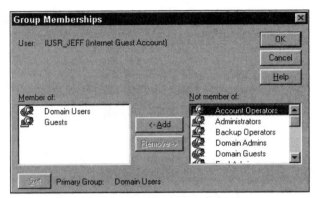

Figure 10-14: Group Memberships dialog

4. After finishing with Groups, click the Account button. The account should never expire and should be a Global account, as shown in the Account Information dialog box in Figure 10-15. Click OK.

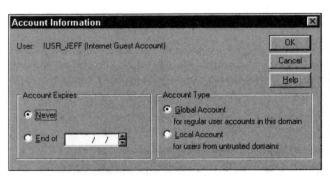

Figure 10-15: Account Information dialog

5. Go back to the list of users in User Manager. Pick User Rights from the Policies menu. Figure 10-16 shows the resulting User Rights Policy dialog. Confirm that IUSR_JEFF has the rights "Log on locally" and "Access this computer from network." Each right can be accessed from the dropdown list next to the label "Right."

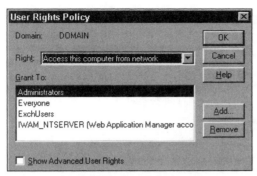

Figure 10-16: User Rights Policy dialog

6. IUSR_JEFF does not appear in the "Grant To" list box in Figure 10-16. Therefore, you need to add this account. You start, as you might guess, by clicking the Add button. Figure 10-17 shows the resulting Add Users and Groups dialog box. If IUSR_JEFF does not appear in the list of names it is because only Groups are shown. You can add the user names to the list by clicking the Show Users button. If necessary, select IUSR_JEFF, press the Add button, and then press OK. Figure 10-18 shows that IUSR_JEFF now is added to the Grant To list box.

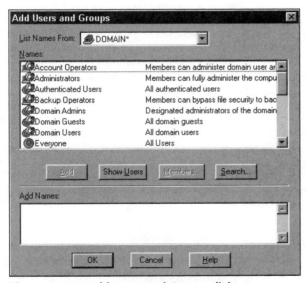

Figure 10-17: Add Users and Groups dialog

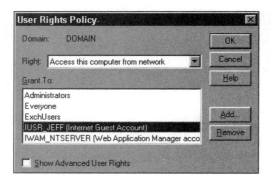

Figure 10-18: Success! User account added

The fact that the user will almost surely be accessing Outlook Web Access from a different computer from the Outlook Web Access server, while explaining the need for the user to have the "Access this computer from network" right, appears to contradict the need for the user to have the "Log on locally" right. The reason for that is that IIS responds to user requests by *impersonating* the user. IIS acts as if it were a user logging on locally to the server. Therefore, the impersonated user needs the "Log on locally" and "Access this computer from network" rights.

While IIS impersonates the user regardless of the authentication method, the rights of the user do matter. IIS runs under the *security context* of the particular user. The purpose of a security context is to give the process running on behalf of the user the same access to files and resources (and no more) than the user would have if he or she were physically accessing the process from the same machine.

You also should verify that IUSR_JEFF is being used for Anonymous Access. Figure 10-19 shows the Anonymous User Account dialog, which specifies the user account through which anonymous access will occur. Access this dialog by clicking the Edit button in the Allow Anonymous Access section of the Authentication Methods dialog box shown in Figure 10-9. We accessed the Authentication Methods dialog box previously through the Internet Service Manager (the Microsoft Management Console snap in). Right-click on NTServerWebsite, choose Properties from the context menu, choose the Directory Security tab, and click the Edit button in the Anonymous Access and Control panel.

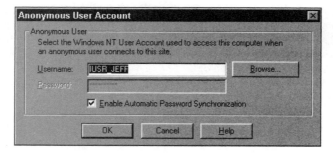

Figure 10-19:
Anonymous User
Account dialog box

Clicking the Browse button in the Anonymous User Account dialog will enable you to select another account, but in this case we are satisfied with the account selected, IUSR_JEFF. You should also check the Enable Automatic Password Synchronization checkbox. The Web site and Windows NT password settings for the anonymous account must be the same. Checking this checkbox will automatically synchronize your Web site password settings with those set in Windows NT.

As stated earlier, you may use existing or create new user accounts for any user who will use either Basic Authentication or Windows NT Challenge/Response. You can configure existing user accounts the same way we configured the Anonymous Access user account, IUSR_JEFF. You can add a new user through User Manager for Domains by choosing New User from the User menu and then configuring the new user. You should give the new user an Exchange account or mailbox.

Permissions

A favorite response of network administrators to grumbling users excluded from interesting parts of the network is "This ain't no democracy." Indeed, users don't have rights the way U.S. citizens do. Rather, they only have *permission* to access directories and files in the network, including those directories and files used by Outlook Web Access. With apologies to Dilbert, permission is given, and can be taken away, by the CENA (Certified Evil Network Administrator).

Outlook Web Access users need IIS permissions. You can set these permissions in Internet Service Manager by right-clicking on Exchange (which represents Outlook Web Access), choosing Properties from the context menu, and clicking on the Virtual Directory tab. (See Figure 10-20.) There are two areas to consider, the two checkboxes under Access Permissions and the three radio buttons under Permissions.

Access Permissions has two checkboxes, for Read and Write, respectively. These permissions are relatively self-explanatory. Read enables users to read or download files from the directory. Write enables users to modify or delete existing files and to add (upload) new files.

Permissions has three radio buttons, for None, Script, and Execute. These permissions control whether you can run applications in this directory. *None* does not allow any programs or scripts to run in this directory. The opposite is *Execute,* which allows any application to run in this directory, including applications mapped to script engines, such as ASP and Windows Scripting Host (WSH), as well as .dll and .exe files. The compromise is *Script,* which enables only applications mapped to a script engine. Select the Execute Permissions (Including Script) radio button. This enables applications mapped to script engines and .dll and .exe files to run in this directory. This is necessary because Outlook Web Access is an ASP application.

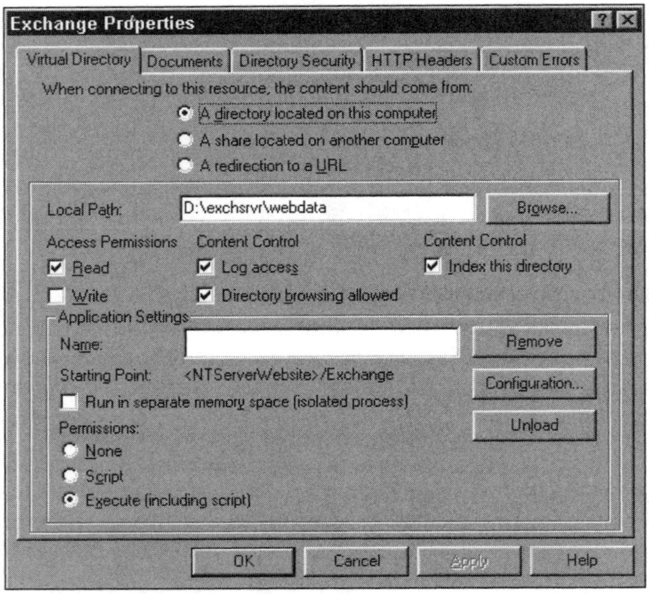

Figure 10-20: Virtual Directory tab for Outlook Web Access

Permissions become more complicated if, as is usually the case, the directory or file is on a Windows NT File System (NTFS) drive, because NTFS also has its own permissions, including Read and Change. Figure 10-21 shows these NTFS permissions, which you can access by right-clicking the directory (shared with the name WEBDATA), choosing Properties from the context menu, clicking the Security tab, and choosing Permissions.

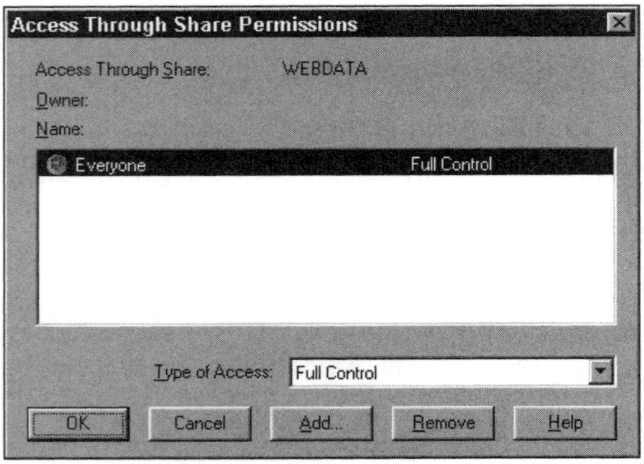

Figure 10-21: NTFS Permissions

While the existence of read and write permissions in both IIS and NTFS may appear to be a duplication, it really isn't. IIS permissions control which Hypertext Transfer Protocol (HTTP) commands are permitted to access HTTP resources. NTFS permissions control the access a user account has to resources on the hard disk.

For example, when a Web user wants to read a Web page, the browser sends a header that specifies the name and location of the resource and the HTTP command GET, which tells IIS that the requestor wants to "read" the resource. If the user does not have Read permission in IIS for that resource, the request fails. If the user does have Read permission in IIS for that resource, and the resource is on an NTFS drive, then Outlook Web Access checks if the user account has an NTFS permission to access that file. If so, access is permitted, but if not, the request fails notwithstanding the IIS read permission.

The rule that the more restrictive setting between IIS and NTFS controls for HTTP requests also applies when the IIS setting is the more restrictive. For example, if a Web user has NTFS permission but not IIS permission to write to a directory, the HTTP request fails.

However, the more restrictive setting rule only applies to HTTP requests. For example, an NTFS change permission enables a network client to modify an HTML file on the server by, for example, finding it in Explorer (assuming the network drive is mapped) and opening and modifying it in Notepad, even if there is no IIS Write permission. IIS permissions only apply to HTTP requests.

Fortunately, there is usually no conflict. When you right-click a directory in an NTFS drive and choose Properties from the context menu, one of the tabs will be named Web Sharing as in Figure 10-22. This tab reflects the IIS permissions. Additionally, IIS configures the NTFS permissions (under the Security tab) to its requirements.

Your users will need to access the WWW and Outlook Web Access services of IIS. By default, the WWW service of IIS is installed in INETPUB\WWWROOT, and Outlook Web Access is installed in EXCHSVR\WEBDATA. In Windows NT Explorer, IUSR_JEFF should have at least Read permission for INETPUB\WWWROOT and EXCHSVR\WEBDATA.

You give Write permission sparingly for obvious reasons. You give Read permission to directories containing information to publish (HTML files, for example). It is a good idea to disable Read permission for directories containing scripts and executables to prevent clients from downloading the application files.

Once you have given permissions, you have completed the configuration of the security of Outlook Web Access and are ready for the fun part: running it.

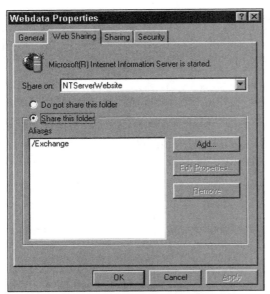

Figure 10-22: Web Sharing tab in NTFS Permissions

A Quick Tour of Outlook Web Access

Figure 10-1 at the beginning of this chapter shows the Outlook Web Access user interface you reach by logging in to Outlook Web Access as an Exchange user. The initial view is of the Inbox. From there, you can create a new mail message, send and receive mail, or post a message. You can access these commands with the toolbar icons, which have ToolTips.

Figure 10-23 shows the mail message form you bring up by clicking the Compose new mail message icon. This mail message form is the HTML equivalent of the mail message form in the Outlook client. The HTML equivalent is necessary because users need the Outlook client to view Outlook forms and not all of your Outlook Web Access users will have it. Later in this chapter you will learn how to install and use the Outlook HTML Form Converter to convert Outlook forms so that any standard browser can view them.

The mail message form in Outlook Web Access is quite similar to the message form in the Outlook client. For example, it has the Check Names functionality and permits you to add attachments and set properties so you will be informed when the message has been delivered and read. However, as will be discussed in more detail in connection with the Outlook HTML Form Converter, not all of the functionality of an Outlook mail message form will translate into the HTML version. For example, clicking the To... button in the Outlook client mail message form opens the Address Book as shown in Figure 10-24, permitting you to select from it the recipients for your message. By contrast, the mail message form in Outlook Web Access lacks this functionality.

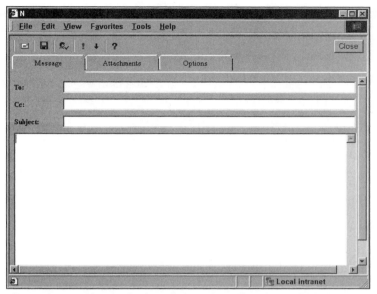

Figure 10-23: The Outlook Web Access mail message form

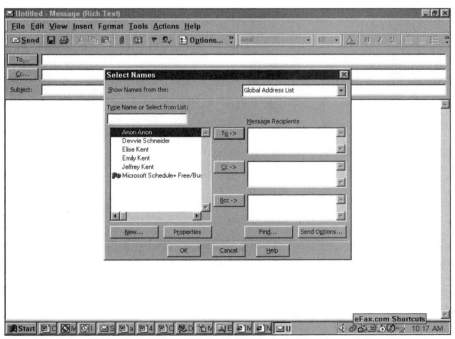

Figure 10-24: Opening the Address Book in the Outlook Client mail message form

The post message form is similar to the message forms used in Internet newsgroups such as `alt.fun.programmers.none`. The dropdown list box permits you to display messages (mail as well as post) by various criteria, including conversation topic. This permits a threaded discussion similar to that of newsgroups.

Calendar and Contacts are similar to Calendar and Contacts in the Outlook client. You can use the Calendar not only to create or view appointments, but also to send meeting requests.

The Find Names dialog is relatively intuitive. The user utilizes this dialog to find an entry in the Exchange Address Book by typing information (such as part of the first or last name) and then clicking the Find button.

The Public Folders feature will display all folders to which the user has access rights. The use of public folders is integral to Outlook Web Access and is discussed in the next section.

The Options and Log Off features are relatively self-explanatory. Clicking of the Log Off icon will bring up the log off page.

Public Folders

The Outlook client, by default, has private folders for your Inbox, Calendar, and Contacts, among others. However, if you want to share the information in these folders, whether totally or just to a limited extent (such as read-only access), then the information should be stored in a public folder. Public folders are the focus of collaborative applications because they contain the information being shared.

The Outlook client is the tool for creating new folders, whether private or public. While private folders do not require Exchange Server, public folders do. However, you cannot create a public folder from Exchange Server. For that, you need an Exchange client. The Outlook client is usually used for this purpose, though you can also use Outlook Web Access.

Creating a Public Folder

Since public folders are created in the Outlook client but hosted in Exchange Server, your Outlook client must be logged on to Exchange Server to create a public folder. Once you are logged on to Exchange Server, you can create a public folder in the Outlook client with the following steps:

1. Choose New from the File Menu and choose Folder. Figure 10-25 shows the resulting Create New Folder dialog box.

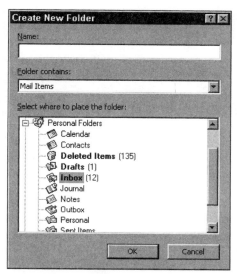

Figure 10-25: The Create New Folder
dialog box

2. Under Name, give the folder a name. We'll call this folder Group's ToDo.

3. Under the "Folder contains" dropdown box, you need to choose the type of items the folder will contain. The choices are Mail, Contact, Appointment, Note, Task, and Journal. A Mail item means that items in this folder will be based on mail message items like the ones in your Inbox, a Contact item means that items in the new folder will be based on Contact items like the ones in your Contacts folder, etc. As you may have guessed from the "ToDo" in the folder's name, the choice is Task. Since the default is "Mail Items," you should choose Task from the drop-down list.

4. Since the folder is public, under "Select where to place" expand Public Folders and select All Public Folders. This will place the folder among the public folders. Then click OK. Figure 10-26 shows the newly created folder.

5. In Figure 10-26 the Group's ToDo folder has a Task icon (the check in a box) next to it since the folder is based on task items. The right pane shows a standard Tasks View (Simple List), which you can change with the menu command View ⇨ Current View.

6. Now that you have created the folder, right-click on the folder and choose Properties from the context menu. Figure 10-27 shows the resulting Properties dialog box for the folder.

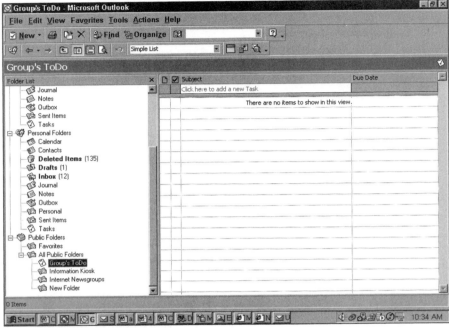

Figure 10-26: The Group's ToDo Public Folder

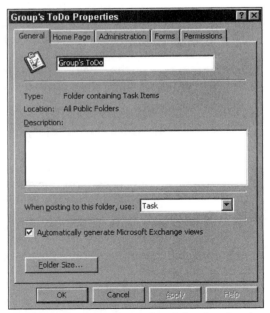

Figure 10-27: The Properties dialog box for the Group's ToDo public folder

Table 10-1 lists and explains the tabs of this dialog box:

Table 10-1 Tabs of the Public Folder's Properties Page	
Name	**Purpose**
General	Contains folder's name and description and specifies whether a post to this folder should be the default Task (in this case) item or a form.
Home Page	Permits assigning a Web page (Internet or intranet) that will appear in Outlook when the folder is selected.
Administration	Contains miscellaneous administrative options.
Forms	Permits assigning forms to the folder.
Permissions	Specifies who can access the folder and what type of access they have.

Tip You can also use Outlook Web Access to create a public folder. Log on as an Exchange user, click Public Folders, and then click the New Folder toolbar with the Create a New Folder tool tip. The user who created the folder also can delete it. However, Outlook Web Access does not provide the same degree of control over the configuration of the public folder as does the Outlook client. For example, right-clicking the folder and choosing Properties from the context menu will bring up only an informational dialog rather than the Property Page shown in Figure 10-27.

Permissions

Your Public folders can be as public as you want them to be. Depending on the purpose of a public folder you can configure it for access even by anonymous users, or only by a select group of users. The Permissions tab is where you determine how public the public folder will be. Figure 10-28 shows the Permissions tab.

The list at the top of the Permissions tab lists the names of the users who have permission to access the folder and their respective *roles*. You can add users to the list with the Add button and remove them with the Remove button. The Properties button opens the Properties dialog of the Exchange Mailbox of the user selected in the list.

Each user has a role. You can set roles in the dropdown list labeled Roles below the list of users. The role will be applied to the user selected in the list of users above.

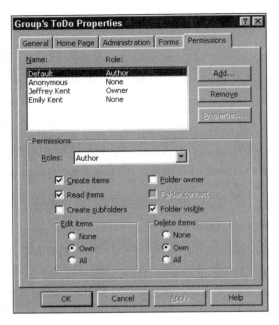

Figure 10-28: The Permissions tab

The role is a shorthand method of setting the properties set forth in the checkboxes and option buttons below the dropdown list:

✦ Create items — Permission to post items in the folder.

✦ Read items — Permission to open (read) items in the folder.

✦ Create subfolders — Permission to create subfolders of the folder.

✦ Folder owner — All permissions in the folder.

✦ Folder contact — Status of folder contact, who receives user requests for permission or other changes and automated notifications.

✦ Folder visible — Permission to see the folder.

✦ Edit items — One of following three:

  • None — No permission to change any item.

  • Own — Permission to change items created by that user.

  • All — Permission to change any item.

✦ Delete items — One of following three:

  • None — No permission to delete any item.

  • Own — Permission to delete items created by that user.

  • All — Permission to delete any item.

Setting a role in the dropdown list automatically sets the values of these properties. Table 10-2 lists the default settings of each role:

	Table 10-2 **Roles**							
Role	*Create*	*Read*	*Subfolder*	*Owner*	*Contact*	*Visible*	*Edit*	*Delete*
Owner	Yes	Yes	Yes	Yes	Yes	Yes	All	All
Publishing Editor	Yes	Yes	Yes	No	No	Yes	All	All
Editor	Yes	Yes	No	No	No	Yes	All	All
Publishing Author	Yes	Yes	Yes	No	No	Yes	Own	Own
Author	Yes	Yes	No	No	No	Yes	Own	Own
Nonediting Author	Yes	Yes	Yes	No	No	Yes	No	Own
Reviewer	No	Yes	No	No	No	Yes	No	No
Contributor	Yes	No	No	No	No	Yes	No	No
None	No	No	No	No	No	Yes	No	No

You are not limited to these combinations of property settings. You can devise other combinations, within reason. For example, if you grant Read permission, you cannot deny Folder Visible permission. If you customize a combination of property settings, the Role is, quite logically, Custom. Different users can have different combinations of property settings. Each Role will be named "Custom" though the combinations differ. "Custom" simply indicates that the Role is not one of the defaults such as Author or Reviewer.

The Roles have a logical hierarchal structure:

✦ The Owner has the maximum permissions.

✦ The Publishing Editor has all but the Owner and Folder Contract properties.

✦ The difference between a Publishing Editor and a Publishing Author is the latter can only edit or delete his or her own items rather than all items.

✦ The only permission of a Publishing Editor that an Editor lacks is the permission to create subfolders.

✦ Similarly, the only permission of a Publishing Author that an Author lacks is the permission to create subfolders.

✦ The only difference between an Author and the Nonediting Author is that the latter can only delete, and not edit (being "Nonediting"), his or her own items.

✦ Reviewers and Contributors can see folders. In addition, Reviewers can Read but not Create, and Contributors can Create but not Read.

✦ None means that the user can only see the folder, unless the user is Anonymous, in which case None means no permissions at all.

Log in as a user with Owner permissions. In this example, one of the co-authors has that permission. The public folder is visible and he can open it, though right now nothing is in it.

You also can see and open the public folder if you log in as an Exchange user whose name is not listed among the users in the Permissions Properties page. The reason for this is that one of the users is Default. Default is in essence a user group for all authenticated users whose names are not listed. Default's default property settings (no pun intended) give users in this group the Author role.

Default does not apply to Exchange users whose names are listed in the user list. Add a User to the list, give the user the role None, and uncheck the Folder Visible checkbox. After logging on as that user, you will not see that folder when you click on Public Folder.

Finally, log in anonymously by clicking the hyperlink "Click here" next to the label "Public Access" on the Outlook Web Access logon page. The name Anonymous in the user list is for Anonymous Access. Anonymous's role is None, but the Folder Visible checkbox is unchecked. When you log in, you'll get a dialog box warning "Unable to render folder. There are no published folders." This is because the Anonymous user has no access to any public folders. Dismiss the dialog box by clicking OK. The Outlook Web Access user interface will appear, with Public Folders being the start, but no public folders will be listed.

Anonymous Access to Public Folders

Next we will create a public folder for, well, the public, who will be using Anonymous Access. The name of this public folder will be Information Kiosk and it will be based on Mail items.

1. In Permissions, the user Anonymous will be given Author privileges. Log in Anonymously. The folder is still not visible. The reason is that you also need to change settings in Exchange Administrator.

   Figure 10-29 shows the Properties page for HTTP (Web) Site Settings. Access the Properties page by opening Protocols under the Configuration container, and either double-clicking on HTTP (Web) Site Settings or selecting it and choosing Properties from the toolbar.

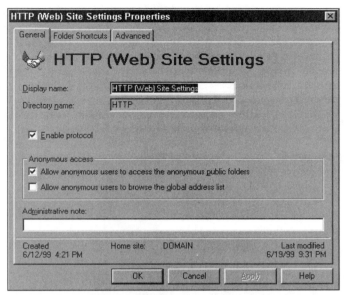

Figure 10-29: HTTP (Web) Site Settings Properties page

2. In the General tab, check the checkbox next to "Allow anonymous users to access the anonymous public folders." Next, click the Folder Shortcuts tab. Figure 10-30 shows that no Folder shortcuts are listed.

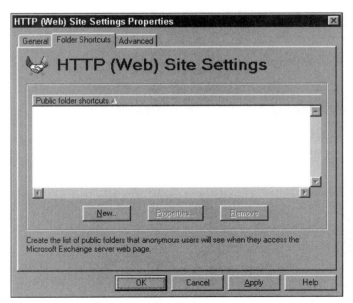

Figure 10-30: Folder Shortcuts Tab

3. You need to add a folder shortcut for the Information Kiosk folder. Click the New button. This brings up the Public Folders dialog. Figure 10-31 shows this dialog after you've clicked on Public Folders to expand the view of all public folders.

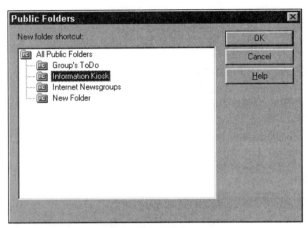

Figure 10-31: Public Folders dialog

4. Select Information Kiosk and click OK. Figure 10-32 shows that Information Kiosk is now listed as a folder shortcut in the Folders Shortcuts tab.

Figure 10-32: Information Kiosk added as a folder shortcut

Now when you log on as an Anonymous User you will be able to see and access the Information Kiosk folder.

Controlling User Access to Public Folders

An Exchange user may view the ability to create public folders as the freedom of self-expression. Exchange administrators usually take a different view, visualizing anarchy as public folders proliferate wildly. Therefore, Exchange administrators typically limit the ability to create public folders to a select few, including, of course, the Exchange administrator. This limitation is imposed by Exchange administrators using, of course, Exchange Administrator.

In Exchange Administrator, choose Configuration from the hierarchy tree. The Configuration container holds the objects used to configure, depending on the object, connections, protocols, servers, recipients and so on. Select Information Store Site Configuration from the right pane. Public folders reside in the information store. Use Information Store Site Configuration to specify, among other properties, which users have the right to create top-level public folders. A top-level folder is, as the adjective implies, a folder at the very top of the public folder hierarchy. Once a top-level folder is created, the owner of that folder can set permissions that allow other users to create subordinate folders below the top-level folder.

Open the property pages of Information Store Site Configuration by double-clicking it or selecting it and choosing the Properties toolbar. Figure 10-33 shows the Top Level Folder Creation page.

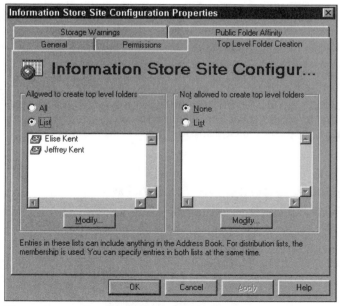

Figure 10-33: Top-level folder Creation page

You can grant permissions to create public folders by means of inclusion or exclusion. "Allowed to create top-level folders" lists all users who *can* create top-level public folders. "Not allowed to create top-level folders" lists all users who *cannot* create top-level public folders.

There are three ways to permit everyone in the Address book to create top-level public folders:

✦ Selecting the All option button in "Allowed to create top level folders."

✦ Selecting the None option button in "Not allowed to create top level folders."

✦ Leaving empty both the "Allowed to create top level folders" and the "Not allowed to create top level folders" boxes.

Choose the List option button for "Allowed to create top level folders" to restrict who can create top-level public folders. Then, click the Modify button. This opens the Address Book, where you can select users to add to the "Allowed to create top level folders" box. Once you have entered a name in the "Allowed to create top-level folders" box, all other users are automatically prevented from creating top-level folders.

The process is essentially the same for adding users to the "Not allowed to create top level folders" box.

HTML Form Converter

Users can view Outlook forms only if they have Outlook. Since the primary advantage of Outlook Web Access is that you can use it to include users who don't have Outlook, your Outlook Web Access application cannot use Outlook forms. However, HTML forms will work since users access Outlook Web Access through a Web browser.

You could create the HTML forms by (ugh) writing the required HTML code. However, converting your custom Outlook forms to HTML is faster and easier. Additionally, your Outlook Web Access applications will often parallel your Outlook applications. Converting your custom Outlook forms to HTML will help you to keep the two in sync.

Installing and Configuring the Converter

The software requirements for the HTML Form Converter are the same as for Outlook Web Access discussed earlier in this chapter. You install the HTML Form Converter by running the fcsetup.exe file in the Formscnv folder of the

Exchange 5.5 Service Pack 1 CD. The executable file is FormConv.exe and by default will be placed in a folder named Microsoft Outlook Form Converter.

Additionally, the developers who will be using the HTML Form Converter will need Read and Write access to the Webdata folder on your Outlook Web Access server. This share also needs to be named Webdata. See Figure 10-34.

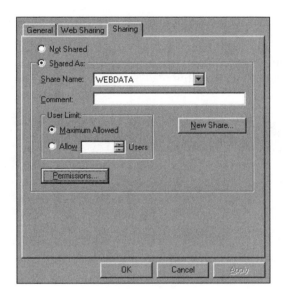

Figure 10-34: The Webdata folder must be shared as "Webdata" for Read and Write access by form developers.

Convertibility of Forms and Controls

Just as not all of the functionality of the Outlook client carries over to Outlook Web Access, Outlook forms are not 100% convertible to HTML forms that are usable by Outlook Web Access. Not all of the forms and controls are convertible, and not all of the features are entirely convertible even in those that are. Nevertheless, in most instances the HTML Form Converter can provide you with a functional HTML version of an Outlook form.

Only forms based on one of the following can be converted:

✦ Mail message (IPM.Note)

✦ Post form (IPM.Post)

✦ Contact form (IPM.Contact)

Thus, a form whose direct or indirect ancestor is a mail message form is eligible for conversion. You can determine ancestry with the `MessageClass` property of the form. For example, a custom form with the message class IPM.Note.CommitteeMtg. LeftCountry can be converted because the first part of its message class, IPM.Note, shows that it is based, indirectly, on the mail message form.

Other types of forms, such as Task forms, are not supported by the HTML Form Converter. However, you can use their interface in an HTML form by copying their controls to a mail message or other form supported by the converter and then converting that form.

Some controls are completely convertible, some partially convertible, and some not convertible. Table 10-3 summarizes the convertibly of controls:

Table 10-3 Convertibility of Outlook Controls	
Control	**Convertible?**
Label	Yes.
TextBox	Yes.
ListBox	Yes.
ComboBox	Partially. If editable (user can add to list), converter changes to noneditable.
CheckBox	Yes.
ToggleButton	No.
OptionButton	Yes.
Frame	Yes.
CommandButton	Partially. Images on button not supported.
Image	Partially. Bitmaps converted to .gif files and sizing of images may differ.
TabStrip	No.
MutliPage	Yes.
ScrollBar	No.
SpinButton	No.

Table 10-4 lists the convertibility of other form and control features.

Table 10-4
Convertibility of Other Form and Control Features

Feature	Supported?
Read and Compose Layouts	Yes.
Type checking and formatting.	Yes.
Form background images.	Yes.
ActiveX controls.	No. The converter only inserts a comment indicating where you need to place the necessary HTML code.
Overlapped controls.	No. Layered controls, for example, will be placed in adjacent locations by the converter.
Initial values.	Yes, except usually not for hidden controls.
Required fields.	Partially. There will be a warning message, but you will need to modify it to be in "plain English" for it to be intelligible to the user.
Formulas.	No. The converter only inserts a comment where you need to place the necessary HTML code.
Calculated fields.	Not really. The calculated fields are static, so changes to the underlying fields will not update it.

Finally, the VBScript code behind an Outlook form is not converted. Instead, it is placed in a text file named script.txt. The location of this and other files used by the converter is discussed later in the section on the Web Forms Library. VBScript is not converted because other browsers, particularly Netscape Navigator, do not support it. Because of the prevalence of Netscape browsers, the two most common workarounds, which may be combined, are using VBScript on the server side only and using JavaScript on the client side.

Converting a Form

You can convert an Outlook form with the following steps:

1. The installation program creates a shortcut to the HTML Form Converter that you can access by choosing Start ➪ Programs ➪ Microsoft Outlook HTML Form Converter.

2. The program uses a wizard. Clicking the Next button on the opening screen of the wizard displays the dialog shown in Figure 10-35.

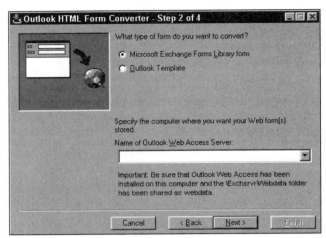

Figure 10-35: Second screen of Wizard — Select form and identify server

3. You need to select between the two option buttons. The choice is between a form in a forms library or an Outlook template (.oft) file. You also need to select from the dropdown list or type the name of Outlook Web Access server where the files will be stored after the conversion.

4. Click the Next button on the second screen. If you chose a forms library in the prior step, the Forms Libraries dialog shown in Figure 10-36 will be displayed, from which you choose a form or multiple forms using the Shift or Ctrl keys. If instead you chose an Outlook template file in the prior step, the Open Outlook Template common dialog box shown in Figure 10-37 will be displayed, from which you choose a file or multiple files using the Shift or Ctrl keys.

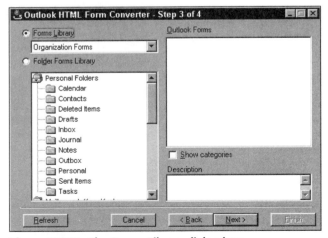

Figure 10-36: The Forms Library dialog box

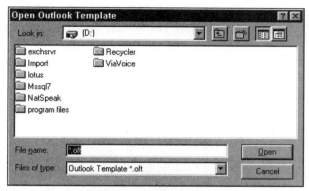

Figure 10-37: The Open Outlook Template common
dialog box

5. Clicking the Next button on the third screen displays the concluding dialog
box shown in Figure 10-38. The first checkbox gives you the option to over-
write your existing form, which you normally will do. The second checkbox
enables Layout Debug Mode. This mode makes visible the borders of tables so
you can see the layout and use the borders to adjust the size and location of
controls. After you've made these choices, click the Finish button.

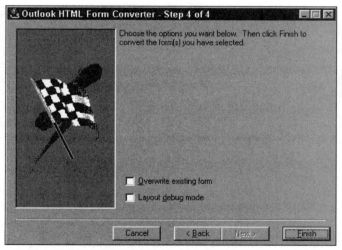

Figure 10-38: The final screen of the HTML Form Converter
wizard

6. Clicking the Finish button on the final screen of the wizard starts the actual conversion of the form or template file. The wizard next displays one of three results for the conversion:

    a. Success!—The wizard notifies you that the form was successfully converted.

    b. Success, but still work to do—The wizard notifies you that the form could be converted to a functional HTML form, but some controls or code in the form need to be modified for their functionality to carry over to the HTML form.

    c. Failure—The wizard does not want to damage your self-esteem with the word "failure," but does notify you that the form could not be converted. This notification will appear if you try to convert a Task or Appointment form, because they are not supported by the HTML Form Converter.

When (not if) you achieve a successful conversion, you can view the converted form with the following steps:

1. Log on to Outlook Web Access.

2. Choose Custom Form from the Compose New dropdown box as show in Figure 10-39, and then click the Compose New hyperlink next to the dropdown box.

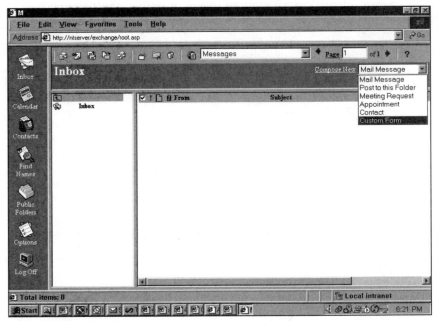

Figure 10-39: Custom Forms are displayed for selection through the Compose New dropdown box

Clicking the Compose New hyperlink will display the Launch Custom Forms dialog box shown in Figure 10-40. This window lists all the custom forms that have been saved in your Web Forms Library, which is discussed below. You launch a form by clicking its name, which is a hyperlink.

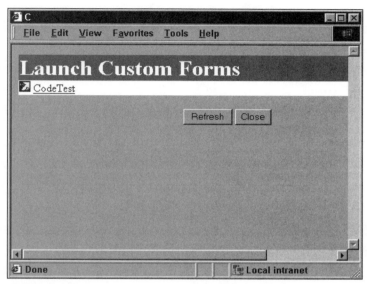

Figure 10-40: The Launch Custom Forms dialog box

Web Forms Library

Chapter 5 reviewed the form libraries used by Outlook, the Organizational Forms library, the Folder Forms library and the Personal Forms library. There is a fourth library that holds the HTML forms used by Outlook Web Access: the Web Forms library.

Directory and File Structure

The Web Forms library is located in the Exchsvr\Webdata folder (assuming you did not change the installation defaults). Figure 10-41 shows the structure of the Webdata folder.

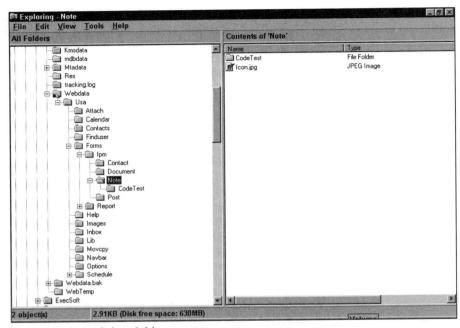

Figure 3-41: Webdata folder structure

The hierarchy, in descending order, is as follows:

- ✦ Webdata — Parent folder.
- ✦ USA — Corresponds to the language pack installed.
- ✦ Forms — Holds the forms.
- ✦ Ipm — Root for message classes.
- ✦ Contact (and Document, Note and Post) — Root for standard forms.
- ✦ First-level custom forms — For example, the necessary files (discussed below) to support the custom form IPM.Note.PleaForMercy would be in a PleaForMercy subfolder.
- ✦ Second-level custom forms — For example, the necessary files to support the custom form IPM.Note.PleaForMercy. Editors would be in an Editor subfolder in the PleaForMercy subfolder, the path being Exchsvr\Webdata\USA\Forms\IPM\Note\PleaForMercy\Editors.

The relative path under the Forms subfolder corresponds to the message class of the custom form whose files reside in a particular subfolder. For example, the custom form IPM.Note.PleaForMercy is in under the Forms subfolder in the IPM\Note\PleaForMercy subfolder. The dots in the message class are replaced by backslashes in the path under the Forms subfolder.

The converter creates and places the following files in the subfolder of each custom form:

✦ FrmRoot.asp — The entry point for the form, just as the Main subroutine is the entry point for a Visual Basic application. The hyperlink in the Launch Custom Forms window is to this file.

✦ Postttitl.asp — The frame of the form, including the toolbar and tab strip. The code in this Active Server Page handles the click events of the toolbar and tab strip.

✦ Page_#.asp — Each page of the form has a separate .asp file. Some pages have names corresponding to the tab name. Custom pages have names such as Page_1.asp, Page_2.asp, etc.

✦ Page_#-Read.asp — If a page has separate compose and read layouts, then if the compose page is named Page_1.asp, the read page is named Page_1-Read.asp.

✦ Commands.asp — This is a hidden file hidden from users that handles both standard and custom actions.

✦ Form.ini — This .ini file contains the form's display name, code page, and whether the form should be hidden in the Launch Custom forms window.

These files can be modified, and additional files may be and usually are placed in the folder for the custom form. These files are discussed at length in Chapter 11 on ASP and CDO.

Enabling Outlook users to use HTML forms

The HTML Form Converter converts a custom Outlook form to HTML to permit users to view the form with a Web browser. Conversely, you may want to enable users to view an HTML form with the Outlook client. For example, if the HTML form is an "original" rather than a conversion of an Outlook form, and it has the functionality you need for an Outlook application, enabling users to view your HTML forms with the Outlook client saves you the time and trouble of creating a corresponding Outlook form.

You do not need to convert an HTML form for users to be able to view it with the Outlook client. Instead, you need only tell Outlook to use the HTML form. The following steps show how to accomplish this in Outlook 2000, but you can do the same in earlier versions of Outlook 97 (version 8.03 or later), Outlook 98, Outlook for Windows 3.1, or Outlook for the (ugh) Macintosh.

1. In Outlook, choose the Tools ⇨ Options menu command.

2. Click the Advanced Options button on the Other tab. This will display the Advanced Options dialog box.

3. Click the Custom Forms button in the Advanced Options dialog box. This displays an Options dialog with one tab, Custom Forms. Click the Web Services button to display the Web Services dialog box, which is shown in Figure 10-42.

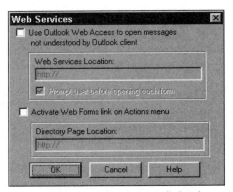

Figure 10-42: Web Services dialog box

4. Check the checkbox labeled "Use Outlook Web Access to open messages not understood by Outlook client." This sets Microsoft Outlook to automatically open an unrecognized form, start your default browser, and display the form in HTML format.

5. In the Web Services Location text box, type the URL for your Outlook Web Access server. This URL will be `http://ServerName/exchange/forms/openitem.asp`. This enables Outlook to search the Web Forms Library if the user attempts to open an item whose message class does not match that of a form in one of the other libraries.

6. Check the "Prompt user before opening each form" checkbox if you want to notify the user that Outlook cannot display the form (because its message class does not match that of a form in one of the other libraries) and ask if he or she wants to view the form using Outlook Web Access.

7. Check the checkbox labeled "Activate Web Forms link on Actions menu" and type in the Directory Page Location text box the URL `http://ServerName/exchange/forms/pickform.asp` to add a Web Forms item on the Actions menu. Choosing this option will launch the user's default Web browser and display the Launch Custom Forms window.

8. Click OK four times.

Including other applications in Web forms library

The Web Forms Library is not limited to containing converted Outlook forms. It may also contain other applications that run from a Web server. You do not have to place your Web applications in the Web Forms Library. However, doing so enables you to use Outlook Web Access authentication to authenticate the users of those applications.

You can add a Web application to the Web Forms Library with the following steps:

1. Create a subfolder under the Forms subfolder to store the files for your application.
2. Create Form.ini and FrmRoot.asp files and place them in the subfolder you created. These files were discussed earlier under Directory and File Structure.
3. Add a jpeg file, naming it Icon.jpg, to the subfolder you created. This will be the icon appearing to the left of the hyperlink to the application in the Launch Custom Forms window.
4. Add the other application files to the subfolder (or subordinate subfolders as your application requires).

Summary

In this chapter you learned about the Web application variant of Outlook, Outlook Web Access. Outlook Web Access is an attractive choice as a Web application because virtually any client can access it and it works out of the box without any custom programming.

In this chapter you learned how to install Outlook Web Access. However, though no programming is necessary, installation is not the end of your task. Security is integral to Outlook Web Access. This chapter covered authentication methods, user and group accounts, and permissions, so you can customize security to the needs of your particular situation.

Public folders are important not just in Outlook Web Access but also in other Outlook applications that interact with Exchange Server. This chapter showed you how to create a public folder, set its permissions, permit anonymous access to it, and control who else can create a public folder.

This chapter also showed you how to convert custom Outlook forms to HTML forms so they can be viewed in Outlook Web Access or another Web application.

Now that you know how to use Outlook Web Access and to create custom HTML forms, the next step is to write code. This involves Active Server Pages and Collaboration Data Objects, the subjects of the next chapter.

✦　　✦　　✦

Active Server Pages (ASP) and Collaboration Data Objects (CDO)

While Outlook is a powerful standalone application, its power is magnified when it can be used as part of a multi-user application spanning a network or even the Internet. You can bring this about with two different but complementary technologies, Active Server Pages (ASP) and Collaboration Data Objects (CDO).

ASP enables you to run the code of a Web-based application on the server rather than on the client machine. This resolves the often-vexing question: Can the client's browser execute my code? That question may have prevented you from using familiar languages such as VBScript because, for example, Netscape Navigator doesn't support VBScript. However, with ASP, this is no longer an issue. The client's browser need only be able to view the HTML resulting from the server's execution of the script.

ASP also provides a structure for your application to keep track of concurrent users. Unlike standalone Outlook applications, server-based applications must be able to distinguish between numerous users who may be logged on at the same time. For example, if your application allows users to read only their own posts, the posts one user will be permitted to read will obviously be different from those that another user will be permitted to read. Your application must "know" the identity of each user and correlate that identity with the user's request to read posts. ASP permits you to assign a unique session to each user, akin to each user having a separate thread.

CDO, on the other hand, is an object model similar in many respects to the Outlook 2000 object library. Indeed, the two libraries cover many of the same collections and objects. However, while the Outlook 2000 object library is designed primarily for stand-alone Outlook applications, the CDO object library is designed for multi-user applications run from a network or Web server. In particular, CDO is designed to work with Exchange Server and public folders.

You can combine ASP and CDO to create applications that function very much like Outlook but run from a central server and are accessible from a Web browser. A prime example of an ASP/CDO application is Outlook Web Access. However, you can combine ASP and CDO to harness the power of Outlook for purposes other than a Web application that mimics Outlook. This chapter will show you how to get started on a server-based Web browser interface application with which users can post their computer problems to a central repository (here a public folder) where tech-support personnel can review and act (hopefully) on the posts.

Active Server Pages (ASP)

Active Server Pages (ASP), at the page or file level, are simply HTML pages that have an .asp extension. Both ASP files and HTML files are text files. HTML as well as ASP files may contain script, which is code written in VBScript or another scripting language. You distinguish ASP script from HTML code by enclosing the ASP script between the characters <% and %>. For example, the following snippet of an HTML page prints out "Today's date is" followed by the actual date, which is returned by the Now function:

```
<BODY>Today's date is <%=Now()%></BODY>
```

The primary difference between ASP and HTML files is *where* the script in these files is executed. HTML files that contain script are executed on the client browser. By contrast, the script in ASP files is executed on the Web server and the results of executing the script are then returned as HTML to the client browser.

As stated in the introduction, Server-side scripting has the advantage of removing the issue of whether the client's browser can execute the script. There are additional advantages to server-side scripting. Since your server does the work of executing the script, the power of the client machine is less of an issue. Server-side scripting enables you to protect your code. Server-side scripts cannot easily be copied as can regular HTML code because only the result of the script is returned to the browser. Users cannot view the scripts themselves.

ASP will work on Web servers running Microsoft Internet Information Server (IIS) version 3.0 and higher. Third party software will permit ASP to run on other Web servers, even those running on non-Windows operating systems like Unix.

Active Server Pages is an ActiveX Scripting Host. While many programmers, and this book, use VBScript for ASP pages, you may use any compatible ActiveX Scripting Engine for your ASP application. The installation of ASP (with IIS) installs scripting engines for VBScript and JScript, the latter being Microsoft's variation of JavaScript. However, other scripting engines, such as PerlScript, a Perl-based scripting engine, are available from third parties.

ASP Object Model

Figure 11-1 depicts the ASP object model:

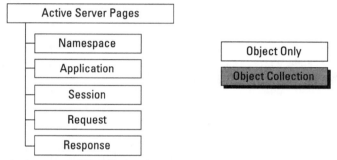

Figure 11-1: ASP object model

ASP, like Outlook 2000, has its own object model, which has the following objects:

✦ Server — The Server object represents, not surprisingly, the Web server on which the ASP application runs. You use the Server object's `CreateObject` method to create CDO objects.

✦ Application — The Application object represents an instance of an ASP application from when the first user accesses it until the Web server shuts down or the IIS administrator unloads the application.

✦ Session — The Session object represents an individual user of the application from when that user first accesses the application until that user exits it. As you might expect, this interval is referred to in ASP programming parlance as a *session*.

✦ Request — The Request object permits you to access information passed from the browser to the ASP application. You often use the Request object to obtain information that the user entered in an HTML form for processing by your script.

✦ Response — The Response object controls the HTML and other content that the server returns to the client browser.

Server object

The Server object has properties and methods that enable you to modify attributes of the server, such as how long a script may run before it is terminated, and to create objects on the server, such as the CDO object discussed later in this chapter.

The `ScriptTimeout` property sets and returns the maximum amount of time (in seconds) a script can run before it is terminated. Its syntax is:

```
Server.ScriptTimeout = NumSeconds
```

The default value of the `ScriptTimeout` property is 90 seconds. However, you may determine that this time interval is too short or long for certain scripts. For example, scripts that access or retrieve data from a data source might require longer than 90 seconds to run.

A user who is waiting for the script to run may believe that the page did not load properly and either leave your application, which is undesirable if the user is a potential customer, or try to reload the page with Stop and Refresh commands, slowing down the server with yet more requests. Therefore, you may want to advise the user that "this may take a while" if you are using a lengthy `Script Timeout` value.

The Server object also has a `CreateObject` method. The `CreateObject` method creates and returns an object on the server (not the client browser). The created object is identified by its ProgID. The syntax of the `CreateObject` method is:

```
Set objvar = Server.CreateObject(ProgID)
```

By default, objects created by the `CreateObject` method have page scope. An object with page scope is destroyed when ASP has completed processing the current page. This limited scope may be acceptable for some objects. However, you will need other objects, such as the CDO object that will be discussed later in this chapter, to persist during the lifetime of the application or a session. You can increase the scope of an object created by the `CreateObject` method by assigning the return value of the `CreateObject` method to variables with Application scope, as discussed next, or with Session scope.

Application object

You use the Application object to create and instantiate variables with global scope. You create a variable with application scope with the syntax:

```
Application("variable name")
```

The following code snippet creates a CDO object variable and then assigns that variable the return value of the `CreateObject` method with a CDO object's ProgID parameter, `MAPI.Session`:

```
Set Application("oCDO") = Server.CreateObject("MAPI.Session")
```

You do not need to previously declare the variable `oCDO` as:

```
Dim oCDO As Object
```

The reason is that in VBScript all variables are of the Variant data type.

The Application object has no properties. It does have two collections:

✦ Contents — Contains the items that have been added to the application through a script command.

✦ StaticObjects — Contains all of the objects created with the `<OBJECT>` tags within the scope of the Application object.

The CDO object variable `oCDO` in the preceding code snippet would be a member of the Contents collection. You use the Contents and StaticObjects collections for debugging to list the items and objects with Application scope. These collections would rarely be used in the application itself.

The Application object has two methods, `Lock` and `Unlock`. The `Lock` method prevents other clients from modifying an application-level variable while one client is accessing it. For example, you would want to prevent more than one client at a time from modifying the value of an application-level variable `numVisits` that kept count of the number of visitors.

The `Unlock` method permits other clients to modify an application-level variable after that variable has been locked by the `Lock` method. You do not need to call the Unlock method to "unlock" a variable that was previously locked. However, if you do not explicitly invoke the `Unlock` method, the variable is unlocked only when the .asp file ends or times out.

The following code snippet demonstrates the use of the `Lock` and `Unlock` methods:

```
<%
Application.Lock
Application("numVisits") = Application("numVisits") + 1
Application.Unlock
%>
```

Session object

You use the Session object to create and instantiate variables that apply to individual users of your application. You create a variable with session scope by using the same syntax that you use for creating a variable with application scope except that you would substitute `Session` for `Application`:

```
Session("friendlyName")
```

Table 11-1 lists the properties of the Session object:

Table 11-1	
Properties of the Session Object	
Name	***Description***
CodePage	Sets or returns an integer that identifies a character set relating to a particular language.
LCID	Sets or returns an integer that identifies a system-defined locale.
SessionID	Returns an integer that uniquely identifies a session.
TimeOut	Sets or returns the number of minutes after which a session will end if in the meantime the user does not refresh or request a page within the application. The default in IIS 5.0 is 10 minutes.

This code snippet sets the `CodePage` property to English, whose character set (as well as the character sets of most European languages), is identified by the integer 1252:

```
<% CODEPAGE = 1252 %>
```

This code snippet sets the `LCID` property so currency will be formatted in pounds (£) rather than in dollars:

```
<%
   Session.LCID = 2057
   Dim curNumb
   curNumb = FormatCurrency(125)
   Response.Write (curNumb)
%>
```

The `SessionID` property uniquely identifies a session within the instance of an application. However, if and when the application ends, such as if the Web server is restarted, the value of the `SessionID` property no longer is valid. Therefore, you should not use the `SessionID` property to generate primary key values for a database application since, if the Web server is restarted, the `SessionID` property values generated by the new application could duplicate those generated by the prior instance of the application.

You may wish to shorten the `TimeOut` property if it is likely that users will be using your application for less than the default time-out period. This will more quickly restore resources to your Web server. The following code snippet sets the time out period to five minutes:

```
Session.Timeout = 5
```

The Session object has one method, `Abandon`. This method will explicitly end a session. Otherwise, a session will end when it times out. You use the following syntax to invoke the `Abandon` method:

```
<% Session.Abandon %>
```

The Session object, like the Application object, has its Contents and StaticObjects collections. These collections are the same as the corresponding collections of the Application object, except that they apply to items and objects with session-level scope rather than application-level scope.

Request object

The Request object permits your ASP code to access information, such as user input in an HTML form, passed from the browser to the ASP application.

The Request object has one property, `TotalBytes`. This property returns the total number of bytes sent in the body of the client's request.

Table 11-2 lists the collections of the Request object:

| Table 11-2 | |
| **Collections of the Request Object** | |
Name	**Description**
ClientCertificate	Retrieves the certification fields (specified in the X.509 standard) from a request issued by the Web browser.
Cookies	Retrieves the values of the cookies sent in an HTTP request.
Form	Retrieves the values of form elements posted to the HTTP request body by a form using the POST method.
QueryString	Retrieves the values of the variables in the HTTP query string.
ServerVariables	Retrieves the values of predetermined environment variables.

An ASP application that requests and displays the e-mail address entered by a user illustrates the ServerVariables, QueryString, and Form collections. This application consists of two HTML pages, one to obtain the user's input and the other to display the output. The application uses the GET and PUT methods to pass input from the client browser to the Web server. The user chooses which method to use.

Figure 11-2 shows the input form. The user has two options for entering his or her e-mail address. The first option ("Let's get your e-mail address") uses the GET method. The second option ("Please post your e-mail address") uses the POST method.

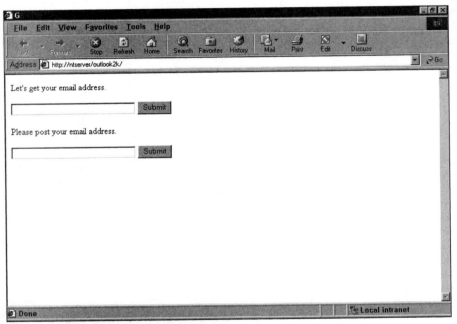

Figure 11-2: Input form for ASP application

Listing 11-1 lists the HTML code for the input form:

Listing 11-1: **HTML code for input form**

```
<html>
<head><title>GET and POST methods</title></head>
<body>
```

```
<form method="Get" action="../Outlook2k/getpost.asp" name
="GetExample">
  <p>Let's get your e-mail address.</p>
  <p><input type="text" name="email" size="30">
  <input type="submit" value="Submit" name="GetSubmit"></p>
</form>

<form method="Post" action="../Outlook2k/getpost.asp" name
="PostExample">
  <p>Please post your e-mail address.</p>
  <p><input type="text" name="email" size="30">
  <input type="submit" value="Submit" name="PostSubmit"></p>
</form>

</body>
</html>
```

Figure 11-3 shows the output file that results if the user chooses the GET method. Figure 11-4 shows the output file that results if the user chooses the POST method.

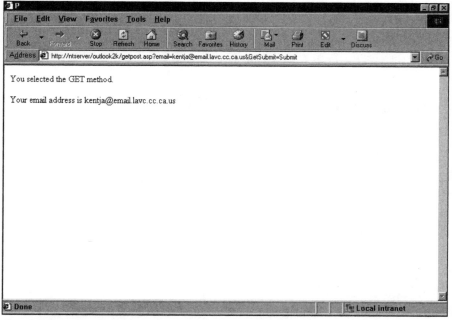

Figure 11-3: Output file resulting from use of GET method

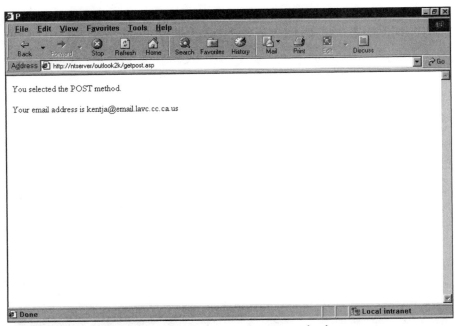

Figure 11-4: Output file resulting from use of POST method

Listing 11-2 lists the code for the ASP form:

Listing 11-2: **HTML code for ASP form**

```
<html>
<head><title>Post and Get ASP Page</title></head>

<%RequestMethod = Request.ServerVariables("REQUEST_METHOD")%>

<body>

You selected the <%=RequestMethod%> method.

<P><%If RequestMethod="GET" then %>
Your e-mail address is <%=Request.QueryString("email")%>

<% else %>
Your e-mail address is <%=Request.Form("email")%>

<% end if %>

</body>
</html>
```

You use the ServerVariables collection to obtain the value of one of many predefined environment variables. REQUEST_METHOD is one of these environment variables. The REQUEST_METHOD environment variable returns the method used to make a request. For HTTP, the request methods include GET and POST. Thus, the following ASP script assigns to the variable RequestMethod the particular method (GET or POST) that the user utilized to send their e-mail address:

```
<%RequestMethod = Request.ServerVariables("REQUEST_METHOD")%>
```

Note There are other useful environment variables. For example, the environment variable HTTP_USER_AGENT returns a string describing the browser that sent the request. This is useful in those all too many situations in which Internet Explorer and Netscape require different code to accomplish the same task. Another useful environment variable is LOGON_USER, which returns the Windows NT account the user is currently logged on to.

The ASP script then branches into an If ... Else structure based on whether the value of the variable RequestMethod is GET or POST.

If the request method is GET, then you would use the QueryString collection to obtain the e-mail address entered by the user. With the GET method, the HTTP query string is appended to the URL of the ASP page following a question mark (?) character. You can use the Address Bar to view the HTTP query string. Figure 11-3 shows the Address Bar of the ASP page after the GET method was used. The string in the Address Bar reads:

```
http://ntserver/outlook2k/getpost.asp?email=kentja@email.lavc.c
c.ca.us&GetSubmit=Submit
```

The HTTP query string identifies two variables, email and GetSubmit, and their corresponding values. These variables were given their names by the <name> tag in the HTML code:

```
<p><input type="text" name="email" size="30">
<input type="submit" value="Submit" name="PostSubmit"></p>
```

In the HTTP query string, the two variables, email and GetSubmit, are separated by the ampersand (&) character, and the values of each variable follow the equals sign (=). Thus, the value of the email variable is email.lavc.cc.ca.us, the value entered into the text box, and the value of the GetSubmit variable is Submit, the value of the Submit button.

You use the name of a variable to retrieve its value from the QueryString collection. Thus, the following statement retrieves the value of the e-mail address:

```
Your e-mail address is <%=Request.QueryString("email")%>
```

If the request method is POST, then you would use the Form collection to obtain the e-mail address entered by the user. As Figure 11-4 shows, unlike with the GET method, with the POST method the variable values are not appended to the URL of the ASP page. Thus, you may prefer the POST method when you do not want the user to be able to view the value of the variables generated by their input. However, since with the POST method the variable values are not appended to the URL, you cannot use the QueryString collection to retrieve their values. Instead, you use the Form collection.

As with the QueryString collection, you use the name of a variable to retrieve its value from the Form collection. Thus, the value of the e-mail address is retrieved for output by the statement:

```
Your e-mail address is <%=Request.Form("email")%>
```

Response object

The Response object controls the HTML and other content that the server returns to the client browser.

Table 11-3 lists selected properties of the Response object:

<table>
<tr><td colspan="2" align="center">Table 11-3
Properties of the Response Object</td></tr>
<tr><td>*Name*</td><td>*Description*</td></tr>
<tr><td>Buffer</td><td>Setting this property to True holds output to the browser until the script has completed; False releases the output immediately.</td></tr>
<tr><td>ContentType</td><td>Specifies the HTTP content type for the response. The default is text/HTML.</td></tr>
<tr><td>Expires</td><td>Specifies the number of minutes before a page cached on a browser expires.</td></tr>
<tr><td>ExpiresAbsolute</td><td>Specifies the day, and optionally time, when a page cached on a browser expires.</td></tr>
<tr><td>IsClientConnected</td><td>Returns whether the client remains connected to the server.</td></tr>
<tr><td>Status</td><td>Specifies the status line to be returned by the server. The status line is a three-digit number that indicates a status code and a brief explanation of that code, such as "401 Unauthorized."</td></tr>
</table>

The Response object's `Buffer` property allows you to hold (buffer) rather than release output to the browser until the script has completed. This enables you to determine if an error has occurred before you release the output.

The `Buffer` property has two possible values, True and False. False means that the server sends the output to the client as the output is processed. True means that the server does not send the output to the client until the ASP scripts on the current page have been processed or either the `Flush` or `End` method (discussed next) has been called.

False is the default value for versions 4.0 and lower of IIS. True is the default value for version 5.0. The syntax for setting the value of the Buffer property (in this example to True) is:

```
Response.Buffer = True
```

Table 11- 4 lists selected methods of the Response object.

Table 11- 4
Methods of the Response Object

Name	Description	Parameter
Clear	Purges any buffered HTML output.	None.
End	Stops server processing of the script and sends any buffered output.	None.
Flush	Sends buffered output immediately.	None.
Redirect	Directs the browser to attempt to connect to a different URL.	The URL to which the browser is redirected.
Write	Writes the parameter to the output.	The value to write to output.

Several of these methods can be used in conjunction with the Response object's `Buffer` property. As discussed above, the `Buffer` property enables you to buffer rather than release output to the browser until the script has completed so you can determine if an error has occurred before you release the output. If no error occurred, then you would use the `Flush` method to send the output. If an error occurred, then you would use the `Clear` method to purge the buffered output. You would then use the `Write` method to warn the user that an error occurred, and finally the `End` method to stop further processing of the ASP script and send the error message to the client.

Creating the ASP Application's Virtual Directory

An ASP application lives in a virtual directory. Outlook Web Access, as explained in Chapter 10, is an ASP application. By default, the virtual directory in which Outlook Web Access is located is named Exchange. You can use the Microsoft Management Console of Internet Information Server (IIS) to view this virtual directory. Figure 11-5 shows that the Exchange virtual directory is under the WWW service and is mapped to the..\exchsrvr\webdata folder on the hard drive.

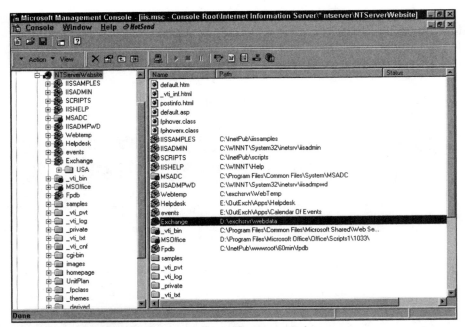

Figure 11-5: Outlook Web Access' virtual directory, Exchange

You can use the virtual directory name to access the ASP application. For example, you may access Outlook Web Access by using the URL *WebServerName*/exchange, substituting for *WebServerName* the name of your Web server. This URL will open the default page. You can set this default page from Microsoft Management Console of IIS. Right-click the Exchange virtual directory under the WWW service, select Properties from the context menu, and choose the Document tab, which is shown in Figure 11-6. Check the Enable Default Document checkbox and make sure that default.asp is first in the list box. This will result in default.asp being the page first accessed when you log on to Outlook Web Access.

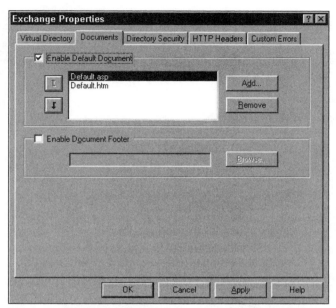

Figure 11-6: Setting default document for ASP application

You could create the ASP e-mail address application discussed in the preceding section on the Request object collections with the following steps.

1. Create a virtual directory. As Figure 11-7 depicts, from the Microsoft Management Console in IIS, right-click the Web service, in this example called NTServerWebsite, choose New from the context menu and Virtual Directory from the submenu. This displays the New Virtual Directory Wizard shown in Figure 11-8.

2. Type a friendly name for the application in the text box. This name will be part of the URL for the application, following the name of the Web server. In this example the friendly name is Outlook2k in honor of this book. After you have entered a name for the application, press the Next button.

3. Figure 11-9 shows the second screen of the New Virtual Directory Wizard. Use the Browse button to enter the physical folder on which the application will be located, and then click the Next button.

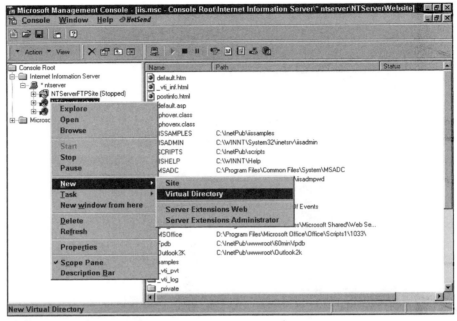

Figure 11-7: New Virtual Directory menu command

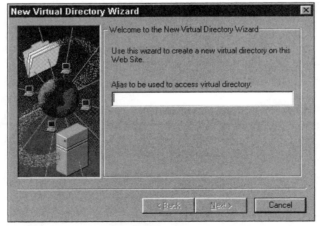

Figure 11-8: New Virtual Directory Wizard—name of application

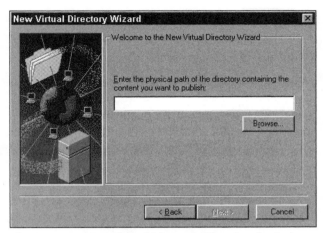

Figure 11-9: New Virtual Directory Wizard — physical location of application

4. Figure 11-10 shows the third screen of the New Virtual Directory Wizard. Enter the access permission. This example allows users Execute access, which is the third checkbox.

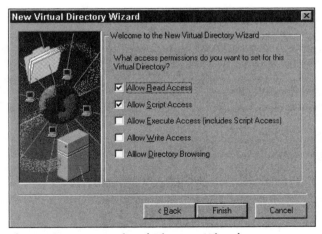

Figure 11-10: New Virtual Directory Wizard — access permissions

5. Press the Finish button. Figure 11-11 shows the new virtual directory in the contents pane.

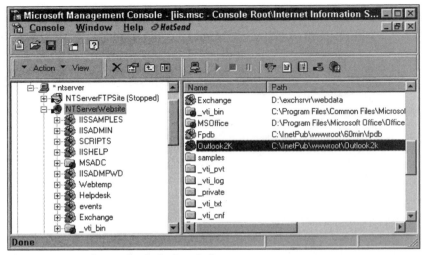

Figure 11-11: The Outlook2k virtual directory

6. Move the input and output files to the physical directory to which the Outlook2k virtual directory is mapped. In this example, the input file (Listing 11-1) is called `default.html` and the output file (Listing 11-2) is called get-post.asp. You must give the output file an .asp extension so that the ASP interpreter will process the ASP script in the file.

7. Figure 11-6 shows the Document page for Outlook Web Access. You would access the Document page for the Outlook2k application similarly by right-clicking the Outlook2k virtual directory under the WWW service, selecting Properties from the context menu, and choosing the Document page. Check the Enable Default Document checkbox and make sure that default.html is first in the list box. This will result in default.html being the page first accessed when you log on to the Outlook2k application.

8. Access the Outlook2k application with the URL `WebServerName/exchange`, substituting for `WebServerName` the name of your Web server. This URL will open the default page, which is `default.html` because of Step 7.

Lifecycle of an ASP Application

When an ASP application begins, the ASP interpreter first attempts to load a file named global.asa in the virtual root of the Web. This is an optional file, though most ASP applications have it, including Outlook Web Access. The file must be named global.asa and it must be stored in the root directory of the application. An application can only have one global.asa file.

The purpose of a global.asa file is to execute code whenever an application or a session starts or ends. The file contains four subroutines:

- ✦ `Application_OnStart` — This subroutine is called when the *first* user makes his or her first request for an .asp file from your application.

- ✦ `Session_OnStart` — This subroutine is called when *any* user makes the first request (for that user) for an .asp file from your application.

- ✦ `Session_OnEnd` — This subroutine is called for a particular user when that user's session with the application ends.

- ✦ `Application_OnEnd` — This subroutine is called when your application ends.

The `Application_OnStart` subroutine is only called when the first user first requests an .asp file. It is not called when additional users make their first requests for an .asp file. Additionally, it only is called when the requested file is an .asp file. It is not called if the user instead requests an .html file.

You use the `Application_OnStart` subroutine to instantiate and initialize global variables that will persist during the lifetime of the application. For example, you could use this subroutine to instantiate and initialize a variable that counts the number of users using your application. The following sample application uses this subroutine to save the name of the server.

The `Session_OnStart` subroutine is called at the first request of *any* user for an .asp file from your application. Therefore, this subroutine will be called after the `Application_OnStart` subroutine when the first user makes his or her first request for an .asp file. However, unlike the `Application_OnStart` subroutine, the `Session_OnStart` subroutine also will be called when subsequent users make their first requests for an .asp file.

You use the `Session_OnStart` subroutine to instantiate and initialize variables that will persist during an individual user's use of an application. The interval from when a user first accesses the application to when he or she leaves it is usually referred to as a *session*, which is represented by the Session object discussed above. The following sample application uses the `Session_OnStart` subroutine to save the mailbox name of the user who is logging on.

A user's session with the application ends, calling the `Session_OnEnd` subroutine, if either your code calls the `Abandon` method of the Session object or the user does not request or refresh a Web page in the applicator for the timeout interval. The timeout interval by default is 20 minutes but you can change it by assigning a different time period to the `TimeOut` property of the Session object

You can use the `Session_OnEnd` subroutine to clean up variables instantiated in the `Session_OnStart` subroutine.

You use Session level variables to maintain the *state* of an application. Many Web applications are *stateless*. This means that, as far as the application is concerned, each time you navigate from page to page within the application, you are a new user. The application does not "remember" that you just visited another page within the application, much less which page that was.

ASP applications can keep state information on a session by maintaining variables global for the user. This information is stored when the user first accesses the ASP application, triggering the Session_OnStart subroutine, and persists until the user exits the application, triggering the Session_OnEnd subroutine.

State information is stored on the user's machine in a file often referred to as a "cookie." In ASP applications, cookies only persist during a session. They are destroyed at the end of the session. Users will receive new cookies when they next access the application.

Note An ASP application can store a cookie on the user's machine only if the settings of the user's browser permit it. The ASP application will work even if the user does not accept cookies. However, the application will not be able to maintain state information on the user.

An application ends, calling the Application_OnEnd subroutine, if either the Web server shuts down or you press the Unload button in the IIS Microsoft Management Console. You use the Application_OnEnd subroutine to release the memory you took when you instantiated global variables in the Application_OnStart subroutine. You also should use it to save variables, such as one that counts the number of users using your application, to disk.

Collaboration Data Objects (CDO)

The Messaging Application Programming Interface (MAPI) has long offered an object model for developers writing mail-enabled applications. However, writing MAPI applications was no easy task. MAPI not only had a complex object model, but also required the C or C++ programming language.

Microsoft, as it released each major version of Exchange Server, released an API to enable developers to write applications using Exchange Server without having to use full-blown MAPI. Microsoft introduced the OLE Messaging library, now referred to as CDO 1.0, when it released version 4.0 of Exchange Server in 1996. Microsoft renamed the OLE Messaging library the Active Messaging library when it released version 5.0 of Exchange Server in the beginning of 1997. The Active Messaging library, now referred to as CDO 1.1, enabled developers to use ASP to access Exchange information. An ASP/OLE Messaging application, Outlook Web Access, was introduced with Exchange Server 5.0.

Microsoft renamed the Active Messaging library Collaboration Data Objects (CDO) when it released version 5.5 of Microsoft Exchange Server at the end of 1997. CDO 1.2 was included in Microsoft Exchange Server 5.5 and CDO 1.21 was included in Microsoft Outlook 98 and Microsoft Exchange Server 5.5 Service Pack 1 or higher.

CDO consists of three libraries that correspond to three dynamic link library (.dll) files:

✦ CDO — This library (`cdo.dll`) lets you add to your application the ability to send and receive mail messages and to interact with folders and address books. This library will be discussed in detail in this section.

✦ CDO Rendering Library — This library (`cdohtml.dll`) renders CDO objects and collections in HTML for use on the World Wide Web. This library was used for the Outlook Web Access forms discussed in Chapter 10.

✦ CDONTS — CDO for NTS Library (Collaboration Data Objects for Windows NT Server, `cdonts.dll`). This is a "lite" version of CDO. CDONTS' functionality is more limited but it is easier to use than the more complex CDO. You use CDONTS for comparatively simple tasks like sending unauthenticated e-mail from a Web page.

The Future of CDO

Neither time nor Microsoft stands still. Microsoft has announced future versions of both CDONTS and CDO.

✦ CDO 2.0 is the successor to CDONTS. CDO 2.0 is included in Windows 2000 (the successor operating system to NT 4.0) Server and Workstation. CDO 2.0 provides basic messaging services, such as the ability to send e-mail and post discussions/news, and support the SMTP and NNTP protocols and inbound protocol events and agents. However, it does not provide access to mailboxes.

✦ CDO 3.0 will be the successor to CDO 1.2. CDO 3.0 will be included in the next release of Microsoft Exchange Server (likely named Exchange Server 2000), which according to Microsoft was supposed to be released about 90 days after Microsoft Windows 2000, but has been delayed. (As of the writing of this book, Release Candidate 2 of Exchange Server 2000 was the most current.) CDO 3.0 will have a different object model from CDO 1.2 and will include extensions to the OLE DB and ADO programming models. It will be a superset of CDO 2.0 and will enable new functions, such as voicemail, fax, and pager support, as well as enhanced support for scheduling, task and contact management. Last but not least, a future release of Microsoft Outlook will also support CDO 3.0.

Microsoft has maintained the backwards compatibility of CDO through its successive versions. Thus, an application written with OLE Messaging can be run with the CDO 1.21. There is no indication that backwards compatibility won't continue with CDO 3.0.

The most current library of CDO (cdo.dll) and the CDO HTML Rendering library (cdohtml.dll) are installed with the Microsoft Exchange Server 5.5 Service Pack 2. The CDO HTML Rendering library (CDOHTML.DLL) is used in Active Server Pages applications (e.g., Outlook Web Access) and you can install it on the Microsoft Exchange Server 5.5 computer by choosing the option Outlook Web Access.

Cross-Reference   Installing Outlook Web Access is covered in Chapter 10.

CDO Object Model

CDO, like seemingly everything else in this book, has an extensive object model. These objects include:

✦ Session — This object is the gateway to the application.

✦ InfoStores — The InfoStores collection is comprised of all message stores available to the session based on the permissions of the user logged in. You can use the InfoStores collection to access the folders in both Public Folders and the user's mailbox. Related folders comprise a Folders collection, and each folder is a folder object. This is analogous to the Folders collection and MAPIFolder object discussed in Chapter 3.

✦ AddressLists — The AddressLists collection is comprised of all address lists available to the session based on the permissions of the user logged in. Each Address list is an AddressList object, and its entries comprise the Address-Entries collection, which contain AddressEntry objects. These collections and objects are analogous to those address book collections and objects covered in Chapter 4.

✦ Messages — The Messages collection is comprised of AppointmentItem, MeetingItem, or Message objects. These objects are parallel to the Outlook items of the same names discussed in Chapter 4.

✦ Recipients — The Recipients collection object contains one or more Recipient objects. Each Recipient object represents a recipient of a message. The Recipients collection and Recipient object correspond to the collection and object of the same name discussed in Chapter 4.

✦ Attachments — The Attachments collection contains the attachments to a message, each of which is an Attachment object. The Attachments collection and the Attachment object are akin to the collection and object of the same name discussed in Chapter 4.

✦Fields — The Fields collection is comprised of Field objects. Each Field object represents a field, which may be in an InfoStore or folder, an address list or entry, or a message, appointment, or meeting item.

The CDO object library and the Outlook 2000 object library cover many of the same collections and objects. Indeed, the Outlook 2000 object library covers some items that the CDO object library either does not cover at all (contact items) or does not cover as deeply. Nevertheless, the CDO object library is not an inferior duplicate of the Outlook 2000 object library. The Outlook 2000 object library, while quite adequate for standalone Outlook applications, is not designed for multi-user applications run from a network or Web server. CDO is designed for that environment.

Exploring CDO Through the Tech-Support Application

The Outlook 2000 object model represents a standalone application, Outlook 2000. By contrast, CDO does not represent a particular application. Instead, CDO is used to enhance the functionality of applications. Therefore, CDO's many collections and objects, each with a number of properties and methods, can best be explained in the context of a working application. The following section will use a tech-support application to explore the CDO object model.

Synopsis of tech-support application

1. Users, upon entering the URL of the application in their Web browser, will be directed to the log-on page shown in Figure 11-12, where they will then be asked to enter their Exchange mailbox name.

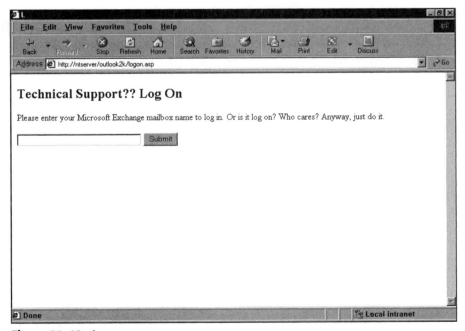

Figure 11–12: Log-on page

2. If the users are authenticated, they will be shown the menu displayed in Figure 11-13 and given the choice of making a help request or logging off.

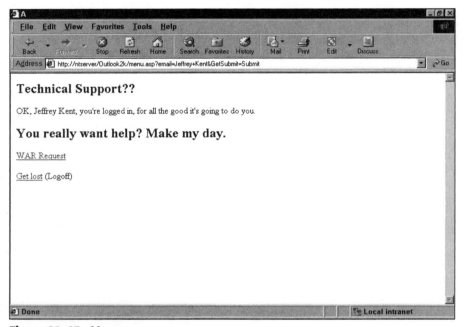

Figure 11–13: Menu page

3. If the users make a help request, then they will be shown the help ticket displayed in Figure 11-14 with those fields describing the user (name, phone number) already filled in.

4. After the users complete and submit the help ticket, a message is posted to an Exchange Server public folder. Figure 11-15 displays that folder. Figure 11-16 shows the custom form representing that item, which you displayed by clicking on the item in the view.

5. The users, after they have submitted the help ticket, will be shown a menu page similar to that displayed in Figure 11-13 and will be given the choice of making another help request or logging off.

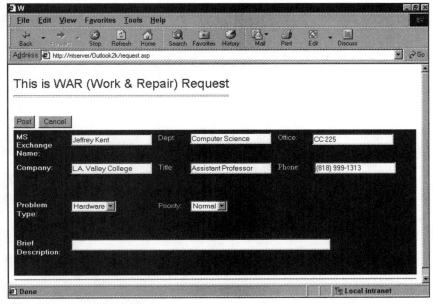

Figure 11–14: Help ticket

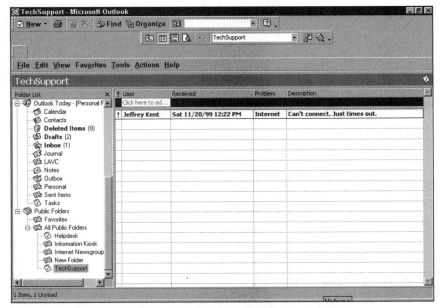

Figure 11–15: Public folder view showing posted help ticket

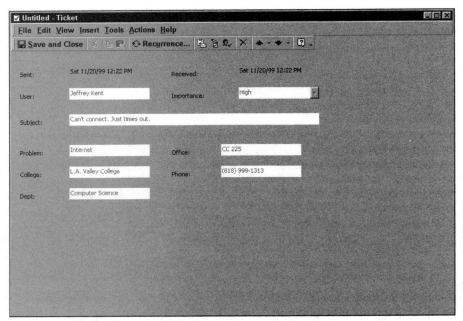

Figure 11–16: Public folder form showing posted help ticket

Using the logon method

The first steps you must take in your CDO application are to create a Session object and then to use the Logon method of that object to log onto the server. You need a Session object to access other CDO objects, and you cannot access any Exchange Server data without successfully logging on.

You can create a Session object with the CreateObject method of the Server object, as discussed in the preceding section:

```
Set objSession = Server.CreateObject("MAPI.Session")
```

You can then use the Session object variable objSession to invoke the Session object's Logon method. That method has the following syntax:

```
objSession.Logon( [profileName] [, profilePassword] _
    [, showDialog] [, newSession] [, parentWindow] _
    [, NoMail] [, ProfileInfo] )
```

Which of the seven optional parameters you use and the values you give them depend on which of three log-in scenarios you use in your application:

✦ Authenticated logon using an existing profile — Your user is logging on to a machine, usually his or her own, on which he or she has an existing user profile.

✦ Authenticated log on using a dynamically created profile — You want to authenticate the user, but he or she is logging on to a machine on which he or she does not have a profile. This is the usual scenario when the user is accessing another machine on the network or the Internet.

✦ Anonymous Access — Many Internet applications do not require, and in fact encourage, access by guests. These applications permit anonymous access.

Table 11-5 describes the parameters of the Logon method:

Table 11- 5 Parameters of the Logon Method		
Name	**Description**	**Comments**
ProfileName	Optional string that specifies the profile name to use. Profiles are listed in the Choose Profile dialog box displayed in Figure 11-17.	You use the default value, an empty string, unless you intend authenticated log on using an existing profile and you do not want to prompt the user for a profile using the showDialog parameter.
ProfilePassword	Optional string that specifies the profile password.	You use the default value, an empty string, unless you intend authenticated log on using an existing profile and you do not want to prompt the user for a password using the show Dialog parameter.
ShowDialog	Optional Boolean value. The default, True, displays a Choose Profile dialog box.	You should specify the value False unless you intend authenticated log on using an existing profile and you want to prompt the user for a profile or password.
NewSession	Optional Boolean value that determines whether the application opens a new MAPI session or uses the current shared MAPI session.	You should use the default, True, which opens a new MAPI session, unless you intend authenticated log on using an existing profile.
ParentWindow	Optional long value that specifies whether the currently active window is to be used as the parent window for the log-on dialog box.	The default value of zero specifies that the dialog box should be application-modal. This parameter is ignored unless showDialog is True.

Continued

	Table 11- 5 *(continued)*	
Name	**Description**	**Comments**
NoMail	Optional Boolean value that specifies whether the session should be registered with the MAPI spooler.	You normally should use the default value of False, which registers the session with the MAPI spooler, unless Anonymous access is used.
ProfileInfo	Optional string that contains the server and mailbox names separated by a linefeed (vbLF) character.	This parameter is only used by applications interfacing with Exchange Server and is ignored if ProfileInfo is supplied.

Figure 11-17: Choose Profile dialog box

The following code could be used for authenticated log on using an existing profile MS Exchange Settings with the password password:

```
objSession.Logon "MS Exchange Settings", "password", _
    False, False, 0, True
```

The exchange server and mailbox names are concatenated with a separating linefeed character and assigned to the profileInfo parameter. In the following code for authenticated log on using a dynamically created profile, the exchange server's name is NTSERVER and the mailbox name is Jeffrey Kent. This information can be obtained from the Exchange Server Service Profile dialog box depicted in Figure 11-18.

```
strServer = "NTSERVER"
strMailbox = "Jeffrey Kent"
strProfileInfo = strServer + vbLF + strMailbox
objSession.Logon "", "", False, True, 0, True, strProfileInfo
```

Anonymous access (assuming the Exchange Server administrator enables it) also uses the profileInfo parameter. However, the syntax of creating that parameter is different from creating it with authenticated log on using a dynamically created profile. With authenticated log on using a dynamically created profile, the exchange server's name and the mailbox name are con-catenated with a separating linefeed character. With anonymous access, the exchange server's *distinguished* name (a unique name used as an identifier of an object) and the mailbox name are concatenated with *two* separating linefeed characters.

Figure 11-18: Exchange Server Service Profile Dialog Box

The syntax for the server's distinguished name, with the variables italicized, is:

```
/o=enterprise/ou=site/cn=Configuration/cn=Servers/cn=server
```

You should replace the `enterprise` parameter with the name of the Exchange Server organization, the `site` parameter with the Exchange Server site to be accessed, and the `server` parameter with the name of the Exchange Server machine.

You can obtain these parameters from the Registry using the `LoadConfiguration` method and the `ConfigParameter` property of the RenderingApplication object. The log-on example in Listing 11-4 uses the `LoadConfiguration` method and the `ConfigParameter` property of the RenderingApplication object to obtain the server name for a dynamically created profile.

Logon page

The example above used the following code for a dynamically created profile:

```
strServer = "NTSERVER"
strMailbox = "Jeffrey Kent"
strProfileInfo = strServer + vbLF + strMailbox
objSession.Logon "", "", False, True, 0, True, strProfileInfo
```

Hardcoding the names of the exchange server and the user's mailbox works fine if the exchange server's name happens to be NTSERVER and the user's mailbox name is Jeffrey Kent. Obviously neither will always be the case.

The server's name is stored in the Registry of the Web server. The ASP application, residing on the Web server, has access to the system registry of the server. Therefore, the ASP application can retrieve from the registry the name of the server for the dynamically created profile.

By contrast, the user's mailbox name will not be stored on the server. Therefore, the user's mailbox name will have to be obtained from the user by the application asking the user to log in with the mailbox name.

Additionally, unless your application is either very private or very unsuccessful, you will have more than one user at a time. The application will need to keep one user separate from the other.

Figure 11-12 showed the log-on page, logon.asp. This page is similar to the example of the GET and POST methods in Figure 11-2.

Users can be directed to the log-on page when they navigate to the URL of your application either by making the log-on page the default page for the application as shown in Figure 11-6 or by using the Redirect method of the Response object to redirect the user from the default page to the log-on page.

Listing 11-3 shows the HTML code for the log-on page:

Listing 11- 3: **HTML code for log-on page**

```
<html>
<head><title>Logon</title></head>
<body>
<h1 align="left"><b><font size="5">Technical Support?? Log
On</font></b></h1>
<p align="left">Please enter your Microsoft Exchange mailbox
name to log in. Or
is it log on? Who cares? Anyway, just do it.

<form method="Get" action="../Outlook2k/menu.asp" name
="GetExample">
  <p><input type="text" name="email" size="30">
  <input type="submit" value="Submit" name="GetSubmit"></p>
</form>

</body>
</html>
```

The log-on page uses the GET method to obtain the user's mailbox name. The action parameter refers to the menu.asp page, which is shown in Figure 11-13.

Obtaining the server name

As mentioned earlier in this chapter in the discussion of ASP, the ASP interpreter looks for a global.asa file when the application first attempts to access an .asp file. The Application_OnStart procedure in the global.asa file runs when the ASP application first starts. Listing 11- 4 lists the code for the Application_OnStart procedure in the global.asa file:

Listing 11- 4: **Application_OnStart procedure in global.asa**

```
Sub Application_OnStart
    On Error Resume Next
    Set objRenderApp =
Server.CreateObject("AMHTML.Application")
    Set Application("RenderApplication") = objRenderApp
    objRenderApp.LoadConfiguration 1, _
        "HKEY_LOCAL_MACHINE\System\CurrentControlSet\" & _
        "Services\MSExchangeWeb\Parameters"
    Application("ServerName") =
objRenderApp.ConfigParameter("Server")
End Sub
```

You use the Application_OnStart procedure to obtain the server name from the Registry. You will need the server name to build the dynamically created profile.

The code first creates an instance of the RenderingApplication object, which is an object of the CDO Rendering Library.

```
Set objRenderApp = Server.CreateObject("AMHTML.Application")
Set Application("RenderApplication") = objRenderApp
```

The AM in AMHTML stands for Active Messaging, one of the predecessor names of CDO.

The code next invokes the RenderingApplication object's LoadConfiguration method:

```
objRenderApp.LoadConfiguration 1, _
    "HKEY_LOCAL_MACHINE\System\CurrentControlSet\" & _
    "Services\MSExchangeWeb\Parameters"
```

Table 11-6 lists the parameters of the LoadConfiguration method:

Table 11-6			
Parameters of the LoadConfiguration Method			
Name	*Required?*	*Data Type*	*Purpose*
eSource	Yes	Integer	The CDOHTML configuration source, represented either by the constant CdoConfigRegistry (1), the standard Registry key name for the CDO Rendering Library, or CdoConfigDS (2), the Exchange directory server.
bstrSection	Yes	String	The name of the section in the configuration source to load the information from. This is ignored if the eSource parameter is CdoConfigDS.
varSession	No, optional	Object	The Session object the messaging user is logged on to, if any. Ignored if the eSource parameter is CdoConfigDS.

The LoadConfiguration obtains registry information from the following registry key:

```
HKEY_LOCAL_MACHINE\SYSTEM\CurrentControlSet\Services\MSExchange
WEB\Parameters
```

Figure 11-19 shows the Registry values and data for this key.

As Figure 11-19 shows, one of the Registry values is the name of the server. This value is retrieved by the ConfigParameter property of the RenderingApplication object and stored in an Application-level variable called ServerName:

```
Application("ServerName") =
objRenderApp.ConfigParameter("Server")
```

Note   For anonymous access the ConfigParameter property also can retrieve the Enterprise **and** Site **values.**

The variable ServerName should have application scope. The server name will not change throughout the life of the application. Therefore this value should only have to be retrieved once.

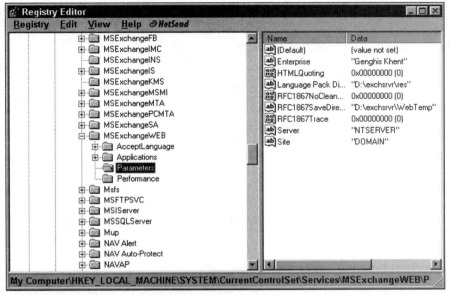

Figure 11-19: Registry configuration information

Initializing session-level variables

As we mentioned earlier in the discussion of ASP, when the user attempts to log on, the ASP interpreter next runs the Session_OnStart procedure in the global.asa file. Listing 11-5 lists the code for the Session_OnStart procedure in the global.asa file:

Listing 11- 5: Session_OnStart Procedure in Global.asa

```
Sub Session_OnStart
    On Error Resume Next
    Session("imp") = 0
    Set Session("sesCDO") = Nothing
End Sub
```

The Session_OnStart procedure has two Session-level variables. The variable imp represents the handle to the security context for the current user. As discussed in Chapter 10, IIS responds to user requests by *impersonating* the user and runs under the security context of the particular user. The variable sesCDO represents the Session object for the user. Since the ASP interpreter calls the Session_OnStart procedure before the user has been authenticated, imp is set to 0 and sesCDO is set to Nothing.

Centralizing Authentication Procedures with the Include Directive

The ASP script calls two procedures, AuthenticateUser and CheckSession, to determine if the user is authenticated. The menu.asp page does not contain the procedures AuthenticateUser and CheckSession. Instead, these procedures are contained in another file named logon.inc. The procedures AuthenticateUser and CheckSession could be contained in the menu.asp page. However, these procedures also will be called from other .asp files in the application. Therefore, these procedures should be contained in one file, here logon.inc, which can be accessed by the various .asp files that need them.

The menu.asp page and the other .asp files that use AuthenticateUser and CheckSession procedures access the logon.inc file with the server-side include directive #include. This directive is similar to the preprocessor directive #include in C and C++. This directive inserts the contents of logon.inc into menu.asp before the Web server processes menu.asp. The syntax of the include directive is:

```
<!-- #include virtual | file ="filename" -->
```

The virtual and file keywords indicate the type of path you are using to include the file. You must use one and only one of these two keywords. The parameter filename is the path and file name of the file you want to include. The included files do not require a special file name extension, but it's conventional to give included files an .inc extension.

You use the virtual keyword to indicate a path beginning with a *virtual directory*. For example, the logon.inc file is located in the library folder of the Outlook2k virtual directory, the root of which is the location of menu.asp. Therefore, the include directive using the virtual keyword would be:

```
<!-- #include virtual ="/Outlook2k/library/logon.inc" -->
```

You use the file keyword to indicate a *relative* path, which begins with the directory that contains the including file. Since the logon.inc file is located in the library folder of the Outlook2k virtual directory, the root of which is the location of menu.asp, the include directive is:

```
<!-- #include file="library/logon.inc" -->
```

Authenticating the user

Once the Session_OnStart procedure completes, the menu.asp file begins to execute. The ASP script for the menu.asp page begins with the statements:

```
<!-- #include file="library/logon.inc" -->
<%

Dim objCDOSession
```

```
AuthenticateUser
CheckSession
Set objCDOSession = Session("sesCDO")
If objCDOSession Is Nothing Then
    Response.Redirect "logon.asp"
Else
    Response.Write "OK, " & Session("mailbox") & _
        ", you're logged in, for all the good" & _
        " it's going to do you."
End If
%>
```

The concept of the menu.asp page is straightforward. The code checks if the Session-level variable sesCDO points to a valid session or instead to Nothing. If sesCDO points to a valid session, then the user was authenticated, and the menu. asp page displays with menu choices. However, if sesCDO is Nothing, then the user was not authenticated, and is redirected to the log-on page.

Determining the authentication type

The next step is to determine which authentication method the server is using. This application will require Basic or Windows NT Challenge/Response authentication. Anonymous Access will not work in this application.

The ServerVariables collection of the Request object includes AUTH_TYPE. AUTH_TYPE returns a string representing the authentication method used by the server. It will return an empty string ("") if Anonymous Access is used, "Basic" if Basic Authentication is used, and "NTLM" if Windows NT Challenge Response authentication is used.

The menu.asp file first calls the function AuthenticateUser to confirm that the server is using either Basic or Windows NT Challenge Response. If the server is using Anonymous Access, then the user will be given the dreaded "401 Unauthorized" message and will not be able to proceed. Listing 11-6 lists the code for the function AuthenticateUser in logon.inc:

Listing 11- 6: Code for the Function AuthenticateUser in logon.inc

```
Public Function AuthenticateUser
On Error Resume Next
AuthenticateUser = False
strAuthType = Request.ServerVariables("AUTH_TYPE")
If InStr(1, "_BasicNTLM", strAuthType, vbTextCompare) < 2 Then
    Response.Buffer = True
```

Continued

Listing 11- 6 *(continued)*

```
        Response.Status = ("401 Unauthorized")
        Response.End
Else
        AuthenticateUser = True
End If
End Function
```

You should use the VBScript function InStr (also used in Visual Basic to parse the string returned by AUTH_TYPE). InStr takes four parameters:

1. The starting point of the search, here 1.

2. The substring to search for, here _BasicNTLM.

3. The string to search for, here the value of the AUTH_TYPE ServerVariable.

4. The type of comparison, here textual rather than binary.

The InStr function searches the second parameter (_BasicNTLM) for the presences of the third parameter, the string returned by the AUTH_TYPE ServerVariable. If a match is found, then InStr will return the position in the second parameter at which the match starts. That value will be 2 if Basic is the authentication type or 7 if NTLM is the authentication type. However, if the value of the third parameter is an empty string, as would be the case if Anonymous Access were permitted, then InStr will return the first parameter, the starting position, 1. Thus, the value returned by InStr will be greater than 2 only if the server uses Basic or NTLM as the authentication type.

Note   The second parameter starts with an underscore to distinguish the presence of the Basic authentication type (returning 2) from Anonymous Access (returning 1). Without the underscore the Basic authentication type also would return 1.

Checking for a valid Session

Once you have confirmed that the server uses Basic or NTLM as the authentication type, the next step is to see if you have a valid Session object by using the function CheckSession in logon.inc. Listing 11-7 lists the code for CheckSession:

Listing 11- 7: **Code for the Function CheckSession in logon.inc**

```
Public Function CheckSession()
On Error Resume Next
Dim cdoSession
CheckSession = False
```

```
Set cdoSession = Session("sesCDO")
If cdoSession Is Nothing Then
    NoSession
    Set cdoSession = Session("sesCDO")
End If
If Not cdoSession Is Nothing Then
    CheckSession = True
End If
End Function
```

The Session-level variable sesCDO was instantiated in the Session_OnStart procedure in global.asa and represents the Session object for the user. If sesCDO points
to a valid Session-level object, as it will after the first time it is called for the user,
then CheckSession will return True, and menu.asp will continue to execute. However, sesCDO will point to Nothing the first time CheckSession is called by the ASP
application for that user since at that point there is no dynamically created profile
for the user. In that event, the ASP application, which already has the server name,
needs to obtain the user's mailbox name and attempt to form a dynamically created
profile.

Retrieving the mailbox name

After you have confirmed that the server uses Basic or NTLM as the authentication
type, and that the user does not have a valid Session object, then you first need the
user's mailbox name before you can attempt to form a dynamically created profile.
You obtain the user's mailbox name with the function NoSession in logon.inc.
Listing 11-8 lists the code for NoSession:

Listing 11- 8: **Code for the Function NoSession in logon.inc**

```
Sub NoSession()
On Error Resume Next

Dim strMailbox
Dim strServer
Dim strProfileInfo
strServer = Application("ServerName")
If Session("mailbox") Is Nothing Then
    strMailbox = Request.QueryString("email")
    Session("mailbox") = strMailbox
Else
    strMailbox = Session("mailbox")
End If
AuthenticateUser
Err.Clear
Set objSession = Server.CreateObject("MAPI.Session")
Set objAM = Application("RenderApplication")
```

Continued

Listing 11- 8 *(continued)*

```
strProfileInfo = strServer + vbLF + strMailbox
objSession.Logon "", "", False, True, 0, True, strProfileInfo
If Err.Number = 0 Then
    Set objInbox = objSession.Inbox
    If Err.Number <> 0 Then
        objSession.Logoff
        Set objSession = Nothing
        Response.Write "Log on unsuccessful<br>"
    Else
        Set Session("sesCDO") = objSession
        Session("imp") = objAM.ImpID
    End If
End If
End Sub
```

The code next checks the value of a Session-level variable called `mailbox`. If `mailbox` points to a preexisting mailbox name, as it may after the first time the user accesses the ASP application within a given session, then that name is assigned to the local variable `strMailbox`. However, the first time the user accesses the ASP application within a given session, `mailbox` will point to `Nothing`. Since the log-on page used the `GET` method, the QueryString collection of the Request object will contain the mailbox named entered by the user. That value then is assigned to the local variable `strMailbox`.

```
If Session("mailbox") Is Nothing Then
    strMailbox = Request.QueryString("email")
    Session("mailbox") = strMailbox
Else
    strMailbox = Session("mailbox")
End If
```

Dynamically creating a profile

You can attempt to dynamically create a profile since you now have the user's mailbox name as well as the server name. The code creates a session object and then invokes the Session object's `Logon` method, passing as the final parameter the server and mailbox names separated by the linefeed character.

```
strProfileInfo = strServer + vbLF + strMailbox
objSession.Logon "", "", False, True, 0, True, strProfileInfo
```

The fact that the `Logon` method does not return an error does not necessarily mean that the server and mailbox names are valid. The `Logon` method does not verify the validity of either the server name or the mailbox name in the `ProfileInfo` parameter. The method may return successfully even if both of these names are incorrect.

Therefore, when you log on using a dynamically created profile, you should attempt to open the Inbox folder to verify that the server and mailbox names are valid. If either is not, attempting to open the Inbox folder will cause an error. In that event, it is time to log off and clean up.

```
If Err.Number = 0 Then
    Set objInbox = objSession.Inbox
    If Err.Number <> 0 Then
        objSession.Logoff
        Set objSession = Nothing
        Response.Write "Log on unsuccessful<br>"
    Else
        Set Session("sesCDO") = objSession
        Session("imp") = objAM.ImpID
    End If
End If
```

However, if you are able to open the Inbox without causing an error, then you can assign values to the two Session-level values declared in the Session_OnStart procedure in global.asa.

The Session-level variable sesCDO, which represents the Session object or the user, is assigned the reference of objSession, which had successfully invoked the Logon method.

The Session-level variable imp represents the handle to the security context for the current user. As discussed in Chapter10, IIS responds to user requests by impersonating the user. IIS runs under the *security context* of the particular user. The purpose of a security context is to give the process running on behalf of the user the same access to files and resources (and no more) than the user would have if he or she were physically accessing the process from the same machine. The handle points to that security context.

The ImpID property returns the security context handle for current user. This handle is then saved in the Session-level variable imp. The Impersonate method will later use the handle to impersonate the current user.

After NoSession is called, the code in CheckSession returns. The Session-level variable sesCDO, having been set to a valid Session in NoSession, now results in CheckSession returning True. The user has been logged in using a dynamically created profile, and the code in menu.asp continues by displaying the menu.

The menu.asp page will display if the user is authenticated. The address bar in Figure 11-13 shows:

```
http://ntserver/Outlook2k/menu.asp?email=Jeffrey+Kent&GetSubmit
=Submit
```

Accessing CDO Objects

You can access CDO objects once you are logged on.

The Session object has four immediate child objects:

- ✦ Inbox — The default Inbox folder.
- ✦ Outbox — The default Outbox folder.
- ✦ InfoStores collection — All message stores available to the session based on the permissions of the user logged in. You can use the InfoStores collection to access the folders in both Public Folders and the user's mailbox.
- ✦ AddressLists collection — All address lists available to the session based on the permissions of the user logged in.

Using AddressLists to access user information

The menu choice WAR Request is not a request to start a war. Rather, it is a Work and Repair request. At a college at which one of the co-authors teaches, this request is required paperwork for those who wish to beseech the technical staff to fix a computer-related problem.

Figure 11-20 displays a request *before* the user fills in any fields.

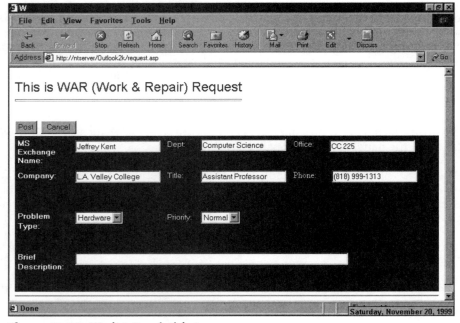

Figure 11-20: Work & Repair ticket

The name, company, department, title, office, and phone fields are already filled in. You obtain the value for these fields from the entry for the user in the Global Address List on the Exchange Server. Figure 11-21 shows the user's entry in the Global Address List:

Note   The WAR Request is on the file request.asp in the companion CD. The request.asp file has two components. One is HTML code to create the form displayed in Figure 11-20. The other is script executed by the ASP interpreter.

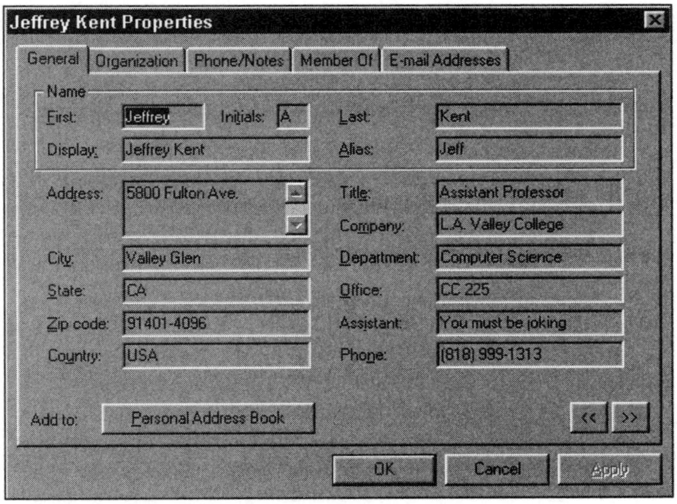

Figure 11-21: User's entry in Global Address List

You can use the AddressLists property of the Session object to access the user's address lists. The AddressLists property, with no parameters, returns the AddressLists collection, which comprises all of the user's address lists. You can use the AddressLists property to obtain a particular address list by passing either the list's one-based position in the collection or its name. The following code iterates through the user's AddressLists collection and prints out the name and number of entries in each list:

```
For Each AddressList in objSession.AddressLists
    Response.Write "<b>AddressList name = " & _
     AddressList.Name & "</b><br>"
    Set objAddressEntries = AddressList.AddressEntries
    Response.Write "Number of Addresses = " & _
     objAddressEntries.Count & "<br>"
Next
```

You can use the `GetAddressList` method of the Session object to access directly either the Global Address List or the user's Personal Address Book without having to iterate through the user's AddressLists collection. This method takes one argument. The argument must be either `CdoAddressListGAL` (0) to access the Global Address List or `CdoAddressListPAB` (1) to access the Personal Address Book. The request.asp file uses the following statement to access the Global Address List:

```
Set objAddressList = _
objCDOSession.GetAddressList(CdoAddressListGAL)
```

The next step is to access the entry for the user in the Global Address List. This entry is an AddressEntry object. Each AddressList object has an AddressEntries collection representing all of the entries in the address list. You can use the `Item` property of the AddressEntries collection to access individual entries, which are AddressEntry objects. The `Item` property retrieves an entry by either its one-based position or its name. The user's name is stored in the Session-level variable `mailbox`. The request.asp file uses the following statement to access the user's entry in the Global Address List:

```
strMBox = Session("mailbox")
Set objAddressEntry = _
objAddressList.AddressEntries.Item(strMBox)
```

The AddressEntry object has a `Fields` property. The Fields property, with no parameters, returns the Fields collection, which represents the individual entries for the user, such as for the user's name, phone number, and so on. You use the `Items` property of the Fields collection to obtain a particular field. You can pass the Items property the field's one-based position in the collection. However, you usually would not know the relative positions of the fields. Therefore, you usually identify a field by its `proptag`. The `proptag` is a constant with a hexadecimal value. The file constants.inc on the companion CD-ROM contains the constants used in this application.

The request.asp file uses the following statements to access the value of the user's company, department, title, office, and phone fields in the Global Address List:

```
Set objFields = objAddressEntry.Fields
fldDept = objFields.Item(CdoPR_DEPARTMENT_NAME).value
fldCompany = objFields.Item(CdoPR_COMPANY_NAME).value
fldTitle = objFields.Item(CdoPR_TITLE).value
fldPhone= objFields.Item(CdoPR_BUSINESS_TELEPHONE_NUMBER).value
fldOffice= objFields.Item(CdoPR_OFFICE_LOCATION).value
```

The code then checks if any of these fields are empty strings. If they are, then their value is replaced with "None specified" so the user of the application won't be misled by empty spaces in the form to believe that there is something wrong with the application. The following code snippet does this for the department field:

```
If fldDept = "" Then
    fldDept = "None specified"
End If
```

Once the values have been retrieved from the Global Address List, you can insert them in the HTML table using the Write method of the Response object. The following code snippet relates to the entry for the department name:

```
<INPUT TYPE="Text" NAME="Dept" value="
<% Response.write fldDept %>"
```

Using the InfoStores collection to access the public folder

After the user fills out the WAR request, he or she clicks the Post or Cancel buttons. Clicking the Post button will post the information entered by the user into the TechSupport public folder. Chapter 10 discusses how to create public folders. The TechSupport is based on task items.

The TechSupport public folder is represented by a Session-level variable named TechSupportFolder. It is logical to store a reference to the TechSupport public folder in a Session-level variable since that folder will be accessed throughout the session when users post requests to it.

You can access the public folders through the InfoStores collection of the Session object. This collection contains all message stores available to the session based on the permissions of the user logged in. Each message store is an InfoStore object. Each InfoStore object has a root folder from which users may access other folders in a folder hierarchy. The following ASP script prints out the name of each InfoStore, followed by the name of each folder in it:

```
For Each InfoStore in objSession.InfoStores
    Response.Write "<b>InfoStore name = " & _
        InfoStore.Name & "</b><br>"
    Set objRootFolder = InfoStore.RootFolder
    Response.Write "* Root Folder = " & _
        objRootFolder.Name & "<br>"
    Set objFolders = objRootFolder.Folders
    For Each Folder In objFolders
        Response.Write "** " & Folder.Name & "<br>"
    Next
Next
```

The output of the ASP file is as follows:

```
You are logged on as DOMAIN\Administrator
InfoStore name = Public Folders
* Root Folder = All Public Folders
** Group's ToDo
** Information Kiosk
** Internet Newsgroups
InfoStore name = Mailbox - Jeffrey Kent
* Root Folder = Top of Information Store
** Calendar
** Contacts
** Deleted Items
** Drafts
```

```
**  Inbox
**  Journal
**  Notes
**  Outbox
**  Sent Items
**  Tasks
```

This code first accesses each InfoStore object by using the `InfoStores` property of the Session object:

```
For Each InfoStore in objSession.InfoStores
```

Only two InfoStore objects are accessed: Public Folders and Mailbox – *Username*. These are the only two InfoStore objects created by the Exchange Server for a dynamically created profile.

After using the `Write` method of the Response object to output the name of each InfoStore, the code then accesses the root folder of each InfoStore:

```
Set objRootFolder = InfoStore.RootFolder
```

After again using the `Write` method of the Response object, this time to output the name of each root folder, the code uses the Folders property of that Folder object to access and then iterate through the Folders collection of the root folder:

```
Set objFolders = objRootFolder.Folders
    For Each Folder In objFolders
        Response.Write "** " & Folder.Name & "<br>"
    Next
```

Tip

A common "gotcha" is the error MAPI_E_FAILONEPROVIDER. This error can be misleading because you may not receive it when you log on, but rather when you are trying to access a particular mailbox or folder. The problem may be that you were authenticated, but only for Anonymous Access. Consequently, you were permitted to log on, but not to access a particular mailbox or folder. You can check the account for which you were authenticated with the following code:

```
Response.Write("You are logged on as " & _
    Request.ServerVariables("LOGON_USER") & "<br>")
```

If you are logged in under the Anonymous account, you will receive a blank string back. In the preceding code example, which accesses public folders through the InfoStores collection, this line returned the string:

```
You are logged on as DOMAIN\Administrator
```

However, you cannot use the InfoStore object's `RootFolder` property to access the root folder of the Public Folders if your application is running as a Windows NT service. Doing so will raise an error. Instead, you must use the InfoStore's `Fields` property to obtain the Microsoft Exchange property `R_IPM_PUBLIC_FOLDERS_ENTRYID`, property tag &H66310102. This represents the top-level public folder. You then pass this value as the first parameter to the Session object's GetFolder method to access the root folder.

The following code in menu.asp uses these techniques to store a reference to the TechSupport public folder in a session-level variable:

```
Set colInfoStores = objCDOSession.InfoStores

For Each objInfoStore In objCDOSession.InfoStores
    If objInfoStore.Name = "Public Folders" Then
        Exit For
    End If
Next

strRootID = objInfoStore.Fields(&H66310102)
Set fldRoot = objCDOSession.GetFolder(strRootID,
objInfoStore.ID)

Set colFolders = fldRoot.Folders
Set fldTechSupport = colFolders.Item("TechSupport")
Set Session("TechSupportFolder") = fldTechSupport
Session("InfoStoreID") = objInfoStore.ID
```

Tip The second parameter of the GetFolder method, the StoreID, is a string that specifies the unique identifier of the message store containing the folder. This identifier is the ID property of the InfoStore object. This parameter is optional. However, the authors found that passing it was necessary, at least in the computer configuration they used.

Posting a message in the TechSupport folder

Now that you have a reference to the TechSupport public folder, the next step is to post the user's WAR request to that folder. Clicking the Post button brings into play the ticket.asp file, the code for which is in Listing 11-9:

Listing 11-9: **Code for ticket.asp**

```
<!-- #include file="library/logon.inc" -->
<!-- #include file="library/constants.inc" -->
<%

Dim objCDOSession
AuthenticateUser
CheckSession
Set objCDOSession = Session("sesCDO")
If objCDOSession Is Nothing Then
```

Continued

Listing 11-9 *(continued)*

```
        Response.Redirect "logon.asp"
End If

If InStr(Request.form("Action"), "Post") Then

    Set objFolder = Session("TechSupportFolder")
    Set oMessage = objFolder.Messages.Add

    With oMessage
        .Sent = True
        .Unread = True
        .TimeSent = Now
        .TimeReceived = Now
        .Type = "IPM.Task.Ticket"
            .Importance = Request("Priority")
        .Fields.Add "User", 8, Request.Form("User")
        .Fields.Add "Description", 8, Request("Description")
        .Fields.Add "Problem", 8, Request("Type")
        .Fields.Add "Phone", 8, Request("Phone")
        .Fields.Add "Dept", 8, Request("Dept")
        .Fields.Add "Office", 8, Request("Location")
        .Fields.Add "College", 8, Request("College")
          .Submitted = FALSE
          .Update
    End With
    Set oMessage = Nothing

Else
    Response.Redirect "menu.asp"
End If
%>

<html>
<head><title>Authentication Page</title></head>
<body>
<h2><b><font size="5">Technical Support?? </font></b></h2>
<h2>You really want help? Make my day.</h2>
<a href="request.asp">WAR Request</a><P>
<a href="logoff.asp">Get lost</a> (Logoff)<P>
</body>
</html>
```

The code, like the corresponding code in the other .asp files, confirms that the user has a valid Session object. The code then uses the If ... Else control structure to see if the user clicked the Post or the Cancel button in the request.asp file. If the user pressed the Cancel button, then the user is redirected to the menu.

If the user pressed the Post button, then the code creates, assigns values to, and then posts a message to the TechSupport public folder. The code first sets a reference to the TechSupport public folder using the Session-level variable TechSupportFolder, and then adds a new message to that folder:

```
Set objFolder = Session("TechSupportFolder")
Set oMessage = objFolder.Messages.Add
```

The Folder object has a Messages property. This property returns the Messages collection belonging to that folder. That collection's Add method creates and returns a new message to the collection's folder.

The next step is to determine the type of message. The TechSupport folder contains task items by default. However, a custom form may be better suited to your application than a generic task item. Chapter 5 discusses how to create a custom form. Figure 11-16 shows the custom form, whose fields correspond to information in the request form. Figure 11-22 shows the custom form in design view, with the text box labeled Problem mapped to the custom field Problem. Therefore, the Type property of the message is assigned the custom form's message class, IPM.Tasks.Ticket.

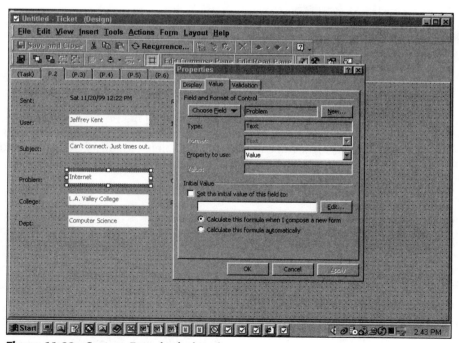

Figure 11-22: Custom Form in design view

Additionally, you should add the custom form to the forms available to the Tech-Support public folder. Figure 11-23 shows the Forms tab of the properties dialog box of the TechSupport public folder:

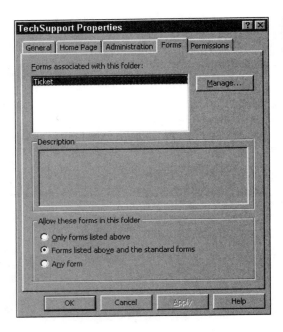

Figure 11-23: Making Custom Form available to TechSupport folder

The next step is to add fields to the message, including the Problem field mentioned earlier. The Message object has a `Fields` property. That property returns the Fields collection for that message. You can add a custom field to a message by using the `Add` method of the Fields collection. Table 11-7 lists the parameters of the `Add` method:

Table 11-7
Parameters of Add Method of Fields Collection

Parameter	Required?	Data Type	Description
Name	Yes	String	The name of the custom property.
Class	Yes	Long	The data type of the custom property. 8 represents a string. Others include 11 (Boolean), 7 (Date), 2(Integer), 3 (Long), 4 (Single) and 12 (Variant).
Value	No, optional	Variant	The initial value to be assigned to the property.

The following code in ticket.asp adds the custom fields and assigns their values from the entries in the request form:

```
With oMessage
    ...
    .Importance = Request("Priority")
    .Fields.Add "User", 8, Request.Form("User")
    .Fields.Add "Description", 8, Request("Description")
    .Fields.Add "Problem", 8, Request("Type")
    .Fields.Add "Phone", 8, Request("Phone")
    .Fields.Add "Dept", 8, Request("Dept")
    .Fields.Add "Office", 8, Request("Location")
    .Fields.Add "College", 8, Request("College")
    ...
End With
```

Additionally, you must set certain intrinsic properties of the message before using the Update method to post it to the TechSupport folder. The reason is that when you post a message to a public folder, as in this application, the MAPI messaging system will not set the values of these intrinsic properties for you.

The Sent property returns a Boolean value reflecting whether the message has been sent through the MAPI messaging system. You as the programmer need to set this property manually to True before the message can be posted to a public folder.

The Submitted property returns a Boolean value reflecting whether the message has been submitted to the MAPI messaging system. You need to set this property manually to False before the message can be posted to a public folder.

You also need to set the Unread property manually, in this case to False because the message has not yet been read.

The value of the TimeSent property is the time the user sent the message, and the value of the TimeReceived property is the time the folder received the message. These properties also need to be assigned values. The code uses the Now function to set both properties to the current date and time.

Once these properties are set, the Update method posts the message to the TechSupport folder. Figure 11-15 shows the message in the folder and Figure 11-16 shows the message displayed with the custom Outlook form.

Summary

In this chapter you learned how to harness a powerful technology, Active Server Pages. ASP enables you to run the code of a Web-based application on the server rather than on the client machine. Since the server executes the code and the client need only read the HTML returned by the server, you no longer need to worry about whether the client's browser can execute your code.

ASP also provides a structure that enables your application to keep track of concurrent users. Unlike standalone Outlook applications, server-based applications must be able to distinguish among numerous users logged on at the same time. In this chapter you learned the ASP lifecycle subroutines that enable you to use the ASP object model to assign a unique session to each user, which is like to each user having a separate thread.

You also know how to create a virtual directory for your ASP application. The URL of your ASP applications is based on the name of the virtual directory.

In this chapter you also learned how to use Collaboration Data Objects. CDO is an object model similar in many respects to the Outlook 2000 object library, and indeed, the two libraries cover many of the same collections and objects. However, while the Outlook 2000 object library is designed primarily for standalone Outlook applications, the CDO object library is designed for multi-user applications run from a network or Web server. In particular, CDO is designed to work with Exchange Server and public folders.

With the tech-support application in this chapter we demonstrated how to use the CDO Object Model in combination with ASP. We also used the application to show solutions to critical issues in CDO programming, such as authenticating the user and accessing CDO Objects like folders and address lists. The application, of course, is a teaching tool, not a finished product. However, by using the knowledge you obtained from analyzing the tech-support application, you can create powerful ready-to-use applications of your own.

✦   ✦   ✦

What's on the CD-ROM

The CD-ROM contains source code examples from Chapters 6 and 7, as well as a .pdf version of the entire book. Adobe Acrobat Reader v4.05 (which allows you to read .pdf files) is also included.

ZipOut 2000, from MicroEye, Inc., is a 30-day evaluation version of software that automatically compresses attachments to outgoing messages and items stored in your mailbox or personal folders. ZipOut can send attachments to recipients in a .zip or self-extracting file. If you do not have a Zip utility, ZipOut provides an integral Zip file viewer. Attachment compression is done on the fly with no user intervention required. With ZipOut 2000 you can also manage attachments in your mailbox or personal folders. You can compress attachments on all items in a folder and subfolders, remove HTML stationery, or simply delete attachments from a selection of messages. You can schedule automatic attachment compression in your mailbox based on a single or recurring Outlook task, and display the compression results in an Office 2000 Web component.

While the contents of the CD-ROM were the most current as of the publishing of the book, you should check the URLs in Appendix B for updated versions.

Table A-1 outlines the contents of the CD-ROM that accompanies this book.

Table A-1 Contents of CD-ROM		
Name/Version	Supported platforms	System requirements
Source code from Chapters 6 and 7		
ZipOut 2000 (Evaluation – 30 day trial)	Outlook 2000	Outlook 2000
Complete text of *Microsoft® Outlook® 2000 Programming Bible* in .pdf format	Windows 95/89/NT4/2000	
Adobe Acrobat Reader v4.05	Windows 95/89/NT4/2000	

✦   ✦   ✦

Outlook Resources

The Internet has numerous resources on Outlook 2000, as well as on related applications such as Exchange Server and Internet Information Server and related technologies such as Collaboration Data Objects and Active Server Pages. You have two sources for these resources: Microsoft and "The Rest of the World." You also can access different types of interactive resources, such as newsgroups and mailing lists, in addition to the traditional white papers.

Since the available resources would fill a small book, this appendix cannot include them all. However, many of the resources listed here also provide links to additional resources.

The links were verified when this book went to print. However, links change frequently, particularly Microsoft links.

Microsoft

Outlook, Exchange Server, and Internet Exchange Server each have home pages, which are convenient entry points to further information on these applications.

- ✦ Outlook — `http://www.microsoft.com/office/outlook/`
- ✦ Exchange Server — `http://www.microsoft.com/exchange/`
- ✦ Windows NT Server Web Services (includes IIS) — `http://www.microsoft.com/ntserver/web/default.asp`

Microsoft continues to improve (or debug, it depends on your point of view) Office 2000 products. The Office 2000 Update site dedicated to Outlook is `http://officeupdate.microsoft.com/welcome/outlook.asp`.

Microsoft continues to enhance Outlook 2000 with add-ons. This book discusses two of them, Team Folders Kit and Digital Dashboard. The sites from which you can obtain further information on these add-ons, or download them, are:

+ Team Folders Kit — `http://www.microsoft.com/Exchange/collaboration/tfwizard_eng.htm`

+ Digital Dashboard — `http://www.microsoft.com/solutions/km/DigitalDashboard.htm`

Outlook problems can drive you crazy. If you need help, you can go to the Microsoft Personal Support Center, 2000 at `http://support.microsoft.com/support/`. The site does not provide psychological help (not yet, anyway), but the assistance it does give you may save you from needing it. The support sites specific to Outlook 2000, Exchange Server, and IIS are:

+ Outlook 2000 — `http://support.microsoft.com/support/outlook/default012k.asp`

+ Exchange Server — `http://support.microsoft.com/support/exchange`

+ Internet Information Server — `http://support.microsoft.com/support/iis`

Microsoft has several sites dedicated to developers. One is the Microsoft Office 2000 Developer Home (`http://msdn.microsoft.com/officedev/`). Another is the Microsoft Developer Network (MSDN), located at `http://msdn.microsoft.com/`. MSDN has a wealth of online information on Outlook, Exchange Server, and the technologies they use, such as MAPI and CDO. Useful sites within MSDN include:

+ Exchange Developer Center — `http://msdn.microsoft.com/exchange/default.asp`. Primarily Exchange Server development, but much information on Outlook and CDO also.

+ Platform SDK Components for Component Library Developers — `http://msdn.microsoft.com/downloads/sdks/platform/complib.asp`. Code samples for CDO, MAPI and Exchange Server.

+ MSDN Exchange/Outlook Online Special-Interest Group (OSIG) — `http://msdn.microsoft.com/osig/exchange/default.asp`

+ MSDN Exchange/Outlook Support newsgroups.

While MSDN is an excellent resource for programming issues, Microsoft TechNet (http://www.microsoft.com/technet/) is the resource for technical issues such as bug reports and fixes. Additionally, it provides Exchange Application Downloads (http://www.microsoft.com/technet/download/exchange/default.asp), a central clearinghouse for custom Microsoft Exchange applications written by third-party developers — a very useful source of code!

Finally, the Microsoft Office 2000 Resource Kit has a section on New Tools for Outlook 2000 (http://www.microsoft.com/office/ork/2000/journ/OutToolsIntro.htm).

The Rest of the World

Slipstick Systems Outlook & Exchange Solutions Center (http://www.slipstick.com/) was perhaps the first and still one of the best sites on Outlook and Exchange.

The Outlook and Exchange Developer Resource Center (http://www.outlookexchange.com/) provides resources, including code examples, for Outlook and Exchange Server Development.

The Outlook 2000 resource center (http://www.microeye.com/outlook/) has code examples and information on Outlook 2000 COM Add-Ins.

The Microsoft Exchange Software site (http://www.exchangefaq.com/) has a list of books and add-ons related to Microsoft Exchange Server and Microsoft Outlook.

Collaborate Today (http://collaborate.glazier.co.nz/) focuses on colloboration applications using Exchange Server features. The site also includes a list of Microsoft Exchange/Outlook-related newsgroups and a discussion group.

CDO Live (http://www.cdolive.com/) is the premier site for Collaboration Data Objects.

Exchange Code Exchange (http://www.exchangecode.com/) has numerous code examples for Outlook and Exchange Server.

ExchangeFAQ.org: (http://www.exchangefaq.org/) is an excellent resource site for Exchange administrators with lots of information, including a discussion forum.

✦　　✦　　✦

Index

Continued

Continued

Continued

IDG Books Worldwide, Inc. End-User License Agreement

READ THIS. You should carefully read these terms and conditions before opening the software packet(s) included with this book ("Book"). This is a license agreement ("Agreement") between you and IDG Books Worldwide, Inc. ("IDGB"). By opening the accompanying software packet(s), you acknowledge that you have read and accept the following terms and conditions. If you do not agree and do not want to be bound by such terms and conditions, promptly return the Book and the unopened software packet(s) to the place you obtained them for a full refund.

1. **License Grant.** IDGB grants to you (either an individual or entity) a nonexclusive license to use one copy of the enclosed software program(s) (collectively, the "Software") solely for your own personal or business purposes on a single computer (whether a standard computer or a workstation component of a multiuser network). The Software is in use on a computer when it is loaded into temporary memory (RAM) or installed into permanent memory (hard disk, CD-ROM, or other storage device). IDGB reserves all rights not expressly granted herein.

2. **Ownership.** IDGB is the owner of all right, title, and interest, including copyright, in and to the compilation of the Software recorded on the disk(s) or CD-ROM ("Software Media"). Copyright to the individual programs recorded on the Software Media is owned by the author or other authorized copyright owner of each program. Ownership of the Software and all proprietary rights relating thereto remain with IDGB and its licensers.

3. **Restrictions On Use and Transfer.**

   (a) You may only (i) make one copy of the Software for backup or archival purposes, or (ii) transfer the Software to a single hard disk, provided that you keep the original for backup or archival purposes. You may not (i) rent or lease the Software, (ii) copy or reproduce the Software through a LAN or other network system or through any computer subscriber system or bulletin-board system, or (iii) modify, adapt, or create derivative works based on the Software.

   (b) You may not reverse engineer, decompile, or disassemble the Software. You may transfer the Software and user documentation on a permanent basis, provided that the transferee agrees to accept the terms and conditions of this Agreement and you retain no copies. If the Software is an update or has been updated, any transfer must include the most recent update and all prior versions.

4. **Restrictions on Use of Individual Programs.** You must follow the individual requirements and restrictions detailed for each individual program in Appendix A of this Book. These limitations are also contained in the individual

license agreements recorded on the Software Media. These limitations may include a requirement that after using the program for a specified period of time, the user must pay a registration fee or discontinue use. By opening the Software packet(s), you will be agreeing to abide by the licenses and restrictions for these individual programs that are detailed in Appendix A and on the Software Media. None of the material on this Software Media or listed in this Book may ever be redistributed, in original or modified form, for commercial purposes.

5. Limited Warranty.

   (a) IDGB warrants that the Software and Software Media are free from defects in materials and workmanship under normal use for a period of sixty (60) days from the date of purchase of this Book. If IDGB receives notification within the warranty period of defects in materials or workmanship, IDGB will replace the defective Software Media.

   (b) **IDGB AND THE AUTHORS OF THE BOOK DISCLAIM ALL OTHER WARRANTIES, EXPRESS OR IMPLIED, INCLUDING WITHOUT LIMITATION IMPLIED WARRANTIES OF MERCHANTABILITY AND FITNESS FOR A PARTICULAR PURPOSE, WITH RESPECT TO THE SOFTWARE, THE PROGRAMS, THE SOURCE CODE CONTAINED THEREIN, AND/OR THE TECHNIQUES DESCRIBED IN THIS BOOK. IDGB DOES NOT WARRANT THAT THE FUNCTIONS CONTAINED IN THE SOFTWARE WILL MEET YOUR REQUIREMENTS OR THAT THE OPERATION OF THE SOFTWARE WILL BE ERROR FREE.**

   (c) This limited warranty gives you specific legal rights, and you may have other rights that vary from jurisdiction to jurisdiction.

6. Remedies.

   (a) IDGB's entire liability and your exclusive remedy for defects in materials and workmanship shall be limited to replacement of the Software Media, which may be returned to IDGB with a copy of your receipt at the following address: Software Media Fulfillment Department, Attn.: *Microsoft Outlook 2000 Programming Bible*, IDG Books Worldwide, Inc., 10475 Crosspoint Blvd., Indianapolis, IN 46256, or call 1-800-762-2974. Please allow three to four weeks for delivery. This Limited Warranty is void if failure of the Software Media has resulted from accident, abuse, or misapplication. Any replacement Software Media will be warranted for the remainder of the original warranty period or thirty (30) days, whichever is longer.

   (b) In no event shall IDGB or the authors be liable for any damages whatsoever (including without limitation damages for loss of business profits, business interruption, loss of business information, or any other pecuniary loss) arising from the use of or inability to use the Book or the Software, even if IDGB has been advised of the possibility of such damages.

(c) Because some jurisdictions do not allow the exclusion or limitation of liability for consequential or incidental damages, the above limitation or exclusion may not apply to you.

7. **U.S. Government Restricted Rights.** Use, duplication, or disclosure of the Software by the U.S. Government is subject to restrictions stated in paragraph (c)(1)(ii) of the Rights in Technical Data and Computer Software clause of DFARS 252.227-7013, and in subparagraphs (a) through (d) of the Commercial Computer — Restricted Rights clause at FAR 52.227-19, and in similar clauses in the NASA FAR supplement, when applicable.

8. **General.** This Agreement constitutes the entire understanding of the parties and revokes and supersedes all prior agreements, oral or written, between them and may not be modified or amended except in a writing signed by both parties hereto that specifically refers to this Agreement. This Agreement shall take precedence over any other documents that may be in conflict herewith. If any one or more provisions contained in this Agreement are held by any court or tribunal to be invalid, illegal, or otherwise unenforceable, each and every other provision shall remain in full force and effect.

my2cents.idgbooks.com

Register This Book — And Win!

Visit **http://my2cents.idgbooks.com** to register this book and we'll automatically enter you in our fantastic monthly prize giveaway. It's also your opportunity to give us feedback: let us know what you thought of this book and how you would like to see other topics covered.

Discover IDG Books Online!

The IDG Books Online Web site is your online resource for tackling technology — at home and at the office. Frequently updated, the IDG Books Online Web site features exclusive software, insider information, online books, and live events!

10 Productive & Career-Enhancing Things You Can Do at www.idgbooks.com

- Nab source code for your own programming projects.

- Download software.

- Read Web exclusives: special articles and book excerpts by IDG Books Worldwide authors.

- Take advantage of resources to help you advance your career as a Novell or Microsoft professional.

- Buy IDG Books Worldwide titles or find a convenient bookstore that carries them.

- Register your book and win a prize.

- Chat live online with authors.

- Sign up for regular e-mail updates about our latest books.

- Suggest a book you'd like to read or write.

- Give us your 2¢ about our books and about our Web site.

You say you're not on the Web yet? It's easy to get started with IDG Books' *Discover the Internet,* available at local retailers everywhere.

CD-ROM Installation Instructions

The CD-ROM that accompànies this book contains source code examples from Chapters 6 and 7, a .pdf version of the entire book, Adobe Acrobat Reader v4.05, and ZipOut 2000 v2.0.2245. Each item on the CD is contained in a separate directory.

Please see Appendix A for a more detailed description of the CD contents, supported platforms, and system requirements.